Workplace relations
in Colonial Bengal

Critical Perspectives in South Asian History

Series Editors
Janaki Nair (Jawaharlal Nehru University, India)
Mrinalini Sinha (University of Michigan, USA)
Shabnum Tejani (SOAS, University of London, UK)

Editorial Board
Nira Wikramsinghe, Leiden University, Netherlands
Willem van Schendel, University of Amsterdam, Netherlands
Carole McGranahan, University of Colorado Boulder, USA
J. Devika, Centre for Development Studies, Trivandrum, India
Farina Mir, University of Michigan, USA
Daud Ali, University of Pennsylvania, USA
Samira Sheikh, Vanderbilt University, USA
Nandini Chatterjee, University of Exeter, UK
Sunil Amrith, Harvard University, USA

Critical Perspectives in South Asian History publishes critically innovative scholarship on South Asian history from the ancient world to the present day. It focuses on three broad scholarly developments; a growing engagement with public history in South Asia, a conceptual shift that assigns agency to South Asia as the *generator* of research rather than the *object* of it, and a concerted effort to study histories of neglected regions, peoples, methods and sources.

Published

Forms of the Left in Postcolonial South Asia: Aesthetics, Networks and Connected Histories,
Edited by Sanjukta Sunderson and Lotte Hoek

Forthcoming

Towards a People's History of Pakistan: (In)audible Voices, Forgotten Pasts,
Edited by Kamran Asdar Ali and Asad Ali

The YMCA in Late Colonial India: Modernization, Philanthropy and American Soft Power in South Asia, by Harald Fischer-Tiné

The Emergence of Brand-Name Capitalism in Late Colonial India: Advertising and the Making of Middle-Class Conjugality, by Douglas E. Haynes

Political Imaginaries in Twentieth-Century India, by Mrinalini Sinha and Manu Goswami

Workplace relations in Colonial Bengal

The Jute Industry and Indian Labour 1870s–1930s

Anna Sailer

BLOOMSBURY ACADEMIC
LONDON • NEW YORK • OXFORD • NEW DELHI • SYDNEY

BLOOMSBURY ACADEMIC
Bloomsbury Publishing Plc
50 Bedford Square, London, WC1B 3DP, UK
1385 Broadway, New York, NY 10018, USA
29 Earlsfort Terrace, Dublin 2, Ireland

BLOOMSBURY, BLOOMSBURY ACADEMIC and the Diana logo
are trademarks of Bloomsbury Publishing Plc

First published in Great Britain 2022
This paperback edition published 2023

For legal purposes the Acknowledgements on pp. xi–xiii constitute
an extension of this copyright page.

Series design: Jade Barnett
Cover image: Man in front of Megna Jute Mills gate, July 1949. Dundee Heritage Trust.

A catalogue record for this book is available from the British Library.

Library of Congress Cataloging-in-Publication Data
Names: Sailer, Anna, 1982- author.
Title: Workplace relations in colonial Bengal : the jute industry and
Indian labour 1870s-1930s / Anna Sailer.
Description: London ; New York, NY : Bloomsbury Academic, 2022. |
Series: Critical perspectives in South Asian history |
Includes bibliographical references and index.
Identifiers: LCCN 2021038610 (print) | LCCN 2021038611 (ebook) |
ISBN 9781350233539 (hardback) | ISBN 9781350233546 (pdf) |
ISBN 9781350233553 (ebook)
Subjects: LCSH: Labor movement–South Asia–History–19th century. |
Labor movement–South Asia–History–20th century. | Jute industry–South
Asia–History–19th century. | Jute industry–South Asia–History–20th century. |
Organizational change–South Asia–History–19th century. | Organizational
change–South Asia–History–20th century.
Classification: LCC HD6815.8 .S35 2022 (print) | LCC HD6815.8 (ebook) |
DDC 331.880954–dc23/eng/20211014
LC record available at https://lccn.loc.gov/2021038610
LC ebook record available at https://lccn.loc.gov/2021038611

ISBN: HB: 978-1-3502-3353-9
         PB: 978-1-3502-3356-0
         ePDF: 978-1-3502-3354-6
         ePUB: 978-1-3502-3355-3

Series: Critical Perspectives in South Asian History

Typeset by Integra Software Services Pvt. Ltd.

To find out more about our authors and books visit www.bloomsbury.com
and sign up for our newsletters.

Für meinen Vater.

Contents

Illustrations

Acknowledgements

I first developed the ideas of this book as part of my PhD project 'Workplace Matters. The Bengal Jute Industry between the 1870s and the 1930s' at the Georg-August-University of Göttingen. This project would not have been possible without support from the Heinrich-Böll-Foundation, which funded large parts of it. In addition, I received support in the form of a fellowship at the German Historical Institute in London and a fellowship at the Göttinger Graduiertenschule für Geisteswissenschaften. My subsequent employment at the Centre for Modern Indian Studies, Georg-August-University of Göttingen, allowed me to further develop this project and turn it into a book. I want to thank these institutions, as well as their staff for their support.

I am grateful to the staff in the archives I visited, and where my research started to take shape. In particular, I want to thank the staff at the West Bengal State Archives, Calcutta; the Special Branch of Police Archives, Calcutta; and the Dundee University Library; the British Library, London; the Centre for South Asian Studies, Cambridge.

During my research I had the great pleasure to meet former Scottish employees of jute mills, who worked as overseers, assistant managers and engineers in Bengal in the 1940s and 1950s. Our conversations taught me a great deal about the process of production in this period, and helped me make sense of the technical descriptions in archival reports that I was consulting at the same time. They described the noise, the dust and the smell of jute mills, and helped me 'see' the mills in a way that managerial and police reports could not have conjured up.

Many people accompanied me on the path of developing and finishing this project. Ravi Ahuja supervised my PhD thesis and was a constant source of encouragement. His comments at various stages of my work, as well as the many discussions we had, helped me greatly in developing my thoughts, and in transcending the limits of my initial ideas about this project. His inexhaustible patience is greatly appreciated!

Marcel van der Linden acted as second supervisor for my thesis. His comments were immensely encouraging, and his feedback on my work helped me to develop it further from a PhD project to a book. Frank Perlin's advice and comments on my work were unfailingly generous and suggestive. I was fortunate to have met Alexis Wearmouth, a fellow student of the history of the jute industry, early on during this project. I am grateful for his generosity in sharing important materials, and I am grateful for our conversations about the Bengal jute industry.

Discussions of labour history in general, and of the jute industry in particular, helped shape the ideas that went into this book. I want to thank Samita Sen for her insightful engagement with my work, and for her own pioneering work on the jute industry. I am also grateful for conversations with Dilip Simeon, Peter Birke, Klaus-Peter Wittemann, Ritajyoti Bandyopadhyay, Saikat Maitra and Görkem Akgöz. Radhika Singha's encouragement was crucial in turning this project into a book.

My long-running engagement with the Association of Indian Labour Historians in Delhi has profoundly influenced my work. Chitra Joshi, Prabhu Mohapatra and Rana Behal have been an unfailing source of encouragement, warmth and critical engagement for many years. By organizing the bi-annual labour history conference in NOIDA, they have created a remarkable space for global conversations about labour history. The late and greatly missed Sabyasachi Bhattacharya made invaluable comments on an early draft of this work, and I regret that he could not see its completion.

I was lucky to be able to share my archival journey with fellow travellers, who made the experience even more rewarding and enjoyable – I would like to thank Patrick Hesse, Anirban Bhattacharya, Ishan Mukherjee, Anwesha Roy, Kaustubh Sengupta and Debarati Bagchi.

The extended CeMIS community and its periodic visitors provided for a great network of support and exchange. I particularly wish to thank Maria Framke, Nitin Sinha, Heike Liebau, Nitin Varma, Shahana Bhattacharya, Anwesha Sengupta, Maria Pomohaci, Michaela Dimmers, Sebastian Schwecke, Robert Rahman Raman, Vidhya Raveendranathan, Arun Kumar, Arnaud Kaba, Enrique Martino, David Mayer, Svenja von Jan, Rohan Dominic Mathews and Jana Tschurenev.

Like all projects, this project too was sustained by close friendships. Rukmini Barua, Ahmad Azhar, Naveen Chander, Camille Buat, Razak Khan and Martin Christof-Füchsle have been vital throughout, as a source of both academic and personal sustenance. Somak Biswas, Matteo Mazzamurro and Laura Schwartz have also been a great source of encouragement. Ulrike Crodel has been an important part of my life since childhood, and I am honoured that she continues to be so. Liz Davies and the late Mike Marqusee made London feel like home immediately, and I will always be grateful.

Above all, my family has been a constant anchor through the ups and downs of this project. Sumit and Tanika Sarkar have supported me constantly and in so many ways. At the beginning of my project, after my first archival visits in Calcutta, I used to read out the 'latest' developments of the 1929 general strike to them. The mix of excitement, warmth and insight with which they responded turned into a continuous feature accompanying my project, and I feel lucky being part of their family.

Ursula and Dietmar Pacl have in their generosity provided an important basis of love and support for me, without which I would not have been able to begin my project in the first place. Jörg Pacl, Maia Krenkler, Moritz and Helene Pacl have just always been there for me when I needed them – unconditionally. Sukumari Bhattacharji helped make me feel home in Calcutta, and I will always miss her.

Aditya Sarkar has sustained both this project and me from the beginning. He has always encouraged me in pushing further with my work, listened to my extended descriptions of blockages and apparent impossibilities, and engaged with my thoughts into the small hours of the morning. While I might say that this project would not have developed like it did without him, this would be redundant, for I cannot imagine my life without him. It was a historical necessity that we met.

Joachim Sailer is at the core of who I am. He introduced me to philosophy, literature, art and life. Unfortunately, this book only remained a beginning for him, and he never got to witness its conclusion. I will always be proud to be his daughter, and I will never stop looking up to him. This book is dedicated to him.

1

Introduction

In 1894 Marie Imandt and Bessie Maxwell, two journalists of the *Dundee Courier*, undertook a 'tour around the world', reporting to their readers from various locations in Europe, Asia and America.[1] In July they reached Calcutta, a destination which was of special interest to their readership. Dundee and Calcutta were home to the most important centres of jute production in the world. Earlier in the year, a number of mills on the Hugli had increased their hours of work from seventy-two to ninety hours per week, after installing electric light; one mill had even increased its weekly hours to 122.[2] Not surprisingly, this triggered concerns in Dundee. Legal restrictions, as observers argued, prevented a similar excess in hours, resulting in an unfair advantage to the jute industry in India. Just one month before Imandt and Maxwell arrived in Bengal, the Conservative MP John Leng had raised the issue in Parliament, calling for a check upon the exploitation of workers, which it sustained. The Dundee Chamber of Commerce followed a few months later, addressing the Secretary of State for India on the matter.[3]

The concerns in Dundee account for the priority placed by the journalists and their audience upon labour conditions in Bengal jute mills. In a series of articles, Imandt and Maxwell reported about rhythms of work, wage levels, as well as about the general conditions of the industry. Upon their arrival, Marie Imandt described her first impressions of the rhythms of work in a Bengal jute mill as follows:

> The jute mills in Calcutta are opened in the morning, and work goes on continuously until sunset. If three men or women are at a machine three go to work in the morning. At seven a fourth man or woman goes in, and so on until there are three or four extra men or women for each machine. These relieve the workers at meal times, and during the frequent breaks in the day they demand.[4]

Imandt's snapshot of a working day in a Bengal jute mill revealed the image of a workplace which was populated by workers and 'extra' workers, entering or leaving the workplace at various moments of the day. These 'extra' workers were strictly speaking not at work. Rather, their purpose was to relieve other workers who were employed at the mills' machines. The rhythms of substitution, in which both sets of workers engaged, enabled the former to take breaks for meals or other purposes, while the latter took over the work at the machines. Just as the mills' engines ran continuously, then workers and 'extra' workers seemed to engage in a parallel motion through the mill, sustaining a seemingly continuous process of work, and of breaks.

Trying to account for her observations, Marie Imandt had recourse to two explanations. Her first explanation was that this rhythm of work was a general feature in India. The irregular and constant shifts between work and break, carried by the motion of workers and 'extra' workers, were accordingly necessary, because of the habits of Indian workers. They had no true sense of time – or, as Imandt put it: they did not understand the idiom 'that time is money'. The result of these apparently ingrained habits was that Indian workers could and would not comply with a 'normal' routine of industrial work. Instead, workers in India required frequent breaks for a drink, a smoke or for a bath in the river, which, as Imandt added, was 'so important a matter in the Hindoo religion that nothing will prevent these people from going at certain hours to bathe'.[5]

Based on these apparently general habits, Marie Imandt provided also a second explanation for the rhythms of work she had just witnessed: the prevalence of the multiple-shift system in Bengal jute mills. At the heart of this system of work-organization lay the employment of groups of workers, or small work gangs, rather than individuals. The number of workers in each gang exceeded the number actually required to run the machinery. The result of this arrangement was that at any given moment in the working day, more workers were present at the site of production than the number of workers employed on machines, or employed for specific tasks. The multiple-shift system, thus, was based on a structure of *excess labour*.[6] Despite the continuous and uninterrupted rhythm of the mills' engines, workers could take breaks on an informal basis, as they could always share their work with 'extra' workers. Excess-employment, from this perspective, appeared as a necessary result of the prevalence of workers' habits, since, as Imandt pointed out, 'the natives would refuse to work at all' if 'these frequent goings-outs were to be stopped'.[7]

The two explanations given by Marie Imandt, in order to account for the rhythms of work she had just witnessed, presented a well-known image of industrial work in colonial India. Practices of substitution, in this reading, appeared to be an expression of the fact that workers' practices in the mill were determined by a set of 'pre-modern' habits, which opposed the time of the 'modern' workplace.

Workers' rhythms, accordingly, were marked by a lack of discipline and bad time keeping; sloth, dilatory habits of work; and by a general 'inability' to work for prolonged periods of time.[8] Similar rhythms of work were to be found throughout colonial India. Depicting patterns of work in a Bombay cotton mill in a concurrent manner, a member of the Indian Trades Association reported:

> Anybody who has been to a mill in Bombay any time of the day when it is working cannot have failed to notice that even during the hours when these workmen ought to be at their work they leave if off, go out and spend their time as if they had nothing to do. Every five minutes you see them coming out by twos or threes, one washing his mouth, another smoking and a third eating his tiffin.[9]

Mill compounds in Indian industries, then, appeared to be inhabited by workers who were not at work – quite in contrast to the European workplace, as colonial officials were never tired of pointing out.[10]

Practices of substitution, however, seemed to fulfil a second function in the Indian workplace. The motion of workers and 'extra' workers, who relieved one another at the mills' machines, after all, sustained a continuous process of production. In the case of the jute industry, this meant, more precisely, an uninterrupted process of production that ranged from twelve to twenty-two hours per day.[11] 'Pre-modern' practices of work, in this reading, seemed to meet the demands of the 'modern' workplace. They appeared to be inextricably linked to a 'modern' industry, which was certainly highly profitable. The Bengal jute industry was not only famous for its fabulous rates of profits and its high returns. Rather, the mills on the Hugli managed to establish a virtual monopoly over the production of jute goods. The increase in hours of work in the mid-1890s, in fact, marked the beginning of a new boom, which would eventually serve to outrank the jute industry in Dundee. This, in turn, would establish the dominant position which the mills on the Hugli held in the years to come.[12]

The success of the Bengal jute industry was to some degree unique – at least insofar as this was the only case in which an industry in the colonial periphery managed to outrank its counterpart in the centre.[13] Yet the principal problem, that irregular rhythms of work seemed to enable a regular process of production, appeared to be a general feature of the 'Indian' workplace. The fact that groups of loitering workers in mill-compounds seemed to reflect 'pre-modern' habits of work, while simultaneously being an expression of a continuous process of production, was not restricted to the Bengal jute industry alone. Indicative of a resulting tension in the depiction of the 'Indian' workplace are observations made by members of the 1890 Factory Commission:

In a woollen mill in the United Provinces, working on an average only 10 ½ hours a day, accurate statistics have been collected for some years, and it was found that on two selected days, one in May and one in November, about 44 per cent. of the workmen remained inside the mill during the whole of the working hours; the average operative there does not leave his work for more than half an hour in the day. In Agra, on the other hand, where the operatives come from the same part of the country, but where the working day varies from 13 ½ to 15 ¼ hours, we were particularly struck with the listless, lazy manner of the operatives, and with the large number loitering about in the compound. Similar comparisons obtruded themselves upon our notice throughout the tour; the system in force in Delhi, for example, compares most unfavourably in this respect with that obtaining at the Empress Mills in Nagpur, or the Buckingham and Carnatic Mills in Madras.[14]

The members of the commission briefly speculated about the possibility of a connection between long hours of production and workers' habits of 'loitering'. Yet they eventually concluded that practices of work were essentially the expression of workers' habits, leading to the ambiguous statement that 'the' Indian worker, 'while naturally disposed to take work easily, possesses considerable adaptability' – an ability, which accordingly determined 'to some degree' the manner in which he worked, without, however, detaching this manner from the realm of 'pre-modern' habits.[15]

We thus have a peculiar problem here. Practices of substitution – and, in effect, practices of work – simultaneously reflected the 'pre-modern' time of workers and the 'modern' time of the mill. The constant motion of workers, relieving one another in the course of the working day, accounted for the fact that practices of work remained caught in the realm of the 'pre-modern', even at the moment of facing the universal time of the machine. The internal division of the 'Indian' workplace seemed to be inscribed into the process of production itself, which was composed of two distinct spheres – each unfolding according to its own internal logics of time and discipline. While the mill could not control the former, workers were not prepared to follow the latter. The sphere of the 'pre-modern' and that of the 'modern', in turn, appeared to sustain the same process of production, without corresponding to one another. The Indian workplace, in other words, appeared to be a *paradox*. Rephrasing Parimal Ghosh's expression of an 'atypical type', by which he described the worker-turned-peasant', it might be said that at the shop-floor it was the 'Indian' workplace which presented itself as 'atypical'.[16]

When trying to account for the prevalence of these two opposing spheres at the site of production, contemporary observers used to present two distinct explanations. The first, and more important one, was excess-employment. Mills and factories in colonial India, accordingly, used to employ 'extra' workers, in order to compensate for the gap between what workers were prepared to do and the demands of the 'modern' workplace. Excess-employment, in this reading, enabled workers to fill the gap between the time of the 'pre-modern' and the time of the 'modern', by substituting one another at the machines. Workers, after all, were 'allowed' to share their work on an informal basis, as managers and state representatives pointed out on various occasions.[17] Attributing this rhythm to the realm of 'habits', the secretary of the Bengal Chamber of Commerce (BCC) explained that workers' 'lack of persistency is partially met by the ease with which they work for many hours together'.[18] Regularly employed workers, too, were allowed to share their work with a 'fellow-worker' or 'joriwalla'.[19] They were, thus, contributing to the continuous motion of workers at the site of production, which sustained a continuous process of production.

Excess-employment, in this reading, compensated for the 'deficiencies' of workers' habits. Yet it did so not by solving the underlying tension between the sphere of the 'pre-modern' and that of the 'modern'. Rather, it functioned to drown the articulations of workers' 'habits' under a mass of excess labour, by turning a multiplicity of interrupted rhythms of work into a regular motion at the machines. The process of production was in this reading sustained on account of excess-employment, precisely because workers did not need to enter 'normal' production relations in order to meet the demands of the 'modern' workplace. Instead of contradicting each other, then, the two spheres of the Indian workplace sustained the process of production by remaining parallel to one another. Indian workers could retain their 'pre-modern' habits, while the mills' workforce sustained a 'modern' process of production. Habitual practices of work, then, seemed to bear no relation to the space in which they were being practised. The mill, in turn, appeared to operate autonomously from the 'pre-modern' habits of workers.[20]

The price for drowning the articulations of workers' 'pre-modern' habits by employing 'extra' workers was an increase in labour costs. Comparing the 'Indian' workplace with its idealized 'European' counterpart, contemporary observers highlighted that the 'habits' of Indian workers required the employment of more workers per machine (or per task) than in Europe.[21] Excess-employment, while in principle sustaining the process of production, meant that the defects of the Indian workplace were still visible in the efficiency of production. The systematic employment of 'extra' workers appeared to divert the problem of the 'Indian' workplace from the point of production to the appropriation of profits.

A second set of explanations, which seemed to indicate why managers were compelled to let workers so continuously evade the 'normal' routine of industrial work, concerned problems of labour shortage. Workers in India were, according to these explanations, slow to enter mills and factories, leading to constant problems of labour supply in emerging industries. Making matters worse, workers often did not remain in industrial areas for extended periods, as contemporary observers informed us. Rather, 'Indian' workers left mill towns regularly, in order to search for other jobs or return to their rural homes. A variety of other reasons seemed to contribute to this tendency of Indian workers. These included the epidemics that periodically broke out in congested mill neighbourhoods and were seen to scare workers away; as well as the relatively high wages earned by workers, which, observers suggested, allowed them to sustain themselves for a few months and relieved them of the compulsion to work in the first place.[22]

Among the various reasons why workers left mills and mill towns, the most important one for contemporary observers was certainly that Indian workers seemed to sustain tight links to the rural areas from which they had migrated. Elaborating on the effects of this feature of Indian workers, as members of the 1890 Factory Commission wrote,

> it follows that the Indian operative is, in general, independent of factory work to the extent that he does not rely exclusively upon factory employment in order to obtain a livelihood; at most seasons he can command a wage sufficient to keep him [...] The position of the operative has been greatly strengthened by the fact that the supply of factory labour undoubtedly is, and has been, inadequate; and there is, and has been, the keenest competition among employers to secure a full labour supply. These two main causes – the independence of the Indian labourer, owing to the fact that he possesses other and congenial means of earning a livelihood, and the deficient labour supply – govern the whole situation.[23]

The argument that Indian workers remained 'peasants' indicated, in this context, not only particular notions of time and discipline that seemed to inform the sphere of 'habits'. Rather, it suggested that mill authorities were unable to reduce the gap between the time of the 'pre-modern' and the time of the 'modern'. Or, in turn, that they were unable to reduce the quantity of excess labour that was necessary in their mills. For, as already Marie Imandt had informed her readers, workers would 'refuse to work at all' if managers attempted to change the form of work organization in Indian industries.[24]

While the mill appeared to be functioning autonomously at the point of production due to excess-employment, it remained dependent on workers' habits at the point of profit making. This dependency appeared to be based on the fact that workers always retained the option to refuse to work, and to return to their rural homes instead. Managers' apparent compulsion to allow workers to express their 'habits' at the workplace and in mill-compounds, then, seemed entirely shaped and sustained by the forces of custom, community and neighbourhood. In other words, it appeared as entirely *external* to the workplace. The 'Indian' workplace, in this reading, seemed only to leave space for the question of when those structures and traditions, which sustained the sphere of the 'pre-modern' in neighbourhoods and villages, would vanish. Or, to put it differently, when and if 'Indian' workers would be forced to give up these aspects of their 'pre-modern' habits, that restricted the possible range of managerial interventions and blocked the emergence of a fully 'modern' workplace.

These questions of whether workers' 'habits' were indeed changing in Indian industries, and if rhythms of work were becoming more regular in mills and factories, were discussed frequently in contemporary debates. The tendency of workers to leave the workplace during hours of work appeared in principle to be declining. While the Factory Commissions of 1890 and 1908 described at length 'loitering' workers in mill compounds, members of the Whitley Commission hardly mentioned the issue in 1931.[25] Surely enough, workers' apparent tendency to evade the 'normal' rhythms of industrial work during the working day turned into a source of managerial complaints again in the 1930s – a problem that found new solutions.[26] Habitual practices of work, which indicated the prevalence of a sphere of the 'pre-modern' at the site of production, then, seemed to share a fate with the figure of the *jobber*, whose position, as Rajnarayan Chandavarkar pointed out, appeared to be declining in a 'periodic, almost cyclical' manner.[27] Factory systems based on structures of excess-employment, too, seemed to experience a continuous decline throughout the early twentieth century, while, at the same time, remaining a defining feature of Indian industries. The workplace appeared to be caught in a second tension – between an ongoing decline of workers' 'habits' in the mill-space, and the essential continuity of a division into the realm of the 'modern' and of the 'pre-modern', that seemed to stall further development of industrial relations.

Questions about changes in workplace relations in Indian industries also informed historiographical debates. Approached in terms of transition, uneven development and transformations, or, alternatively, as an essentialized absence of change, scholars tried to analyse that which appeared as the sphere of the 'pre-modern' in colonial representations. The underlying division of the workplace, into a terrain in which workers' 'habits' unfolded, and into a space at the site of production where the articulations of these practices were rendered invisible, continued to inform these debates, as we shall argue in more detail below. The result was that while the realm of workers' 'habits' appears in several accounts to be shaped and re-shaped, the workplace itself remains an unchanging, at times even a-historical, terrain. Developments, after all, seemed to occur in a sphere that appeared to be external from the vantage point of the 'modern' workplace. The underlying opposition between the spheres of the 'modern' and the 'pre-modern', more precisely, remained a structural feature of the binary that historians tried to overcome. This was a problem which in principle also informed studies which stressed continuity over change.

Early traditions of labour studies scholarship in India were informed by modernization theory and identified worker commitment to industry as the central problem faced by capitalism in Third World societies. In these analyses, the frequent absenteeism and apparent indiscipline of Indian industrial workers, set against a norm based on the experiences of advanced capitalist economies, were located in a narrative of transition from traditional to modern society. The habits and customs of workers, which stemmed from their pre-industrial roots in rural society, appeared as an impediment to capitalist development, and accounted for managers' complaints about absenteeism and labour market shortages.[28]

Morris David Morris offered an influential critique of this view; yet, he too remained within the fold of the narrative of pre-modern societies making a 'transition' to an industrial modernity whose patterns were known and could be predicted. Forms of absenteeism and labour turnover – the two central markers of workers 'habits' in colonial debates – were accordingly 'more likely a consequence of employer policy than of worker psychology and social attachments'.[29] That which appeared in colonial debates as the sphere of workers' habits was in this interpretation bound to economic conditions and rendered in terms of managerial strategies.

While this argument was an important one, Morris also made a crucial distinction between different forms of work-irregularity. Patterns of migration and workers' periodic returns to their rural homes were in this reading certainly a considerable phenomenon, linked to low wages and underdeveloped urban spaces. Practices of leaving the workplace in the course of the day, in contrast, were read as a result of managers' complaints and exaggerations. Based on statistical data that colonial officials gathered from the 1920s, Morris pointed out that the average rate of absent workers 'was probably always below 10 per cent, and we would suggest that this was not a very high figure, especially when we consider that illness alone probably contributed substantially to the total'.[30] Practices of substitution, in this reading, did not actually belong to the realm of habits nor to the workplace in Indian industries. They also did not belong to the set of managerial strategies which shaped the workplace in colonial India. This was, according to Morris, a general feature.

There are two crucial implications which result from this reading. One is that the pool of practices which constituted the peculiarities of the Indian workplace, in colonial debates, were stripped of precisely those elements which appeared to run counter to the demands of the 'modern' workplace at the site of production. Irregularity of work was only a problem when analysing questions of migration and of labour recruitment. A second implication, closely related to the first one, is that the workplace itself appears as unchanging. While patterns of migration might be subjected to changes – in particular if wage levels and conditions in mill-towns improved – the rhythms of work at the site of production did already meet the demands of the 'modern' workplace.

Morris's analysis, arguably, played a central role for later debates on labour relations in colonial India. Even when contesting his conclusions, historians largely accepted the frame of analysis he established, where recruitment and migration patterns became the central problems of labour history. This in turn tended to accentuate, rather than diminish, the division of the workplace into a dynamic 'outside' (where the irregularities of migration, neighbourhood and community mattered) and a static 'inside' (where the workplace itself appeared as largely immune to change). The impression that the opposition between the realm of the 'pre-modern' and that of the 'modern' did not actually pose a problem at the site of production, after all, was not the result of a particular employment strategy – that of excess-employment – but the result of the fact that there never was an opposition at this point in the first place. The workplace in Indian industries seemed exclusively to raise the question of how patterns of migration and forms of recruitment unfolded.

In response to histories that were informed by modernization theory, and tried to understand labour relations in colonial India in terms of transition, several critical histories emerged from the 1980s onwards. One important intervention came from Dipesh Chakrabarty in his study of the Bengal jute industry. Chakrabarty's work is widely acclaimed for its rejection of the notion that practices of workers could be understood in purely economic terms. Chakrabarty argued in favour of attending to the forms of culture and authority which governed workers outside the workplace and were translated into workplace practices of domination as well as resistance.[31] 'Theirs was', as

Chakrabarty argued, 'a precapitalist, inegalitarian culture marked by strong primordial loyalties of community, language, religion, caste, and kinship'.[32] Labour relations, accordingly, were characterized by the mutual incomprehension and incompatibility between workers and managers. The persistence of a peasant identity meant that workers remained at a certain level pre-industrial. Culture, as Chakrabarty's critics have argued, acquires a somewhat static, *deus ex* machina status in his explanation of labour relations.[33]

It has been pointed out that Chakrabarty's interpretation of labour relations in the Bengal jute industry effectively reproduced the image of 'Indian' workers which colonial officials and other contemporary observers presented.[34] Considering the implications of his arguments for the structure of the 'Indian' workplace, this argument might be stretched further to some degree. Practices of work, after all, were informed by a culture which essentially opposed the demands of the 'modern' workplace. Workers' culture, more precisely, indicated a notion of time and discipline which was essentially different to linear notions of time as presented by the 'modern' workplace. Notions of time are in this reading not singular elements, tied to particular practices, but deeply embedded in the realms of the 'Indian' and of the 'bourgeois' culture. Or, put differently, different notions of time were part of essentially different understandings of traditional hierarchies and of equality, of community and of modern individualism, or of religion and secularism.[35] Needless to say, what we are encountering here is the original opposition between the sphere of the 'modern' and that of the 'pre-modern', each of which is explained in terms of culture.

In his analysis, however, Chakrabarty does not simply follow the contemporary representations of the 'Indian' workplace, but he takes another path in two respects. In contrast to contemporary depictions of workplace relations, the two spheres of culture appear as two features which, indeed, could never meet. This is, first and foremost, apparent in relation to the question of change. Colonial officials still anticipated that the sphere of workers' 'habits' would eventually give way to a fully modern workplace or that, alternatively, workers were at least able to adapt to some degree to the demands of the 'modern' workplace. In Chakrabarty's account, in contrast, this option does not seem to exist, as both 'Indian' workers and European managers could not understand one another, and as their cultural heritages could not correspond. The sphere of the 'modern' and of the 'pre-modern' appears not simply as opposites or as different. Rather, they turn into incommensurables at this point, as Chakrabarty himself pointed out later.[36]

The second implication is that he uses the separation between the sphere of the 'modern' and that of the 'pre-modern' in order to clear the category of culture from economic concerns. 'Pre-modern' rhythms of work, then, did not remain a feature because of a shortage of labour supply, but simply because they were part of workers' culture. On the side of the mill, this meant that the concern with labour supply was a purely economic matter. The result was that the problem of labour supply appeared as the other side of a lack of the knowledge of the other aspects of the working classes.[37] This was most apparent in the figure of the *sirdar*.[38] This figure, after all, played a central role in recruiting outside the mill, as well as a crucial role in falsifying registers and other documents of employment at the shop-floor. In Chakrabarty's analysis, the *sirdar* stands for managerial lack of knowledge or, rather, the managerial unwillingness to learn about the workforce. So at the very point at which the worker acted as a worker, when engaged at the point of production, we encounter a peculiar situation where managerial authority seems to dissolve. The workplace itself therefore appears yet again as a space where the 'pre-modern' characteristics of workers are rendered invisible – not because of the impact of an excess-employment, nor because of industrial modernization, nor because of a deficiency among workers, but because of the casual attitude of managers towards securing adequate knowledge of their employees.

Chakrabarty's work marked the beginning of a new trend in Indian labour history, which began to move outside the workplace and explore a wide set of issues beyond the direct study of industrial relations. Industrial labour history, and more specifically the study of working-class identity, came to centre on the neighbourhood, migration networks and rural homes, family structures and gender relations, or the lived contexts of the urban poor.[39] The practices, beliefs, social relations and community structures, which colonial debates presented as belonging to an unchanging sphere of workers' 'habits', are in recent studies analysed through the lenses of identity formation, resistance and subversion, and everyday life. The category of culture plays an important role in these processes as well, though as part of a variety of interactions and relations that were constantly shaped and re-shaped.[40]

Workers' history, in these studies, appears to be increasingly vibrant. Workers in mill and factories negotiated their identities in everyday interactions at tea-shops, urban housing areas or in villages, while these histories are increasingly embedded in wider narratives, pointing to the influence of the colonial state or of the national movement. Seemingly 'static' features – such as the continuous importance of rural–urban connections – are widely seen to be based on survival networks that sustained workers in underdeveloped urban areas, as well as in a highly insecure labour market. The rural–urban connection, in this reading, appears to become part of the process of identity formation.[41]

While the studies of workers' practices and identities certainly have added a lot to our understanding of workers' histories in colonial India, they remain to some degree caught in the binary that was laid out by colonial observers. This problem is, first of all, reflected in a tendency to scrutinize the constitution of working-class culture in an increasingly diverse field, which lay outside of mills and factories. It is secondly – and most obviously – apparent when turning to the workplace. The workplace, in several studies, appears to play the function of a background, in which negotiations over identities, which originated in neighbourhoods, were being continued. The workplace as the site of production, in contrast, appears as an invisible and unchanging aspect – at least from the vantage point of the formation of workers' identities. The site of production, rather, appears to be a sphere that was shaped by the mills' claim of authority over workers – a feature that was fundamentally unchanging. One example here is Subho Basu's study of the jute industry. Jute mills, in his reading, appear as spaces that were dominated by the despotism of managers and European supervisors – a feature that expressed itself in excessive violence at the site of production.[42] The workplace is simultaneously presented as a site in which workers negotiated identities, community ties and solidarities through categories of honour and respect. The latter, however, appear to take shape in an undefined space, as the relation between workers' practices and the mills' claim to authority remain unexplored. Both elements of the everyday experiences of work, then, appear to unfold parallel to one another.[43]

Moving into another direction, several authors – and here foremost Chitra Joshi – argued that workers' identities at the site of production were reflected in practices of subversion and in forms of resistance. The category of agency appears crucial in this context, in order to understand the vibrancy of workers' worlds of labour. Workers, on this reading, used to work slower, or, alternatively to leave the site of production, in order to actively question and negotiate the limits of authority that were spelt out by the mill. Moments when workers interrupted their work, further, did not remain moments of subversion, but they were also moments during which they chatted and discussed with other workers, thus turning into a source of workers' experiences and of identity formation.[44]

In this reading, however, it seems that the category of agency takes on a specific function, insofar as it appears to create a distance between the moment in which workers were subjected to the mills' authority at the machines and those moments in which they actively shaped their identities. Agency, thus, seems to function in a way, which renders the workers' experiences and identity formation processes in terms of permanent opposition to the 'normal' rhythm of industrial work. The result is that workers' experiences, as part of a vibrant and dynamic field of working-class culture, appear to rest entirely on those moments when they did not act as workers. Their identities, in turn, were shaped in a similar fashion.

This brief overview of different studies of labour relations in colonial India reveals a peculiar tension. While historians sought to move beyond the division between the sphere of the 'modern' and the 'pre-modern' outside the site of production, this same division continued to structure histories of labour in colonial India. It was, more precisely, the 'Indian' workplace which continued to be understood in terms of two spheres or *moments* functioning parallel to one another. While the sphere of 'pre-modern' habits took different shapes in the various approaches, the latter – the sphere of the 'modern' – was persistently defined by a set of managerial strategies. These were unchanging, since they circulated in a realm of problems – labour supply, flexibility, efficiency – that remained constant.[45]

An interesting reversal, in other words, can be seen in the study of industrial labour relations in India. Colonial observers tended to explain blockages in the development of capitalism in terms of workers' unchanging habits. Some of the most sophisticated and fruitful recent scholarship, by contrast, attributes what were earlier seen as workers' deficiencies and irregularities, to the effects of managerial practices of authority, recruitment strategies, ideologies and ignorance of workers' life worlds. These managerial 'defects' now appear as an unchanging motor of a deadlock in the development of capitalism, just as workers' habits once did. At a certain level, then, the successful challenge to older understandings of labour relations has ended up mirroring some of its oppositions.

Workplace matters

This study seeks to move beyond the deadlock outlined above by reconsidering the workplace in Indian industries, and, more precisely, by tracing the changing organization of work in the Bengal jute industry between the 1870s and the 1930s. Contrary to commonly held assumptions, the organization of work at the site of production was transformed substantially in this period. On a broader level, this development was marked by an increasing regulation of workers' practices of cooperation at the shop-floor, and within the mill space. This was, firstly, reflected in managerial attempts to regulate the deployment of work gangs in Bengal jute mills between the 1870s and the First World War; it was reflected in the introduction of an individualized system of labour deployment in the 1920s and 1930s, and it was expressed in the regularization of the modalities of employment of workers in the late 1930s. The changing organization of work was, secondly, reflected in contestations over the modalities of labour deployment – both among capitalists, and between capital and labour. These contestations were strongest at moments of intensified change, and we will in particular consider the escalating labour conflicts of the late 1920s and the 1930s against the backdrop of the changing organization of work.

At the outset, the transformations of work in jute mills were driven by attempts to rationalize the process of production – a development which has been noted by several scholars with regard to Indian industries in this period. The transformations of work, however, were also a response to trends towards a standardization of jute goods and towards the introduction of newly specified products. This implied the introduction of new measures of managerial control, calculation of workers' skill and output, and of restrictions of workers' movements at the site of production. While the first jute mills in Bengal could not export jute goods due to their products' uneven quality, the industry started exporting sacking products after changing the organization of work in the 1870s, and started exporting hessian bags after another intervention at the site of production in the 1890s. The abolition of gang work in the 1920s and new changes in the 1930s, meanwhile, were a basic condition for producing finer hessian bags of different types.[46] These latter developments resulted in processes of formalization of labour relations in jute mills, which would continue to impact capital labour relations after the Second World War.

The transformations of work in jute mills, further, corresponded to the changing situation of the industry in jute belt. Questions of labour supply had been a source of concern in the early years of the industry, when mills relied exclusively on local sources of labour supply. These concerns were inscribed into the regulation of work gangs in the late nineteenth century in the form of excess-employment. By the early twentieth century, sources of labour supply had expanded to include Bihar and the United Provinces, and an internal labour market had emerged in the increasingly industrialized hinterland of Calcutta, accompanied by a drop in excess-employment within work gangs in the first decade of the twentieth century, and by the formal abolition of excess-employment under the new system of individual deployment.[47] With increasing levels of militancy among workers in the 1930s, attempts to retain control over workers in their neighbourhoods, too, came to be part of the organization of work in Bengal jute mills. This included, as we shall see, measures such as propaganda campaigns in workers' neighbourhoods, but also changes to the modalities of the employment of workers.

From the perspective of labour, the changing organization of work implied managerial infringements on established social relations that sustained practices of work at the site of production, and that sustained workers in their neighbourhoods. Survival networks, on which workers relied on in mill towns, were deeply embedded in the networks that workers relied on at the shop-floor. The changes in the organization of work affected among others the range of options that workers had to help secure jobs for friends and family members, and the ways in which workers could establish a hierarchy between sections of the workforce – such as (Hindu) spinners and (Muslim) weavers. The abolition of gang work in the 1920s also implied that the working day was regularized, as workers were required to remain at the shop-floor throughout their shift. This, in turn, implied restrictions for Bengali workers who had to walk several miles to the factory; it had implications for Muslim weavers who wanted to leave the workplace early during *Ramadan*; and it had an impact on the everyday rhythms of women at the shop-floor who had to look after children in the course of the day. The transformations of work in jute mills, in other words, spelt out interventions in the *social formation* of labour that had impacts both at the shop-floor and beyond.

The changing organization of work indicated a field of contestations of industrial relations that shaped labour conflicts in the 1870s, 1890s, late 1920s and in the second half of the 1930s. In the latter decades, managerial interventions intensified due to a deepening crisis of the industry and intensified attempts to adjust the process of production. Workers responded to these changes with militant strikes, and with refusal to implement the demanded changes. The contestations of industrial relations in this period were accompanied by emerging forms of organization of workers at the shop-floor in form of workers' committees, and the development came to intersect with the emerging trade union movement. Whereas the former affected labour conflicts at the level of individual mills (to be negotiated with the mills' manager), the latter meant that localized labour conflicts could emerge as broader conflicts, affecting the entire jute industry (to be negotiated with the Indian Jute Mills' Association and the Government of Bengal).

Tracing the transformations of the workplace in the Bengal jute industry in the following study, we will consider the regulation of work gangs between the 1870s and the early 1920s in Chapter 1. In this period, the organization of work in Bengal jute industry was based on distinct modes of regulating work gangs that came to be known as a *multiple-shift system*. The introduction of the system in the late nineteenth and early twentieth centuries has to be understood in correspondence to the expansion of the industry, as well as in connection with changes in the process of production that allowed for the production of finer hessian goods. At the outset of the First World War, however, the system's implementation in the industry came to be increasingly contested. This was driven by a growing crisis of overproduction, experienced by the Bengal jute industry as well as by conflicts between capital and state, as the specific modes of deploying work gangs in Bengal jute mills prevented the administration of the Indian Factories Act.

In Chapter 2, we shall turn to the modalities of work under the multiple-shift system in the 1920s. The deployment of work gangs under the system was at that point highly regulated. It was, further, an important source of contemporary images, commonly used to describe 'Indian' labour by contemporaries – such as absenteeism from the workplace, excess-employment or the power of *sirdars* over workers. Considering the modalities of the system more closely at this moment, then, is a crucial basis for re-conceptualizing the workplace in Indian industries. It is, further, an important backdrop, against which the implications of the changing organization of work in the 1920s and the 1930s can be mapped.

Chapter 3 will analyse the implications of the abolition of the multiple-shift system between the mid-1920s and the early 1930s. This change was marked by the deployment of individuals, instead of work gangs. The introduction of individualized labour deployment was driven by managerial concerns over measures of rationalization and labour control that targeted specific sections of the workforce. The change was accompanied by mass dismissals of 'excess labour', and by restrictions of workers' practices at the site of production, that they had hitherto relied on to sustain work at the machines.

The final two chapters of the book re-consider the strike movements in the Bengal jute industry in the late 1920s and in the 1930s. This period appeared as a conjunction between the growing militancy among jute workers over the changing organization of work and an emerging pan-Indian trade union movement. This meant, firstly, that the scale of struggles in the jute industry changed. What had previously been a series of localized strikes in the hinterland of Calcutta could emerge as broader strike movement, including two general strikes, in 1929 and 1937 (Chapter 4). It secondly correlated with impressive forms of workers' organization at the level of the factory, through which workers contested managerial rights to arrange work in jute mills in the first place. Managers responded by expanding measures of labour control from the workplace and into mill neighbourhoods. We will consider this development in Chapter 5.

Throughout the chapters of this book, the workplace and its transformations will be the central point of departure for investigating changing industrial relations in the jute industry, between the late nineteenth and mid-twentieth centuries. This analytical focus stems from the book's contention that the workplace in Indian industries has not been adequately analysed or theorized historically. Such an analysis can both re-contextualize broader developments of the jute industry and open up new questions for Indian labour history. However, there is also a clear limit to such an analysis. Its focus on the workplace implies a restriction in relation to themes that have been central to newer labour histories. These include the changing position of *sirdars*, the question of working-class consciousness as expressed in forms of subversion and resistance, the changing gender relations within the workforce, the complex relations of authority and pressure between workers' militancy and trade union organizations controlled by *bhadralok* activists, and the frequently violent communal segmentations between Hindu and Muslim workers. These themes, which have been the source of the richest insights of Indian labour history since the critical turn occasioned by Chakrabarty's work, do crop up recursively through the book. But they do so more episodically than substantively, and principally insofar as they connect with the book's main theme – the nature and consequences of transformations in the organization of work itself. The Conclusion to this book, therefore, takes up and attempts to disentangle some of these issues, and to relate them in new ways to the question of the historical constitution of the industrial workplace.

Sets, squads and shifts – the emergence and development of the 'Multiple-Shift' system

In 1908, D.R. Wallace published a series of articles in a Calcutta journal, in which he recounted the history of the Bengal jute industry. His narrative began in the mid-1850s, when the first two mills were built on the Hugli; dwelt on the 1870s, when the industry expanded into one of the major industries of colonial India; and ended in Wallace's own present, when the Bengal jute industry had established a global monopoly over the production of jute goods. Due to the immense interest in his articles, Wallace soon re-published them in the form of a book, with the title 'The Romance of Jute' – a name that reflected the author's interpretation of this story of industrial growth and expansion.[1]

Around the same time, Wallace was interviewed by the members of the 1908 Factory Commission as one of the representatives of the jute industry. A central concern of the commissioners during these interviews was to make sense of the multiple-shift system, as well as to understand the reasons for its application. The multiple-shift system was at that point a dominant feature of the Bengal jute industry, and was exclusive to it. Its structural features and functions, however, puzzled the commissioners. In their final report, they remarked on the complexity of the system, while giving accounts of the interrogations of workers, which they had conducted in an attempt to ascertain that the system was, in fact, applied in Bengal jute mills.[2]

In his response, Wallace described the origin of the multiple-shift system as part of the history of the jute industry, pointing out that the system had emerged at two distinct moments in the late nineteenth century:

> In the seventies, when so many jute mills were erected, the hours gradually grew longer as the result of competition, and a shift system followed. The system was perfected [in the 1890s,] when electric light was introduced.[3]

While placing the origin of the multiple-shift system in its contemporary form in different moments of the industry's past, Wallace further hinted at the fact that the 'shifts' had come up in the preparing and spinning departments of jute mills.[4] The vaguely defined 'perfection' of the system, as Wallace's argument implied, described the introduction of a second mode of regulation in the weaving and finishing departments in the mid-1890s. The term multiple-shift system acquired a new meaning in this time, as it came to describe distinct modes of labour deployment in preparing and spinning departments, but also the regulations of work in the weaving and finishing sections of Bengal jute mills.[5]

In 1908, Wallace was not the only one who presented the multiple-shift system this way. Several managers used the term in a way which indicated that it had been applied since the early days of the industry, while it was, simultaneously, presented as having been introduced recently, when referring to the entire mill.[6] From the perspective of the commissioners, the terminology of the multiple-shift system certainly contributed to the uncertainty in defining the system. In contrast to the commissioners, however, Wallace did not seem particularly interested in the multiple-shift system. While connecting its history to the expansion of the industry when asked about the matter by the commissioners, he did not include the topic in his 'Romance of Jute', neither as a factor for the growth of the industry, nor as a particular factory system.[7]

Twenty years later, Wallace published a second edition of the 'Romance of Jute', in which he included new sections on the history of the industry. In contrast to his earlier interpretation of the industry's past and present, the multiple-shift system now figured prominently in the book, taking up substantive parts of the additions. Instead of elaborating distinct forms of regulation at the shop floor, he highlighted the deployment of work gangs as a basic (or, in Wallace's reading: essential) feature of the system. The deployment of work gangs under the multiple-shift system accordingly granted workers the freedom to leave the site of production during hours of work that they needed.[8] It simultaneously served the needs of capital, as its application meant that the mills on the Hugli could regulate the output of jute goods flexibly. The key for both these advantages was a structure of excess labour. This, according to Wallace's analysis, meant that the mills had access to a 'conserved' productive capacity of labour when they wanted to adjust hours of work, while workers could always rely on 'extra' workers when leaving the site of production in the course of the day. The multiple-shift system, thus, appeared as a condition for prolonging the 'Romance of Jute' in Bengal.[9]

The new departure in Wallace's descriptions of the multiple-shift system points us less to a new perception of the organization of work than to a new situation within the industry itself. In contrast to the early 1900s, the application of the multiple-shift system was highly contested within the industry. After the previous periods of growth, the mills on the Hugli were faced with a growing threat of overproduction. According to the opponents of the multiple-shift system, the systematic deployment of work gangs posed a threat to the industry, due to the 'conserved' productive capacity of the mills. A second set of problems, connected with the deployment of work gangs, was the problem of labour control – more specifically, the apparent limitations to the establishment of proper managerial control at the site of production. This problem was not raised only by managers and managing agents, but also by the colonial state. The inspector of factories, in particular, complained repeatedly that it was impossible to regulate working hours as long as even the mill managers had no means of controlling the rhythms of substitution of their excessive workforce.[10]

We will discuss the specific reasons for, and dynamics of, conflicts over the multiple-shift system in the 1920s in more detail below. For now, it may suffice to return to Wallace, and to point out that he was responding to a situation in which the application of the multiple-shift system was increasingly contested. The underlying form of work-organization – the deployment of work gangs – had become a problem. A growing number of mills abolished the multiple-shift system in this decade, introducing a regular single-shift system in its place.[11] Wallace's new statement on the principal features of the multiple-shift system was a response to these developments, focusing on the presumably essential functions which the multiple-shift system had to offer the industry and its workforce.

Wallace's observations from 1908 and 1928 reflected general patterns in the way contemporaries used to present the organization of work in Bengal jute mills. These may be summarized in two ways. First, the multiple-shift system described a specific factory system based on the deployment of work gangs. It emerged between the 1870s and the 1890s, combining two modes of work-gang regulation. It was applied in this form until the late 1920s. Second, the multiple-shift system shaped the prospects of industrial development, since its application rested on a structural excess in employment which served the needs of industry and (Indian) workers alike. Between the early 1900s and the 1920s, however, the deployment of work gangs seemed to turn into an impediment for the industry. By the late 1920s, then, the system had come to be identified with problems of overproduction and of labour control. In a growing number of mills, it was replaced by a single-shift system, which was based on the deployment of individuals, rather than work gangs.

In studies of the history of the Bengal jute industry, the multiple-shift system has barely been discussed. More so, questions of work-organization and factory regulation entered history books predominantly in the form of generalized remarks, which hardly served to identify the features of the multiple-shift system in their specific historic contexts, nor in their processes of change. Symptomatic of this problem is that the majority of historians presented the case as if the multiple-shift system was introduced in the mid-1890s, when a number of jute mills installed electric light and increased their hours of work. According to this reading, the multiple-shift system was introduced as a fully developed factory system, which neither evolved nor was grounded in changing forms of regulation of work at the site of production. Instead, its sole purpose was to enable an increase in hours of work during periods of high demand for jute goods. Scholars treated the multiple-shift system as a standard double shift system, which was introduced and abolished by the mills of IJMA in order to regulate hours of work.[12]

Some historians have taken another path and placed the origin of the multiple-shift system in an undefined past, without further specification of its origin or development. Even Ranajit Das Gupta – a historian not otherwise prone to vague formulations – wrote that the multiple-shift system had been introduced 'quite early', when discussing strikes in the 1890s.[13] In this, and in similar cases, the multiple-shift system entered the narrative of histories of the jute industry only in the last years of the nineteenth century, when it had been fully developed as a factory system, and the mills of the IJMA had increased their hours of work.[14] The different chronology of factory regulation in Bengal jute mills was thus still embedded within a similar periodization of labour relations, and in a narrative which effectively reduced the multiple-shift system to a standard double shift system.[15]

The problem about equating the multiple-shift system with a double shift system lies not so much with the name for the system.[16] 'Double shift system' was one of the terms that contemporaries used as well.[17] While this is probably an important reason for the choice of this term by historians, it contributed to the confusion over the system. A double shift system refers to the deployment of individual workers during each shift rather than work gangs. The regulation of work in Bengal jute mills, in turn, appeared to be determined only by a longer duration of the working day, rather than by an organization of work based on the deployment of work gangs. The problem of excess-employment, meanwhile, appeared to bear no relation to the mode of labour deployment either. Rather, it, appeared to be an additional feature, grounded either in workers' migratory habits, or in the demand of the industry for excessively long hours of work.[18]

Even in studies where the multiple-shift system was not treated as a regular double shift system, this division was apparent. Dipesh Chakrabarty, for instance, noted that the multiple-shift system was a unique feature of Bengal jute mills. He further suggested that the everyday rhythms of work in this system were an expression of workers' culture which managers had conceded. The existence of the multiple-shift system, then, seemed to confirm the inapplicability of the 'modern' factory system to India. Notwithstanding this apparent origin of the multiple-shift system, however, its abolition in the late 1920s, in Chakrabarty's account, seems to have had little effect on workplace relations – neither in terms of 'modernizing' the workplace nor in terms of triggering conflicts at the site of production. Chakrabarty, in other words, reverts at this point to treating the problem of shift-systems and the organization of work as two distinct features which inhabited different temporal realms.[19]

Rather than merely indicating a scholarly omission, the problems encountered in identifying the multiple-shift system are, arguably, a reflection of a blockage in the study of the process of production. The separation of the *organization* of work from the *regulation* of work under the factory system in Bengal jute mills – as well as the de-historicization of both – was a result of the fact that the process of production has the status of an abstraction in previous histories of the Bengal jute industry. Historians generally contented themselves with pointing out that individual tasks in the process of production in jute mills were simple and that managers rarely invested in new machinery, thus concluding that the process of production remained continuously simple as well. The apparent simplicity of the production process, then, seemed to account for managerial strategies, which were concerned with hours of work, but not with workplace relations. Other managerial strategies – such as excess employment – were subjected to the problem of hours of work, enabling a flexible regulation of the latter.[20]

This blockage contributed to the impression that the multiple-shift system was not subject to historical change. For if the process of production and labour relations at the point of production were continuously simple and unchanging, then the 1870s would, indeed, be no different in this respect from the 1920s. Attempts, by contemporaries, like Wallace, to present the multiple-shift system as an eternal feature of the Bengal jute industry in the midst of the crisis of the system, then, seemed to be confirmed retroactively by the concerns of historians, while simultaneously reinforcing these very concerns. The consequence of this is, ironically, that evidence about work-organization gathered from the very period of irreversible change has been mobilized in explanations which effectively assume the unchanging character of work-organization.

To move beyond these blockages, we need to begin by re-considering the history of the Bengal jute industry. The development of the multiple-shift system as part of the history of the Bengal jute industry should, arguably, be understood as a cumulative regulation of work gangs, which performed different functions in the context of the industry, as well as at the site of production. In the 1870s, the deployment of work gangs was formalized in a way which established excess employment as the dominant feature of labour deployment. This served to incorporate a reserve army of labour, in a context of recurring labour shortages. The expansion of the multiple-shift system in the mid-1890s, however, indicated a qualitatively new development. It entailed increased attempts to control workers at the site of production, by restricting the motions of groups of workers at the site of production. While this expansion at first only affected workers who occupied key positions in the process of production, the new regulation of work gangs was expanded further in the early years of the twentieth century. This signalled a growing de-naturalization of the deployment of work gangs, which Wallace observed in the 1920s.

1.2

Work gangs, sets and multiple-shifts – the introduction of the 'Multiple-Shift' system in the 1870s

In the early decades of its existence, the Bengal jute industry experienced a slow yet steady growth. In the 1850s, the first two jute mills opened their gates on the Hugli. By the late 1860s, three more mills had come up. Situated at various spots in the hinterland of Calcutta, they produced one type of coarse packing material, the so-called 'sacking' cloths and bags. Their products were sold exclusively in British India and Burma. While the five mills made sound profits, the limited range of products in this period meant that profit margins were not too impressive and did not leave much space for further expansion.[1]

In the early 1870s, the situation of the industry changed crucially. In 1872, jute mills began to export their products to foreign markets, which resulted in a sudden increase in profits made in Bengal. This was, not surprisingly, followed by a rush of capital into the young industry, and between 1873 and 1875, twelve new mills were built on the Hugli.[2] Summarizing the changes in the industry, the correspondent of the Dundee Advertiser wrote in 1879:

> Not a decade ago the Jute mills did not exceed five in number, with about a thousand looms at the outside. Their number now is twenty, with 4800 looms, representing an invested capital of over two and a half millions sterling.[3]

While the productive capacity of the jute industry soon outstripped the demand for its goods, anticipations of an imminent growth in demand mounted in the following years. The growing global demand for trading goods contributed to these hopes, as jute products emerged as central packaging material for trading goods in the second half of the nineteenth century. A representative of the Dundee jute industry explained in 1872 that the jute industry was the 'the most expansive of any trade now in existence', arguing that the volume of global trade would grow fourfold in the next ten years.[4]

Until the early 1880s, then, new mills were still being built, while older mills proceeded to install new looms. By the early 1890s, the number of looms in the industry had increased to over 9,500.[5]

The 1870s also witnessed a change in the organization of work in Bengal's jute mills. In 1872, a number of mills introduced a 'crude' system of 'relieving-squads' in their preparing and spinning departments.[6] At the heart of this system was the employment of work gangs arranged into 'sets' – batches at the site of production. The number of workers per set exceeded the requirements of the process of production. This mode of work-organization was not in itself new, as the first jute mills in Bengal had already deployed their workers in sets.[7] Rather, the novel feature of the newly introduced 'relieving-squads' was that existing sets of workers were divided into workers and 'extra' workers. The relation between excess employment and sets of workers at the site of production, in other words, was *formalized*. While excess-employment continued to be a structural feature of the organization of work in Bengal jute mills, it acquired a new status, as the fact of an excess in employment turned into a visible, and measurable, category.

In the following years, the system was developed further in the spinning and preparing departments of jute mills, developing in the course of the decade into the multiple-shift system. In contrast to the earlier mode of arranging sets, mills working with a 'shift'-system deployed three sets of workers in the course of one working day. In the words of contemporary observers, each of these was arranged in the form of relay shifts.[8] However, given that the basis for these relays was sets (or groups) of workers, and not individuals, this structure might better be described as *relay-sets*. This change, then, served to fix the degree of excess-employment, which was retained in the course of the working day, at a higher level than in 'single-set' mills.

The changes in the organization of work in the 1870s meant that on an average three workers were employed for two tasks. An exemplary set of three workers would be comprised of two workers at machines, and one worker who was technically speaking employed without a task. In overall terms, the degree of excess-employment was fixed between 25 and 30 per cent of the requirements of the production process.[9] In the 1870s, when the mills on the Hugli worked seventy-two hours per week, just as in the late 1890s, when the mills of the IJMA increased their weekly hours to ninety, the degree of excess-employment remained largely the same in mills applying a multiple-shift system.[10] It was only in the 1920s, when hours of work were reduced to fifty-four, that some mills reduced the number of relay-sets, thus changing the ratio between workers and 'extra' workers. This, in turn, led to a reduction of excess-employment to 10 per cent of the requirements of production.[11]

The formalization of the relation between sets of workers and excess-employment, however, also implied that the relation between sets and work gangs was affected. Work gangs, which were a stable element in the process of recruitment through *sirdars*, and sets of workers deployed at the site of production, were formally detached from one another. The recruitment and the deployment of workers, in other words, were formally separated. Providing a glimpse into this problem, in 1894, Marie Imandt reported an interview she conducted in the Titaghur Jute Mills, with a group of five women workers. The women seemed to work together as a group, without being deployed in the same 'set'. Being asked about the rhythms of their shifts, they responded:

> Q: *When do you go to work in the morning?*
> A: The old ones at nine, the young ones at six.
> Q: *How many times do you go out to rest?*
> A: The old ones three times, the young twice.[12]

While each of the members of the group of five, then, had different hours of work, they distributed the rhythms of relay-sets in their group according to the relations among themselves, in this case on the basis of age.[13] As part of a work gang, however, the group of five women was employed throughout the day.

Whereas the introduction of the multiple-shift system spelt out decisive changes in the organization of work in the preparing and spinning departments, the rhythms of workers in the weaving and finishing departments remained largely unaltered. In this part of the mill workers continued to be deployed in single sets. Rather, indications suggest that as late as the early 1890s, workers in core departments such as weaving were simply contracted for the day, which suggests that work gangs and sets of workers remained largely identical.[14] Describing the rhythms of work in the weaving department, the manager of the Serampore Jute Mill declared with some enthusiasm that workers

> are at liberty to go out and to their work at their own convenience; this suits them well and makes the work in the mills very popular with them as there is no restriction whatever put up on them as regards going out and in.[15]

While the degree of excess-employment was not formalized as under the system of relay-sets, workers in the weaving and finishing departments still participated in the same process of production as workers in the preparing and spinning departments. Managers and managing agents seem to have calculated the degree of excess employment on the basis of the entire workforce in the department, as 'extra' workers were not specifically deployed in particular sets. The degree of excess-employment was, accordingly, fixed indirectly in these parts of the mill.

At the point of its introduction, and in the midst of a hitherto unprecedented period of growth, a central function of the multiple-shift system was, clearly enough, to enable an increase in hours of work. Under the earlier 'single set' system, workers in Bengal jute mills had worked about ten hours per day, as jute mills ran their machines for twelve hours daily, with two-hour breaks in the course of the day. Under the multiple-shift system, in contrast, jute mills increased their daily hours of work to twelve or fourteen (depending on sunlight) by deploying sets of workers continuously through the day. Sets in the preparing and spinning departments were arranged in relays, while sets in the weaving and finishing departments were simply deployed without specified break-periods.[16]

Increases or reductions in hours of work in Indian industries, by adjusting the deployment of sets of workers, were in themselves neither new nor uncommon. Mills and factories commonly changed the number of workers employed per set in order to regulate the hours of work flexibly. This method was, for instance, commonly used in seasonal factories. Workers in these units were employed in work gangs; yet, the number of workers per gang changed in response to the changing workload through the year. Members of the 1908 Factory Commission, thus, noted that in phases of intensive work,

> the gins are usually worked for periods up to 15, and in rare cases 18, hours, with one set of hands; but a certain number of additional workers are generally engaged, so that the operatives can have periodical intervals of rest.[17]

The commissioners did not see any substantial problem with this approach, and their question rather was if enough 'additional' workers had been employed per ginning mill, in order to balance the long hours of work.[18]

In the weaving and finishing departments of Bengal jute mills, the increase in hours of work seems to have been achieved in a similar manner – by simply employing 'extra' workers in those departments.[19] In the preparing and spinning departments, however, the deployment of workers without formal break-periods seems not to have been an option. Managers remained silent on the reasons for this, but the requirements of the process of production might have contributed to this apparent limitation. When contrasting the development of the overall hours of work with the hours of workers in the preparing and spinning departments, the continuity of this 'limit' is striking. In the latter, workers always worked between nine and ten hours a day and they always had specified break-periods – under the system of single sets in the 1860s, just as much as under the multiple-shift system in the 1870s, the 1890s and the 1920s. Even in the Hastings Jute Mill, where working time was increased to twenty-two hours a day in the mid-1890s, the structure of relay-sets ascertained that workers in the spinning mill were formally deployed for nine to ten hours.[20] The reorganization of sets of workers into relay-sets in one part of the mill, then, appeared to be the basis for raising the hours of work in the entire mill in the years when the industry experienced its first major boom.

The introduction of the multiple-shift system, however, had a second purpose, which was reflected in the establishment of an increased and, more importantly, fixed degree of excess-employment. Excess-employment itself was, arguably, grounded in the vagaries of the labour market situation faced by jute mills, which corresponded to the problems faced by capitalist industry across colonial India. Factories functioned in a situation of generalized labour abundance, which was, however, combined with contingent labour shortages.[21] Between the 1870s and the early 1900s, this was a stable characteristic of the jute industry. In aggregate terms, the mills had access to a sufficient supply of labour, drawn from local sources. At the same time, epidemics, famine, the rapid expansion of the industry and the growing demand for labour by new mills acted as counterweights that restricted the supply of labour. Further, the absence of subsidiary forms of casual employment in the vicinity of the mills, to help sustain workers in times of low demand, meant that the jute industry suffered from the absence of a fully stabilized labour force. This was what grounded the need to maintain a surplus supply of labour at the workplace itself, and to formulate means of work-organization that gave this surplus a formalized, systematic character: the retention of an internalized reserve force of labour.

The formal detachment of work gangs from sets of workers under the multiple-shift system, then, established the dominance of excess-employment as a defining function of labour deployment in this period. In the words of capitalists, the multiple-shift system served to 'conserve' labour in Bengal jute mills.[22] J. Sime, the head of the IJMA in 1928, explained in a similar manner:

> The real truth is that there is surplus labour in the double shift [multiple shift system]. There are more hands than there should be, and we know that all were not working.[23]

Excess-employment, therefore, in the form of 'extra' workers at the point of production, was a mechanism that helped guard against periodic fluctuations in the supply of labour. Excess-employment, integrated with a factory system in the form of gang work, can be understood as a structure of mediation between structural labour abundance on the one hand and contingent labour shortage on the other. The multiple-shift system, then, combined the purposes of enabling an increase in the hours of work and that of conserving a permanent reserve supply of labour.

Surely enough, this second concern, too, was reflected in the structure of the multiple-shift system. The preparing and spinning departments proved to be a continuous source of managerial trouble, from the earliest days of the industry. The principal problem here was that Bengal jute mills combined two industrial units which had hitherto been separate: spinning mill and weaving factory. In Dundee, the processes of spinning yarn and weaving cloth were always conducted in separate units, which were rarely even in the hands of the same company.[24] In Bengal, in contrast, the Borneo Company, usually identified as the second jute mill in Bengal, combined the two functions in one mill unit.[25] This allowed the company to successfully control the entire process of production of jute from the arrival of the jute plants to the finishing of jute clothes in one industrial unit. However, the combination of spinning mill and weaving factory proved to be a weak point in the process of production. Raw jute was of a particularly uneven nature, making constant adjustments in the process of production of jute yarn necessary.[26]

A second problem, closely related to the first, was apparent in the process of softening the raw jute: the hitherto best-known substance for this step was whale oil. Bengal jute mills, however, used cheaper mixtures of vegetable and mineral oils, which, in turn, rendered the production of yarn of an even quality even more difficult.[27] The result was that the connection between spinning mill and weaving factory was a fragile point in the production chain. Throughout the history of the industry, the problem was apparent in various ways. Industrial reports, for instance, indicate a tendency of the industry to produce too little yarn. Strikes, too, brought problems of inadequate yarn supply into the open time and again.[28]

The attempt to increase the stability of production was reflected in the formalization of sets in the preparing and spinning departments. While the overall degree of excess employment was frozen at a high level, the internal separation of sets into workers and 'extra' workers functioned to render this increase a more efficient one from the perspective of the mill. The employment of three workers for two jobs implied, technically speaking, that 'one and a half' workers were employed for one task. Giving an indication of the advantages of this formula from the perspective of capital, the manager of the Champdany Jute

Mill stated, when asked about the necessity of a regulation of hours of work of children in the spinning mill:

> Now, in face of such an enforcement, the basis of which we fail to see for thereby, as at present labour is very scarce with us, and instead of requiring one and a half young persons and children per shift, we would be compelled to employ two, which of course would materially increase our costs of production.[29]

The separation of work gangs and sets of workers, then, appeared to be a side effect of the attempt to increase excess employment.

The concerns about securing the stability of production by ensuring a regular flow of workers were, lastly, grounded in the specific contexts of the industry. Jute mills were comparatively large industrial units. While information about employment rates in the industry remains scattered until the 1890s, it seems certain that the industry employed an impressive number of workers in the 1870s.[30] The Baranagore Jute Mill, for instance, employed more than 4,000 workers daily by the 1860s, while the Samnuggur Jute Mill employed 'upwards of 1,500 natives' in the mid-1870s.[31] Describing the emerging industry, a contemporary report noted:

> The most remarkable manufacturing feature of the present time, however, is the great development, in the neighbourhood of Calcutta, of large steam mills for the spinning and weaving of jute and gunny bags, in establishments of a European character under European management. There are 15 to 20 large jute factories in and around Calcutta; and the tall smoking chimneys recall associations of the manufacturing cities in Europe.[32]

This vivid impression of an emerging urban-industrial area, however, had a crucial flaw: the mills were not situated in urban areas, but in the hinterland of Calcutta. They had been built on strips of land squeezed between the river and dense forests. Jute mills were, further, not placed near roads or rail stations. The transport of raw materials and goods was conducted exclusively by river. For this purpose, a number of mills built 'private' railroads, leading from the mill to the river.[33]

The location of mills as well as the spatial structure of the industry, in other words, became crucial dimensions of the labour market situation, since they affected the accessibility of mills.

The reasons for choosing spots along the river, from Budge-Budge to Naihati, had to do with cheap land prices and lower tax rates in rural municipalities.[34] Cheap land, in particular, was an important concern for mill owners. In order to be prepared for the next increase in demand, mill owners regularly bought some 'extra' land in the vicinity of their mills for the purpose of future extension. While constructing new mills, managing agents already anticipated future loom installations.[35] By 1895 when John Leng visited the Bengal jute belt, mills owned spare land, in anticipation of the next industrial boom.[36]

Another reason for placing jute mills in the hinterland of Calcutta was the belief shared by most industrialists that this would secure a sufficient and a cheap supply of labour. Given that until the 1890s jute mills drew their workforces mainly from local sources, it is not surprising that a good location was considered one with an 'abundant' labour supply in the vicinity, and without competing mills in the immediate neighbourhood. Otherwise, went the worry, mills would be subject to intense wage-competition.[37] The district magistrate of Hooghly complained in 1879:

> In Serampore the establishment of four jute mills has increased the competition on the part of employers of all kinds to obtain labour, and the result has been that the wages not only of the mill hands but of labourers of all sorts have been greatly raised.[38]

Fears of increasing competition over workers remained a staple of the industry in the years to come. In the early 1880s, the owners of the Samnuggur Jute Mill tried to prevent the building of the Victoria Jute Mill in the neighbourhood of one of their concerns, by initiating legal proceedings against their rival mill owners. Their case was lost, however, and the new mill was built.[39]

Mill owners enjoyed uneven success in their search for locations with abundant labour supply. Some notable success stories included the Gourepore Jute Mill, which was situated near an already-existing town and reported few concerns with labour supply; so too the Howrah Jute Mills, which had been erected near Calcutta.[40] In other cases, however, the location chosen turned into an important source of problems with labour supply. The Fort Gloster Jute Mill was not only not located near an existing town, but its location rendered the mill hard to access for workers walking longer distances:

> Fort Gloster is the name of a pergunnah or villah, situated on the banks of the Hooghly, about 12 miles from Calcutta, on the opposite side of the river. It is not very readily accessible to Calcutta save by water, the only other way being to drive down the road to Budge Budge, and to cross the river there to Fort Gloster, just opposite – a somewhat tedious and tiresome journey.[41]

Given the isolated location of the mill, it is hardly surprising that the Fort Gloster Jute Mill was among those which were reported to suffer from labour shortages.[42]

In addition to the relative isolation of jute mills, the location of mills between rivers and forests also increased the risks of diseases. Take, for instance, the Samnuggur Jute Mill:

> The mill is very fairly supplied with labour, but the situation is unhealthy, and much fever prevails there during the rainy season. The wind blowing over an unhealthy tract of forest or jungle before it reaches the mill, it certainly is not the most desirable spot in a sanitary point of view upon which to have located a Jute mill.[43]

Malaria, in particular, regularly took epidemic form in the jute belt, a problem apparent throughout the history of the industry.[44] As late as 1930, a health survey among jute workers stated that levels of malaria among them were 'abnormally high'.[45] After a fresh epidemic outburst in the Waverly Jute Mill, the Inspector of Factories reported:

> It is thought that the prevalence of the disease is due to large tracks of jungle in the vicinity of the mill. The manager of the mill states that until such jungle is entirely cleared, the workers and other residents in the district will continue to be liable to such attacks.[46]

In the 1930s, the jute belt had changed considerably, as we shall see. The Waverly Jute Mill was, in fact, located in an important centre of the jute industry, near Barrackpore, where large numbers of jute workers were concentrated. While the managers of the Waverly Jute Mill apparently promised to clear the forest on and near their mill compounds, the peculiar mixture of industrial areas and forested surroundings seems to have changed only gradually.[47]

1.3

The extension of the multiple-shift system in the 1890s and the emergence of the jute belt

In the mid-1890s, the Bengal jute industry entered a new period of growth, marked by the production of an increasing number of hessian cloths and bags. Hessian cloths, in contrast to sacking cloths, were of a higher quality, and had hitherto been the main commodity produced in Dundee.[1] With the new scope of production, the expansion of the Bengal industry exceeded previous limits, and new mills mushroomed all along the Hugli. Within a brief period, the number of jute mills nearly doubled, while the number of looms installed in Bengal increased from about 9,500 in the early 1890s to over 30,000 in 1908.[2]

The industry's second boom was, yet again, combined with a change in the organization of work. The multiple-shift system came to be extended to the weaving department. As with the organization of work in the preparing and spinning departments, the newly introduced regulation among weavers implied a formal division between workers and 'extra' workers at the site of production. Sets of workers and work gangs, previously largely identical in the organization of work, were formally detached from one another. In contrast to the regulation of the 1870s, however, this separation did not serve to establish a determinate degree of excess-employment. Weaving sets barely incorporated any 'extra' workers under the extended multiple-shift system. In large sections of the department sets were comprised exclusively on the basis of one worker per loom. It was only in the hessian side of the department that weaving sets included 'extra' workers without a specified task.[3]

One result of this was that the importance of additional 'extra' workers in the everyday rhythms of work, as well as their concrete distribution in weaving departments, remained unspecified in managerial accounts. It however seems likely that the number of additional workers employed was flexible and hinged on the length of the working day, as well as on the availability of workers at any given moment. In the mid-1890s, when the mills on the Hugli had increased their hours of work to fifteen per day while the industry was expanding rapidly, the 'extra' workforce was probably more important than it was in the 1920s, when mills on a multiple-shift system had reduced their daily hours of work to thirteen and a half and when, as capitalists stated, labour shortages had ceased to be a problem.[4]

Either way, the new modalities of the deployment of weavers signalled a different set of concerns about the regulation of the workforce at the site of production. This was, firstly, grounded in the requirements of the process of production. The specific focus on the weaving department was the outcome of concerns of managerial control over workers at a particularly crucial point in the process of production. We shall discuss the implications of this change on the everyday rhythms of weavers in more detail in the next chapter – for now, it may suffice to point out that the reduced number of 'extra' workers in the weaving department meant that managers had better oversight over the work done by individual members of a set. Weavers occupied the only position classified as semi-skilled, and concerns about the quality of work in the weaving department posed an ever-present source of managerial worries.[5] With the increasing importance of finer hessian products, these concerns gained a new urgency.[6]

The externalization of excess-employment corresponded with the growing importance of new sources of labour supply and, in turn, with a change in the composition of the workforce. Before the 1890s, jute mills had nearly exclusively employed Bengali workers. In the early 1890s, an increasing number of migrant workers began to come to the jute belt. The majority of these workers came from Bihar and the United Provinces and were classified as 'up-country'. This development accelerated in the course of the expansion of the industry from the mid-1890s.[7] By the early twentieth century, Bengali workers had become a minority in jute mills, and about 80 per cent of jute workers were 'up-country' migrants. In the following years, new groups of migrant workers from Orissa and the northern parts of Madras Presidency joined the trend.[8]

The changing composition of the workforce was distributed unevenly. Whereas weaving departments were soon filled exclusively with 'up-country' workers, the workforce in spinning mills, and in particular spinning departments, remained dominated by Bengali workers. Managerial strategies seem to have played a crucial role in this development – particularly in relation to the dominance of 'up-country' workers in weaving departments.[9] While managers, as so often, remained silent about such measures, workers' responses were clearer, as the mid-1890s saw an increasing number of strikes. Conflicts between newly employed 'up-country' weavers and Bengali workers were an important trigger in this context.[10]

The extension of the multiple-shift system had another implication which contributed to the changing composition of the workforce. The reduction of excess labour to its bare minimum implied that weavers' options of arranging hours of work among themselves had been restricted as well. Practices of substitution, after all, hinged in the first place on the presence of extra workers. Making matters worse, managers also implemented a number of measures to ascertain the attendance of individual weavers at the beginning and at the end of the working day, in order to further increase their control over weavers' movements at the site of production.[11] The extension of the multiple-shift system, in other words, implied an increasingly *regular* working day for weavers.

This posed a problem for Bengali workers in particular. While generally classified as 'locals', Bengali workers mostly lived in villages that bordered jute mills and were compelled to walk several miles to reach their workplace.[12] 'Up-country' workers, in contrast, generally lived in mill towns. Bengali weavers, then, faced new disadvantages when they tried to combine mill work with staying in their rural homes. In the spinning mill, in contrast, the system of relay-sets meant that workers still had the option to turn up for the second or third shift, beginning their working day earlier or later. In the structure of relay-sets, further, break periods were often comparatively long, enabling workers who lived in villages closer to the mill to walk home during lunch breaks.[13]

In the late nineteenth and early twentieth centuries, when the jute mills worked fifteen hours per day, the increasing difficulties faced by Bengali weavers in reaching the mill were often presented as a problem of hours of work, rather than a problem of extended deployment. While a representative of the Kankinarrah Jute Mill explained in 1908 that in his mill, Bengali workers 'would not come at five A.M., and at present, they started with the second shift', a weaving *sirdar*, who had worked in the same mill for twenty-six years, explained:

> Before electric light was introduced many of the local Bengali men came to work, but they did not come now on account of the long hours. No workers in the Kankinara mill approved of such long hours; they were unanimously opposed to them. The operatives had absolutely no time at home for their domestic concerns. They got home at about 9 P.M. and did not get to bed till about 11 P.M. Then they had to get up about 3 A.M., prepare their food, wash, and so on, and get to work by 4 A.M.[14]

In the 1920s, when hours of work had been reduced to fifty-four per week, this problem remained. Mills working with a multiple-shift system distributed their weekly hours over four working days of thirteen and a half hours of work, leading to extensively long days when the mills' gates were open.[15]

The inflow of migrant workers coincided with the construction of new mills along the river. The boom of the 1890s led to an unprecedented escalation and in the hinterland of Calcutta, new labour centres emerged. The area was increasingly covered with jute mills, or, as John Leng put it: 'now the new mills on the Hooghly are clustering more together and filling up intervening spaces'.[16] In the process, towns and villages, such as Barrackpore or Titaghur, rapidly turned into mill towns. In and around Barrackpore, for instance, nine jute mills opened their gates in close proximity to one another, among them the Anglo-India Jute Mills, which combined four complete mill units in their compound.[17] In Titaghur, just south of Barrackpore, five mills were opened between the 1880s and the 1910s, two of which were among the largest mills on the river, each employing over 10,000 workers per day.[18]

In contrast to the 1870s, then, when a small number of isolated mills operated in the hinterland of Calcutta, the area became a large and distinct jute belt by the late 1890s, connecting individual mills near forests and the river to industrial centres in the north and the south of the city. The expansion of the jute industry occurred in tandem with the growth of other industries and workshops, such as the Lilloah railway workshop in Howrah, oil industries in the south of 24-Parganas, paper mills in Titaghur and near Barrackpore, as well as cotton and rice-mills. All this contributed to the emergence of an industrial area in and around Calcutta.[19]

The increasing density of industries in the hinterland of Calcutta meant that workers were increasingly able to sustain themselves and their families in the jute belt, despite the flexibility of production (and the resulting irregularities of employment). The mills on the Hugli could, in turn, rely on the availability of an internal labour market. Dagmar Curjel, visiting the area in the early 1920s, for instance, noticed that a large proportion of women workers in the Upper Hooghly Jute Mill was the wives or relatives of men employed in the nearby Lilloah railway-workshop. Similar patterns become apparent in rare glimpses of workers' biographies. Take, for instance, Kamala, who worked in the Howrah Jute Mill. She reported in the late 1920s to members of the IJMA that her father had worked 'on the railway' and had been shifted to Howrah about twenty years ago. After his death, she and her mother had taken up a job in the Howrah jute mill.[20] Bochu Nikanto, a drawing *sirdar* in the Samnuggur Jute Mill, had started to work as a shifter in the India Jute mill after his father's death. While his mother had not been able to find employment in the same mill, she managed to find a job in the nearby Serampore Cotton Mill.[21]

Further, the possibility of taking up other jobs (at least temporarily) could be important when living in the jute belt. Take, for instance, Narsama Kurmi, who worked as a rover feeder in the Howrah Jute Mill. She reported in the late 1920s that she had arrived in this mill five years ago. As she described further, she had

> not been in Howrah all the time; for after a while she had trouble with a *sirdar* and was obliged to leave, when she went up to Serampore, and from there to Titaghur. Has also worked in Rishra. Came back to Howrah [...] as she found the *sirdar* who had annoyed her gone.[22]

Or Biro, who described his occupation as 'calender coolie' in the Champdany Jute Mill.[23] He had at first worked in the Rishra Jute Mill, after which he returned home, trying to live off his small plot of land. When this failed, he 'came to Champdany and obtained a job of a gardener in the European quarter of the mill'. He then tried to return home but was forced to take up work in the jute belt once more after ten months. This time, he worked in a press-house near the Champdany Jute Mill. Eventually, he found employment in the Champdany Jute Mill.[24] Another example is Mongal, who worked in the Batching Department of the Victoria Jute Mill:

> He [...] set off with his wife and daughter to look for work on the railway and was in the employment of the Bengal Nagpur Railway for about a year. He then went to Fort Gloster Jute Mill where he worked in the Batching Department for about eight months. This place, however, did not suit him or his family very well, so, knowing that his brother-in-law Bhikari was a Recruiting *Sirdar* at Victoria mill, he made up his mind to try and get work there. Bhikari looked after them on their arrival and got them taken on in the Batching Department, where they have now been working for the last nine years.[25]

Mohan, meanwhile, who had been working in the Victoria Jute Mill for forty years, explained that he originally started working in the Samnuggur Jute Mill as a young boy. He reported further that after giving up his job in the mill, he and a family member

> crossed the river and obtained work as mason's collies at Victoria Mill which was then under construction. When the mill was completed and started they both got work as hand hemmers. Mohan remained in this job for over three years and then he changed to the machine sewing where he has been working ever since.[26]

One result of the widening networks of workers in the jute belt, as well as of the emergence of networks which sustained them in the industrial hinterland of Calcutta, was that managers and managing agents' fears of imminent labour shortages appeared to diminish. The directors of the Titaghur Jute Mills reported to their shareholders in 1900:

> Labour has been both abundant and satisfactory during the year, notwithstanding, that a new Mill has been started in the immediate neighbourhood, which seems to prove that large labour centres are a decided advantage to the Mills.[27]

From the perspective of the Duff Company, this development seemed unexpected. The directors of the Titaghur Mills reported similar 'news' to their shareholders in the following years. Only in 1906 did they stop reporting about labour supply, as the 'abundant' supply of workers no longer seemed newsworthy.[28] In 1914, the general manager of the company declared that labour shortages in the Bengal jute industry were a problem of the past.[29]

The high concentration of jute workers in a number of industrial towns implied that these new labour centres were unevenly distributed through the jute belt.[30] The scarcity of roads, meanwhile, remained a problem. Most transport for the industry was still organized through the river. This included not only the transport of raw material and finished goods, but also wage payments, for which money was picked up in Calcutta and brought via the river to mills along the Hugli.[31]

Attempts to build roads in various parts of the jute belt, meanwhile, turned into a new source of conflicts in the 1920s. Conflicts emerged over questions of maintenance of roads, as well as over the question of who bore responsibility for their construction – managing agencies or district authorities. In cases like the Grand Trunk Road, which led from Calcutta through the most densely populated mill towns in 24-Parganas, mill managers and local authorities shared the responsibility of maintaining the road. The responsibilities for road maintenance, however, were not settled. In the late 1920s, for instance, the IJMA reported about a conflict over the Goshpara Road:

> At the request of a member of the Association, the Committee in June, made representations to the Government of Bengal on the subject of the condition of the up-keep of the Goshpara or Main North Road. The Committee stated that the mills in the membership of the Association could not accept liability of the up-keep of the road, which, to all intent and purposes, was the main thoroughfare of the district; and in requesting that the Government of Bengal should consider that desirability of taking over the road in the same way as they had the main road from Calcutta to Barrackpore.[32]

The conflict over responsibility for roads in mill areas led to a conflict in Budge-Budge too. In 1914 the mill manager had improved the road in front of the mill gates and connected it with other roads nearby. After the changes, local authorities claimed that the road was now public property. In the course of the dispute, local police forces intervened in a conflict with workers, claiming that the mill managers had commanded the workers to attack local police forces. In an initial court ruling, the manager was held guilty, but this was eventually overruled in a second hearing.[33]

Meanwhile, the expansion of a road in the northern part of the jute belt led to a different dispute. Near Gourepore, local mills had built a road, which partially occupied the land of a private landowner. He himself had agreed to the building of the road. But after his death this was reversed by his son, who had inherited the land. Given that the Land Acquisition Act was not applicable in the hinterland of Calcutta, the road had to be torn down again. Soon afterward, the area witnessed one of the most serious riots during the general strike of jute workers in 1929, as we shall see in more detail in Chapter 4. During these events, police forces had trouble reaching the affected areas in time.[34]

Due to the establishment of industrial centres in an area with scattered possibilities for transport, the problem increasingly affected the colonial state as well. Not only was the quality and density of roads uneven, but jute mills were often not built near existing railway stations, and the industry was scattered on both sides of the river. A report about a communal riot in Kankinara concluded that it could have been prevented if the police 'had taken a faster train to Naihati and marched from here to Kankinara'. Instead, the police had taken a slower train to Barrackpore – a station that, however, was closer to the mill.[35] In Budge-Budge, on the other hand, a police constable had to take a ferry in order to cross the river, and call for reinforcements, in the course of a serious riot in 1928. The reinforcements took a ferry as well and thus arrived several hours later after the riot had ended.[36]

Altogether, the developments in the Bengal jute belt at the turn of the century indicated that excess-employment, as a mode of securing a stable supply of labour, diminished in importance. Among weavers and beamers, the reduction of excess-employment was, in principle, implied in the mode of regulation of sets of workers – at least as a possibility. Given that managers and managing agents, during the expansion of the multiple-shift system, did not anticipate the future changes in the jute belt, this possibility should rather be seen as a side effect of the attempts to increase managerial control. In the spinning mill, in contrast, the system of relay shifts meant that the degree of excess-employment remained fixed. This reflected the intensified attempts by managers to secure stability of production in this side of the mill.

In contrast to the problems of securing a stable supply of workers, the problem of stability of production remained a matter for managerial concern. The problems in the combination of spinning mill and weaving factory were a structural feature of the industry, despite advances in the process of production. Industrial reports and labour conflicts point us in particular to recurring problems with insufficient supplies of yarn that led to restrictions in production in the weaving factory.[37] The regularly voiced contemporary complaint, that 'up-country' migrant workers tended to leave for their homes at regular intervals, presumably contributed to the tendency of managers and managing agents to not deploy 'up-country' workers in those parts of the mills where the process of production itself posed a problem with regularity of supply.

Until the late nineteenth century, Bengali workers remained, as we have seen, the dominant group of workers in the spinning mill. With the expansion of the industry, as well as with the growth of individual mills, this appeared increasingly unsustainable, at least in the northern parts of the 24-Parganas, where the highest number of jute mills was concentrated in a small area. From the early twentieth century on, thus, managers and managing agents increasingly tried to settle 'madrassi' workers in spinning departments in these areas. In contrast to 'up-country' migrants, 'madrassi' workers usually brought their families with them and returned home less frequently. Given that the majority of women and children were, in any case, employed in the spinning mill, 'madrassi' families often worked jointly.[38]

The new attempts to secure the stability of production by 'changing' the composition of the workforce were also reflected in the coolie lines of jute mills. In many of these, 'madrassi' workers, until the early 1930s, paid significantly lower rents than other sections of the workforce (with the possible exception of sweepers or *durwans*).[39] In mills like the ones in Titaghur, the largest parts of the lines comprised the so-called 'madrassi' lines, which had been built specifically for south Indian workers.[40] As one manager pointed out later, these concessions 'dated from the days when such labour was recruited to fill gaps in the local force', as 'madrassi' workers were said to be a more stable workforce.[41]

Another measure, which Dagmar Curjel noticed during her visit to the jute belt in 1922, was that mills began to offer healthcare facilities for women (however weakly developed) in order to attract more families – and, more specifically 'madrassi' families – to settle in coolie lines.[42] Managers, in other words, used welfare measures as a means of incorporating families in order to secure the stability of the workforce in the spinning mill. The work gang as a unit of employment, then, was secured by relying on another type of unit, which served to keep workers tied to the mill by means of mutual dependency on family income.

The situation was rather different in the south of Calcutta. In this part of the jute belt, Bengali workers remained the dominant group of workers in the spinning mills. The gradual abolition of the multiple-shift system in the 1920s – and along with it the system of relay-sets – however, implied that workers had to attend to their jobs throughout the day. The single-shift system, after all, was based on the deployment of individuals, not of sets. Mr Williamson, the manager of a mill that had abolished the multiple-shift system briefly, only to re-introduce it soon after, explained:

> One particular reason [for the re-introduction of the multiple shift system] is this, that under the multiple shift system and particularly in the place where that mill was, we draw labour from Akla and Diamond Harbour. Under the single-shift system the workers have very little time to spend with their people.[43]

The experience of Mr Williamson was certainly no exception. In the late 1920s, the distribution of 'madrassi' and Bengali workers in the preparing and spinning departments was, arguably, also reflected in the spatial distribution of mills that continued to work with a multiple-shift system. Whereas in the late 1920s about 50 per cent of the industry had abolished the older system of 'shifts', this almost exclusively affected mills in the northern parts of the jute belt, as well as a few in the direct vicinity of Calcutta.[44] The only exception here was the Birla Jute Mill, which was situated in the far south of the jute belt.[45] The emergent distribution of Bengali and 'madrassi' workers signalled more than simply a shift in the way the stability of production was to be sustained. It also implied a tension between the northern and southern parts of the jute belt at the point of the actual abolition of the multiple-shift system.

'The bogey man of the 60 hours' – conflicts between managing agencies over the hours of work

The two changes in the organization of work gangs under the multiple-shift system, in the early 1870s and the mid-1890s, were each interlinked with a new phase of expansion of the Bengal jute industry and, in turn, with an increase in hours of work. These moments of growth were followed by periods of overproduction, which lasted, with brief interruptions, from the late 1870s until the early 1890s, as well as from the early 1900s till the late 1920s (and beyond). Increases in hours of work, then, were regularly followed by attempts to reduce hours of work again in order to curtail production.[1] Crises of overproduction were becoming increasingly prolonged in the early decades of the twentieth century. In this period, in fact, the mills of the Indian Jute Mills' Association (IJMA) remained on short-time agreements nearly continuously, with the First World War as the only major exception.[2]

In the context of recurring crisis, it is hardly surprising that the multiple-shift system was never entirely undisputed in the industry. The system came to be at the heart of conflicts over short-time agreements between managing agencies. Until the turn of the century, the system of relay-sets had been at the heart of industrialists' conflicts, and several mills changed this mode of arranging sets in order to return to a 'single-set' system in the spinning mill and weaving factory.[3] In the early twentieth century, however, the idea of abolishing the multiple-shift system altogether began to gain in importance. These implied a move away from the deployment of work gangs, followed by the introduction of a regular single-shift system.[4] In contrast to the earlier moments when the multiple-shift system was temporarily abolished and then reintroduced, the introduction of the single-shift system implied a comprehensive change in the organization of work at the site of production.

The introduction of the single-shift system was also guided by increasing concerns over matters of labour control, as we shall see in more detail in the next section. For the present, it is more important to point out that the multiple-shift system continued to dominate labour deployment until the late 1920s, *despite* the industry's repeated tendency to crisis, and despite the increasingly escalating conflicts among managing agencies. The continued importance of the system was, arguably, the outcome of conflicts between capitalists in this period. To indicate this aspect of the development of the multiple-shift system, we will begin by outlining the conflicts over short-time agreements in the late nineteenth century, before discussing the conflicts in the early twentieth century.

After its first major expansion, the Bengal jute industry entered a phase of severe crisis in the second half of the 1870s. A considerable number of mills went bankrupt in the course of this slump, just a few years after having opened their gates. The correspondent of the Dundee Advertiser reported rather dramatically:

> The dividends have become smaller by degrees and beautifully less, and the sun
> of many a concern has now, we fear, sank for ever beneath the dividend horizon,
> leaving nothing but debenture debts behind.[5]

Or, as Wallace put it later: 'Looking back, it is surprising that the mills did not suffer more than they did during the subsequent ten years' struggle for markets.'[6] The events in the second half of the 1870s forcefully demonstrated the risks of investing in a jute mill in Bengal. After the rush of capital in the previous years, the industry was certainly established as a highly competitive one. Investments in mill construction and machinery, meanwhile, were comparatively expensive, and the machines used had a very low 'scrap value', since they could hardly be used for anything else.[7]

In the course of the crisis of the late 1870s, only five mills abolished the system of relay-sets, in order to reduce their costs of production and hours of work.[8] A more immediate reason for abolishing the system of relay-sets, however, was that these mills could simply not afford to work seventy-two hours per week while 'conserving' extra workers. The directors of the Seebpore Jute Mill – which was to go bankrupt soon after – thus reported:

> The depressed state of the bag market continued during the greater part of
> the past half-year. The 14 hours daily work, with double set of hands [= relay-
> sets], was discontinued by your Directors, as proposed at the last meeting of
> shareholders, rather than temporarily close the mill and lose the workpeople,
> and the old system of 10 hours daily work with a single set of hands re-adopted.[9]

The directors' statement also indicated a crucial problem with discontinuing the system of relay-sets: the problem of labour supply. Most of the mills which abolished the multiple-shift system in the 1870s had few problems with labour supply, as they were in the neighbourhood of Calcutta or of other towns.[10] In the event of a sudden rise in demand, then, these mills could again increase their hours of work relatively easily, as they had better access to local sources of labour supply.

The continuance of the multiple-shift system in the majority of jute mills during the crisis of overproduction, in addition, points us to the role of managing agencies. Keeping the production of jute goods at a high level was certainly in the interest of the agencies, which were usually remunerated on the basis of the number of pieces produced, rather than on the basis of profits.[11] The dispute in the late 1870s, however, entailed another element in the relationship between managing agencies. A short-time movement, it was broadly agreed, would lead to better prices for jute goods and, in turn, to higher profits. Yet the change in shift-rhythms by a minority of mills hardly made any difference to the overall production of jute goods in Bengal. Or to let the correspondent of the Dundee advertiser speak again:

> To be successful every short time movement should be general. If this is not so, those mills that continue to work full time do so at the expense of those working short time.[12]

Mills which had been forced to adopt a single-shift system in the course of the crisis, then, did not gain much of an advantage. On the contrary, the fierce competition between managing agencies seemed to ensure that the multiple-shift system would not be abolished, despite the resultant increase in the impact of the crisis. The result was a situation which Paul Benthall would later describe as a 'survival of the fittest' in the course of which the bankruptcy of new mills balanced the problem of overproduction.[13]

In 1884, when the industry's crisis continued, capitalists founded the Indian Jute Manufacturers 'Association (in 1902 renamed the Indian Jute Mills Association, or IJMA), with the objective of implementing short-time agreements among its members.[14] In the following years, the association implemented a series of agreements with the purpose of curtailing production. These short-time agreements, however, restricted not the hours of work but the number of days per week during which its members were allowed to run their machines.[15] Due to the different options of arranging sets of workers in the spinning mill, the difference between working hours and working days was not merely semantic.

Mills working on a multiple-shift system could work longer hours per week than those mills which had adopted a 'single set' system.[16] While the arrangements between the members of the IJMA served to balance out the industry's tendency towards crises of overproduction, this balance remained uneasy, as the power relations between managing agencies continued to be represented in the terms of the agreements. The result was that managing agencies which could afford to continue the multiple-shift system enjoyed an advantage over those mills which could not.

In the aftermath of the second boom in the jute industry, the importance of establishing working time agreements to restrict production rapidly grew more intense. The productive capacity of Bengal jute mills was expanding disproportionately, marking a trend which, with brief interruptions, continued until the late 1930s.

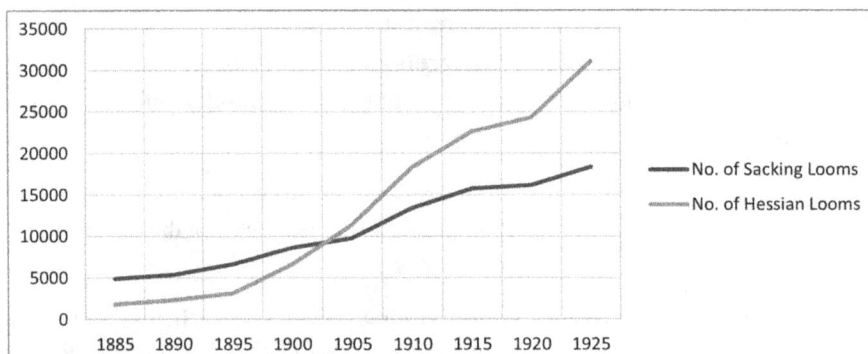

Figure 1 Diagram of the number of looms in Bengal jute mills. / Data from: D.R. Wallace. *The Romance of Jute. A Short History of the Calcutta Jute Mill Industry. 1855–1927.* Second Edition. London: W. Thacker & Co., 1928.

This meant that the industry's tendency to overproduction was intensified rather than overcome. The development, however, also led to the establishment of a global monopoly over the production jute of goods by the mills of the IJMA. The impact of the IJMA's short-time agreements on prices for jute goods increased massively, while the risks of failing to establish new agreements rose considerably. The slump which would potentially follow the end of the restrictive policy of the IJMA, after all, threatened to be much worse than that of the late 1870s.

The expansion of the industry, then, was accompanied by a continuing series of short-time agreements, each of which lasted between six months and two years. After each cycle of restrictions, new agreements followed to be implemented in the months to come. The most noteworthy exception in this chain of agreements was the First World War, when, due to major hikes in demand for jute goods for both civil and military purposes, the mills on the Hugli were able to use their full capacity. After the war, however, the mills of the IJMA resumed their policy of restricting hours of work, which once again took the form of a continuing chain of temporary agreements, lasting with brief interruptions until the Second World War.[17]

The effect of these agreements was that the mills of the IJMA managed to keep global prices for jute goods comparatively high, thus securing an impressive flow of profits. Due to the sudden drop in demand in the aftermath of the First World War, and possibly also driven by the success of their earlier short-time agreements, the IJMA mills implemented a series of restrictions from 1922, which, for the first time, limited the hours of work rather than specifying the number of working days in the week. They restricted the hours of work to fifty-four per week, to be applied in multiple and single-shift mills alike. They also agreed to not install new looms in their mills unless managing agents could provide exceptional reasons for doing so.[18] While jute mills broke these agreements regularly, by working longer hours, or by secretly installing new looms, the restrictions were still sufficient to reduce the levels of overproduction, and to keep the prices for jute goods high. The profits made by Bengal jute mills remained impressive through most of the decade and were, in fact, among the highest in the history of the industry.[19]

The high profits which could be made from the production of jute goods, however, also contributed to the growth of jute industries outside the IJMA. In the early 1920s, the first Indian-owned jute mills opened their gates on the Hugli. They eventually joined the IJMA on the condition that they could work longer hours than the older mills on the river.[20] In the second half of the decade, however, two new Indian-owned mills opened their gates, refusing to join the IJMA even with these concessions in place. Concurrently, new jute industries emerged in a number of other countries. In particular, attempts to establish a jute industry in Poland raised anxieties on the Hugli, as Polish labour costs were cheaper than in other European countries.[21]

These developments led to escalating conflicts within the IJMA over the matter of short-time agreements. While the special conditions for the new Indian-owned members proved to be a matter for constant negotiation, the question of how to deal with the prospects of growing competition outside the IJMA generated increasingly tense debates among the members of the association. A number of managing agents insisted that the restriction of the hours of work to fifty-four hours per week should be continued in order to sustain high profits, despite outside competition. The largest section of managing agents, however, agreed that an increase in hours of work to sixty was the best solution to the problem. This measure would lead to a considerable increase in production, and, in turn, to a fall in profits throughout the industry. While this implied losses for all companies involved in the production of jute goods, the mills of the IJMA would be able to sustain such a (controlled) crisis of overproduction. In the course of the First World War, the jute mills had acquired impressive savings on which they could rely in the course of the anticipated slump. New jute mills in India and elsewhere, in contrast, had no such option. Instead, they were usually burdened with unpaid debts, which capitalists had incurred in the course of establishing new units.[22]

Without a consensus on the matter of short-time agreements, the members of the IJMA continued to argue among each other, implementing only brief short-time agreements lasting six months or a little more. The inconclusiveness of the internal debate, and, alongside, the threat of an end to even temporary short-time agreements, loomed over the industry throughout the 1920s. Such a scenario implied the revival of the 'survival of the fittest', which had led to the bankruptcy of a considerable number of mills on the Hugli in the past.

The three largest managing agencies on the river – the Yule Group, the Bird Company and the Duff Group – responded to this scenario by preparing themselves for a potential failure of the IJMA restrictions. These three agencies continued to apply the multiple-shift system until its permanent abolition in 1931. This, in turn, meant that they could increase their hours of work to eighty-one per week, if needed. These were also the agencies that had installed the majority of new looms in the previous years, either in some of their older units, or by building new jute mills. By the early 1920s, they shared among themselves about 45 per cent of the looms on the river. In this decade, they seem to have been responsible for the majority of secretly installed looms, with the result that they increased their relative dominance within the Bengal jute industry, combining 55 per cent of the looms of the IJMA in 1935.[23]

Managing agencies with smaller numbers of looms, in contrast, tended to respond to the continued short-time agreements by abolishing the multiple-shift system. This step implied an increase in productivity, instead of conserving a potential increase in the productive capacity of their mills. They sought to achieve this increase in productivity by implementing new measures of labour control, which accompanied the introduction of the single-shift system. Trying to prove that the new system was more productive, and that it allowed for a more efficient regulation of workers' labour, the managing agents of the Anglo-India Jute Mill presented a calculation of work under the single-shift system, including:

1.   % increase in tonnage production.
2.   % decrease in cost per ton of production.
3.   There is a certain amount of faulty cloth, due to weaving defects, etc. Just prior to changing to single-shift, this faulty hessian cloth amounted to 1% of our hessian production. It now amounts to 0.1%, or a reduction of 90%.
4.   We pack our hessian production within certain definite weight limits. The cloth manufactured against order but outside these weight limits is termed 'Outweight' cloth. This 'Outweight' cloth has been reduced by about 80%.[24]

The introduction of the single-shift system, while spelling out advantages as long as the short-time agreements lasted, also implied that, in the case of a failure to agree on new restrictions, mills could only increase their hours of work to sixty per week if they did not want to break the regulations of the Indian Factories Act.

The problem of hours of work under the multiple-shift system turned into a source of bargaining power in the midst of increasing competition inside and outside the IJMA. R.B. Laird, a representative of the Duff group of mills, explained in 1930 that his group continued to apply the multiple-shift system in their mills, because

we might have to work more hours with the existing mills. We may start new mills at some future date.[25]

The possibility of an increase of production, which Laird drew on, did not so much hint at the anticipation of a future growth – certainly not at the outset of the Great Depression. Rather, it implied a more or less open threat to those mills inside and outside the IJMA, which had no such option. Summarizing the different anticipations and fears afloat in the industry, a representative of the Anglo-India Jute mills stated that

the bogey man of the 60 hours working has been frightening the market for too long, and I think everyone will agree it is time he was scotched. Our group have for a long time advocated that in our opinion the best way to place the Jute Mill industry on a sound basis was for all mills to work 60 hours a week on the single-shift working, and in our opinion, it is economically the soundest system under which to run any mill. Be that as it may, opinions differ, and there is a school of thought who consider the single shift system to be not as good as the double shift system with the result we have roughly 50% of the Mills on the river each working the two different systems. The single shift mills cannot work longer than the 60 hours per week, whereas it is always open to the double shift mills to work 81 hours per week, so that even if it is decided to extent the working hours of all mills to 60 hours per week, the bogey of something above 60 hours working will always remain![26]

By the late 1920s, the anxieties about the present and future course of the industry had led to a deadlock. By then, about half the mills of the IJMA had abolished the multiple-shift system, while the other half had made no such attempt. The Bird Company, the only one of the three largest managing agencies to have introduced the single-shift system (in two of their six mills), in fact, considered the reintroduction of the multiple-shift system in both mills by the late 1920s.[27]

In 1928, the mills of the IJMA agreed to experiment with an increase in the hours of work to sixty per week. This was to be implemented in 1929, but the question of how long the IJMA would sustain this increase continued to be a matter of debate. Another point of conflict was the question of how to proceed after interruptions in production, such as strikes or the breakdown of machinery. As long as the mills on the Hugli worked fifty-four hours per week, single and multiple-shift mills alike used to increase their hours of work temporarily after stoppages of production in order to make up time lost. The planned increase in hours of work to sixty per week, however, implied that only multiple-shift mills retained this option. The multiple-shift mills agreed eventually to not make up time lost after interruptions in production. While, then, the *Times of India* explained enthusiastically that the IJMA had finally decided to 'kill the competition', Paul Benthall from the Bird Company showed himself less optimistic on the success of the endeavour, as he feared (among others) that their mills would be 'at the mercy of our labour'.[28]

Due to the impact of the Great Depression, the experiment of an increase in hours of work in order to 'kill' the competition was cut short harshly. In 1930, the IJMA was forced to restrict production to unprecedentedly low levels, as the prices for jute products collapsed, while the problem of emerging jute industries was taken care of to a considerable degree at the same time. In order to pay stable dividends to their shareholders throughout the crisis, the members of the IJMA decided to use up large parts of their savings. Meanwhile, the multiple-shift system was abolished completely in 1931, thus solving also the problem of the 'bogey of something above 60 hours' for the years to come, as the mills on the Hugli had neither the financial nor the practical means to do so.[29]

Overlapping- vs single-shifts – conflicts over the problem of labour control, and the advance of the single-shift system

The conflicts among capitalists over short-time agreements were augmented by a second set of conflicts, which emerged in the early twentieth century and especially in the 1920s. These conflicts unfolded over questions of labour control in its broadest sense. The prevalence of work-substitution at the site of production, as well as the structural excess employment in Bengal jute mills, meant that working hours could not be identified with any determinacy – not even on a formal level. The continuous motions of workers and 'extra' workers, replacing each other at their machines at seemingly random moments of the day, after all, were not simply a side effect of the application of the multiple-shift system. Rather, they were at the heart of the organization of work in sets, on which the system rested. For the purposes of mill regulation, as well as for the regulation of factory law, this posed severe problems, which were raised with increasing insistence by mill managers, as well as by representatives of the colonial state.

The multiple-shift system, not surprisingly, came to occupy a central position in these debates over the deployment of work gangs. The onset of the single-shift system, more specifically, seemed to expose the multiple-shift system as the major obstacle to the proper regulation of workers in jute mills. The single-shift system rested on the deployment of individuals, rather than groups of workers as principal units of labour. In the first decade of the twentieth century, the multiple-shift systems' 'opposite' had been a form of 'single-set' system, which was in principle associated with the same problems. In 1912, this situation began to change, as five jute mills introduced a regular single-shift system, as we have seen in the previous section. The change in shift systems, however, was reversed before it could develop into a trend. With the outbreak of the First World War, the global demand for jute goods rose unprecedentedly. The mills on the Hugli responded by increasing their hours of work to eighty-one per week, and the five single-shift mills were forced to re-introduce the multiple-shift system.[1]

In 1922, the multiple-shift system was abolished in a number of jute mills. This time the step did not remain a temporary one, and a growing number of mills introduced the single-shift system in the following years.[2] Until 1925, single-shift mills remained in a minority on the river. In 1926, when seventeen mills changed shift systems, however, the balance began to change, as nearly 50 per cent of the industry had adopted the new system. While the ratio between single and multiple-shift mills on the river remained largely stable until the late 1920s, the multiple-shift system, nonetheless, had emerged as a problem in this period, and the single-shift system had emerged as its solution.[3]

From the perspective of managers and managing agencies, the change in shift systems between 1912 and 1931 was guided by three consecutive objectives. First, the abolition of the multiple-shift system signalled the end of the deployment of work gangs – and, in turn, of the organization of groups into sets at the site of production. The change in shift systems, secondly, signalled attempts to extend managerial control over workers, which seemed to depend on the possibility of identifying individual workers at the workplace. These two steps were the basic condition for the third: increasing labour productivity and introducing new measures of rationalization in jute mills.[4] Measures of rationalization, which, as has been noticed elsewhere, picked up speed in the 1920s, then, were tied to the organization of work, or, more specifically, to the problem of shift systems.[5]

Attempts to increase labour control at the site of production, however, were not reflected solely in the increasing opposition between multiple and single-shift mills. Rather, the multiple-shift system itself was adjusted in order to allow for better managerial control over workers. This was most apparent in the weaving factory. The formal separation between workers and 'extra' workers, on which the re-organization of sets in the weaving department hinged, was expanded to the other departments of the weaving factory. By the 1920s, the entire workforce employed in Bengal jute mills came to be regulated under the multiple-shift system, or in formalized sets.[6] In contrast to the earlier changes in the organization of work gangs, the requirements of the process of production provided no apparent reason for this adjustment nor does there seem to have been a particular moment at which the change was introduced throughout the industry. The implementation of the multiple-shift system, rather, ceased to be a feature designed to respond to *specific* problems in the process of production, or in the general context of the Bengal jute industry.

A second adjustment of the modalities of the multiple-shift system concerned the role of *sirdars* in the weaving department. Throughout the mill, *sirdars* and clerks were responsible for ascertaining the attendance of workers at the beginning and at the end of the working day. In the weaving department, however, managers and managing agents discontinued this practice in the aftermath of the extension of the multiple-shift system. The European overseer of the department, now, was responsible for controlling the attendance of workers, thus ascertaining that each member of a set was indeed present throughout the day. The employment of weavers, in other words, was formally regulated by the mill. *Sirdars*, in turn, only retained a role in weaving departments in matters of supervision, but no longer in the registration of workers.[7]

The advance of the single-shift system was orchestrated by increasingly escalating conflicts over matters of labour between capital and state. The principal problems of the dispute were already apparent during the visit of the 1908 Factory Commission. The commission had been set up after a series of conflicts in the Bombay cotton industry. After an increase in hours of work to fourteen hours per day around the turn of the century, the industry experienced an increasing number of strikes, while prominent mill owners called for a legal restriction of hours of work.[8] Responding to these events, an earlier commission on the working conditions in textile factories had recommended in 1906 that the 'period of employment' of men should be restricted to twelve hours per day.[9] The task of the 1908 commission, then, was to determine if hours of work were excessive in Indian industries, and whether a general restriction of the working day was necessary or not.

At the outset of the investigation, the commissioners defined 'excessive hours' of work, stating that this expression was

> to denote cases where operatives have been actually worked, in any one day, for a period exceeding 12 hours. The expression 'working hours' or 'hours worked' will […] be applied to the period for which the operative remained on duty, after deducting all intervals of rest of a definitely ascertained character.[10]

While this definition seems not to have caused any serious confusions in view to the textile industry in Bombay, the matter was different in the case of the Bengal jute industry. Jute mills, applying a multiple-shift system, ran their machines for fifteen hours per day. Sets of workers, too, were engaged for fifteen hours at a time – at least in the weaving factory. Individual members of each set, however, never worked more than twelve hours per day, managers and managing agents assured the commissioners. The organization of work in sets, as well as the structural excess in employment, after all, implied that workers were allowed to arrange for a sufficient amount of breaks in the course of the day, by substituting one another.[11] These break periods were, needless to say, not of a 'definitely ascertained character'; yet, mills and factories working with an 'approved shift system' were not required to introduce determinate intervals of rest in the first place.[12]

The problem which the commissioners faced concerned more than the determination of 'excessive hours' of work in the Bengal jute industry. In addition, the question of whether the working day was to be restricted to twelve hours of work per day or not revealed a crucial tension. A restriction of the overall *working day* to twelve hours per day would have implied that jute mills had to run their machines three hours less per day. A restriction of workers' *hours of work*, in contrast, had no further consequences, since they already had the option of working only twelve hours per day. C.A. Walsh, the inspector of factories for Bengal and Assam, who assumed that the latter was the case, articulated the problem rather sharply, stating:

> There are roughly speaking 22,000 women working in jute mills alone, and 16,000 children, the latter under 14 years of age; the majority averaging 9 or 10 years, and half these infants are compelled to leave their homes at 4-30 A.M. to be present in the mills at 5 A.M. I have carefully read the proposed amendments of the Act, but fail to see that these children or their mothers will be benefited by any of the recommended clauses, to say nothing of the European Assistants, who, throughout the year, spend their days from early morning till night in the mills or mill compound.[13]

In the interviews with representatives of the jute industry, too, the uncertainty over the objective of the commission was striking. Some managers and managing agents seem to have assumed that the question concerned the working day, while others discussed the implications of a restriction of hours of work. There were others who combined both options, pointing out that a restriction of hours of work was not necessary, but a restriction of the working day would be of an advantage for the industry. Not surprisingly, then, the members of the 1908 Factory Commission faced severe difficulties in their investigation of the Bengal jute industry.[14]

In their final report, the commissioners concluded that a general restriction of hours of work in India was not necessary, as extensive abuses 'in the matter of excessive hours' were primarily a problem in cotton and jute textile industries. Instead, they recommended implementing a series of 'indirect' restriction which would affect mainly these industries. The first of these was the introduction of a 'young persons' class, whose daily hours were to be restricted by the Indian Factories Act. This measure would, accordingly, initiate a reduction of working hours in Bombay cotton mills, which employed considerable numbers of 'young persons'. The second indirect restriction was aimed at the Bengal jute industry, and implied a compulsory interval or rest, even in factories with an 'approved shift-system'.[15] The commissioners noted that this would render the application of the multiple-shift system 'uneconomical' and, in turn, would force jute mills to abolish the practice of deploying sets of workers throughout the day.[16]

The hopes of the commissioners proved to be premature, as the special status of 'approved' shift systems in Bengal was retained.[17] When the new Factories Act was introduced, jute mills continued to deploy their workers without formal break-periods, as they received an exemption from the requirement to apply the rule from the Government of Bengal. Despite the failure to force an abolition of the multiple-shift system, this episode was still remarkable. None of the earlier enquiries into the conditions of work in Indian industries had identified the multiple-shift system as a source of confusion.[18] Members of the 1891 factory commission, as well as representatives of the 1906 textile labour commission, had even indicated that the multiple-shift system could be a positive example for other industries. Far from being a questionable exception, it seemed to be a possible model for other mills.[19] The doubts raised in 1908, then, appear as a new concern in the history of the colonial state's investigation of working hours in Indian industries. The multiple-shift system was for the first time identified as a problem by representatives of the colonial state.

In the aftermath of the 1908 Commission, the multiple-shift system continued to be seen as a problem for factory regulation. More precisely, the *administration* of hours of work in Bengal jute mills emerged as a central source of conflicts between capital and state. The question of how to regulate hours of work had been another task of the 1908 commission. In contrast to the problem of excessive hours, the commissioners seemed to treat this issue as secondary. In their final report, they noted that the administration of the Indian Factories Act differed considerably across colonial India, and that its regulation was altogether insufficient. They concluded that the matter needed closer consideration.[20]

In 1911, a new Factory Act was implemented based on the recommendations of the Commission, restricting hours of work to a maximum of twelve hours per day for adult male workers. One year later, 1912, an amendment to Act was implemented. The 'second' problem of administration had been considered as well, with the result, that the Government of India introduced compulsory registry books in mills and factories, in order to ascertain the attendance of individual workers in the course of the day.[21] Debates about registry books were not new in themselves. Already in the late 1870s, when the Government of India debated the initial introduction of factory regulation among children and women, the issue had been raised. Registry books appeared to be a crucial element in the implementation of state regulation in factories. However, the prevalence of gang work and practices of work-substitution in Indian industries seemed to render the introduction of registry books a futile endeavour.[22] The amendment of the Indian Factories Act in 1912, then, implied a crucial shift in the policy of factory regulation. This shift can be seen as an expression of the greater emphasis on implementing the law, which happened in the wake of the scandal around Bombay factories in 1905 and fanned outwards, and which can perhaps be seen as a precursor to the much more elaborated forms of state-led industrial development after the First World War.

It was the inspector of factories who articulated the problem of the multiple-shift system after 1912 repeatedly. He raised the issue virtually every year in his report. In 1928, for instance, he noted:

> In mills working on the multiple shift system, flagrant abuses of the provisions of the [Indian Factories] Act for the protection of labour still continue. Efforts to enforce proper registration and strict observance of specified hours of work for all persons employed, have met with only a small measure of success.[23]

In 1926, when nearly 50 per cent of the industry had introduced the single-shift system, and when the complete abolition of the multiple-shift system seemed possible, he addressed the Bengal Chamber of Commerce, the Government of Bengal and the Government of India on the matter – probably in an attempt to speed up the development that he understood to be unfolding.[24]

This attempt, however, failed. By the late 1920s, when the Whitley Commission examined the jute industry, the inspector of factories appeared to be rather bitter on the question of factory regulation in jute mills. When being asked on employment registers, he admitted that he had practically given up to attempt to control them. At the beginning of the year, he had begun to resume control 'just for the benefit of the Royal Commission; otherwise I should have been more or less quiet in regard to that'.[25]

The emerging conflict between capital and state encountered a second set of conflicts, which evolved among capitalists. Back in 1908, the questions of the members of the Factory Commission had revealed a tension between managers and managing agents. This was, primarily, a conflict over hours of work in jute mills. The recent hike in working hours also affected managers and European overseers.[26] Managers used the occasion to stage their own discontent publicly or at least to present it to the representatives of the colonial state. George Spence, the manager of the Titaghur Jute Mill, expressed this directly in 1908. While stating that a restriction of the working day in Bengal jute mills was not necessary, and not in the interest of the industry, he concurrently stated that 'speaking on behalf of jute mill managers, he knew they would welcome a 6 to 6 day'.[27] Other managers argued in a similar manner.

A second aspect of the conflict between managers and managing agents, which was raised in 1908, concerned the question of labour control. T.W. Clark, who managed the Kankinarah and Kamarhatty Mills, pointed out that under a single-shift system,

> the overseers would get to know their workers individually, and have more control over the accuracy of the pay-sheets than they can possibly have under the continual shifting of the sets.[28]

This line of arguments against the multiple-shift system was to increase in importance in the years to come. In 1922, when Dagmar Curjel interviewed managers in jute mills, the majority of them gave detailed accounts of how workers – in particular, women and children – were exploited in their mills, as they themselves had no means to ascertain the movements of workers under the multiple-shift system. As Curjel put it:

> It was the general opinion of the managers that multiple shifts lead to many abuses which they were unable to control, both among the men and women workers.[29]

A focus of these statements was the fact that managers had no means to ascertain the regulations of the Indian Factories Act in their mills in the first place.

The intervention of the inspector of factories in 1926 put an end to managers' attempts to stage their discontent. It silenced factory management, as it brought the degree of the conflict between managing agencies forcefully into the open. The pressures of state intervention and industrial change, in other words, met at this point: the pressure exerted towards the abolition of the multiple-shift system on the part of the factory inspector intersected with the emerging deadlock among capitalists over the matter of short-time agreements. The factory inspector's interventions accelerated this rift within the ranks of capital, at least at the level of managing agencies. Managers, in turn, took recourse to expressing the opinion of their managing agencies on matters of labour control.[30]

By 1929, when the Whitley Commission prepared to interrogate Indian industries, the issue had fully emerged as a problem of labour regulation from the perspective of the colonial state. The multiple-shift system now appeared as a genuine obstacle to labour legislation, as well as to industrial development. Workers employed under the new single-shift system, according to the commissioners, were 'healthier' and 'happier' than workers in mills working with a multiple-shift system.[31] The members of the IJMA, on the other hand, had agreed to take no formal position on the matter of shift systems in 1926. They reverted to expressing their conflicts over hours of work indirectly, using the commission as a background to debate matters of labour control. An illustration of this was the intervention of Alexander Murray. Murray was a representative of the Bird Company and also a regular member of the Whitley commission.[32] This tension led to a rather peculiar situation, in which he eventually interviewed himself, in order to bring home the point that the multiple-shift system, in fact, did not allow for proper control over workers:

> Q (Mr. Murray): You said that the single-shift working eliminated to a large extent the power of the sardar?
> A (Mr. Murray): Yes.
> Q: How does that come about?
> A: Simply because the European assistant in charge gets to know his workers and it is impossible for the sardar to dismiss or take on workers as he pleases.
> Q: In the case of double shift working you have only got a percentage more?
> A: But they are changing over all the time throughout the day.
> Q: To get to know the workers here also does not seem to be an insuperable thing?
> A: The assistant goes out and comes back and finds new faces on the same machine. It is not possible to know the workers so easily.[33]

In other passages in the interviews, however, he intervened in order to state that the multiple-shift system did not pose a problem for labour regulation, or alternatively, to state that he had no opinion on the matter. Only after the abolition of the multiple-shift system did he publish a more decisive statement on the matter. In 1934, looking back upon the developments of the industry in the past decades, he identified the publication of D.R. Wallace's 'Romance of Jute' as a key moment in which a new trend towards increased managerial control took shape.[34] In contrast to Wallace, who had written his book as an invocation of the constant and durable qualities of the jute industry, Murray interpreted it in terms of his own present, as part of a straight line leading to the abolition of the multiple-shift system.

Uninterrupted hours of work and frequent breaks – the modalities of shared work and excess-employment at the shop-floor

Bengal's jute mills were enormous workspaces, comprising large rooms where hundreds and sometimes thousands of workers were present at any given time, amidst a cacophony of noise, machines humming and a perpetual swirl of dust. People were constantly on the move within the spaces of the mill, some of them carrying materials from one department to another; others sharing their work with each other, or leaving their individual tasks to take breaks; while unemployed workers wandered through the mill in the hope of finding a job for the day.[1] To any casual observer, these everyday rhythms of the mill must have presented themselves as immediate impressions of chaos and disorder. The workplace appeared as a site in which managerial authority was severely limited. Workers and 'extra' workers, in turn, appeared to experience a considerable degree of 'freedom', as they were allowed to evade the 'normal' rhythm of the industrial work throughout the day.

In contrast to the apparent disorder, and the erratic rhythms of workers at the site of production, mills applying a multiple-shift system sustained a continuous process of production. The disorder at the shop-floor unfolded in the course of an excessively long working day, which workers and substitute workers alike were subjected to. Illustrating the implications of this aspect of the working day, J. Sime, a representative of the Yule Group of mills, complained in 1926:

> We are the only textile trade in India, which starts and stops its machinery at the extreme hours permitted by law. We are the only textile industry in the world outside Japan and China, and possibly Russia, in which the operatives start work at 5-30 a.m. and, with intervals of rest, stop work at 7 p.m. [...] Mill buzzers [in Bengal jute mills] blast out at 4 a.m. the intimation that it is time for those who have 3 or 4 miles to walk to get ready to be at their work at 5-30 a.m. then with intervals of rest of about 4 hours they stop work at 7 p.m. and return the same dreary roads, always in the dark to their homes and I assure you they are dreary roads in the rainy season.[2]

Sime's statement was part of the conflict among capitalists over the hours of work in the late 1920s. Yet, he still pointed to a general feature of working hours in jute mills: the rhythms of work in the course of the working day suggested that the mill subjected workers to the incessantly long rhythms of the machines. This indicated that managers did not lack control over their workforces at this point.

The different impressions of the rhythms of work in jute mills, surely enough, bring us back to the two opposing features of work in Indian industries, which we have discussed earlier. Practices of work were accordingly shaped by workers' 'pre-modern' habits, while, concurrently, being the basis for long, and continuous, hours of work. As a result, the process of production seemed to be composed of two distinct spheres, each of which followed their own logics of time and discipline. In this presentation, the rhythms of workers and the time of the workplace remained in an *unmediated* opposition to one another, despite sustaining the same process of production. The feature of excess-employment, in this reading, seemed to solve this apparent paradox, as it served to drown the articulations of workers' 'habits' at the site of production. Mills and factories in colonial India, then, functioned autonomously from the 'deficiencies' of Indian workers, as workers' 'habits' did not require meeting the demands of the 'modern' workplace.

The two aspects of the working day were also inscribed into the structural features of the multiple-shift system. While sets of workers were deployed throughout the day, individual workers were allowed to substitute one another with other members of their set, as well as with 'extra' workers, who had been employed in addition to these sets. The concrete features of the multiple-shift system, further, determined the ways in which sets of workers were regulated in the different sections of the mill. The system defined the parameters within which sets of workers were deployed, and within which individual workers could arrange their hours. It orchestrated these parameters according to the specific needs of the industry, adjusting them at different points of its history.

Before turning in the following chapters to the introduction of the single-shift system, and to the question of what this change implied for workers and mill managers alike, it seems useful to consider the modalities of the multiple-shift system more closely. Shared work is arguably the key concept through which we can identify the expression of the work gang at the site of production, as well as the problem of labour control over individual workers. We will argue that the key link we need to consider, in order to approach workplace relations, is the practice of substitution or of shared work. At the outset, this practice appeared as a feature, which workers used in order to subvert the daily rhythm of work. Workers and 'extra' workers negotiated the terms of their substitution for one another. In order to ensure perennial work at the perennially running machines, however, workers had no choice but to substitute one another. Shared work was from this perspective a condition for the mills' regulation of workers and 'extra' workers according to the requirements of the process of production.

The practice of shared work, then, was at the heart of the contradictions of the multiple-shift system, insofar as it expressed the two opposing appearances of this system. These appearances were not the cause, but the result of a system of industrial work which combined informal work-arrangements and formal employment of groups of workers, by inscribing the practice of shared work into its regulatory frame. The organization of working processes on the basis of shared work was, further, the condition for the possibility of a structural excess-employment in the first place. While 'extra' workers were technically speaking not at work as individuals, they were still always (and necessarily) part of a group of workers who attended to the machines. The multiple-shift system, thus, has to be understood as a regime of industrial control, which enabled an excess in employment, by regulating the practice of shared work at the site of production.

In the following chapter, we will trace the modalities of shared work under the multiple-shift system in a reversed order. The system of 'relay sets' was first introduced in the spinning mill in the 1870s, as we have seen, before being expanded to the weaving department in the 1890s. It seems, nonetheless, useful to begin our discussion with the latter. The degree of excess labour was among the lowest in this department, allowing us to identify the problems posed by this system of work-organization more clearly than in other parts of the mill. This will provide a backdrop, against which we can address the regulation of work gangs in the weaving factory and in the spinning mill.

The modalities of substitution in the weaving department

The weaving department was one of the largest departments in jute mills, and about one-third of the workforce of an average mill was employed here.[1] Weavers occupied the only position in the workforce of Bengal jute mills, which was categorized as 'semi'-skilled. This meant that while their job required some skill, the mill did not provide for apprenticeships, or similar forms of training. Rather, weavers were expected to acquire their skills on the job. Other jobs in jute mills were categorized as 'unskilled'.[2]

In the weaving and finishing sections of Bengal jute mills, workers generally received piece-wages. Weavers were an exception, as they did not receive a regular piece-wage, but a wage composed of a basic weekly payment (if they attended their looms through the week) and a bonus payment. The latter was paid if they had produced a certain number of pieces, or 'cuts', in the course of one week. If they under-produced, weavers lost their bonus payment and risked dismissal.[3] This practice of wage payment, combining a remuneration for regular attendance and a remuneration for output, originated in the mid-1890s, when the multiple-shift system was expanded to the weaving department. Up until this point, weavers received a regular piece-wage, while *sirdars* received a wage payment that was composed of a weekly payment and a bonus payment.[4]

Under the multiple-shift system, sets of weavers were deployed uninterruptedly throughout the day. They had recourse to different ways of organizing their periods of work and break. One option was the casual employment of additional workers for the weaving department. Additional workers were employed on a daily basis – as *badli* workers. This was in contrast to weavers deployed in sets, who were generally employed on a regular basis.[5] Unlike the formal structures of excess labour, contemporary observers mentioned this mode only generically, treating it as a 'flexible' addition to the multiple-shift system. Due to the lack of sources on the matter, the importance of this 'additional' workforce for the everyday practices of substitution remains hidden.[6]

Weavers deployed in sets had recourse to options of work-substitution with other members of their group. Weavers working on small looms were simply 'allowed' to substitute one another. In the case of broad looms, the mill provided for a determinate number of substitute workers. This meant either that the mill employed one 'extra' worker for four regular workers or, alternatively, that groups of regular weavers received 'extra' wages in order to hire another worker themselves. In contrast to his colleagues, the 'extra' weaver's wages were time-based, calculated on the basis of the hours during which the set was deployed.[7]

The size of the machinery determined the separation between sacking and hessian-weavers, since only a marginal proportion of broad looms was placed in the sacking-side, while virtually no small looms were used in the hessian-side of Bengal jute mills.[8] The mill, then, provided hessian-weavers with more options to substitute one another in the course of the day, as sets of workers in this side of the department retained a higher degree of excess labour than in the sacking-side. In the following, we will discuss the implications of the different combinations of a *formalized* and an *additional* excess-employment in the two sides of the department separately.

The sacking-side

When approaching the rhythms of work among sacking-weavers under the multiple-shift system, the first problem is striking, when considering the formal employment of workers: at first glance, there was no structural excess in employment inscribed into sets, as only one weaver was employed per sacking-loom. 'Extra' weavers, who were employed flexibly, and in addition to the machines' requirements, were not part of the formal rhythms of work.[9] Despite the apparent absence of a formalized excess in employment, however, sacking-weavers were still 'free' to share their work with other members of their set in order to leave the site of production in the course of the day. Let me illustrate this by quoting from the testimony of Shama Charan Samuth, who was employed in the weaving department of the Budge-Budge Jute Mills in the 1890s. The commissioners summarized his statements in the following way:

> He, being a weaver, is supposed to work continuously all day, and not in the shifts that are worked by the operatives in the [spinning-] mill. Being unable to work continuously, an arrangement prevails among themselves by which he gets 1 ½ hours' leave at 9 o'clock for eating his breakfast. Then again half an hour in the afternoon, about 3.30 or 4, for eating sweetmeats. For the two hours he is

away the man at the next loom does his work, and he in a similar way does that man's work when he is away. A man can work two looms for a time, but he could not possibly work two looms for the whole day. Besides the periods above stated, he can go out for short periods two or three times for necessary purposes.[10]

The first striking aspect of this is that one weavers' break necessarily meant that another worker *had* to stay behind in order to attend the looms. Shama Charan Samuth, after all, could only leave his own loom if the weaver on the 'next loom' took over Samuth's work as well. Considering that looms in jute mills were always constructed in sets of two, this man at the 'next loom' can be specified further as the weaver on the adjoining loom.[11]

Further, both of them were employed as regular weavers. The choice of a break at a given moment of the day, then, was not only dependent on another worker. Rather, the possibility of leaving the workplace depended on a *specific* worker who was employed as a regular weaver as well. While both members of a group, thus, might have agreed *ad hoc* on a break for 'necessary purposes', the very act of negotiating this spontaneous break was necessarily based on a relationship of *mutual dependency*, which constituted both weavers' working days on a regular basis.

It was during these moments, in which one member of a set worked for two that he turned into his colleagues' substitute. He could, thus, combine the role of a regular worker (at his own loom) with that of an 'extra' worker (at his colleague's loom). The result was that even at the moment of one weaver's break, work would never be interrupted at either of the looms. If Shama Charan Samuth, for instance, decided to leave the mill for a drink, a smoke or a bath in the Hugli, work would still be conducted at his machine. During his break, it was not only his tireless loom that kept running. His colleague, too, was waiting, as he could only work on two looms for a limited period. Meanwhile, both weavers' *wages*, too, were being calculated, as their wage payments depended on the number of pieces, which had been produced on each of their looms in the course of the week. While weavers, then, exercised the option of leaving their workplace, they never really left their work behind. The ever-running loom on the one hand as well as the social relations which sustained the 'bathing' weaver's rhythms of break were still at work.

On its most principal level, then, the excess in employment appeared as an *articulation* of a mutual dependency between the two weavers, which had been appropriated by the mill. The interdependency between both members of the set was established at the moment that they faced the ever-running loom, and the need to produce an incessant number of 'cuts'. The *possibility* of working at two looms at a time, however, only emerged as such due to the practice of sharing work. These practices would, in principle, persist under an individualized system of labour deployment, such as a regular shift system. However, the key difference was that, under the multiple-shift system, these practices of shared work constituted a determinate mode of exploitation. They were, in other words, a basic source of excess-employment.

Indicated in the testimony of Shama Charan Samuth is a second, very crucial aspect, which helps us to further delineate the source of an excess in employment in the everyday rhythms of work. The act of sharing work always also meant a period of *intensified* work. The moment during which the first weaver left the mill was necessarily the moment during which the second weaver had to increase his own efforts, in order to work for both of them. Likewise, after having returned from his break, it was the first weaver's turn to substitute his colleague, being now the one who worked at both looms. Each break taken in the course of the day had to be *negated* by an equal amount of work. During each break, one member of the set had to apply a quantity of *labour power* which was sufficient to match the temporary absence of the second weaver. The two weavers, then, did not simply share their work 'freely', as representatives of capital (and other observers) liked to express it. On the contrary, both weavers needed to share their work in such a way as to generate a *determinate* amount of 'extra' labour power, in order to meet the rhythm of the machine, as well as in order to receive their full wages at the end of the week.

The result of this arrangement was that in the course of a working day of, for instance, fifteen hours, both weavers might have worked 'only' twelve hours (as managers liked to point out), but they always had to 'invest' an amount of labour power which would equal the total hours during which the machines were running. Their working hours were necessarily composed of a set of formally uneven hours, as their hours of work were a combination of a set of *individual* hours at one loom, plus of a set of *shared* hours at two looms. This meant, for instance, that one working day of altogether fifteen hours could be composed of a set of nine hours of 'individual' work, plus a set of three hours of shared work. Accordingly, each weaver in this example would have worked nine hours on one loom, and three hours on two. In addition to these twelve hours of uneven work, both of them then had three hours of break (or a break period, which was equal to the amount of shared work). If, however, the two weavers chose to take four hours of break instead, their working day would again have included an equal amount of shared work – four-hour breaks needed to be compensated by four hours of shared work, leaving the remaining seven hours for 'individual' work at one loom.

At this point, it is possible to specify what was informal about the organization of work under the multiple-shift system. The distribution of 'individual' and of shared hours of work could, from the perspective of the mill, only be assumed, but it could not be known. The problem of formally uncertain break regulations was not so much the question of whether workers invested a sufficient amount of labour power in order to match each other's breaks. Rather, the way in which workers distributed their hours of shared and of individual work was the uncertain element. In theory, both workers had a wide variety of options – ranging from six hours of shared work for both (thus granting each other half a day off) to working without a break all day long (and thus breaking the regulations of the Indian Factories Act). Alternatively, they might have shared their work on an unequal basis (thus combining the options of excessive work and excessive leisure). While these extreme options are obviously unlikely, they indicate the possible range of uncertainties on the side of capital, as well as on the side of the colonial state.

The range of possibilities of work-time arrangements among the members of a set, arguably, implied a need for *adaptability* from the perspective of workers. The possibility of a break for one weaver, after all, depended on the amount of time another worker *could* work on two looms at once – an option, which depended not only on individual workers' abilities, but also differed throughout the year. During the heat of the summer months, for instance, weavers' capacity to sustain a continuous process of production on two looms was most likely reduced (while the option to take a bath in the river gained in importance). Diseases and recurring epidemics, too, can be seen as a factor which affected the capacity of weavers to intensify their work, and which sets of workers needed to negotiate. The quality of yarn coming from the spinning department, as well as the break-down of machinery, constituted another set of sources of uncertainty in the everyday rhythms of work, which weavers needed to respond to.[12] The absence of sanitary housing arrangements for workers, as well as the lack of investment in new machines, then, was to some degree outweighed by the flexibility of time-arrangements between workers.

The regulation of hours of work and of break among sacking-weavers, lastly, raises the question of the role of *sirdars* at this point. *Sirdars* were formally not involved in the work-time arrangements among weavers. They had, moreover, no authority over the daily employment of sets of weavers. Not only were weavers employed on a regular basis, but their attendance was controlled by the European overseer of the department, in contrast to other sections of the mill. One side effect of this mode of regulation was that managers and managing agents hardly mentioned the presence of *sirdars*, when explaining the everyday rhythms of work in weaving departments. On the contrary, they presented the case as if the authority of *sirdars* had been abolished – or at least curbed – under the multiple-shift system.[13] This, in turn, renders the identification of *sirdars'* concrete role at this point fairly difficult.

Two aspects of the organization of work appear as crucial in regard to this problem. *Sirdars* were, firstly, employed as supervisors in weaving departments, formally overseeing the constant flow of sets. In the everyday rhythms of work, they thus retained crucial functions by observing a continuous flow of work, conducted by sets of weavers.[14] *Sirdars* also supplied groups of workers to the mill, which arguably strengthened their authority at this point. The initial employment of workers through *sirdars* suggests that a set comprising two weavers was concurrently part of the same work gang. The formal detachment from work gangs and sets under the multiple-shift system remained grounded in the relations among work gangs. This, however, should not lead us to assume that the two types of groups were identical. An average work gang, as has been pointed out, was usually composed of about fifteen to twenty workers.[15] Weaving *sirdars*, in turn, were responsible for several sets at the same time, each of them working in a labyrinth of machines, and each of them taking breaks at various moments of the day. This renders it unlikely that *sirdars* would have intervened extensively in the arrangements of breaks between weavers – at least, as long as the members of each set managed to organize their hours of work and of break without conflicts.

In terms of 'additional' extra workers this situation was, presumably, different. In this case, the mill employed these weavers in addition to the existing structure of sets. Managers, more importantly, seem to have employed 'daily' weavers without further specification as to which loom (or as part of which set) they were supposed to work in the first place. Keeping in mind that 'daily' weavers, too, were usually part of a work gang, it can be assumed that the authority of *sirdars within* work gangs served to establish a relationship of interdependency between sets of weavers and 'daily' weavers at particular moments of the day. The gap between the number of workers formally required to run the machines and the number of workers who sustained the process of production, was, in other words, mediated by reliance on the relations within work gangs. The *sirdars'* mediatory role at this point was, strictly speaking, an *external* one, as their authority functioned to secure the set as a basic unit of work, whose relations were, henceforth, subsumed under the continuous rhythm of the loom. The flexibility of employment under the multiple-shift system was enabled by this interrelation between sets and work gangs. While the former were hired on a regular basis, managers could rely on the latter in order to hire additional workers *ad hoc*, if and when required.

The hessian-side

Moving to the hessian-side of the weaving department, the first striking difference was the deployment of one 'extra' worker on a regular basis. The usual example, which managers gave in order to illustrate rhythms of work-organization in the hessian-side, was that of a group of five workers working on four looms.[16] This exemplary group consisted of four regular weavers, each of them being employed on one loom. The fifth worker was a 'daily' or *badli* weaver. He was employed without being assigned a specific loom; yet, in contrast to 'additional' extra workers, he was necessarily part of a specific set of workers. The fifth member's task was to substitute each of the four regular weavers in the course of the working day, in order to enable each of them to take breaks.[17]

Members of the Whitley Commission were presented with the table below by the IJMA, illustrating this mode of deployment. Four exemplary weavers were employed as piece worker and per four looms, whereas a fifth worker was employed for the day or as a *badli* worker.

The formal rhythm of work-organization, which specified the way in which hessian-weavers were to arrange their mutual periods of break, however, appears to have been virtually impossible to follow. If each of them wanted to take a lunch break of two hours, then they would have had to organize a chain of ten hours of consecutive breaks. They would have had to start with their lunch breaks at eight o'clock in the morning, if the last one of them wanted to finish his break at eight o'clock at night, when the mills' gates were about to be closed for the day. Including the added 'extra' hour for each weaver, this meant that this chain of breaks would have stretched throughout the entire working day.

The problem here is that it seems unlikely – if not absurd – that weavers would have organized an uninterrupted chain of breaks, which stretched throughout the day. The result was that the practice of generating a certain amount of 'extra' labour power, by means of intensifying work, was common in this side of the department as well. We of course cannot know what shapes this took, since

Shifts among Piece Workers in the Weaving Department

6	7	8	9	10	11	12	1	2	3	4	5	6	7	Shift	Total Hours
A.M.													P.M.		
														A	11
														B	11
														C	11
														D	11
														Daily Weaver	10

(Daily Weaver employed as Time Worker)

Figure 2 Shifts in weaving department.

managers did not know about the actual rhythms of breaks, and since colonial officials never enquired about this problem either when interviewing workers. A multiplicity of options, thus, could be imagined. These options possibly also depended on the skill of the daily weaver. Sources indicate that skilled workers, who were too old to work as regular weavers, could become daily weavers just as much as workers who wanted to train themselves to work at the looms. Take, for instance, Khedoo Miah, who worked in the Victoria Jute Mill. When interviewed in the late 1920s, he told members of the Whitley Commission that he had worked in the mill 'for 28 years', before he decided to become a daily weaver, because 'he was an old man now'.[18] Jumanrathi Miah, in contrast, who worked at the same time in the Kinnison Jute Mill, told the commissioners that he had come to the jute belt twelve months ago, where he had secured a job as a daily-weaver with the help of a relative. Until that point, he had no prior experience of working a 'power-loom', and he had not entered a jute mill before that point. The position of 'daily' weaver helped him to secure a job as a regular weaver after a few months.[19]

The working day in the hessian-side of the weaving department, then, was in principle comprised of a set of 'uneven' hours as well. In contrast to their colleagues on the sacking-side, hessian workers did not have to make up for the entire amount of time spent on breaks by means of intensifying their own work. Instead, the 'extra' weaver, or perhaps another member of the group, substituted one (or two) of the other weavers at particular (and limited) moments of the day. The composition of individual hours and of shared hours of work varied in even more ways than in the sacking-side.

There is another form of effort apparent in this side of the department, which involved all members of the group alike. For, if the five weavers wanted to organize an uninterrupted rhythm of work, they had to rely on the networks among themselves in order to negotiate their breaks. The fact that work at their ever-running machines was sustained by a relationship of mutual dependency was arguably even more pronounced in the hessian-side, where more looms needed to be attended to by a set of weavers. The possibility to negotiate moments of break (and their duration) was complicated by the specific conditions of the workplace. Weavers not only had to arrange their breaks while surrounded by the rattling noises produced by their machines. In order to communicate in the midst of this noise, weavers had to use signs and gestures, as words would hardly carry far enough.[20] Workers' sign for the arrival for the manager in a mill to the south of Calcutta was for instance a signal that implied the arrival of a fat (or well-fed) man.[21]

Ad hoc discussions, or maybe even disagreements, over the arrangements of breaks at the workplace were hardly possible. Instead, decisions to take breaks always required a pre-defined set of gestures and signals. These gestures had to have been developed already before entering the noisy workplace, if miscommunications at the site of production were to be avoided and, if possible, conflicts were to be prevented.[22] The physical condition of the workplace, then, suggests that the act of arranging breaks could hardly have been restricted to the site of production itself. Rather, workers had to take this question back with them before entering the deafening workplace again.

The necessary efforts in coordinating the tasks within the set, lastly, bring us to the problem of how the set of five workers was *composed*. In the sacking-side of the department, as we have seen, two regular weavers, assembled at adjoining looms, constituted a set. In the hessian-side, one daily weaver was deployed per set. Neither weavers nor *sirdars* had the authority to employ these daily weavers. The European overseer of the department decided in the morning who would be employed for this job. This was a formal feature, designed to increase managerial control over weavers. In the everyday rhythms of the mill, it seems unlikely that Scottish overseers *could* have chosen the 'extra' worker for every set of weavers. The weaving department was one of the largest departments in Bengal jute mills; yet, only one or two European overseers were employed.[23] European overseers, further, could hardly communicate with workers, leave alone determine which constellation of workers could function as a group in the course of the day.[24] The point of this rule, then, seems to have been less about determining specific workers for the job. Rather, it appeared to be a measure aimed at ascertaining that each set was, indeed, composed of five weavers.

The ways in which sets of weavers were composed, however, could differ in the hessian-side. The previously discussed form of four regular weavers and one badly weaver seems to have been the most common. Nonetheless, some mills used another model, deploying three weavers, who received 'extra' wages in order to employ an 'extra' worker themselves. This was, for instance, the case in the Budge Budge Jute Mills, where hessian-weavers described their rhythms of work in 1908 in the following way:

> Our working hours are at present from 5 A.M. to 8 P.M., but, we are arranged in sets of three looms each, and we either relieve each other, or engage a 'daily' worker at our joint expense, so that each of us gets a 2 hours' interval for food before noon, and one hour again in the afternoon. Thus, we actually work only 12 hours a day, and get 3 hours off. But we [...] must all come at 5 A.M. and stay till 8 P.M., otherwise our looms are given to others; so that it would be no use our employing extra 'daily' hands at our own expense.[25]

In contrast to the example of sets of five weavers, the three hessian-weavers had the option of acting as sub-contractors, in order to adjust the size of the group when they needed it. This apparent freedom was met by another restriction, as the condition for receiving the additional wage was that each of them was present at their loom at the beginning and the end of the working day. The mutual dependency between weavers, which mills drew on when deploying sets at the ever-running machines, then, was utilized by the mills' management in order to sustain sufficient control over the production of the group of workers.

If we consider the overall structures of the working day in the weaving department, two things have become apparent. The first striking feature is that one weaver's capacity to leave the mill always also meant the compulsion of another weaver to stay behind. The crucial problem of the practice of shared work was not so much the worker who left the mill, but, rather, the worker who worked at his loom instead; or, in the case of the hessian-weavers, the group of workers who stayed behind. In both cases, this problem was principally the same, since sacking and hessian-weavers alike could only share their work in sets, which were defined by the perennially running machines. The image of the bathing weaver in the river was in itself not an expression of a lack of discipline or of other 'ingrained' habits. Rather, it was an expression of the necessary act of sharing work, or of the fact that work was still conducted at the loom, and that the social relations sustaining this very break were still at work as well.

The second striking feature of the working day was that the act of sharing work always meant that workers had to generate a certain amount of 'extra' work, thus generating the possibility of an excess in employment as a mode of exploitation. In the case of the two sacking-weavers, this meant that they themselves had to invest an amount of labour, which would add up to the total hours of production. The presence of an 'extra' worker, as part of the group of hessian-weavers, did not substantially change this situation. Periods of intensified work were still apparent in this side of the department. Rather, it meant that only some of the five weavers needed to intensify their work, if the group wanted to jointly generate a sufficient amount of labour power. At the same time, however, the necessary effort in organizing their breaks increased considerably, as the number of workers per set increased in an environment which rendered the coordination of tasks difficult.

2.2

Rhythms of work and labour control in the weaving factory

While we have so far discussed the problem of how continuous production could be organized by means of sharing work in sets, we will turn in the following section to the question of how these practices could be controlled by the mill. The principal problem here, we argue, was a split at the heart of the working day. While the constant application of labour power throughout the hours of employment was regulated by the mill, the actual arrangement of hours of work was necessarily indeterminate from the perspective of managers and overseers alike. This situation gives rise to the question of how the mill could actually regulate the former, given that managers had no direct control over individual workers' hours.

A central theme, which illustrates the problem at stake, concerns the modalities of wage payment. Weavers were employed as piece workers, receiving a combination of a basic payment and a bonus payment. They received the latter if they had produced a certain number of cuts on a given loom. This, at least, was how managers used to explain this mode of wage-calculation to representatives of the colonial state, as well as to other observers. Keeping in mind that work was necessarily shared at the looms in the course of the day, and that weavers' concrete arrangements of work and of breaks were uncertain, it is apparent that this statement contains a crucial contradiction. Each cut produced at a given loom necessarily contained the shared labour of an indistinguishable number of workers. This number was indistinguishable, because the act of sharing work was *practised* informally, while, at the same time, being a formal *practice* within the structure of the mill. The basic unit of actual work was, after all, not an individual worker, but always a group of workers. Thus managers, in turn, could not have paid individual workers for the number of pieces they had produced at a given loom.

In order to illustrate this problem, we should turn to another description of the rhythms of work in the weaving department, this time from the perspective of the manager of the Titaghur Jute Mill. In 1930, he was questioned about wage payments by the puzzled members of the Whitley Commission. Trying to explain the problem, he used the example of the fifth worker in the hessian-side of the department, pointing out:

> For working four looms we have five men; the fifth man is a badli. These four looms work all the 13½ hours, and the weaver is paid for full-time though he does not work all the time.
> *How many hours does a weaver work?*
> He works 11 hours a day, but he is paid for 13 ½ hours.
> *Are you paying to the weaver for what the badli does?*
> Yes, it comes to that.[1]

The problem which members of the Whitley Commission struggled with is striking: four weavers were paid on the basis of a number of cuts they had not actually produced during their thirteen and a half hours of employment, while the mill paid a fifth weaver for an amount of time he had not actually worked. The regular weavers, as well as the *badli* worker, were paid for a period in which none of them was supposed to work. The result was a paradoxical situation, in which the five weavers' wages were calculated as if there was no practice of shared work in the mill, despite the presence of an extra worker. The formal rhythm of uninterrupted employment (according to which wages were paid) and the formal organization of work (which was shared by the five weavers), then, seemed to be in conflict with one another.

To understand this, it is necessary to take the split at the heart of the working day seriously. The working day was divided into (1) a period of uninterrupted work, conducted by a group of workers, and (2) several indeterminable periods of individual workers' work. It is necessary, first, to consider how the mill ascertained the uninterrupted application of labour power by groups of workers and, second, what the indeterminacy of individual workers' work meant in the everyday rhythms of work. This twofold step implies that the category of control itself was divided into a field of control at the level of the mill, regulating workers' labour power, as well as into a field of managerial control over individual workers.

The act of sharing work among groups of weavers was, as we have seen, the basis for a constant application of labour power at the continuously running looms. Two or more weavers had necessarily worked on one loom in the course of a day, in order to allow the regular weaver on this very loom to take a break. This meant, on the one hand, that the substituting weavers worked in the regular weaver's name. It meant, on the other hand, that the regularly employed weaver was at any moment of the day *responsible* for realizing a continuous process of work at his loom. If the substituting weaver(s) decided spontaneously to leave the mill as well, the result was a loss of wages for the regularly employed weaver. If, alternatively, the regularly employed weaver decided *ad hoc* to extend his break for an hour or two, it was yet again his wage which would be reduced at the end of the week. The discrepancy between formal hours of employment and informal hours of work, then, was an essentially arbitrary one. Parallel to the excess of labour at the workplace, the mill's claims on the weaver's labour power were present throughout the day, represented in the uninterrupted rhythm of the loom.

From this perspective, then, the mills' apparent lack of control did not result in an actual loss of control. While the number of pieces produced on a given loom could not have been the expression of an individual weaver's labour power, these pieces still represented the applied labour power for which the regularly employed weaver had been responsible. The tension between the loom as the smallest unit of control and the group of workers as the smallest unit of actual work turned into a problem faced by workers at this point. In addition to having to negotiate break-arrangements, they also had to tackle the problem of potential wage reductions caused by bad work done by either one of them. In this respect, it seems quite certain that the effort involved in negotiating the excess in employment increased at the end of the week, when wages were paid and bonus payments calculated.

While the *continuity* of production in the course of the day, then, was ascertained despite the apparently informal practice of sharing work, a lack of managerial control emerged at the point of ascertaining the *quality* of production. The crucial problem here was that the mill could not identify the work of individual weavers and, thus, could not determine whose work had been good. The first result of this was that managers could not fine weavers directly. Neither the mill manager nor the overseer of the weaving department, after all, could establish the quality of an individual weaver's work with certainty. A woven piece of jute cloth did not reveal whether one, two or maybe even three weavers had shared a loom when producing this piece. This is, of course, not to say that weavers did not suffer fines under the multiple-shift system.[2] Managers, however, could not know whether fines were directed at workers who had actually made a mistake. In effect, weavers were more or less fined at random.[3]

Closely related to the problem of fines was the question of skill. In a jute mill, weavers were the only category of workers classified as semi-skilled, while the rest of the workforce was classified as unskilled. The problem of identifying the work of individual weavers meant that it was virtually impossible to establish the skill levels of individual weavers. The enthusiasm of the manager of the Samnuggur North Mill, who reported to his directors after the multiple-shift system was abolished in his mill in 1931, may illustrate the problem at stake here:

> With the introduction of this system of working [single shift system], it was possible to dismiss the Daily Weavers, who were to a great extent responsible for, and certainly received the credit for, the bad work coming from the looms. It was also possible to weed out the poorer classes of Weavers, and employ only the more experienced ones.[4]

Leaving aside the question of whether the daily weavers were indeed responsible for the 'bad work' in the department, the predicament of the mill managers' is quite striking. While he himself seemed to be certain who the culprit was, he could not establish this apparent fact at a *formal* level. In turn, his options in dismissing 'bad' workers were limited as well. Under the newly introduced single-shift system, in contrast, workers still engaged in practices of work substitution, as we shall see in more detail in the next chapter. In this case, however, individual workers were, at any moment, responsible for the quality of work coming from their looms, thus increasing the managers' options to threaten and dismiss those workers, from whose looms bad work had been coming. This was a crucial difference, which certainly contributed to the enthusiasm of the manager of the Samnuggur Jute Mill.

Trying to circumvent the problem of identifying workers at the site of production, managers and overseers relied on *sirdars*. This was, again, most apparent with regard to fines. *Sirdars* determined which member of a set had been responsible for a mistake, and which worker, accordingly, should receive the fine.[5] The point of this rule was, arguably, not so much to establish the work of individual weavers with certainty. Even *sirdars* could hardly have known where a mistake originated, while neither managers nor overseers saw them as a source of reliable information in the first place. Rather, the practice implied that it was up to *sirdars* and workers to settle the problem of wage reductions among themselves. Fines, then, were established as an indirect mode of labour control in the hands of managers and overseers by drawing on the authority of *sirdars* among workers.

Surely enough, then, *sirdars* took on another mediatory function at this moment. They mediated the gap between the units of work and of production, in order to negotiate wage reductions among workers without conflicts that would render the practice of shared work impossible to sustain. In contrast to the earlier moment of mediation by *sirdars*, this can be described as an *internal* form of mediation. It functioned to sustain the process of production, because *sirdars* acted as part of the group of workers. Or, put differently, the mill put the relations within work gangs to work in order to establish indirect control over sets of workers. At the site of production, the constant presence of these relations was not only the outcome of the mode of employment through *sirdars*. It was also constituted in housing arrangements, as workers – in particular, weavers – often lived in *sirdars'* houses and, thus, depended on them to remain in the jute towns in the first place.[6] The lack of direct managerial control over workers in the process of production, ironically, ended up constituting a field which seemed to affirm the dependence of workers on work gangs.

With regard to the question of determining levels of skill, this indirect mode of labour control contributed to managerial uncertainty. According to the statements of the managers of the Duff Company, *sirdars* generally identified daily weavers as 'culprits' for bad work, thus presenting the work of regularly employed weavers' as flawless.[7] The result was that those workers who had been hired for the day appeared to be responsible for the vast majority of mistakes, whereas those weavers, whose jobs hinged on the number of pieces they had produced in the course of one week, seemed to work without mistakes. Far from being merely a traditional role, then, the authority of *sirdars* was at this point just as much the outcome of the organization of work in Bengal jute mills – or, put differently, it was an outcome of the conditions of the modern workplace.

Indicative of the continued importance of *sirdars* in negotiating wage reductions among piece workers were attempts to temporarily introduce regular double shift systems in Bengal jute mills in the 1940s – well after the abolition of the multiple-shift system. War requisitioning during the Second World War led to temporary mill closures in some areas of the jute belt. In order to make up for the loss, affected managing agencies responded by deploying the workforce of their closed mill unit in one of their functioning ones.[8] This measure instantly led to conflicts among piece workers, when the workforce of one mill was employed on the first shift, and the workforce of the second mill on the second shift. The regular double shift system could only be applied if workers from the same mill were employed on the same machines throughout the day – or in two parallel double shifts. This was even the case if the closed mill was in the same compound. In the Titaghur Jute Mills, for instance, it was the Titaghur Mill No. 2, which had been requisitioned by the US military, while the Titaghur Jute Mill No. 1 was to combine the workforces of both mill units. There was no significant difference between the workforces of the two mills. Workers, on the contrary, came from the same areas, shared the same neighbourhoods, and frequented the same tea-stalls. The only difference, then, which could account for these conflicts, was the role of *sirdars*, and, with them, the relations that had been established within work gangs, and which managers needed to rely on again during the war.[9]

Returning to the modalities of the multiple-shift system, let us, lastly, consider the rhythms of work in the other sections of the weaving factory. Here, the principal mode of organizing work was similar to the weaving department. In the beaming, winding and finishing department, one worker was employed per machine or, alternatively, sets comprised five workers on four machines. Among winders, further, jute mills had introduced a bonus payment in order to push the speed of production.[10] Employing another worker on their own account, however, seems not to have been an option.

A crucial difference to the organization of work in the weaving department was that the attendance of workers was ascertained by *sirdars*, and not by departmental overseers. Further, workers were employed on a daily basis, as regular positions at the site of production were restricted to the weaving department. The detachment between work gang and set, in turn, was hardly sustainable – even on a formal level. Managers and overseers could not ascertain that workers who had been registered had actually been working in the mill. The difference between the departments of the weaving factory was the outcome of the differing investments in matters of labour control at the point of production. Through measures like the bonus-payment among winders the mill tried to regulate the overall speed at which workers worked, without, however, making an effort to identify the quality of production turned out by individual workers. The mediatory role of *sirdars* at the moment of deployment can, in turn, hardly be seen as an external one longer – at least not from the perspective of the set. Yet even here, *sirdars* presumably had to mediate the tension created by the indeterminacy of individual workers' work in the course of the day, and the remuneration of work through a piece-rate.

2.3

Rhythms of work and labour control in the spinning mill

The formal arrangement of work in the spinning mill was considerably more complex than in the weaving factory. Three sets were usually arranged into a sequence of relay shifts, though in some cases mills seem to have deployed two sets or, alternatively, four or five sets of workers in a sequence of relays.[1] Excess-employment was formalized within this sequence of relays. It was fixed at about 25 per cent of the requirements of the process of production, though this number, too, could differ.[2] Children, moreover, who were mostly employed in the spinning department, had separate shifts. The regulations of the Indian Factories Act, after all, implied that they could not work more than six hours per day.[3] Trying to decipher the formal rhythms of employment in the spinning mill, then, members of the Whitley Commission presented the table below:

General Shifts among groups of Time Workers (I) & among Children (II) in the Spinning Mill

6	7	8	9	10	11	12	1	2	3	4	5	6	7	Shift	Total Hours
A.M.													P.M.	(I)	
														A	8 1/2
														B	9 1/2
														C	9
														(II)	
														A	6
														B	6
														C	6
														D	6
														E	6
														F	6

Figure 3 Shifts in the spinning mill.

Each of the shifts in this table indicated one set, comprising up to three workers. This was in contrast to hours of work in the weaving department, where each 'shift' represented the working hours of one individual worker.

The number of workers per set in the spinning mill could differ within this structure of relay-sets. The Inspector of Factories, for instance, reported a mill in which the 'C' shift was only composed of half a set 'of hands', whereas workers in the 'A' and 'B' shift were employed in a full set. He also noted that even the manager of the mill 'was unable to explain to me the system of working in his mill without reference to a diagram'.[4] The complexities of the multiple-shift system in the spinning mill, then, were baffling even for managers.

The complexity of the system was reflected in the rhythms of work of individual workers. The testimony of Gauri, who worked in the late 1920s in the Standard Jute Mill, gives an account of this problem. Gauri worked on the carding machine in the preparing department, where sets of workers usually comprised three people – two of them on the feeder and the receiver end of the machine respectively, and one of them as a substitute worker. She described her interrupted rhythms of work in the following way:

> I work in the jute department. I throw the jute on to the carding machine: I come to the mill at 5-30 in the morning, work till 9 o'clock and go home and eat my food and return to the mill at 10 o'clock. I then work till 3 o'clock, go home, take my food and sleep and then return to the mill next morning, go home, eat my food and return at 5 o'clock.[5]

Having outlined her hours of work in the course of the day, she further indicated that the jobs she did within this structure differed too.[6]

The constant coming and going of workers in the course of the day, then, was not only the outcome of the practice of sharing work on specific machines. The rhythms of employment, too, implied a continuous motion of people – both in terms of hours of work and with regard to the positions which workers took within sets. The separate sequence of shifts for children contributed to this problem. Yet the spinning mill was also inhabited by children, who were too young to work, and had come with their mothers. Janet Kelman, visiting the jute belt in 1924, noted that only about 20 per cent of women workers were working in the weaving factory – most of them in the hand-sewing department, which was often separated from the rest of the factory.[7] In the spinning mill, then, young children constituted another group, which added another type of movement to the motions of the departments, while women substituted one another in order to not only leave the site of production, but also feed their children at various moments of the day.[8]

In the midst of this pandemonium of relays, rhythms of substitution and of children's play, we already encounter the problem of labour control at the point of ascertaining the formal employment of workers. In the weaving department, as we have seen, managers and departmental overseers could not know which worker had worked at a given machine at a particular moment of the day. This problem was linked to the mode of deployment. In the spinning mill, however, neither managers nor overseers could establish with certainty if workers who had been employed at a given day had in fact been present in the first place. The combination of diverse shifts and rhythms of substitution seemed to forestall this option.

The structures of supervision further contributed to this problem. *Sirdars* and clerks were responsible for ascertaining the presence of individual members of a set during each shift, by entering their names into the mills' registry-books.[9] The European overseer, meanwhile, was responsible for observing the registration of workers' attendance in order to confirm that the entries were correct. This, however, was virtually impossible. European overseers, as managers and managing agents admitted, rarely knew the names of individual workers, and could at best identify workers by sight, once they had worked in the department for a while.[10] During her visit to the jute belt, Janet Kelman described the following incident:

> In one mill where there was a desire to show the working of the system, the name of the first woman who was called up could not be found in the roll book. [...] She was sent back to work, and a second woman was called forward. When her name was looked up it was found that the shift letter on her metal token was the same as that which stood opposite her name in the book, but the name was a very simple Indian one which might have belonged to half a dozen different women. When inquiries were made there was great scurrying to get information. One called to another, and that one shouted to a third, a fourth fled for a book, and a fifth opened it, and three or four gathered round to see what was going on, while one worker after another was abruptly summoned to come forward.[11]

The formal rhythms of work and their regulation, then, resulted in a tension between the number of workers formalized in the sequence of relays, and the actual number of workers who had been working in the course of the day. Whereas the former was strictly *determined* within the regulations of the mill, the latter necessarily remained *undetermined* at the site of production. This was a structural feature of the organization of work in the spinning mill. It was, as we will outline in more detail below, the outcome of distinct managerial concerns, which drove the introduction of the multiple-shift system in spinning mills in the 1870s and which, in turn, shaped its working until its abolition in the 1920s. In contrast to the weaving department, where the main concerns of managers had aimed at establishing control over workers at the site of production, the system of relay-sets had been introduced in order to correspond to a context of a consistently insecure labour supply. The system, in other words, was designed to function *despite* the absence of workers at moments of labour scarcity. Concurrently, it was designed to incorporate a reserve army of workers in periods of improved labour supply.

In the everyday rhythms of work, this meant that there always remained a gap between the number of workers who should have been working in the course of the day and those who were actually present. This, too, was a structural feature, as we shall see. In 1929, a representative of the IJMA gave an example of that feature of work in the spinning mill, when he explained to members of the Whitley Commission that in his mill only 10 per cent of the 'surplus labour' were in fact present in the everyday rhythms of the work, while, formally, 20 per cent more workers were employed (and paid), than required to run the machines. The commissioners, being once more puzzled about the conditions of work in Bengal jute mills, asked further:

> (Q) *You may have 10 per cent of the names on your books who actually do not exist as far as working is concerned and that money goes somewhere?*
> (A) Yes; it is divided among the baboos and the *sardars*, and the man who is doing two men's jobs.[12]

Elaborating on the practice further, he added:

> The company is paying for the [absent] surplus labour; it does not in any way affect the workers. As long as the workers are not harassed there is no necessity for our interference.[13]

The statement that 10 per cent of the workforce in this mill was composed of 'ghost-workers' should not be treated as definite. Due to the lack of control over the attendance of workers, the manager could not establish with certainty how many workers had in fact been missing, or how many workers had done 'two men's jobs'. The number should rather be seen as a formal calculation, indicating the degree to which the absence of workers was considered legitimate from the perspective of management.

For our present analysis of the organization of work at the site of production, the general features of the system of relay-sets imply three steps. First, we need to consider the principal forms through which workers made up for the absence of workers in the everyday rhythms of work or the practices, which were deployed to negate the gap between formally employed, and actually present workers. In a second step, we need to examine how the absence of workers was regulated at various moments, or how these practices came to be applied in the everyday rhythms of work, as well as in the context of a changing supply of labour.

Lastly, we will return to the problem of labour control in order to outline the implications for managerial control at the site of production in the spinning mill.

Beginning with the first problem, the above-quoted statement already indicated a crucial practice, which was deployed to make up for the absence of workers: the intensification of work by the 'man who did two men's jobs' and, as should be added here, by the woman who took over two jobs. Similar to practices of sharing work in the weaving factory, workers in the spinning mill took over two jobs, combining the position of regular and of substitute worker. In contrast to the former, however, this did not necessarily imply that workers worked on two machines at the same time. Spinning frames, for instance, needed to be operated by several workers. This was a general feature which was not restricted to the organization of work under the multiple-shift system. The number of workers formally required to run the machine hinged on the size of the spinning frame; on the number of spindles per frame; the speed applied; the type of yarn which was produced (differing, for instance, between twist and warp on either the sacking or the hessian-side); as well as on the concrete arrangements in individual mills.[14]

Irregular breaks in the course of the day were presumably another source of intensification. For instance, women workers who had come to the mill with their children needed to be prepared to take care of them, whether enough substitute workers were present or not. The specificities of the process of production, as well as the spatial arrangement of the mill machinery, contributed to the difficulties in formally identifying the movements of workers at this point. Describing the condition in preparing departments, Dagmar Curjel wrote in 1922:

> In many cases the women workers in the Preparation Departments were crowded together, in parts of the mill where through ventilation was inadequate, and the air contained much dust and fluff.[15]

In the spinning department, meanwhile, the structure and arrangement of spinning frames implied that workers constantly emerged out of and disappeared in a maze of high machines in order to operate the frames on two sides.[16]

Practices of sharing work by relying on extra workers who were formally employed in each set were, in this context, hardly distinguishable from practices of substitution which made up for the absence of extra workers. The feature of excess-employment in the spinning mill, ironically, seemed to be an important basis for undermining the formal structures of employment in the everyday rhythms of work.

A second mode of compensation for the absence of workers was working longer hours than formally prescribed under the system of relay-sets. Kazi

Zahruddin Ahmad, the president of a workers' organization founded in 1895 in
the northern parts of the jute belt, described this as a central feature of work in
the spinning mill, stating that

> in shift system all the shifts do not and cannot turn up in time with the result
> that the men, women and children are made to work overtime.[17]

He added that *sirdars* played a crucial role in forcing workers to work long hours –
an impression certainly shared by other contemporary observers. During their
breaks, workers often were compelled to remain in mill compounds, in order to
take over machines of absent workers, and, thus, to fill gaps which emerged in
the course of the day. While workers in the spinning mill, then, in principle had
fixed hours of work and break, they had to be prepared to cut their breaks short
in various ways.[18]

The ways in which these different options of compensating for the absence of
workers shaped the everyday rhythms of work are impossible to establish. How
workers made up for the absence of others hinged on a variety of factors – most
obviously, of course, on the number of workers who were absent. During moments
of labour shortage or epidemics, for instance, the number of workers who had
to intensify their own work presumably increased. The implications of being
tied to the mill compound, meanwhile, differed between Bengali and 'madrassi'
workers – the two dominant groups in the preparing and spinning departments
of jute mills. The former usually came from villages in the surrounding areas,
as we have seen in Chapter 1. If their village was close enough, they tended to
leave for their home during lunch breaks. But this was not always the case, and in
particular in the south of Calcutta Bengali workers tended to rent rooms in mill-
towns, in order to stay there during the week.[19] 'Madrassi' workers, in contrast,
usually had their homes inside mill compounds, as they lived in the mills' coolie
lines. The composition of the workforce, in other words, constituted another
factor which affected the ways in which workers could make up for the absence
of others.

The consistent absence of workers in the formal sequence of relay-sets, as
well as the various ways of compensating for this absence, raises the question
of how the organization of work was regulated, and how a continuous process
of production was sustained in the everyday rhythms of work. This problem,
arguably, brings us to the role of *sirdars*. Practices of substitution rested, in
principle, on relations among groups of workers. Workers needed to rely on
relations within work gangs, in order to coordinate the different options of
making up for the absence of others, and in order to sustain a continuous process

of work. The two aspects of *sirdars'* mediatory role, which we have observed in the weaving department, were interwoven at this point. Formally, *sirdars* established the stability of sets at the site of production, thus ascertaining that workers could arrange break-periods among themselves. The act of establishing the stability of sets, however, implied that *sirdars* needed to rely on the authority which they exercised within work gangs, in order to secure a continuous process of production.

From the perspective of the mill it meant that existing relations within work gangs were put to work, thus turning into a mode of exploitation in the process of production. Not surprisingly, then, the authority which *sirdars* exercised over workers was reconstituted through the modalities of the organization of work under the system of relay-sets. This was a feature which we have already seen at work in the weaving department. However, *sirdars* authority was more immediately integrated into the process of production in the spinning-mill. *Sirdars* had the power to hire or dismiss workers throughout the day. Given that workers in the spinning mill were generally employed on a daily basis, this was not simply a matter of initial employment, but it was a structural feature of the rhythms of work.[20] If, further, a worker had to leave the site of production, then *sirdars* had the option to hire a *badli* worker for the rest of the day or, alternatively, to put pressure on those workers who were present by threatening them with dismissal (on the same day or later) as well.[21]

A second, and no less important, problem brings us to the modalities of wage-payment. In the spinning mill, workers were generally categorized as time workers, in contrast to their colleagues in the weaving factory. Weekly wages were paid indirectly. *Sirdars* received the joint wages for sets of workers they had 'provided' to the mill in order to distribute the share of each worker among them.[22] This mode of wage-payment certainly reflected the importance of *sirdars* in supplying workers to the mill. Yet it also meant that the authority which *sirdars* exercised, at this point, was strengthened further. The structural indeterminacy of workers' presence at the shop-floor was, in turn, not the problem of the mill anymore, but had to be negotiated within work gangs.

The degree to which the mode of employment and of wage-payments shaped relations between workers and *sirdars* hinged on the question of labour supply. In order to illustrate this, we should turn to the problem of bribes. In principle, bribes were a general feature of labour relations in the jute industry (and in Indian industries at large), as contemporary observers pointed out time and again. Paying bribes in order to attain a job in the mill was either seen as part of workers' ingrained habits, or as an expression of *sirdars'* power over workers –

or as a combination of both.[23] Yet, during moments of labour shortages, this situation seems to have been different. In 1908, Kazi Zahruddin Ahmad described this problem, stating that

> when there was a shortage of labour the *sirdar* allowed hands to come in without any 'admission fee', but directly labour became plentiful, those operatives had to pay him dasturs or forfeit their appointment. The head *sirdar* received about R30 from the mill, and made at least R100 a month in dasturs. It was perfectly true that the *sirdar* made the hands leave in order to change them about, and allow new hands to come in that gave them more money.[24]

Harilal, a worker in the Titaghur Jute Mill, described the changing role of bribes in the everyday rhythms of work in a similar manner, explaining to members of the Whitley Commission:

> I have been working here for the last six years. I am by caste a Dusadh. I brought my wife here, and she died here. I did not pay any bakshish for getting my job; other people might be paying bakshish to the *sardar*. I am living in the busti with my brother-in-law. When there is a big surplus labour then we have to pay bribes to the *sardar* to get employment, but when there is shortage of labour we get in somehow or other. I came in when labour was short.[25]

These two statements point us to a crucial problem. *Sirdars'* authority at the site of production rested also on their ability to supply a sufficient number of workers to the mill. The relations between workers and *sirdars* were shaped by an *interdependency* at the moment of facing the requirements of the process of production. In a context of labour shortages and a consistently insecure supply of labour, hierarchies between workers and *sirdars* could be affected, if the latter struggled to hire enough workers for the day. The way the organization of work affected the relations between workers and *sirdars*, then, was arguably different in the late nineteenth century and in the 1920s. In the former decade, in contrast to the latter, the industry experienced constant shifts between an insecure labour supply and acute labour shortages during massive booms.[26]

Returning to the problem of labour control at this point, it can be said that the apparent lack of control by managers and departmental overseers over the concrete movements of workers was, in itself, not an expression of an inability to establish managerial control at this point nor of an essential difference of habits or practices on the side of workers. The apparent absence of control by managers, rather, was a very precise one, as it was designed to oversee the regulation of work within work gangs. The possibility of sustaining a continuous process of production, in this context, rested on a complex network of relations among workers and *sirdars*, which were (re-)constituted in the everyday rhythms of work, while responding flexibly to changing situations of labour supply.

The fact that this arrangement turned into an important element in the context of escalating debates over questions of labour control, too, can be seen as a response to the changing supply of labour. Practices like the entry of 'ghost-workers' into the mills' attendance registers by *sirdars*, and the resulting increase in workload or in hours of work for workers, had not been raised as a matter of concern by managers and managing agents in the late nineteenth century. In the 1920s, in contrast, it seemed to be an essential problem, which apparently shaped labour relations in jute mills significantly. Yet, given the structural features of the system, as well as the labour market situation, it would be hard to imagine that this practice had not been common in the late nineteenth century as well. The change, which was reflected in these different presentations of the practice, then, seems to have rather been one of *function*. A practice, which had served the requirements of the workplace in a context of labour shortages, had lost its purpose at a point at which capitalists agreed that labour shortages were a problem of the past. Stripped of its original function, then, the same practice turned into an act of subversion and, along with it, so did the practices of workers and of *sirdars*, which sustained it.

2.4

Reconsidering the workplace

Having so far discussed the organization of work under the multiple-shift system in single departments, we will in this section change our perspective and try to (re-)consider the everyday rhythms of work in Bengal jute mills. From the perspective of the mill, the multiple-shift system appeared like a kaleidoscope of distinct regulations of work gangs. Practices of substitution corresponded to specific requirements in the process of production or of the industry at large. The system, in turn, marked separations between workers according to the ways in which they could organize their hours of work and of break. This included not only the formal regulations of work, but also the ways workers could undermine them or, for that matter, in which they *had* to undermine them.

Moving beyond the site of the mill machinery, the varieties of organizing work as well as their calibration could be stretched further. The occupations in jute mills included jobs such as clerks, *durwans* (or *jamadars*), seasonal workers, sweepers, *mistries*, engineers, carpenters and boatmen.[1] The organization of work among carpenters or boatmen was barely addressed in contemporary reports. Clerks and *durwans*, meanwhile, were not employed in a sequence of sets, as their position was important in establishing the mills' control over the movements of groups of workers.[2] Seasonal workers were contracted through *sirdars* in the summer months, when the new raw jute arrived and needed to be sorted into different godowns. *Mistries* were deployed in a sequence of relay-sets similarly to the system in the spinning mill. According to managers and managing agents, this had the advantage that *mistries* could combine the regular attendance of machines more efficiently with sudden increases in workload due to the breakdown of machines.[3]

The different modes of organizing work rested on two distinct *moments*. Practices of substitution (either by intensifying one's own work or by working longer hours) were an articulation of relations (1) among groups of workers faced with the mills' machines, as well as of relations (2) within work gangs.

In the midst of the varieties of regulating groups of workers, these interrelated moments constituted a general feature of work under the multiple-shift system. It was at the heart of the impression that the employment of additional workers could drown the variations of workers' practices in an industry that was itself subject to historical change. We have at this point, clearly enough, returned to the impression of a division of the 'Indian' workplace into a sphere of the 'modern' and of the 'pre-modern', which we have discussed at the beginning of this study.

The two moments of the process of production were further reflected in the way in which workers expressed their agency at the workplace. In the hessian-side of the weaving department, we have already encountered the importance of the question of who would become a daily worker in the first place. Old workers, who were too old to work throughout the day, just as much as young workers, who wanted to train themselves on the looms, could become extra weavers. People who would otherwise not have been employable under a 'regular' system of work, or a system which required the attendance of workers throughout the day, could be included into the reserve army of labour, by deploying networks among workers. Networks generally understood to have sustained workers in mill towns were also constituted at the site of production.

Practices of substitution among workers were also apparent beyond the immediate boundaries of departments. Noormahamad, an 'up-country' worker who worked as a weaver in the Titaghur Jute Mill, reported the following when interviewed by representatives of the IJMA in 1929:

> [He] was only a boy of 20 when his mother was compelled to send him to work in some of the jute mills near Calcutta, being advised to do so by many of her well-wishers, some of whom were mill employees of this province. He started as a shifter boy, but very soon became a spinner. Now as many of his villagers were in the weaving [department] and as he saw, they had a good income he cherished an ambition to be a weaver and, in order to fulfil this object, used to go in his leisure to the Weaving Department to help his villagers in their work. Noormahamad thus acquired good practice in the art of weaving. Soon afterwards, he was fortunate enough to secure a weaver's job. He has become a skilled weaver now [...] and earns about Rs. 40 per month.[4]

The chain of events, which Noormahamad reported about, was also apparent in other testimonies. Spinners in particular seem to have used their position in order to train themselves to work in the weaving department, thus establishing paths for workers across different departments.

At this point, however, one clarification seems necessary. The testimonies of workers recorded in the late 1920s, by the Whitley Commission, indicated that 'madrassi' and 'up-country' workers entered different parts of the weaving department. 'Up-country' workers were in principle employed on both hessian- and sacking-looms. 'Madrassi' workers, who had originally been employed in the spinning mill, seemed to have exclusively entered the sacking-side of the department. This reflected, arguably, different hierarchies among workers. Wages in the spinning department were considerably lower than in the weaving department. Within the latter, however, wages in the sacking side were on an average lower than in the hessian-side.[5] The work on the coarser sacking material was physically heavier, while the machines produced a constant amount of dust, which covered workers and machines alike. On the hessian-side, in contrast, the production of the finer material required more skill, and it was less dusty. When leaving the mill at the day's end, hessian and sacking weavers were recognizable, as the latter were covered in layers of dust, while the former were comparatively clean.[6]

The language of workers, too, gives us an indication of the higher respectability, connected to the position of hessian-workers. Weavers who earned about Rs. 25 per month described themselves as 'ordinary' or 'simple' weavers. Weavers like Noormahamad, who earned forty rupees per month, described themselves as 'skilled' or 'broad-room' weavers – the latter pointing to the hessian-side of the department.[7] The appropriation of the mill space by utilizing practices of substitution ended up establishing paths within the mill, which defined both the possibilities and the limits for workers to find better jobs in the mill and which, in turn, sharpened hierarchies among sections of the workforce.

The testimony of Noormahamad points us to another aspect of the way workers appropriated practices of substitution: when training in the weaving department, he was not employed there. He was, technically speaking, undermining the regulations of the mill. The same practice of substitution workers was compelled to rely on, could also turn into an act of subversion. How it was interpreted hinged on the decisions made by the European overseer of the department. Noormahamad seemed confident enough about the practice to give this detail to the enquiring commissioners. However, departmental overseers could also decide to insist on the formal rules of the mill, such as in the Central Jute Mill, where, in 1910, a weaver was dismissed when he 'sent as a substitute' another man whom the European overseer of the department 'refused to employ'.[8]

The fact that conflicts like these occurred in the weaving department was a result of the changing position which weavers had within the formal regulations of the mill. With the introduction of finer jute goods, attempts to assert managerial measures of labour control in this department increased. It is against the backdrop of this development, that weavers stated to the 1908 Factory Commission:

> It was common for a weaver to absent himself as many as four days a month from his work; he would send a substitute on these occasions. There were always some men out of employment, for if a weaver fell ill he lost his place.[9]

The line that marked the distinction between substitution as a practice of work or of subversion was contested at this point. While workers needed to rely on networks among themselves, the increasing regulation of practices of substitution implied that the question of how these networks were (re-)constituted in the process of production was contested by the mill.

Kazi Zahr-ud-din Ahmad, whom we have already encountered in the previous section, described another problem, when explaining how signs and gestures could be used in order to track the movements of overseers and managers:

> The wireless telegraphy was well known to the Indian workers long before the great Italian discovered it in Europe. Through a system, more perfect than the recent discovery native labourers know when their master is sleeping, when he is in the bathroom, and when in the dining room. In short, when he is back inside the mill he finds that his babu, *sirdars*, and the workers are at their respective duties, and gets highly pleased and receives a laugh at the back from his workers.[10]

Workers, then, responded to the fact that the workplace was a space constantly filled with noises that were too loud to allow for verbal communication by utilizing a 'wireless telegraphy', which both sustained the process of production, just as much as it undermined the authority of the mill. These forms of communication were, in principle, not restricted to the multiple-shift system, and it may well be assumed that this was one reason for the difficulties which managers and departmental overseers faced when trying to abolish practices of substitution.[11] The line between defiance and subversion, however, was no longer blurred, and the practice itself had become a form of subversion.

Defending the spaces and rhythms of the workplace – labour conflicts over the change in shift systems

On 8 March 1926 the Gourepore Jute Mill, situated about twenty-six miles to the north of Calcutta, changed its method of working – the multiple-shift system was abolished and replaced with a single-shift system.[1] At first this change did not lead to conflict, as work went on without noteworthy interruptions. About a month later, however, the situation changed. On 7 April the weaver Jagnarain Singh requested leave on account of sickness. It was still early in the morning, and work in the mill had just begun. His request was refused by J. Spence, the departmental overseer, who sent the weaver back to his loom. Jagnarain, not accepting this decision, soon afterwards returned to Spence's office repeating his request.[2]

Witnesses later described this encounter between the European overseer and the worker. Jagnarain was 'standing with folded hands' in front of Spence, while the latter was waving 'his hands' decisively, reiterating that Jagnarain should 'go away'. Jagnarain, however, did not leave. Spence responded by beating and kicking Jagnarain Singh brutally.[3] At 8.30 am, after Spence had left, Ram Sinhasan Pande, a co-worker of Jagnarain, entered the overseers' office, as he wanted to drink some water from the tap in the room. Instead, he found Jagnarain Singh, lying on the floor. Pande and some other weavers escorted the wounded, who could barely walk, out of the room, and out of the mill. A few hours later, at about 11 am, Jagnarain died. The medical report later stated that the cause of death was a fracture in his skull – the result of the beating.[4] Spence himself was arrested the same day.

On the next day, on 8 April, the weavers of the Gourepore Jute Mill went on strike. They were joined by workers from other departments, resulting in a closure of the entire mill. The strikers' central demand was a sufficient compensation for the mother of the deceased, but they also raised issues concerning wage reductions and working conditions, presumably in connection with the change in shift systems.[5] In response to the attack on Jagnarain Singh, a number of strikers attacked Europeans residing at the mill, wounding several overseers as well as the mill manager. Newspaper reports claimed that the entire workforce of about 9,000 workers participated in the attack.[6] While this was probably exaggerated, it is still clear that the number of workers participating in the attack was impressive and unexpected. Spence had already been arrested the day before, and none of the Europeans who were attacked had been involved in the crime. At the same time, Hindu–Muslim tensions were running high in the area, rendering a concentrated attack by workers unlikely, at least according to the European staff. In the second half of April, these tensions would lead to massive communal riots in Calcutta, as well as in its industrial hinterland – especially in Jagatdal and Kankinarah, where the Gourepore Jute Mill was situated.[7]

The attack on the European staff stopped soon. A small police force was still present in the mill vicinity after the assault on Jagnarain Singh. Further reinforcements arrived within the hour, putting an end to the outburst, and rescuing the supervisory staff of the mill.[8] When the battle ended, three Europeans had been wounded – one of whom, the mill assistant George Ireland, later died from his injuries.[9] While the European staff of the mill do not seem to have been attacked again in the following days, the strike still went on until 20 April. Trade unionists of the Bengal Jute Workers' Association (BJWA) became involved in the workers' struggle. Santosh Kumari Gupta, of the Gourepore Works' Employees' Association, supported the workers in legal action against Spence.[10] The involvement of labour activists increased the workers' bargaining power, and the manager of the mill agreed to pay a 'sufficient' compensation for the death of Jagnarain Singh. He also promised to 'look into' the other grievances which workers had raised.[11]

The events in Gourepore were exceedingly violent and bitter. Starting as an everyday disagreement at the site of production, they led to the apparently sudden outburst of workers' militancy directed at the mill, and its supervisory staff, followed by strike action, which was supported by large sections of the workforce. The chain of events in Gourepore was symptomatic of conflicts over the abolition of the multiple-shift system. The conflict over the multiple-shift system as it was emerging between capital and state, as well as between industrialists, evolved in tension with another set of conflicts, which workers' responses gave account of. The change in shift systems was the single most important trigger for workers' unrest in the 1920s.[12]

The year 1926 witnessed the largest number of mills yet change their shift systems, and levels of industrial conflict reached a peak. In April and May workers of the Anglo-India Jute Mills, just south of the Gourepore Jute Mill, went on strike, fighting with *durwans*, and attacking them with stones and lathis, damaging the mill building, and wounding police officers who tried to intervene.[13] In June, workers of the Bally Jute Mill in the district of Hooghly attacked their manager with shuttles and bobbins, wounding the manager and damaging the mill building in the course of the attack.[14] In November, workers of the Baranagore Jute Mill went on strike and looted the local bazaar, leading to panicked reactions among local shopkeepers in the mill neighbourhood.[15] If we add conflicts which followed the introduction of the single-shift system in other years, the list of damaged mill buildings, wounded managers, departmental overseers, *durwans* or workers could be extended further.[16]

Contemporary observers, trying to explain workers' responses to the change in shift systems, often argued that there was no actual reason to go on strike. The demands that workers raised were, according to them, not based on rational grievances. In 1926, when weavers claimed that the change in shift systems led to wage reductions, the inspector of factories countered that workers had actually received wage increases after the introduction of the single-shift system.[17] Managers and representatives of managing agencies argued that workers were confused about the new wages or, alternatively, that *sirdars* had convinced them that they had suffered wage reductions.[18] Another common workers' grievance concerned increases in hours of work. Here, again, contemporary observers declared that this was not true – workers worked fewer hours under the new system. Only a minority of workers worked longer hours, and the increase in their hours was apparently negligible.[19]

Instead, observers argued that the main reason for these conflicts was the dismissal of workers, as the introduction of the single-shift system rendered the 'conserved' workforce unnecessary. A second contemporary explanation was that these strikes had been instigated by *sirdars*, whose authority and influence over the workforce were compromised by the introduction of the single-shift system.[20] In the late 1920s, when radical trade unions emerged in the jute belt, instigations by outside agitators joined the list of reasons for why the change in shift systems led to strikes regularly.[21]

The latter two interpretations of workers' responses were mainly deployed by supporters of the single-shift system, in an attempt to illustrate that workers actually welcomed the abolition of the multiple-shift system despite their responses to it. By contrast, the first explanation, pointing towards the dismissals of *badli* workers, was used by supporters and opponents of the multiple-shift system alike. The inspector of factories tried to demonstrate in 1912 that the strikes in that year had not been caused by actual grievances, but 'only' by dismissals:

> Various reasons, with little or no truth, were given by the operatives for striking, the real cause undoubtedly being the reduction of hands, as many of those workers retained were anxious that their friends and relatives out of employment should be reinstated by adopting the old system of shifts again.[22]

The change in shift systems, in this reading, had a temporary impact, as dismissed workers would soon find another job in the jute belt. The change bore no structural repercussions for those workers who had retained their jobs.

The manager of the Titaghur Mill, meanwhile, pointed out that the introduction of the single-shift system in the mills of the municipality of Titaghur would cause the dismissal of 20,000 workers.[23] The hardships therefore would be shouldered not only by workers, but also by the municipality, which would have to deal with large numbers of potentially dangerous people. Practices of shared work and excess-employment, which representatives of state and capital argued about in the 1920s, accordingly, appeared only as a structural feature from the perspective of regulation and control by capital, but not when considering workers' everyday experiences of work.

Studies of the history of the jute industry have followed, largely, a similar line of argument. While the rhythms of work under the multiple-shift system have not been subjected to focused research so far, strikes against the introduction of the single-shift system have often been read as protests against dismissals of workers.[24] Other issues – like processes of rationalization under the new single-shift system – have also been cited as a reason for workers' unrest. But even in this case, the dismissals appeared to be the principal problem and the reason for workers' discontent.[25] Demands concerning wage hikes or reductions in hours of work constituted a second source of conflicts in the 1920s. Yet these demands appeared to be unconnected to the change in the organization of work altogether.[26]

If we follow historiographical debates about the jute mill industry more closely, we find that this gap has had serious consequences. One particular debate may serve as indicative of this. Ranajit Das Gupta explained the violent strikes in jute mills in the 1890s as *quasi*-Luddite forms of worker resistance to capitalism, and typical of early industrial development.[27] Dipesh Chakrabarty pointed out that there was a teleology implicit in this account. Chakrabarty's own concern was understanding the violence of workers' protests as symptomatic of cultural forms of managerial authority and the basically peasant form of resistance to it. In support of this point, he drew attention to the fact that violent protest was endemic not only in the 1890s, but also in the second half of the 1920s, as well as in the late 1930s.[28] His identification of these three moments points us in a direction he himself did not take: these three moments were also precisely points at which workplace relations were significantly altered. In the mid-1890s, this meant, as we have seen, the extension of the multiple-shift system and the beginning of a change in the composition of the workforce, as 'up-country' workers began to replace Bengali workers. In the second half of the 1930s, as we shall see in more detail in the following chapters, managers and managing agencies started a consolidated attempt to increase productivity by installing new machines, while, at the same time, instituting labour bureaus, which were designed to further curtail the influence of *sirdars* in the mill.

The mid-1890s, the second half of the 1920s and the last years of the 1930s were exactly the moments at which capital attempted to alter the workplace decisively, and this has been missed out in most historical accounts. It is of course not the purpose of this chapter to suggest that workers' violence can be solely explained through workplace relations, or that cultural forms of authority were unimportant. However, it is at the same time clear that this absence in historical debate has had consequences. By leaving the question of the changing organization of work unaddressed, historians have implicitly rendered the workplace in historically static terms as an unchanging backdrop to the story of industrial militancy and violence. The contention of this chapter is that the problem of workers' militancy, at the moments when it was fiercest, also leads us back to the workplace, whose successive transformations contributed to ruptures in workers' lives both within and outside the mill.

In the following chapter, we will try to approach workers' protests against the change in shift systems, arguing that this was a response to a decisive change in labour relations in Bengal jute mills. This change was framed by two distinct moments – one of disintegration and the other of foundation. Both moments were an outcome of the growing regulation of work gangs, which was reflected in the changing structure of the multiple-shift system, and which was accelerated by the introduction of the single-shift system. Their temporalities, however, differed. While the formal abolition of the multiple-shift system spelt out a sudden intervention into workers practices at the workplace, the introduction of the single-shift system indicated the implementation of a new set of managerial strategies, designed to impinge upon the years to come. The change in shift systems combined a sudden rupture with the establishment of the coordinates for future conflicts.

How to introduce a new regime of production – outlining the logics of change in the mill

The point of departure of changing shift systems was the abolition of practices of sharing work and of a structural excess in employment. While *sirdars* retained an important role in the employment of workers, work gangs now appeared as fully detached from the arrangement of work at the site of production. Links between the practices of employment and the mode of deployment, which had been sustained through the use of sets at the shop-floor, were suspended. The first, and most obvious, result of the change was that the working day in Bengal jute mills was *regularized* as well as *equalized*. Workers in the spinning mill and weaving factory were subjected to specified hours of work and of break.[1] The hours of work in the spinning mill increased formally (though the actual increase hinged on the degree to which individual workers had taken over the jobs of absent workers), while the hours of work in the other part of the mill decreased foremost among sacking-workers, who had fewer options of sharing work and arranging for break-periods under the older system than their colleagues in the hessian-side.

The formal equality of working hours brought differences between workers to the forefront. In order to allow Muslim weavers to leave their workplace half an hour early during *Ramadan*, jute mills working with a single-shift system opened their gates half an hour earlier during the fasting month.[2] Under the multiple-shift system, in contrast, hours of work had not been changed in this period, as weavers arranged their hours of work in such a way that only some members of their set had to remain behind. This was not an option under the single-shift system, since all weavers would have been forced to remain in the mill due to the absence of excess employment. Managers and managing agents probably agreed to implement these recurring adjustments of hours of work because of the important position, which weavers held in the process of production. From the perspective of workers, however, the periodic change in hours of work highlighted differences within the workforce in terms both of religion and skill.[3]

In the everyday rhythms of work, the introduction of the single-shift system meant that each worker was now employed to do one job. Managers and overseers could, in turn, ascribe the output produced on particular machines to individual workers, and determine the quality of their work. Putting the implications of this change bluntly, a representative of the jute industry stated that the application of the single-shift system

> *permits Mills to pick and choose amongst their labour and thus eliminates bad workers to a large extent.*[4]

The manager of the Titaghur Jute Mill gave a more detailed account of the experiences of the supervisory staff in his mill, explaining in 1931 to his directors that

> each Assistant knows the labour in his department. A more accurate check can be kept on the muster roll attendances and each worker can be identified, there being no relieving shift to cause confusion. More time can be devoted to the actual supervision of work by the Overseer, Babus and *Sirdars*, as only two roll calls per day have now to be taken, whereas previously, on the Multiple Shift system, sometimes as many as nine had to be taken. As regards labour on the Single Shift System this is proving plentiful and a better class of worker is available. A higher standard of work can be got from the operatives as they realise there is a plentiful supply of labour in the Bazaar to replace them should their work prove unsatisfactory.[5]

The 'plentiful supply of labour' was also a result of the Great Depression, which had led to unprecedented levels of unemployment in Calcutta and its industrial hinterland. The abolition of the multiple-shift system in the remaining 50 per cent of the industry in that year had contributed to this situation.[6] The principal problem here, however – the implicit threat of dismissal which workers faced if their work was found to be 'unsatisfactory' – was not restricted to the crisis years. This possibility was established as a constant threat under the single-shift system.[7]

The possibility of formally identifying the work of individual workers was a crucial condition for establishing new modes of labour control when the single-shift system was introduced. At the heart of managerial strategies were improved methods of measuring the output of the mill machinery at specific points in the process of production, as well as the re-organization of wage structures and wage incentives. These measures were particularly targeted at controlling the output from the weaving department. The finishing department, where the cloth produced in the weaving department arrived, gained importance for managerial strategies. Questions of how to devise methods for measuring the amount and the quality of the finished cloth proved to be a constant source of concern among managers. In the 1930s representatives of managing agencies visited other mills in order to examine measuring techniques deployed there. The visiting director of the Duff company, for instance, reported with great excitement how the Gagalbhai Jute Mill had managed to improve their method of measuring mechanically, while, at the same time, saving labour costs.[8]

The new position of the finishing department was also reflected in the average wage levels paid in jute mills. The change from multiple to single-shift system implied, in general terms, wage increases for all workers. Yet this increase was distributed unevenly, and some sections of the workforce earned relatively more after the introduction of the single-shift system than others. The highest relative increase in wages was distributed among workers in the finishing department. Taking the data provided by the Inspector of Factories in 1930 as an indication, the differences between the average wage levels in multiple and single-shift mills are striking[9]:

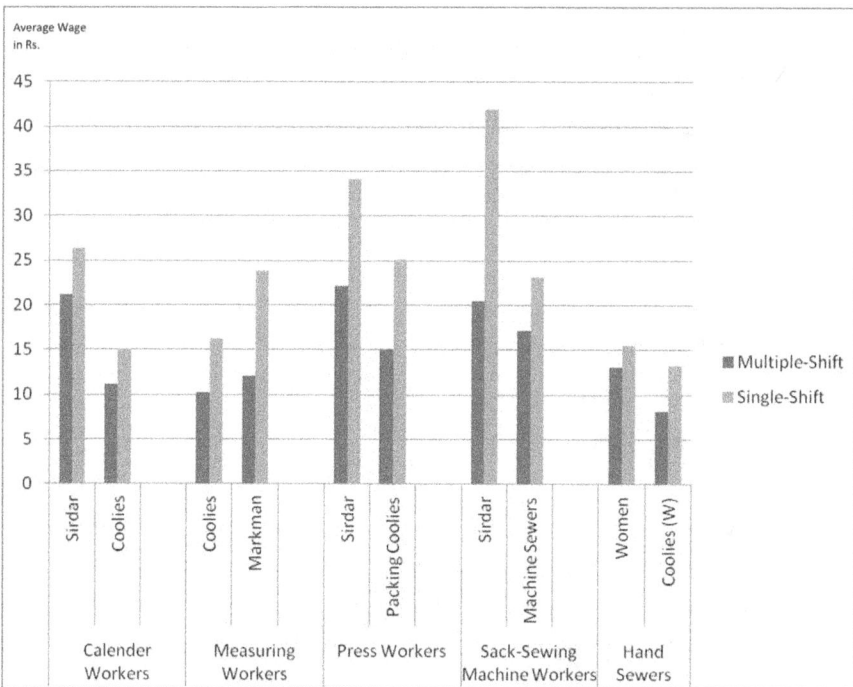

Figure 4 Wages in finishing departments in Bengal jute mills, in Rs. / Data from: Annual Report on the Working of the Indian Factories Act for Bengal and Assam, 1931.

In those sections of the finishing department where the cloth coming from the looms was actually measured, workers – such as markmen – earned as much as 80 per cent more under the single-shift system. These wage increases certainly did not change the fact that wages in the Bengal jute industry were generally low among markmen and other workers of the department.[10] They rather reflected the changed position of the finishing department in the process of production, and affected the position of workers in the internal hierarchy of the workforce.

Relative wage increases were also apparent in the winding department. Here, the yarn was prepared just before entering the weaving department. The winding and finishing department, then, stood out as the two departments where relative wage levels changed most dramatically after the introduction of the single-shift system.

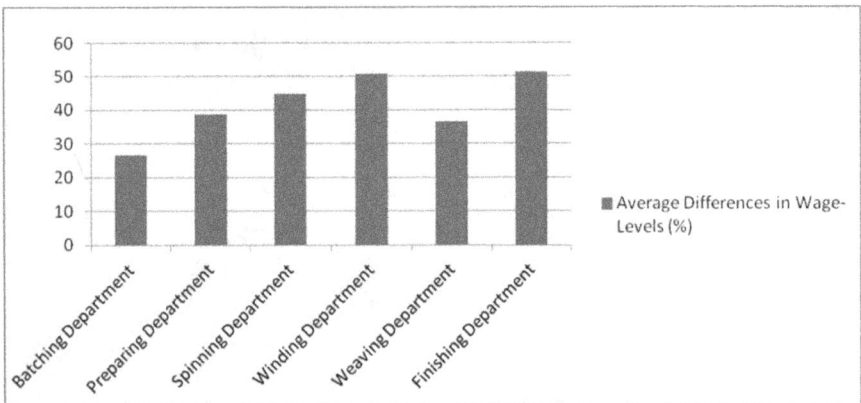

Figure 5 Wage differences between single and multiple-shift mills, in %. / Data from: Annual Report on the Working of the Indian Factories Act for Bengal and Assam, 1931.

The weaving department, in contrast, lost out in the process, as the relative increase in wages was considerably lower here. In accounting for this situation, we need to return, briefly, to the multiple-shift system. Due to the different practices of controlling workers' attendance in the departments of the weaving factory, managers' ability to identify individual workers' work differed too. This implied, in particular, limitations in establishing the movement of workers in the winding and finishing departments. The introduction of the single-shift system, in turn, implied that managers could compensate for the various blockages embodied by the different modalities of work-organization under the multiple-shift system.

The impression that the relative loss in wages experienced by weavers was an effect of the different modes of regulation under the multiple-shift system, rather than a determined attempt by managers to re-arrange their wage structures under the single-shift system, is further accentuated when considering the development of wages *among* weavers. Whereas under the multiple-shift system, hessian-weavers had earned more than sacking-weavers, the situation was exactly reversed after the change. Sacking-weavers, who left the mill at the day's end covered in dust, earned more now than hessian-weavers, previously the highest paid section of the workforce.

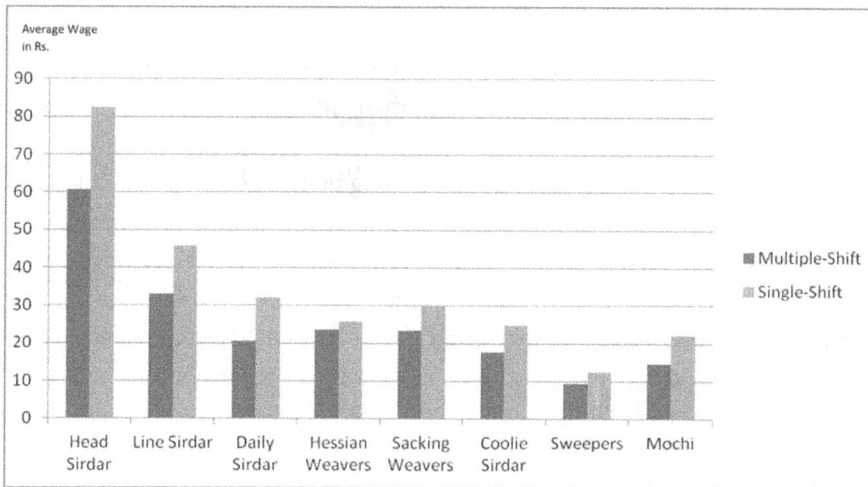

Figure 6 Wages in weaving departments of Bengal jute mills, in Rs. / Data from: Annual Report on the Working of the Indian Factories Act for Bengal and Assam, 1931.

This situation was, in principle, not new: before the extension of the multiple-shift system to the weaving department in the 1890s, sacking-weavers earned more than their colleagues.[11] Under the multiple-shift system, when sacking-weavers had fewer options to substitute one another, they seem to have missed their weekly target of cuts more often than their colleagues, thus suffering relative wage losses.[12] When changing over to the single-shift system, then, managers and managing agents seem to have adjusted weavers' wages without considering the different conditions of work among them.[13]

Attempts to increase the possibility of measuring workers' work led to increased pressures on workers – in particular, as outlined above, since these

steps functioned in sequence with the constant threat of dismissal due to
'insufficient' work. This was, firstly, reflected in the number of accidents in
weaving departments. In 1926, as well as in 1931 – two years, which witnessed
particularly large numbers of mills, changing shift systems – the inspector
of factories noticed increases in accidents at looms, soon after the change.[14]
Managers, too, gave accounts of the new rhythms of production in the weaving
department. The manager of the Titaghur Jute Mill, for instance, reported:

> A great help of course has been the fact that the mills have been working Single-
> shift, but even with this, the weavers would not have been so careful as they are
> today if it had not been for the fact that it is well known that every cut produced
> is being thoroughly examined, not only for gaws and broken warps but also
> snarls, bad selvedges etc. It is a very rare occurrence if any of these faults are
> found in the finished articles nowadays.[15]

The increased options of managerial control over the quality and the amount of
production under the single-shift system, then, affected workplace relations at
the shop-floor significantly.

A second crucial field, in which the changing patterns of control in jute mills
were reflected, points us to the structures of supervision. Managers and managing
agents explained that the re-organization of work based on the deployment of
individuals enabled an increase in labour control, without increasing the number
of European overseers per department. In an attempt to prove that supervision
had not only improved, but could now be efficiently measured, representatives
of the Anglo-India Jute Mills calculated that the introduction of the single-shift
system had led to a 22 per cent increase in the supervision of workers, without
requiring an increase in costs of supervisory staff.[16] The re-organization of
work, however, also affected the position of *sirdars* at the point of production.
According to contemporary observers, the introduction of the single-shift
system had *quasi* automatically broken the power of *sirdars* over workers. The
following exchange during the visit of the Whitley Commission reflected the
apparent changes well:

> (Q): *In your view, does the single shift offer any advantages in control of
> the sardars and diminution of their power to make exactions?*(A): Yes; [...] it
> practically cut out the very vicious *sardary* system and rendered it impotent; it
> put the *sardars* in the position of being technical overseers.[17]

The claim by capitalists, that the 'vicious *sardary* system' had been rendered
'impotent' due to the introduction of the single-shift system, was certainly
inaccurate. Workers usually depended on survival networks in underdeveloped

urban mill areas, in which *sirdars* played crucial roles, as has been pointed out.[18] The fact that dismissals were a constant option under the single-shift system, rather, increased the vulnerability of workers at this point. *Sirdars*, further, were still responsible for the employment of workers. This situation would only change in the late 1930s, when the mills of the IJMA instituted employment bureaus. At this point managers and managing agents would, surely enough, point out that the 'sardary system' had been broken yet again.[19]

The apparent impacts of the single-shift system on the role of *sirdars*, then, were certainly exaggerated by capitalists, as well as by representatives of the colonial state. This, however, should not lead us to miss the fact that the introduction of the single-shift system spelled out crucial changes in the position of *sirdars* at the point of production. The first and most obvious change points us to the problem of dismissals. The constant threat of dismissals due to 'insufficient' work, which was established as a source of managerial control over workers, implied that the power of *sirdars* to simply dismiss workers themselves had been curbed. Similarly, their options to employ 'ghost-workers' had been limited due to the abolition of a structural excess in employment in jute mills.

The specification of their job in the mill as technical supervisors, secondly, marked another set of changes, which affected the hierarchies among them. While managers and managing overseers remained, as so often, silent on the

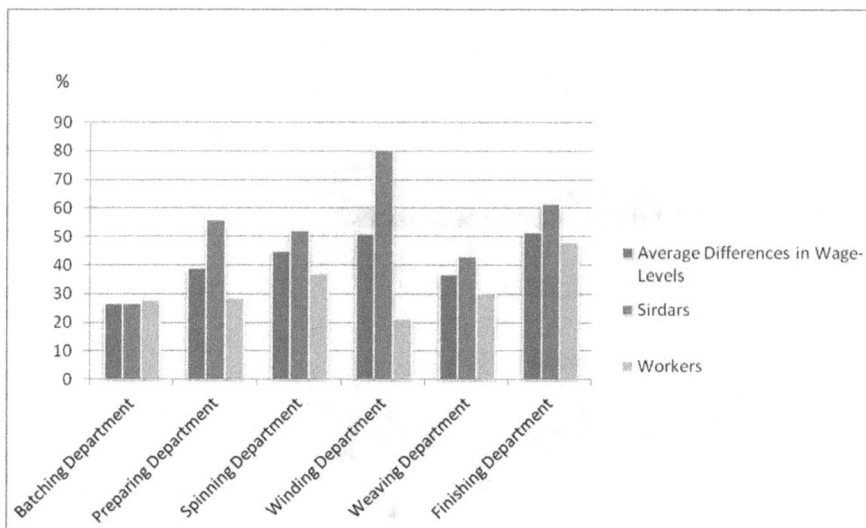

Figure 7 Increase in wages under the single-shift system, in %. / Data from: Annual Report on the Working of the Indian Factories Act for Bengal and Assam, 1931.

concrete implications of this change, the different wage levels between multiple and single-shift mills provide a glimpse into the problem. On an overall level, *sirdars* received by far the highest raise in wages, in relation to the rest of the workforce.

The distribution of the wage increases among *sirdars* reflected the focal points of managerial control, as they were most pronounced in the winding and in the finishing department. In the batching department, where the jobs done by workers were considered to be particularly unskilled, managers' attempts in establishing *sirdars* by means of wage incentives were clearly less pronounced.

Wage differences in multiple and single-shift mills were also apparent *between* different groups of *sirdars*. Head *sirdars* gained considerably more than line *sirdars* did. *Sirdars* responsible for the employment of *coolies* – or for workers not directly deployed on the machines – suffered the steepest loss in wages in relative terms. This change, then, implied a substantial revision of the hierarchy between *sirdars*.

We encounter a peculiar silence in the sources on this matter. *Sirdars* were, in contemporary reports, generally subsumed under an essentially generic category. While their apparent position among workers played a pivotal role in debates over the advantages and disadvantages of the single-shift system, they always appeared as a homogeneous group in these debates. The fact that they held different positions at the site of production seemed to run counter this image. This homogenization of the figure of the *sirdar* certainly contributed to

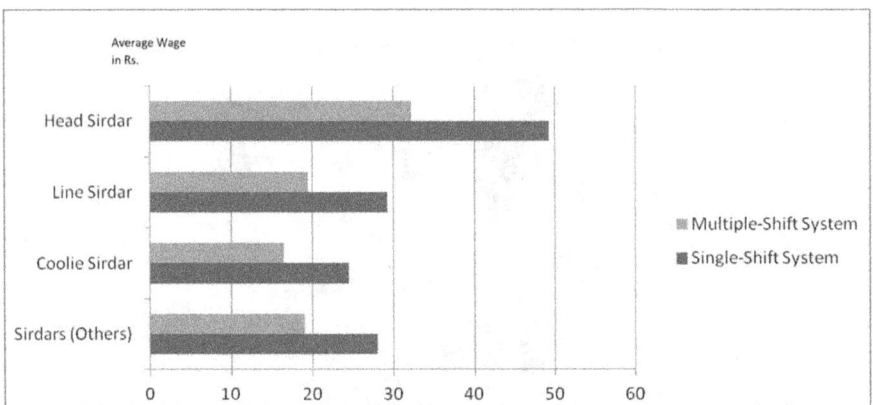

Figure 8 Wages among different groups of *sirdars* in single and multiple-shift mills, in Rs. / Data from: Annual Report on the Working of the Indian Factories Act for Bengal and Assam, 1931.

the absence of discussion of the reasons for wage differentials between *sirdars* in contemporary debates.

The developments in average wages, however, indicate some crucial trends. They reflected a shift *within* the structures of control at the site of production. The growing importance of head *sirdars* was the most striking of these developments. One crucial reason for this change was, arguably, that head *sirdars* were often responsible for implementing the orders of the European overseer of the department. For instance, when a worker had been found to deliver 'insufficient' work, the European overseer would address the head *sirdar*, who, in turn, would talk to the responsible line *sirdar* in order to implement the dismissal of this worker.[20] The changing position of head *sirdars* reflected the attempt by managers to establish a clearly marked chain of command in mill departments, without having to change the structures of supervision altogether. The relative loss in wages among *coolie sirdars*, further, reflected the mills' attempts to improve the structures of managerial control at the most crucial points in the process of production.

3.2

Abolishing excess-employment: Mass-dismissals, rationalization and the re-shaping of the workforce

Mass dismissals constituted a second major development of the change in shift systems. This was principally an effect of the abolition of excess-employment. The number of workers who lost their jobs in the course of this change is virtually impossible to establish. Throughout the 1920s, the mills on the Hugli increased the number of looms installed in their mills considerably – a situation, which effectively over-compensated for the dismissals of workers. Levels of employment in the jute industry rose from 310,000 workers in 1922 to 340,000 workers in 1929, despite the introduction of the single-shift system in this period.[1] In 1931, however, when the multiple-shift system was abolished completely, the members of the IJMA simultaneously restricted the hours of work in their mills and sealed 20 per cent of their looms. This was a response to the crisis of the Great Depression. The combination of these steps led to the dismissal of 60,000 jute workers, without clarifying the degree to which the change in shift systems accounted for this mass retrenchment.[2]

A second problem was that the abolition of excess in employment did not remain an isolated measure when mills changed shift systems. Rather, it came to be linked to measures of rationalization, as well as to attempts to change the composition of the workforce. Similar to the re-organization of modes of labour deployment, which was intrinsically linked to the introduction of new measures of labour control, the implications of mass dismissals for workplace relations have to be understood as part of the process of introducing the single-shift system in Bengal jute mills. In contrast to the problem of labour control, however, the problem of dismissals affected, first and foremost, workers in the spinning mill, as we will outline in the following section.

Let me begin with the dismissal of workers who had formally been employed in excess to the requirements of the process of production. The impact of this step differed considerably throughout the mill, as this feature had been regulated in different ways under the multiple-shift system. In the spinning mill, the degree of excess labour conserved within sets of workers had been considerably higher than in the weaving factory. In the spinning mill, about 20 per cent extra workers were formally employed in sets. In the weaving factory, the degree of excess-employment was less certain, as the majority of extra workers had been employed in addition to existing sets. Contemporary reports, as we have seen, suggested that the number of additional extra workers was falling throughout the first decades of the twentieth century.[3]

Measures of rationalization, further, added to the uneven distribution of dismissals in jute mills. The re-organization of formal rhythms of work proved to be a crucial point of departure here. Measures of rationalization were mainly targeted at the spinning mill. The introduction of regular shifts in place of relay-sets, after all, implied that rhythms of production had to be reorganized more decisively than in the weaving factory. The jobs in the spinning mill, further, were generally considered to require particularly low degrees of skill – an impression probably sharpened by the concurrent increase in managerial concerns over the quality of work in the weaving factory. While machinery was speeded up throughout the mill, attempts to economize work processes under the single-shift system appear to have been most pronounced in the preparing and batching departments of the spinning mill.[4]

The result was again a striking rise in the number of accidents in preparing and batching departments of single-shift mills, in 1926 as well as in 1931.[5] It further meant that the number of workers dismissed due to measures of rationalization increased the overall levels of dismissals already triggered by the abolition of excess-employment in the spinning mill. Let me take the example of the Samnuggur Jute Mills in order to illustrate the problem at stake. In 1931, the mill dismissed 1922 workers, who had previously been employed in excess, when introducing the single-shift system. At the same time, 241 workers had to leave the mill due to the re-organization of processes of production in the preparing and batching department.[6] The introduction of the single-shift system revealed excess-employment both as an outcome of a particular mode of work organization and as a result of blockages, which had prevented further adjustments of working processes.

Measures of rationalization, too, remained a crucial field of activity for managers with regard to the spinning mill. In particular, after the Great Depression, the introduction of high-speed machinery emerged as an important trend in the industry. While individual mills also experimented with new looms or other machines in the weaving factory, the two machines most commonly installed, in a growing number of mills, were roving machines for the preparing department, as well as high-speed spinning frames.[7] The gradual installation of these machines led to fresh dismissals, and, again, to an increase in the overall number of accidents among workers – this time in particular among spinners, who had to work at the ever faster-running machines.[8]

In the course of the 1920s, managers and managing agents had also begun to seize the reorganization of work as an opportunity to rearrange the composition of the workforce. These measures were not *per se* related to the abolition of the multiple-shift system. They can rather be understood as part of the introduction of the single-shift system, as they reflected attempts to 'modernize' the workplace. This development was most pronounced with regard to children. From the mid-1920s, managers and managing agencies began to use the change in shift systems in order to dismiss all the children employed in the mills. This almost exclusively affected the spinning department, where children had worked as shifters under the multiple-shift system. As shifters were still required in the process of production, children were replaced with adult workers.[9]

The dismissal of children in Bengal jute mills was in itself not an exceptional development. The overall number of children employed in Indian industries was falling throughout the second half of the 1920s. The reasons for this development were legal restrictions on the employment of children, as well as general trends towards creating more homogeneous and regularized workforces, dominated

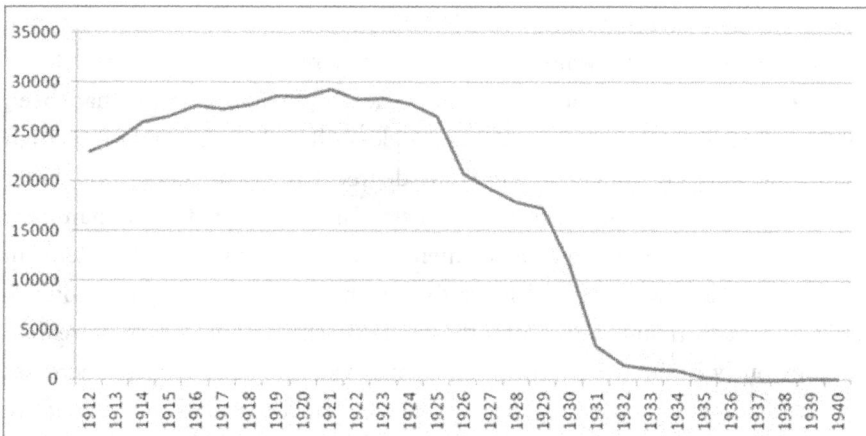

Figure 9 Number of children employed in Bengal jute mills. / Data from: Annual Report on the Working of the Indian Factories Act in Bengal and Assam, 1928–40.

by adult male workers.[10] The jute industry of Bengal was no exception here. In contrast to other industries, however, the dismissal of children came to be intertwined with the change in shift systems – in other words, with a massive change in workplace relations that was already taking place.

The dismissal of children effectively turned into yet another implication of the change in shift systems. The manager of the Titaghur Jute Mill reported to his directors:

> With the introduction of Single Shift and the dismissal of all surplus workers, the opportunity was taken to dispense with all juvenile labour. The Half-Time Shifters were paid off at the expiration of the Multiple-shift System and only Full Time Shifters were engaged which is a more satisfactory arrangement.[11]

A second set of changes, which added to these attempts to homogenize the workforce, concerned women workers. The specific distribution of dismissals after the introduction of the single-shift system meant, *quasi* automatically, that relatively more women workers were affected by the change. The preparing and batching departments were, after all, the departments where the majority of women workers were employed.[12] The formal implications of the abolition of excess-employment, as well as the implementation of new managerial strategies of rationalization, led to a relative decline of women in the workforce. This trend has been pointed out by Samita Sen for this period.[13]

While this development appeared, at first glance, as a side effect of the abolition of the multiple-shift system, managers combined the overall reduction of women workers with a relative reduction in their wages. Women suffered the highest loss in wages – at least in relative terms.

This relative loss in wages was, arguably, a reflection of the new focus on establishing the normalcy of adult male employment, which had been combined with the introduction of the single-shift system. The relatively high rise in the wages of *coolies* was to some degree a result of this trend. Under the multiple-shift system, women had in several cases earned more than male *coolies* working in the same department. Under the single-shift system, in contrast, *coolies* always earned more than women. The lowest paid group of *coolies* in a department would, after the change in shift systems, earn more than the previously highest paid group of women workers. The relative increases in *coolies'* wages appeared as an effect of the priority placed on the relative reduction of women's wages.[14]

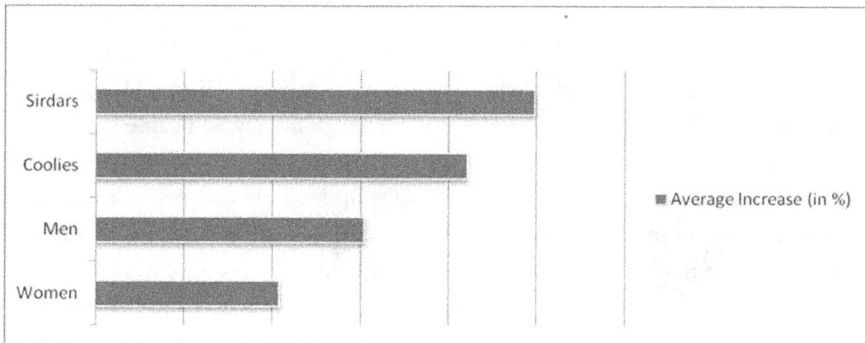

Figure 10 Wage differences according to groups of employees, in %. / Data from: Annual Report on the Working of the Indian Factories Act for Bengal and Assam, 1931.

The dismissal of children and the wage reductions among women workers point us to a third development. The system of relay-sets in the spinning mill was originally designed to increase the stability of labour supply in the context of recurring labour shortages in the late nineteenth century. Managers' attempts to secure the stability of production, by attracting 'madrassi' families to settle in the coolie lines of jute mills, coincided with the falling importance of excess employment in the first decades of the twentieth century. The specific distribution of dismissals at the point of abolishing excess-employment in the 1920s highlighted the fact that the mills' need to retain extra workers had gone. Bengal jute mills no longer needed to try and attract families in order to sustain the stability of production.

From the perspective of 'madrassi' workers, the distribution of dismissals, as well as the adjustment of wage-payments, implied considerable losses in family income. 'Madrassi' workers were, after all, in their majority employed in the spinning mill, which included men, women and children.[15] In an attempt to compensate for the loss in family income, workers seem to have sent their children into local bazaars, where legal restrictions on the employment of children were of no concern. This practice had already come up earlier, as a response to legal restrictions on the employment of younger children. The basic condition for doing odd jobs in the mill neighbourhoods was a rudimentary training in Bengali, as well as in writing of letters and numbers. Lachanao, a 'madrassi' boy-worker employed as a shifter, explained to members of the Whitley Commission how this worked:

When I was a small boy, there was a man in the lines who used to teach me and I learnt a little there. I live in the Standard Mill lines. My father and mother have been working in this mill all along. When I was a little boy, I had a little sister who fell ill and died. My family was badly in need of money, so I came to work. [...] I learnt something from the teacher on the lines for four or five months. I gave up learning three years ago. After I gave up learning and before I joined the mill I was doing odd jobs for the Bengalee shop keepers in the bazaar and earned a little money. I like to go and read provided this does not interfere with my work. (The boy was able to write a few vernacular alphabets and the Arabic numerals.)[16]

The Standard Jute Mill, where Lachanao worked, introduced the single-shift system one year after this interview in 1931. Children like Lachanao, then, most likely had to return to the local bazaars in order to find odd jobs.

The change in shift systems led to an increase of 'madrassi'-schools in Bengal jute mills. In the nearby Titaghur Jute Mill, managers noticed a new 'madrassi' teacher, who had rented two rooms in the coolie lines after the single-shift system was introduced. The classes were, according to mill officials, visited by about forty pupils per day. Since the Titaghur Mill already had a school for workers, the mill managers did not consider enlisting the active involvement of the teacher in the coolie lines.[17] They did, however, rent out the rooms for the school free of charge. The 'madrassi' teacher himself was paid for by workers. He received between four to eight annas per month for each child that was visiting the school.[18] In the Samnuggur North Mill, the mills' manager formed a new school, after he was 'approached by the Madrassis to help them to educate their children'.[19] In this case, too, the school appears to have been well attended, and about forty-five children visited it per day.[20]

Altogether, then, the dismissals in connection with the introduction of the single-shift system cannot be reduced to the question of whether dismissed workers would return to their rural homes. While the vast majority of jute workers certainly sustained links to their homes in Bihar and in the United Provinces, the specific focus of mass-retrenchments, on those sections of the workforce which were more often settled in mill towns and in nearby villages, renders it problematic to see dismissals simply as a matter of 'up-country' workers, as has generally been done in contemporary and in historical accounts of the period.[21] While the majority of 'madrassi' workers were employed in the northern parts of the jute belt, spinning mills in the south of Calcutta were dominated by Bengali workers. In the case of these workers, too, the question of whether they did return to their original homes seems to miss the problem, since it restricts the implications of the change in shift systems for workplace relations to the experience of specific sections of the workforce.

3.3

Intervening in workers' informal rhythms – attempts to suppress practices of sharing work

Contemporary descriptions of the change in shift systems usually avoided discussing shared work as a problem. Rather, the impression was given that the formal abolition of the multiple-shift system simply spelt an end to these practices at the shop-floor. The constant motion of people, substituting one another at seemingly random moments of the day, accordingly, had been stopped when extra workers had been dismissed, and when regular shifts had been instituted.[1] Yet, practices of sharing work had not simply been a formal feature of the multiple-shift system. While being inscribed into the regulatory frame of the mill, rhythms of work substitution were also a central feature of workers' autonomy at the shop-floor. They included not only break-regulations between workers and extra workers, but also arrangements between regular workers and workers from other departments, who wanted to train themselves at particular machines, as well as arrangements between regular workers and people who had not even been employed by the mill – such as friends or family members. The introduction of the single-shift system, then, indicated more general attempts to control the movements of workers, extra workers and outsiders, whose coming and going was tied to informal arrangements inside and outside the mill.

Attempts to suppress practices of sharing work at the site of production came to constitute a central field of conflicts in the change in shift systems. Workers refused the notion that these practices were an act of subversion in the first place, as the rules of the single-shift system implied. The result was a series of interventions from managers in order to curtail informal rhythms of break-arrangements, as well as responses by workers, who did not only adopt or contest these attempts, but also appropriated them in different ways. This led, as we will argue, to a situation, in which workers' autonomy at the site of production was restricted, yet not fully overturned.

The first problem in considering how practices of shared work were restricted in the industry appears when trying to determine if extra workers had, indeed, been dismissed throughout the mill. To put it differently, it was unclear if the abolition of the multiple-shift system did in fact result in the immediate dismissal of *all* extra workers at once, or if this was a more gradual process. Correspondence from the Bird Company indicates that the six mills of the company had followed different paths in this respect. While some of the agencies' mills had dismissed all extra workers, others, like the Union North Mill, had kept a 'complement of spare labour', as Paul Benthall complained as late as 1935.[2] Managers had, accordingly, conceded workers' demands for irregular breaks during the day – a practice known as 'jhol-panni' breaks.[3] The decision to employ extra workers under the single-shift system had in this case been taken unilaterally by the mill manager, leading to a peculiar reversal of the earlier conflict between the managing agency and its managers. Paul Benthall complained strongly about this situation, pointing out that from the perspective of the managing agents 'no allowance for spare labour has been made in the estimates'.[4]

Overall, the abolition of the multiple-shift system led to dismissals of extra workers. However, the organization of work in a manner that excluded practices of substitution was more difficult to implement. This impression is sharpened when we turn to measures directed at regulating practices of sharing work more generally. A crucial set of strategies which managers adopted, in order to tackle this problem, was designed to limit the motion of people at the shop floor. This meant, first of all, that managers tried to define – and control – a boundary between the inside and the outside of the mill compound, by shutting mill gates during hours of work. Neither workers, nor friends, nor relatives were allowed to cross this boundary during the hours of work. Workers, thus, were confined within the compound, while friends and relatives turned into 'outsiders'.[5]

In order to differentiate between those who were allowed to enter the mill compound and those who were not, mills distributed tokens among workers. These were controlled by *durwans*, who had been charged with the task of guarding the gates. Describing his first impressions of the rhythms of work under the single-shift system, the manager of the Titaghur Jute Mill wrote:

> Single Shift working commenced on 2nd March when a good start was made. There were many extra workers looking for employment but only those who were retained for Single Shift working were allowed inside the mill gates and the workers retained had previously been given a token for this purpose.[6]

While the practice of closing mill gates during hours of work was not an unusual feature in industrial facilities, it was a new form of regulation in the Bengal jute industry. Until the first decade of the twentieth century, managers and managing agents used to point out that 'doors in jute mills are always open'.[7]

The main purpose of closing mill gates was to stop the movement of 'outsiders' at the site of production, rather than to control the movement of workers inside the mill. In some of the mills of the Bird Company, as we have already seen, managers still employed a number of extra workers – thus producing the possibility of sharing work in a restricted way. The mills of the Duff company chose another method and introduced a pass-system, under which each worker received a pass in order to leave the mill premises during hours of work for limited periods of time. The time a worker had spent outside the mill was marked on this pass by *durwans* at the mill gates. Once a pre-defined amount of time had been spent outside, the worker was not allowed to leave the mill anymore.[8]

The principal features of this pass-system bear strong reminiscences with those in Indian cotton mills. These had been introduced in the late nineteenth century, in order to specify the amount of time workers could spend outside the workplace during any given break.[9] Like workers in the cotton industry, jute workers employed by the Duff company needed to present a pass in order to leave their workplace for irregular breaks. This form of control was aimed at restricting the practice of sharing work, not preventing it altogether.

A second measure, confirming the impression that managers tried to restrict practices of sharing work, rather than prohibiting them, was apparent with regard to the ways in which managers created incentives for workers to actually stay inside the mill compound. Here, again, the mills of the Duff company left the most detailed accounts behind. In order to prevent workers from going to the local bazaar during their hours of work, the managers of the companies' mills increased the number of tea-stalls and sweetmeat shops inside the compound. In the Titaghur Mill, four new tea-stalls were erected – two for Muslims, and two for Hindus.[10] The manager of the Samnuggur North Mill increased the number of tea-shops and vendors only a few years later, upon noticing that workers still left the mill premises. When reporting to his directors, he wrote:

> It was found necessary during the year to close all means of exit from the compound during the hours the Mill was working, to stop the practice of workers going out for tea, etc. Consequently, two Kutcha huts were erected against the wall of the Compound near the Gates, where tea can be bought by the workers without going outside. [...] Three vendors of Sweets have been allowed to take up a stance inside the compound for the same reason as stated in the previous paragraph.[11]

The establishment of tea-stalls and sweat-meat shops in mill compounds, however, suggests that attempts to restrict workers' movements were directed at particular sections of the work force – in particular weavers. Not only was the number of new tea-stalls fairly small, and unlikely to have been designed to serve substantial sections of the workforce. Rather, before the introduction of the single-shift system, tea-stalls in mill compounds already served mostly weavers. Other sections of the workforce earned lower wages and often could not afford to buy tea on a regular basis, as K.C. Chowdhury pointed out when studying the living conditions of jute workers in 1930.[12]

Keeping in mind that attempts to control workers at the site of production were, in particular, targeted at the weaving department, the specific focus on regulating the movements leading from the weaving department to the spaces outside the mill appears logical. While, in principle, all workers were compelled to stay in the mill compound, managers tried to regulate the movements of those sections of the workforce who were already the objects of attempts to increase labour control. The establishment of tea-stalls and sweat-meat shops, in other words, appeared as an extension of the strategy to control the quality and amount of output coming from the weaving department. This, however, did not so much concern the practices of sharing work between employed weavers who, after all, were being persuaded to take their tea in the mill compound. Rather, the attempt was to restrict the movements of extra workers, who had not been employed by the mill, but who had come due to informal arrangements with regular workers.

The ways in which closed mill gates as well as new tea-stalls and shops in the mill compounds (re-)shaped the mill-space can only be speculated about. However, shops, which on account of wage-hierarchies could only be frequented by a small section of the workforce, certainly increased the visibility of inequalities between workers in the mill compound. Similarly, the visibility of religious communities, who either frequented the tea-stalls for Hindu or for Muslim workers, was sharpened, when the single-shift system was introduced. At the same time, the increased number of tea-shops also provided new spaces for interaction between workers, which could turn into a basis for forging new solidarities. After the general strike of 1937, the manager of the Angus Jute Mill complained that the mills' tea-shops had turned into centres of political discussions and – in the lingo of managers – centres of 'agitation'. The manager, thus, rented the tea-shops to new tea sellers, who were 'loyal' to the company.[13]

Considering, in either case, the measures taken when introducing the single-shift system, it is striking that practices of sharing work were not actually abolished. Managers' reports stay silent as to why they chose to only restrict the movements of workers and 'outsiders', but not the informal break arrangements at the site of production. One set of reasons was certainly that questions of labour control still constituted a problem in jute mills. This was, first of all, apparent when considering the principal structure through which managerial control could be exercised. While the abolition of the multiple-shift system had reduced the number of jute workers throughout the jute belt, mills in Bengal were still massive industrial entities. Large numbers of workers were checked by a small number of Europeans, who had little connection to Indian supervisory staff – a feature that remained unchanged when the single-shift system was introduced. Making matters worse, the Scottish supervisory staff of mills had altogether more breaks than workers in the course of the day.[14] The result was that at regular moments of the day, supervisors could simply not control workers' rhythms and movements at the site of production.

The limited capacities of managers and supervisors to effectively control workers inside the mill were, secondly, complicated, as it proved difficult to control the newly drawn boundary between the inside and the outside of the mill compound. Not only individual mills, but also the surrounding mill compounds, were large entities, rendering it difficult to control all possible entries or exits. A standard compound was, after all, comprised of one or two individual mills; coolie-lines; quarters for the European staff of the mill (usually including a tennis court, in some cases football courts, small soda factories or even an ice factory for the Scottish expatriates); several godowns for raw material, coal and finished goods; water tanks; medical facilities and schools (however inefficient and understaffed).[15] These compounds were further surrounded by over-crowded bustees and bazaars, but also by dense stretches of jungle areas and by the river. Managers and overseers, thus, could hardly have kept track of the many paths which workers and 'outsiders' could use to subvert the new rules of the single-shift system.

The problem of controlling workers inside and outside the mill was intensified by a second set of problems, which was indicated in workers' responses to the attempts to control their movements. Workers regularly resisted the attempts to cut the connections between the mill and their neighbourhoods during the hours of work. The phenomenon of workers who had left the mill while someone else attended to their machines remained a feature of Bengal jute mills. In the weaving departments, where practices of sharing work appeared to be a particularly crucial obstacle, such incidents were mentioned by mill representatives. Attempts by managers or overseers to prevent this, however, were regularly met with resistance by workers. Illustrative of this tendency is an incident which occurred soon after the introduction of the single-shift system in the Titaghur Jute Mill. The manager of the mill reported the conflict to his directors, providing a rare insight into the chain of events at the site of production at the moment when the new rules of the single-shift system were contested. It is thus worth quoting at length:

> About 9 a.m. on Wednesday morning, when Mr. Robertson, Weaving Overseer sent for this weaver in connection with bad work, he discovered that he had absented himself from his loom and had left his brother, who is not employed by us, in his place. Mr. Robertson ordered this man to leave the loom, and another weaver was appointed.
>
> On making his usual inspection at 1-30 p.m., Mr. Robertson found the original weaver together with his brother working the loom and the newly appointed weaver standing aside. He told him that he was dismissed and ordered him to leave the loom, which he refused to do. Instructing the Head *Sirdar* to attend to the matter Mr. Robertson continued his round of the looms.
>
> When attempting to remove the man from the loom the Head *Sirdar* was threatened with a knife. Looms went off, the weavers assumed a threatening attitude towards Mr. Robertson, and the original weaver's brother struck him hard on the head causing a wound behind the ear "2 long, which had to be stitched.
>
> On Thursday morning shortly after the start, the weavers in Mr. Robertson's section stopped and demanded that the dismissed weaver should be reinstated. When told that on no consideration would he be re-engaged they refused to resume work. [...] The looms were stopped till 7 a.m. when full working was resumed unconditionally.[16]

This incident demonstrates the difficulties of controlling workers' everyday rhythms of work. The discovery that two people had entered and left the workplace appeared to be coincidental. According to the new regulations of the mill, the act of sharing work with an 'outsider' was an act of subversion, rendering the dismissal of the weaver legitimate. The entire weaving department, however, opposed this decision strongly and violently – even beginning a brief strike, that too in the midst of the Great Depression.

Between the first dismissal in the morning, and the weavers' response in the afternoon, however, there was a peculiar gap. One reason for this was probably that Mr Robertson had ordered the head-*sirdar* of the department to take care of the matter after the two weavers ignored his decision for the second time that day. In the morning, as well as in the afternoon, when Mr Robertson dismissed the weaver, workers did not appear to react to the situation nor did line *sirdars* or clerks seem to have been inclined to intervene. Neither workers, line *sirdars*, nor clerks, then, took the decision of Mr Robertson seriously. They did not even find it necessary to defend the practice of sharing work at this point, as for them Mr Robertson had no right to take a decision in this matter.

The dismissal of the weaver who had shared his work with his 'brother' interfered directly with established practices of workers, as well as of *sirdars*. The new rules of the mill, which arbitrarily re-defined how workers were allowed to organize their work, did not simply render this practice into a mutually acknowledged act of subversion. The 'brother' at the loom, after all, was not simply an outsider. He was part of an established structure of social relations, which sustained workers in the urban mill areas, as well as at the site of production. Workers refused the very claim of the mill to exercise authority over the ways in which they engaged with people not employed by the mill. The problem then was not so much that notions of authority were based on unchanging *ma-bap* relations, as Dipesh Chakrabarty suggested.[17] Rather, the structure of authority itself was crumbling, as workers' everyday practices were declared to be an act of subversion. It was arguably at this moment, when the mill changed the rules of authority, that the relations of domination at the site of production suddenly became unbearably visible. Workers responded to this by attacking the mill and its supervisory staff.

Considering the difficulties of actually abolishing practices of sharing work, it is quite obvious that neither the dismissal of extra workers nor the closing of mill gates resulted in the introduction of a proper single-shift system. The structures of authority and control in the mill rendered it difficult to actually sustain these measures. The new single-shift system appeared rather as a temporary compromise between managers' attempts to abolish the multiple-shift system and workers' attempts to defend spaces of autonomy in the mill. This compromise was certainly still an arbitrary one. While managers could not fully control the movements of workers and 'outsiders', measures such as the closing of mill gates meant that these practices had been restricted considerably. The terms on which these conflicts were staged, then, changed substantially. People who were not employed by the mill, but wanted to enter it, could not do so through the mill gates anymore. Correspondingly, the risks of sharing work had increased. If another worker was detected at a given machine, the result could be an immediate dismissal if the departmental overseer noticed it. Similarly, the sharing of work with an inexperienced worker (who maybe wanted to train himself to become a weaver in the first place) bore heightened risks, as the mill controlled the quality and amount of weavers' output more thoroughly. All 'gaws and broken warps but also snarls, bad selvedges etc.', which another worker or an 'outsider' had produced in the name of a regularly employed weaver, thus, could lead to an immediate dismissal as well.

Indicative of the degree to which the change in shift systems led to a gradual change in the ways workers organized their work was the problem of skill. The problem of de-skilling is usually seen as a result of processes of rationalization.[18] The attempts to restrict workers' rhythms in the jute industry, which were the condition for introducing new modes of increasing productivity, however, led to a process of *skilling*. This was particularly striking in view to spinners and weavers. While the former had originally been categorized as unskilled, weavers were classified as semi-skilled workers. This meant that weavers were expected to train themselves while working on the looms. Spinners accordingly required neither formal nor informal training at the spinning frames.[19]

A few years after the multiple-shift system had been abolished, however, the industry started to encounter an increasing lack of skilled workers. In particular, skilled spinners and weavers were rare. In a number of mills, the situation started to cause losses in production, leading to various attempts to solve the problem, such as the employment of shifters as spinners, in the assumption that tasks in both jobs were similar enough.[20] Eventually, at the end of the decade, the mills of the IJMA instituted a very rudimentary system of apprenticeships for spinners and weavers. Spinners and weavers, accordingly, were allowed to train their sons at their spindles or looms for the duration of six months. After this period, these apprentices had the chance to be registered as *badli* workers, with the option of being employed on a regular basis if their work was found to be reliable. During their training period, however, they did not receive any wage.[21]

Needless to say, this scheme was not particularly successful. A number of weavers seem to have used this option, but hardly any apprentices wanted to work in the spinning department, where young persons could work as shifters and actually earn a wage.[22] Yet this step indicated that the increased pressure on workers to not share their work with 'outsiders' meant that not enough new workers could be trained any more, in order to sustain the informal system of apprenticeships which had been a feature of the multiple-shift system. The gradual restriction of practices of shared work, then, was reflected in the emerging system of apprenticeships, in which workers were allowed to share their work with relatives again, under conditions that were regulated by the mill.

3.4

Trade union responses

A fourth development, which came to be connected to the change in shift systems, was a rise in working-class militancy throughout the jute belt. Workers' responses to the abolition of the multiple-shift system were marked by intense violence, which was directed at the workplace and at mill buildings, as well as against persons who represented the authority of the mill – such as managers, European overseers or *durwans*. This was a continuous feature of the change in the organization of work, and already in 1912, striking workers 'occupied themselves' by throwing stones and brickbats at their mill, as the *Times of India* put it.[1]

This was paralleled by the apparent intensification of solidarity between workers against management. Conflicts often triggered responses by sections of the workforce that had not originally been involved. In 1925, for instance, a dispute between a *durwan* (*jamadar*) and a weaver in the Presidency Jute Mill resulted in instant strike action, supported by large sections of the workforce. In the course of the conflict, workers chased the mill manager and the *durwan* through the mill, and attacked an overseer.[2] This conflict was followed by a strike in the Lawrence Jute Mill in the same month, when about 4,000 workers downed their tools, after eighteen shifters had left their workplace.[3] In the Gourepore Jute mill, as we have seen, nearly the entire workforce responded to the encounter between Jagnarain Singh and George Spence in the weaving department in 1926 – in the midst of communal riots in the same area.[4] In the same year, workers of the Bally Jute Mill attacked their manager with shuttles and bobbins, while also damaging the mill building in the course of the attack.[5] In the Ganges Jute Mill in 1927, meanwhile, workers in the beaming and winding department went on strike. Their protest soon found support from workers in the nearby Fort Williams Jute Mill, who struck work as well.[6] In 1928, workers of the Fort Gloster Jute Mill attacked the European staff of the mill, as well as policemen who had been sent to prevent a riot. The police were severely outnumbered, while workers had cut through the telephone line, with the result that further reinforcements only arrived several hours later.[7]

While these strikes were a response to a profound shift in industrial relations, this was not what was seen to be at stake in accounts of the dynamics of industrial conflict in the 1920s. This problem was already apparent with regard to the demands raised by workers on the one hand, and the interpretation of these demands by contemporary observers on the other. Weavers, for instance, stated regularly that they had to suffer wage reductions due to the introduction of the single-shift system. In relative terms, their wages had, indeed, been reduced – a problem which also affected their position within the hierarchy of the workforce. Yet, in absolute terms, their wages had been increased. From the perspective of the Inspector of Factories, their demand appeared to be irrational, while other observers seemed to understand weavers' protests as a demand for a general wage increase among jute workers.[8]

Underneath the received narrative of industrial conflict in this time, we find state, workers and trade unions all responding to the transformation of the organization of work on the factory floor. The tensions between the different responses to this change developed into a significant feature of these strikes, which accounted for a particular *dynamic* of industrial action in the jute belt. This was, as we would like to show, the outcome of a type of conflict, which evolved around the organization of work. Rephrasing Gareth Stedman-Jones at this point, we might describe this type as a conflict over the appropriation of labour, in contrast to conflicts over the appropriation of profits.[9] Stedman-Jones argued that conflicts over the appropriation of labour take place *within the labour process*. They are, in other words, disputes over the organization of work at the site of production. They are marked by 'exceptional militancy among skilled workers' in times, when 'new methods of production' are introduced.[10] Conflicts over the appropriation of profits, in contrast, take place *in the sphere of circulation*, and can be seen as 'a struggle for the betterment of the situation of the worker on the basis of the wage contract'. They include short-term wage demands, as well as long-term political goals, which contest the capitalist ownership of industry.[11]

Stedman-Jones, further, pointed out that the dynamics of both struggles are different, as of conflicts over the appropriation of labour

> renders problematic the coexistence between the short term and the long term.
> Industrial discontent and the political expression of that discontent tend to
> converge. Struggles of this kind necessarily begin with the defence of a relatively
> privileged position in production, and they may retain a conservative or even

reactionary form. Whether or not they do so will depend partly [...] upon the political situation in which they take place.[12]

Conflicts over the appropriation of labour, then, are always more and less radical than conflicts over the appropriation of profits. Illustrating this dynamic with regard to the jute industry, it can be said that weavers' complaints over a (relative) loss in wages appeared at its outset as a conservative demand, defending a privileged position within the mill. These conflicts, however, were a response to a comprehensive change in the organization of work and were expressed in strikes that were joined by large sections of the workforce in increasingly militant strikes. Instead of 'simply' defending the position of one section of the workforce, then, complaints over (relative) wage losses were interlinked with workers' demands to decide how managers could organize processes of work at the mill machinery in the first place.

Contemporary observers, meanwhile, tended to 'translate' workers militancy into demands around the wage contract, or 'betterment of the situation of the worker'. Capitalists and representatives of the colonial state rejected the apparent need for such a betterment, while trade unionists largely defended it. In the context of the late 1920s, the specific dynamics acquired further momentum. The implementation of the Trade Union Act and the Trade Dispute Bill in 1927 and 1929, respectively circumscribed how trade unions could represent workers. These acts served to establish a legal framework for the registration of trade unions, as well as for the arbitration of industrial disputes. They were designed, as has been pointed out, to restrict the emerging labour and trade union movement in colonial India, firstly by defining what was a legal and what was an illegal strike, and secondly by determining the conditions for trade unions to be recognized as potential arbiters in labour conflicts.[13] As the parameters of industrial disputes legislation were sketched out, the designation of normative disputes – over wages, hours of work or dismissals – and the exclusion of others, too, were marked. Demands that can be placed within the realm of capitalist welfarism were principally marked as legitimate ones – at least if capital and state agreed that the underlying grievances were legitimate, and if these demands were raised through a recognized trade union. Conflicts over workers' right to organize production, then, were excluded. In addition, the specific conflict over the multiple-shift system was already at the centre of escalating conflicts between capital and state, as the system clashed with the state's attempts to administer the Indian Factories Act. This, in turn, marked the change in shift systems *a priori* as political problem within the terms of the Trade Union Act and the Trade Dispute Bill.

This situation, not surprisingly, had an impact on the ways in which trade unions approached the strikes of jute workers. In the 1920s, there were three sets of trade unions active among jute workers. The oldest was the Kankinarrah Labour Union (KLU), which had been founded in the course of the strikes in the early 1920s by Moulavi Latafat Hossain and K.C. Roy Chowdhury. It was the only trade union among jute workers which was officially recognized under the Trade Union Act.[14] This union supported peaceful negotiations between workers and employers, modelled, as Chowdhuri pointed out, on the 'plan followed in the textile mills of Ahmedabad'.[15] In principle, the KLU supported the multiple-shift system. This was, however, a strictly conservative demand, and the unions' support weakened considerably once the single-shift system had been introduced. The KLU's politics, after all, revolved around the readjustment of existing workplace relations, rather than mounting a fundamental opposition to the organization of work by employers.[16]

Around 1923 and 1925 respectively, two new trade unions were founded, which worked together closely, and eventually merged. In 1923, the Gourepore Works Employees' Association was founded by Santosh Kumari Gupta, a local activist, who had connections to the national movement.[17] In 1925, the Bengal Jute Workers' Association was founded in Bhatpara in 1925, by Kalidas Bhattacharya, a former jute mill clerk, who later became a member of the communist Workers' and Peasants' Party.[18] Both unions supported workers in their everyday conflicts, and over matters of violence by European overseers.[19] The BJWA, further, helped workers in claiming compensation for accidents, ran a school for workers' children and opened a recreation centre for workers.[20] Neither of the unions supported conflicts over the abolition of the multiple-shift system. In 1926, when six mills changed shift systems in the neighbourhood of Bhatpara, both unions only got involved in the strike in the Gourepore Jute Mill, where the trigger had been the death of Jagnarain Singh.[21]

Around that time, the situation of both unions changed. The Gourepore Works Employees' Association was incorporated into the BJWA – or, as Tulsi Das Ghosh, a former member of the Gourepore Works Employees' Association stated later: 'this Union was captured by the Bengal Jute Workers' Association'.[22] Despite its growth, however, the new BJWA was immediately weakened in its work among jute workers, as it was not registered as an official trade union under the Trade Union Act. Still, in 1927 the trade union had worked with local authorities to support workers in their everyday conflicts. The Commissioner for Workmen's Compensation reported about the work of the BJWA, that the union continued during the year to assist its members to obtain compensation, both by agreement and by application to the Commissioner where agreement could not be reached.[23]

The union's status under the Trade Union Act, however, implied that the cooperation between state authorities and the BJWA came to an abrupt end at that moment. The Commissioner for Workmen's Compensation, not surprisingly, did not mention any form of cooperation with the union any more in the years to come.[24] Tulsi Das Ghosh, meanwhile, lost his job as a mill clerk the same year – presumably because his trade union's status as an illegal organization made it easier for the mill manager to dismiss him.[25]

Probably in an attempt to reclaim its right to represent workers, the BJWA responded by expanding its influence and opening up new branch offices in different parts of the jute belt. Strikes, too, were increasingly encouraged and supported by the end of the 1920s.[26] Illustrative of these developments was the involvement of the BJWA in a strike in the Wellington Jute Mill. In April 1928, three members of the BJWA rented an office in Mahesh, a small town near Rishra. Soon, a billboard was put up, indicating with huge letters in Bengali, Hindi and English, that this was a new branch office of the trade union. Tulsi Das Ghosh was commissioned to run this branch office, as well as another new opening of the BJWA in Howrah.

A few months after the office was opened, the management of the nearby Wellington Jute Mill introduced the single-shift system. This step triggered, surely enough, strikes among the workers of the mill. Weavers were the first to leave the workplace, protesting against the (relative) wage reductions they had suffered due to the change. The strike ended after about a month, without success. Two weeks later, the weavers of the Wellington Jute Mill went on strike again. This time, they protested against a temporary increase in hours of work from fifty-four to sixty hours per week. The mill manager had implemented the increase in order to make up for the time lost due to the first strike. This second strike, too, was unsuccessful, and work commenced after two weeks.[27]

In the course of the first strike, the newly founded branch office of the Bengal Jute Workers' Association turned into an important centre of strike activities, demanding an (absolute) increase in wage payments on behalf of the workers. The union distributed rice and *dal* to workers. Kalidas Bhattacharya came to Mahesh several times, and organized meetings among workers, while also establishing connections with communist trade unions, which had emerged in the south of Calcutta. Communists like Radharaman Mitter and Phillip Spratt came to speak, and workers from the nearby Lillooah railway workshop, who were at that time entrenched in an impressive industrial dispute themselves, came along to express the trade unions' solidarity with the strikers in Rishra.[28]

The new policy of the Bengal Jute Workers' Association, and their increased support of strikes in the jute belt indicated a certain, yet limited, degree of radicalization within the union. The emergence of communist trade unions in the southern parts of Calcutta played an important role here. In 1928, the Chengail and the Bauria Jute Workers' Unions were founded in the course of the strikes in the Fort Gloster and the Ludlow Jute Mills. The trade unions were led by the communists Kishori Lal Ghose and Radharaman Mitra, as well as by Bankim Mukharji, who was a member of the Indian National Congress with close contacts to the communist movement. They were tightly connected to the Workers' and Peasants' Party. In order to support workers during strikes, people like Radharaman Mitter or Bankim Mukharji often moved into the mill towns during this time, where they were joined by other labour leaders like Philip Spratt.[29]

In contrast to either the KLU or the BJWA, the communist labour activists generally supported workers in their struggles over the multiple-shift system. The strikes in the Ludlow and Fort Gloster Jute Mills had, in fact, been triggered by the change in shift systems, and workers in both mills demanded the re-introduction of the multiple-shift system. The reason for the support for the workers' struggle in this case was not that the demands which communists raised coincided with the demands of jute workers. It was, rather, that communist unions tended to support workers' struggles more generally, and as part of a growing working-class movement.[30]

After the first strike in Rishra, the activities of the BJWA in the area more or less broke down. When workers went on strike against the increase in hours of work, the office of the Bengal Jute Workers' Association had already been shut, as Tulsi Das Ghosh had abandoned it. In September, the manager of a mill in Howrah offered Ghosh a job, if he helped to end a strike in that mill. This strike, too, had been triggered by a change in shift systems. Ghosh accepted the offer, thus giving up his career as a trade unionist.[31] The episode revealed two important moments of trade union politics in this period. The first was a conflict over the radicalization of trade unions, which also affected rank-and-file members. While he was presumably relieved to find employment again, his testimony also reflected his frustration with the increasing radicalization of trade unionism in the jute belt. The growing cooperation with communist labour activists, then, may have contributed to his decision to abandon the BJWA.

The episode revealed, secondly, the difficulties in establishing trade union networks throughout the jute belt. Kalidas Bhattacharya seems to have learned about the closure of the office in Rishra only a few months after Ghosh had left.[32] Establishing networks among workers in different mill areas posed a difficulty in terms of organizing the trade union itself, and in controlling the activities of local labour activists. While the BJWA had supported workers during the first strike, the trade unionists' attempt to establish themselves in the area on a permanent basis failed for the time being, as the office had been abandoned already.

The second strike in Rishra also brings us back again to the implications of the change in shift systems, and to the conflictual responses to workers' militancy in this context. In the late 1920s, more precisely, when trade union involvement in the conflict over the change in shift systems was rising, and when, simultaneously, labour conflicts were increasing throughout colonial India, workers in the Bengal jute industry began to protest against the temporary increase in hours of work, on account of making up time lost due to strikes. The entire workforce of weaving departments left their workplace after having observed their regular hours of work and were followed out by other sections of the workforce.[33] The practice of increasing hours of work to make up time lost was, in itself, not new in the industry. It had been a common occurrence since the earliest days of the industry, and it continued throughout the 1930s and the 1940s.[34]

In contrast to the problem of wages, which could be interpreted in relative and in absolute terms, the practice of increasing hours of work placed the matter more prominently in the realm of conflicts over the 'appropriation of labour'. The practice of increasing hours of work was, after all, not exactly illegal, as jute mills were formally allowed to run their machines for sixty hours per week. Workers' objection to an increase in hours of work was arguably driven by a resulting increase in the number of working days per week. The abolition of the multiple-shift system had already led to an increase in working days from four to five per week. A further increase in weekly hours implied a working week of six days. The number of off-days, during which workers were not compelled to work in the mill, were, in turn, reduced – and this is what they objected to. One important theme, illustrating the importance of off-days, was the practice of wood gathering in nearby forests, mostly for purposes of fuel. This came up in workers' testimonies at various moments. Palia, a *sirdar* in the Presidency Jute Mill, also reported that after the birth of his daughters, he and his family

> began to collect wood from the distant forests on the off days and would sometimes sell it in the neighbouring markets.[35]

At the time of the interview, he was heavily indebted, which, presumably increased his dependence on this extra income.[36]

Agricultural work, too, was an important source of additional income, in particular among Bengali workers. These workers came from the surrounding areas, and often kept a small piece of land. The additional off day, then, gave them the option to sustain themselves by combining both types of work. In fact, Shama Charan Samuth, whom we have encountered in relation to the modalities of work under the multiple-shift system in the weaving department, told the members of the 1891 commission that he used to work on his own plot of land on the off-day, and, thus, preferred a four-day week.[37] K. C. Roy Chowdhuri, meanwhile, reported about another practice, which was apparently common among 'madrassi' workers. He described that

> [t]he Madrassi women wear only one piece of cloth with no other garments. Their saris are usually six yards long against the usual five yards used by other classes. They invariably use their provincial hand-woven saris. These saris are locally produced by some weavers in coolies in their off time.[38]

The fact that under the multiple-shift system a four-day working week had turned into a *quasi*-structural feature of the Bengal jute industry, then, had also been interwoven with practices which sustained workers' identities in the mill areas.[39]

The BJWA never supported strikes among jute workers over an increase in hours of work. An increase of working hours to sixty was, after all, in line with the Indian Factories Act. Attempts at being recognized as an official trade union rendered it difficult to support strikes over a demand which effectively implied workers' right to work shorter hours than permitted under the law. Communist trade unionists, meanwhile, generally supported workers in their conflicts, including over hours of work. They sought to represent workers not through legal recognition, but with the backing of a growing working-class movement. When 'translating' workers' grievances into demands, they tended to render them in terms of demands made by a broader labour movement. With regard to hours of work in the jute industry, that meant that the question of hours of work turned into a demand for an eight-hour working day – or, for a regular working week of five days. This was a demand which workers objected to, while it was also a demand that turned conflicts in the jute belt into a part of a broader struggle of workers in India and elsewhere.[40] The support offered to the strike in Rishra by trade unionists, then, ended up displaying tensions over their solidarity. These tensions, however, were not so much the result of a genuine impossibility of understanding between workers and trade unionists, but, rather, it was the result of a radicalization of workers' politics, which had been encouraged precisely by the solidarity from the union in the first place.

We should at this point be careful to not reduce tensions over strike demands to questions of trade union authority (as argued by Dipesh Chakrabarty) or workers' agency (as argued among others by Subho Basu).[41] While debates about the nature of the relationship between workers and trade unionists have been important, they tended to focus on the analysis of specific aspects of this relationship – that of authority and its' opposite, agency. In taking the workplace as a point of departure, we are highlighting here a different type of tension. Long-term political goals – such as the establishment of a broader network of trade unionists and of a wider labour movement (with unified demands) – were *a priori* in conflict with demands over the re-introduction of shift system, that was unique to the Bengal jute industry. Rather than attempting to answer the question of authority versus agency at this point, we have sought to broaden the scope of analysis here.

4

'Various Paths Are Today Opened' – working-class politics and the general strike of 1929

In April 1929, a programmatic article was published in a Bengali paper called *Swadeshi Bazar*, about an imminent workers' struggle and its possibilities.[1] The author explained the contemporary situation as follows:

> Various paths are today opened before the workers of the nation. The workers, according to their own capacity, must each pick out a path and travel along it. [...] A struggle must be carried on with the opposing power from various directions [...]. At the present moment new workers are being bewildered at the sight of different ways and different parties. The worker must first choose his path, and thereafter choose the party.[2]

The article appeared in the middle of an intense phase of workers' militancy in colonial India, which was sustained by a growth of working-class movements as well as of trade unions and labour organizations. Between 1928 and 1929, many industries and labour regimes in Bengal witnessed significant upsurges of industrial action: for instance, railway workers in Lilloah, oil-workers in Budge-Budge and scavengers in Calcutta.[3] Most of these struggles were supported or led by the communist Workers' and Peasants Party, and were also supported by revolutionary terrorists.

Among these upsurges was the unprecedented militancy of jute workers, who embarked on the first general strike in their industry's history, after an increase

An earlier version of this chapter has been published in: Anna Sailer, '"Various Paths Are Today Opened". The Bengal Jute Mill Strike of 1929 as a Historical Event', in *Working Lives & Worker Militancy. The Politics of Labour in Colonial India*, ed. Ravi Ahuja (New Delhi: Tulika Books, 2013), pp 207–56.

in the hours of work by the mills of the IJMA on 1 July 1929. Led by the Bengal Jute Workers' Union (BJWU) under Prabhabati Das Gupta and Kali Sen, the strike movement spread rapidly, and by 6 August, about 240,000 jute workers had left their workplaces. Faced with a threatening upsurge of workers, the government intervened and pushed for an end to the strike. Mediated by the government of Bengal, a settlement was achieved, and the IJMA was forced to agree to the demands posed by the BJWU on behalf of the workers. The strike ended on 16 August.[4]

The general strike brought two distinct developments together. First, the growing militancy among jute workers since the second half of the 1920s, which was driven by the changing organization of work. The rising number of strikes in this period testified to this development. Second, the growing political mobilization of workers by an emerging, putatively pan-Indian trade union movement. With regard to the jute belt, this development had become apparent in the late 1920s, when nationalist and communist trade unionists had become involved in strikes in the jute industry. By 1928, labour activists had established networks among workers in different parts of the jute belt, and, more importantly, had begun to cooperate with one another, in order to establish a wider political representation of jute workers. What had previously been a series of localized strikes could now assume the form of a general strike under the leadership of a centralized trade union.

In the late 1920s, however, the establishment of a centralized trade union for jute workers was still in its formative process, as we have seen in the previous chapter. This involved, firstly, the mechanisms of expansion of trade union activities in this area. In order to establish networks between labour activists in mill neighbourhoods, trade unionists needed first to move to mill towns and cities in different parts of the jute belt. In order to navigate through the jute belt, they needed to rely on train networks and on ferries – at times only bringing them to locations a few miles from workers' neighbourhoods.[5] Road transport, too, was an option, which, however, required the availability of cars. The involvement of important organizers in the strike, then, began with attempts to hire a car in order to reach jute workers.[6]

The formation of a larger representation of jute workers, was, secondly, marked by conflicts over the political direction of the emerging centralized trade union organization. Moderate, nationalist and communist labour activists were involved in this process. This affected the kinds of labour conflicts that trade unionists wanted to support, and the ways in which they interpreted workers' demands, as we have seen. It was, further, reflected in the ways in which labour conflicts in the jute belt were conceptualized within the politics of the time. The ways in which labour activists remembered the general strike are illustrative of the different readings that emerged out of the event – or, of the 'different paths' that were offered to workers. In 1938, at a meeting among jute workers, a labour activist read out a poem on workers' struggles, that began with the lines of a popular Bengali poem on Bhagat Singh, and that stated that the general strike of 1929 had been part of a battle for independence, beginning in 1857.[7] A few weeks later, at another labour meeting in the same area, trade unionists talked about the general strike of 1929 as an event that had been organized and led by the BJWU (now renamed as Bengal Chatkal Mazdoor Union) under the undisputed leadership of communist trade unionists.[8] Both narratives presented distinct meanings of the general strike as part of broader political conflicts – which had an impact on the strike's objectives, as well as its modalities of organization.

Conflicting interpretations of the general strike were an expression of diverging political priorities within trade union politics.[9] Difficulties and tensions in establishing a trade union *organization* in the jute belt rarely entered these narratives. Instead, the narratives about the general strike were interwoven with ongoing political conflicts, and they tended to assure communist or nationalist labour activists of their respectively dominant role in previous labour conflicts in the jute belt. The conflictual narratives about the general strike also shaped the memory of the event in the 1930s and beyond. As interpretations of the general strike as part of a nationalist struggle lost importance with the decline of revolutionary terrorism in Bengal in the second half of the 1930s, interpretations of an event that was led and organized by communist trade unionists seemed to dominate the memories of the general strike of 1929 among trade unionists in the early 1950s. Areas in the south of Calcutta, where communist trade unionists had taken a leading role, turned in this context into the epicentre of the strike, while the northern parts of the jute belt were largely erased from representations of the event.[10]

The chain of memory and forgetting also had an impact on the interpretation of the event at the point at which it turned from lived experience into history.[11] Historians working on the jute industry took note of conflicts between communist and more moderate trade unionists, which accordingly broke out – and were resolved – at the end of the general strike, when communist trade unionists took over the BJWU. The spatial features of the jute belt, in the meantime, were in these readings generally homogenized, and the mechanisms of trade union organization turned into abstractions. Workers' conflicts in mill towns and near forests, then, were treated as if they took place in highly concentrated and urbanized environments like Bombay – or as if the Calcutta jute industry had indeed been located *in* Calcutta. Expanding trade union activities in the late 1920s, then, turned into a matter of addressing workers in ubiquitous neighbourhoods, not so much in how to actually organize and control the emerging trade union organization itself.[12]

Before turning to the conflicts over the changing organization of work under the single-shift system in the 1930s, it seems necessary, then, to consider the general strike of 1929 on its own terms – to analyse it as an event. This is an important basis on which to reconstruct the ways in which the political mobilization of workers by an emergent pan-Indian trade union movement intersected with the growing militancy among jute workers, and how this conjuncture shaped workers movements in the jute belt in years to come. We will follow the narrative of the event mainly chronologically. In the *first phase*, localized strikes broke out in the north of Calcutta. The BJWU became involved in some of these strikes, though the question of whether strike action was to be supported at all was contested at this point. On 29 July new strikes broke out during the *second phase* of the strike. The BJWU represented workers in both cases and played a crucial role in connecting otherwise localized strikes to a wider strike movement. The *third phase* began with the proclamation of the general strike on 6 August. The general strike was politically defined under the leadership of Prabhabati Das Gupta. Workers' militancy, however, transcended this attempt at defining the strike, and spread the conflict beyond the reaches of the BJWU. The *fourth phase*, in my analysis, comprises the aftermath of the general strike, after a settlement was arrived at on 16 August. Strikes that had been connected through the BJWU were now localized again. While the settlement signalled the end of the political representation of workers' conflicts as a general strike, the ongoing struggles implied that the movement, which had sustained the event, had gained importance in workers' neighbourhoods.

The beginning of the strikes

In November 1928, the IJMA decided to increase the hours of work in their mills from fifty-four hours per week to sixty. The change was to be implemented from July 1929, and was aimed at triggering a fall in prices of jute goods, in order to put pressure on competing mills outside the IJMA.[1] Between November 1928 and May 1929, members of the IJMA continued to argue among themselves about how the new hours of work should be implemented in their mills, and how managers should proceed after stoppages of production due to the breakdown of machinery, or due to strikes. One decision taken was to discontinue the payment of *khoraki* in multiple-shift mills. *Khoraki* was a bonus payment in kind (a food allowance), which had originally been introduced in mills of the IJMA during the First World War. Jute mills which were running on a single-shift system had already discontinued the payment of this allowance.[2] A second decision taken was to not allow members of the IJMA to increase hours of work after stoppages in production. The legal limit of sixty hours per week under the Indian Factories Act meant that only multiple-shift mills would have had the chance to make up time lost. This would have meant an unfair advantage to multiple-shift mills – at least according to managing agencies running their mills on the single-shift system. Commenting on the decision that no mill was to make up time lost anymore, Paul Benthall from the Bird Company declared in a dramatic fashion that the companies' mills would now be 'at the mercy of our labour'.[3]

While the IJMA was debating the increase in hours of work, attempts by labour leaders to create a more general representation of jute workers in the jute belt, in the wake of the increasing militancy among jute workers, led to the formation of the Bengal Jute Workers' Union towards the end of 1928. This trade union was a merger between the BJWA, which had come up in the northern parts of 24-Parganas, and the Chengail and Bauria Jute Workers Unions from Howrah and Budge-Budge.[4] Under the banner of the BJWU, then, local trade unions and labour activists, who had become active in different parts of the jute belt, came together. The new trade union was to be led by Kalidas Bhattacharya, who had previously led the BJWA in Barrackpore, and the union's new head office was set up in Calcutta.[5]

The organization of a large strike movement, however, does not seem to have been an immediate concern for the BJWU at this point. Rather, a central objective for the trade union was to improve the levels of political organization among jute workers. Indicating the difficulties he saw in organizing strikes among jute workers at this point, Kalidas Bhattacharya explained in January 1929 that:

> Generally speaking, the bulk of the mill-workers of jute mills or presses [...] are neither so expert nor so wide awake to their own interests as the operatives of railway, tramway, and other big workshops.[6]

The planned activities of the BJWU were, however, interrupted immediately after its foundation. In March 1929, labour leaders and (suspected) communists throughout colonial India were arrested in connection with the Meerut Conspiracy Case. This included several labour leaders who had organized strikes in Bengal in 1928, as well as leading members of the BJWU – including Kalidas Bhattacharya.[7]

In May 1929, Prabhabati Das Gupta was elected president of the BJWU. She was by then a well-known labour leader in Calcutta, after organizing and leading a strike of city sweepers in 1928. Das Gupta had not been active in the jute industry before, but because of her charisma and because she was able to combine different political approaches, her involvement in this situation was welcomed.[8] Her election as president of the BJWU was supported by Kalidas Bhattacharya.[9] Kali Kumar Sen, who had been briefly active in the jute unions in Howrah, became general secretary.[10] In contrast to the union's president, he regarded himself as 'communist by conviction', as Suchetana Chattopadhyay has pointed out.[11] Kali Sen had joined politics in the late 1920s, and in 1928 he became the co-editor of the socialist paper *Ganabani*.[12] He was, however, also connected to the revolutionary-terrorist paper *Swadeshi Bazar*, which had published the earlier quoted article about the 'Future Revolution'.[13]

In the formation process of the BJWU, the planned increase in hours of work in IJMA mills turned into an important point of contention, reflecting different visions of trade union politics among its leading members. Prabhabati Das Gupta supported a more moderate outlook for the BJWU. On 11 and 12 May, she joined a labour conference with representatives of the BJWU, the moderate KLU, as well as with local labour activists. At this conference, the majority of speakers were 'all in favour of an amicable settlement by discussion and against strike methods'.[14] Kali Sen, meanwhile, supported a radical course for the union, and agitated for a general strike among jute workers as response to the planned increase in hours of work. In order to trigger a strike among jute workers, he and his supporters spread the rumour that all 'mills are introducing a compulsory single-shift system from the 1st July'.[15] While this rumour was not true, it reflected widespread anxieties among jute workers in the late 1920s, which Kali Sen tried to draw on.

While the different factions of the BJWU fought over the future course of the trade union, strikes broke out in two areas of 24-Parganas. One week after the introduction of the new hours of work, weavers of the Baranagore Mills went on strike on 5 July, demanding a return to the fifty-four-hour week. On the same day, workers of the Meghna Jute Mill went on strike, followed by the Alliance and Craig Jute Mills on the 6th and the Waverley Jute Mill on 13 July.[16] The unrest emanated from the weavers of these mills, who

> simply left work after doing the usual fifty-four hours work and resumed work on the following Monday as usual.[17]

This form of protest had been a recurring practice among jute workers in the late 1920s. Weavers' demands centred on the modes of wage calculation in the event of being compelled to work longer hours.[18] As managers were unresponsive to workers' demands, the weavers of the four mills stopped work fully on 19 July.[19]

The BJWU under Prabhabati Das Gupta got involved in the unfolding conflict in Jagatdal. The union's president, however, did not yet support strike action against the increase in hours of work, and advised workers at a meeting to resume work. As a compromise between strike and protest, trade unionists suggested that workers produce less when returning to work. Narendra Nath Chatterjee, a local lawyer with revolutionary terrorist connections, had been called in by the workers to support their struggle. He, too, supported the suggestion from the BJWU. On 21 July, the workers resumed work and produced less. The attempted compromise, however, backfired immediately. The reduced production by weavers led to a glut in yarn in the mills' machinery, and the managers of the four mills closed their gates completely on 23 July, shutting out workers.[20]

Due to the escalation of conflicts in Jagatdal, Prabhabati Das Gupta – and along with her the moderate faction of the BJWU – was pushed to supporting strike action. The question of the strike's scale, however, remained disputed within the BJWU. By late July, Prabhabati Das Gupta increasingly supported a general strike against the IJMA. This strike was to be carried out by struggles in Jagatdal, and eventually in Titagarh. Prabhabati Das Gupta's own networks among labour activists in the jute belt seem to have been strongest in the northern parts of 24-Parganas. Her choice to centre a general strike around these areas was probably also an attempt to maintain control not just over the emerging strike into which she was increasingly dragged, but also over the newly formed union itself, whose president she had become. On 28 July, then, Prabhabati Das Gupta asked strikers in Jagatdal to persuade the workers of the nearby Anglo-India, Kankinarah and Reliance Mills to join the strike.[21]

Kali Sen, meanwhile, actively supported a further spread of the strike throughout the jute belt and into *all* the mills of the IJMA. By the second half of July, he started touring particular mill towns in a hired car with 'two red flags in front and one big red flag wrapped at the back', trying to persuade workers to join the emerging general strike.[22] Most of the persons connected to the general secretary of the BJWU were communist labour activists who had been active around Calcutta or in the southern parts of the jute belt. For instance, Moni Singh was the Secretary of the Metiaburuz Labour Union in Garden Reach. This union had originally been set up in order to organize the Bowreah cotton workers in 1928.[23] In July 1929 Kali Sen and Moni Singh travelled to jute mills in Metiaburuz, in order to explain to workers the financial losses they would have to bear due to the increase in hours of work.[24] Akhil Bandhu Bannerjee, another labour activist connected to Kali Sen, was a member of the Workers' and Peasants' Party, and the secretary of the Beliaghata Labour Union near Calcutta. He had already organized meetings in Beliaghata on 14 July, jointly with the local Khilafat Committee, trying to organize a large strike in the jute mill industry, and citing the example of 'the Russian peasants and workers'.[25]

In addition to addressing workers in areas where the main factions of the BJWU had access to previously established networks in workers' neighbourhoods, both Prabhabati Das Gupta and Kali Sen tried to broaden their influence in the jute belt. Titagarh, situated to the south of Jagatdal, turned in the war-driven language of the Intelligence Bureau into the 'pivotal point of attack' for both groups.[26] On 24 July, Prabhabati Das Gupta visited Titagarh in order to talk to 'an upcountry cloth-merchant in the local bazar', as well as to a certain Swami Rajrishi, about 'the present situation in the jute mills' and to ask them 'whether any strike was possible'. Not much is known either about this merchant or about Swami Rajrishi, but it was said the latter had some 'influence' over the workers in Titagarh. Prabhabati Das Gupta left the town right after the talk. Briefly after Prabhabati Das Gupta had left, the police noted the arrival of the motor car 'with a red flag hoisted on it'.[27] Kali Sen had come with a group of supporters to distribute leaflets composed by himself.[28]

Initially, the success of Kali Sen in Titagarh was quite limited. At a meeting which was held on 26 July in order to explain the situation in Jagatdal, only about '50 or 60 people attended'. A party with drums was therefore sent around in order to announce the meeting. This attracted more attention to the group and caused some turmoil, since 'mill workers began to abuse the intending speakers and asked them to go away'. The workers accused the trade unionists of having betrayed workers in Lillooah. Apparently in anticipation of the arguments of the visitors, some of the workers stated that they were not hungry and did not need the trade unionists' help. Similar interruptions went on 'in intervals right up to the end of the meeting'. In addition to this 'anti-propaganda', the meeting was disturbed by 'a diversion nearby in the shape of a Hindusthani theatre', causing the attendance to thin away even more.[29]

The next day, the group around Kali Sen organized another meeting. This time, Swami Rajrishi took part as well. His support seems to have helped Kali Sen considerably, and the police noticed fewer interruptions from the audience. The speakers talked about the importance of forming a union 'for fighting with capitalists', who were living 'at the expense of the poor labourers'. It was further said that if 'all the 71 mills in Bengal could make a united stand then the authorities would surely have to come down and comply with them to act according to their dictation'.[30] Kali Sen underlined this statement by referring to the strike in Lillooah – a topic which had been raised by the workers the previous day. He, however, stated that this particular strike had only failed due to want of support 'from the brother labourers in other parts of Bengal'.[31] He pointed to the lack of solidarity, which had not been the trade unionists' but the workers' failure.

Exactly one hour after this meeting, another meeting was organized in Titagarh, this time with Prabhabati Das Gupta, Bankim Mukharji[32] and Swami Biswananda speaking. Probably in an attempt to increase the authority of the BJWU over the audience, a *sirdar* from the Emperor Jute Mills also addressed the workers in support of the strike. The arguments presented by the group were, in comparison with those by the group around Kali Sen, distinctly more moderate, presenting a strike as inevitable and strongly invoking for its support a combination of concepts of honour and solidarity. During the meeting workers expressed their opinion in several interruptions, arguing that they 'had already heard [,] seen and experienced bitter results of the same'. In response, Bankim Mukharji and Prabhabati Das Gupta pointed out:

> that he was advocating strike knowing full well its bitter results and that his
> labourer brethren were too poor to meet the situation, but then did anybody

ever hear that any man had died of starvation owing to any strike. No there was not a single instance. [...] Will not the authorities take advantage of the knowledge that you are not at all in a position to strike? To this Bankim got no direct answer, only there was a murmur among the audience and he tried to press home his point in the manner mentioned above. [...] She asked the audience why they were thinking from now how and on what they would live in case there is a strike. Supposing they were dismissed what would they do? To this, some of the audience replied that all can not be dismissed at a time. One or two were dismissed if there were any dismissals at all and that in that case the other members of their respective families or even some of their fellow brothers might support them but this was not so in case of a strike.[33]

Swami Rajrishi spoke at this meeting as well. This time, however, he was 'found dead against' the strike. Further, it is reported:

He strongly protested against strike and left the meeting as soon as other speakers spoke in favour of it. He was later on found making anti-propaganda outside the meeting thoroughly condemning strike - the result being that the meeting got comparatively thinner.[34]

There is no known reason for this sudden change of mind. It is, however, not unlikely that the arrival of different factions of the same union within the hour did not make a favourable impression on the Swami. It is also possible that there had been some pressure on him from within the neighbourhoods to not support the strike. The majority of workers in Titagarh were still opposed to strike action.

The strong focus of the 'agitation' of the different factions of the BJWU on Titagarh did not yet result in a spread of the strike, as trade unionists of both factions had trouble gaining the trust of the workers. Given, however, the fact that workers in Titagarh did join the strike just a few days later, the conflict between trade unionists and workers should be understood within an already growing atmosphere of militancy, in which the arguments made by the labour activists strongly appealed to workers. The initial rejection of the trade unionists by workers may well have been caused by their apprehension that the strike demanded by the BJWU had real purchase in their own neighbourhoods. Rumours circulating about a planned abolition of the multiple-shift system in the mills in Titaghur contributed to these apprehensions.[35]

The strike that had started in Jagatdal and was increasingly 'carried' to Titaghar, then, had not so much emerged either out of the unions' or out of the workers' actions, as out of the interplay of the two. The escalation of conflicts in Jagatdal both led to an intensification of apprehensions of strike action among workers in Titaghar, and also to increased conflict within the BJWU over the political direction of the trade union. The ongoing process of formation of the BJWU also determined the areas in which the trade unionists tried to 'agitate' among workers. While both groups drew on previously established networks before concentrating their efforts and resources on competing over Titaghur, workers in Baranagore had gone on strike at the same time as workers in Jagatdal. They remained on strike until the end of September. Neither of the factions of the BJWU seems to have had a previous presence in Baranagore, and with the exception of one visit by Prabhabati Das Gupta, the BJWU seems not to have tried to establish a presence among workers here.[36]

4.2

The connection of local strikes and conflicts over the meaning of 'general'

On 29 July the North Union, Soorah and Beliaghata Jute Mills in Beliaghata went on strike, demanding higher wages.[1] The Soorah and Beliaghata Jute Mills were not members of the IJMA, and had not changed their hours of work, when the IJMA's mills did. Only the North Union Jute Mill was a member of the IJMA and the new rules did apply to that mill. Workers eventually demanded higher wages for working overtime.[2]

The strike was triggered by an assault on two 'boy workers' (possibly by an overseer) in the North Union Jute Mill on the morning of 29 July, after which workers left their workplace. Later that day, the other two mills in the area joined the strike.[3] When workers of the North Union Jute Mill wanted to resume work on 2 August, a dispute arose between them and workers from the Beliaghata Jute Mills. The latter tried to prevent an early resumption of work by those workers who had brought them on strike, underlining the immense pressures created in the neighbourhoods over the question of solidarity during the strike. In the course of the dispute, brickbats were thrown, and, as the Special Branch reported, the 'gates of the mill were closed and even then some of the willing workers went to resume work by scaling over the wall'.[4] At a meeting on 4 August, Akhil Bandhu Banerjee 'promised to try and bring out the workers of other Jute Mills' if they would strike.[5]

The strikes in Beliaghata were not immediately connected to the protests in Jagatdal or in Baranagore. In the increasingly tense situation in the jute belt by late July, however, the emergence of a new centre of strikes in the jute belt increased anticipations of a looming general strike. Trade unionists of the BJWU actively connected these labour conflicts while talking to workers in Titagarh in the following days. On 30 July strikers from Beliaghata started to come to Titagarh, with the support of Kali Sen. The workers from Beliaghata were wearing red badges with the letters 'J.W.U.' – probably meaning Jute Workers

Union – written on them.[6] The group of volunteers from Beliaghata was called
Lal Paltan (Red Army).[7]

Sending delegations of strikers to other workers was a practice which had
been deployed by communist trade unions in the south of Calcutta in 1928. An
instance of this is the case of the strikers in Lillooah, who moved in processions
through the industrial areas around them, and who travelled to the strikers of
the Fort Gloster and the Ludlow Jute Mills, among other destinations. While
in Bauria in 1928, Philip Spratt also recommended that the workers build up a
'union-army' of volunteers (wearing red badges), for supporting and spreading
the strike.[8] For Kali Sen, one of the motives for applying this technique one year
later was probably the attempt to gain more trust and support among workers in
Titagarh, who were increasingly backing Prabhabati Das Gupta.

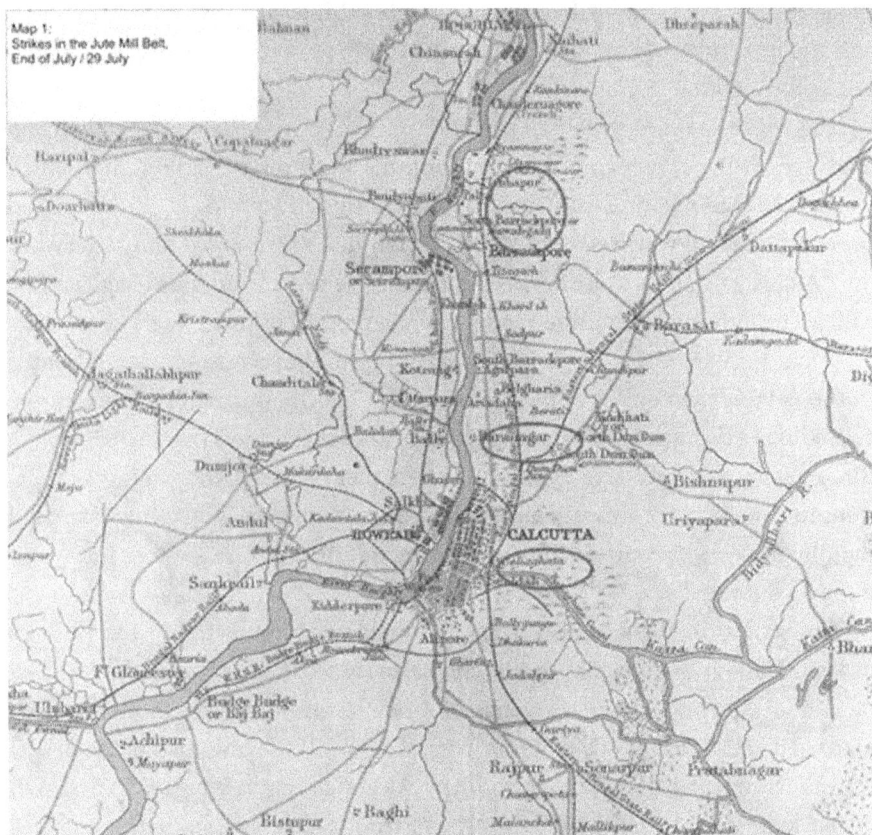

Figure 11 Strikes in the Jute Belt by 29 July 1929. / Map is based on: W.W. Hunter,
The Imperial Gazetteer of India Atlas, Vol. 26. Oxford: Clarendon Press, 1931.

The group around the union's president reacted by recruiting workers from Jagatdal for meetings in Titagarh. Two days after the first time workers from Beliaghata were mentioned in Titagarh, at least twenty-five strikers were reported to have been present at a meeting of the BJWU, wearing 'a white strip of cloth' over their breasts, bearing the inscription 'The afflicted workers of Jagatdal'.[9] Further, workers started to deliver speeches at Prabhabati Das Gupta's meetings. In contrast with the first phase of the strike, *sirdars* were not part of the meetings anymore. On the contrary, speakers at her meetings now explained 'that within a year there would be no *Sardars* anymore'.[10]

In addition to the increased activity in Titagarh, the speeches of Prabhabati Das Gupta, and even more so of her supporters, started to change. Speakers highlighted the broad base of support for a general strike, while also underlining that the general strike was led by Prabhabati Das Gupta, who was by now called 'mataji'. The speeches at her meetings became more pressing, indicating a growing anticipation of a broader struggle – and, along with it, a radicalization. For example, when Abdul Momin spoke first at the meeting on 30 July, he

likened the audience to so many beasts or even worse than that. Even beasts have feelings and sympathy and love for their fellow brothers which are miserably wanting in the labourers at Titagarh. A few of those [who] were present, he said, promised to strike work and get others to strike positively [...] but they did not keep to their word. If they had a drop of human blood in them, if they had ever prided being men, they would never think of what they would do for their living in case of strike. [...] He failed to understand the conduct of the local mill workers, had they any heart? Any respect for their wives and their parents? Any love or responsibility regarding them and their children?[11]

The next speakers at that very meeting explained – after dwelling on the benefits of workers in England in contrast to the workers in India – the need for unity, especially now, when the hours of work had been increased without corresponding increases in wages. When a supporter of Prabhabati Das Gupta spoke, he told the workers,

that 'Mataji', the Lakshmi and saviour of Bengal (meaning Dr. Das Gupta thereby) has taken a vow that she would not rest till all the mills in Bengal struck work. He requested the audience to respect their common mother and to keep her word, if they could not do that or thought it impossible they had better drowned themselves.[12]

He also told the workers that twenty-six mills were already on strike, clearly an exaggeration. Nonetheless, Narendra Nath Chatterjee, who spoke next, developed this point further, when he said 'that workers in England in one and all the mills had already struck work in sympathy with the workers here'.[13] He was probably referring to the cotton mill strike in Lancashire, which was happening parallel to the jute mill strike, but was otherwise unconnected to it – and certainly did not affect all the mills in England.[14] Yet the image of the wide, and even global, support for a strike in Titagarh and Jagatdal seems to have been important and was used in several speeches in order to persuade the workers of the strong basis and good chances for a successful (and short) struggle.

The escalation of the conflict in the first days of August, however, also displayed the tension between the levels of organization in workers' neighbourhoods under the BJWU (which was, after all, still in the process of its formation), and the increasing militancy of jute workers throughout the jute belt. While the BJWU was increasingly successful in connecting localized strikes in order to emerge as a political representative of jute workers, workers started to carry the strike along their own routes, and into areas in which the BJWU had no previous presence. Workers in Jagatdal began to appropriate the situation, and 'bodies of strikers' were noticed in police reports in the following days. The growing intensity of organization is shown by the fact that workers were seen 'admonishing men who crowded on the road, telling them to leave the road clear'.[15] Attempts to induce other mills to strike were reported repeatedly. Picketing workers from Jagatdal, then, travelled to Titagarh, Kankinarah, and to Champdani on the western side of the river, from where picketing moved on to Rishra. Prabhabati Das Gupta, when trying to control these movements of workers, suggested at a meeting in Jagatdal on 30 July the peaceful picketing of the four Anglo-India and the Auckland Jute Mills in Jagadtal.[16] On the next day, however, picketing was reported in Jagatdal, Kankinarah and Titagarh, as well as in Champdani. This massive picketing 'induced' the Alexandra Mills to go on strike the same day.[17]

The increased picketing of workers covered major industrial areas in the northern parts of 24-Parganas as well as in the Hooghly district. The areas into which workers carried the strike were, however, not congruent with the areas in which either faction of the BJWU had been active. Considering the routes taken by workers, the paths taken (or not taken) appear as determinate. An invisible boundary between the northern and southern parts of the jute belt was apparent, which workers did not cross. This was a phenomenon which would again be visible in the general strike of 1937.[18] The river, meanwhile, appears to have been a path used even more commonly than the short overland route between the neighbouring mill towns of Jagadtal and Kankinarah.[19] These patterns in the physical movements of workers suggest sub-surface forms of organization and solidarity among workers, connecting particular neighbourhoods in the jute belt. Workers drew on these networks among themselves, as a response to the growing anticipation of an emerging general strike under a unified leadership. At the same time, they undermined the claims of unified political representation by the BJWU, as they carried the strike into areas beyond the organizational reach of the newly formed trade union.

Anticipations of a large-scale protest also affected responses from police forces. On the eastern side of the river, local police forces were reckoned to be 'adequate' for the situation.[20] Across the river, however, in Champdani and in Rishra, the local authorities panicked when faced with the increasing physical movements of picketing workers from beyond the river. The problems for the police in controlling anticipated conflicts were increased by the weak infrastructure. Several reports, for instance, complain about missing telephone connections. A report of a meeting in Baidyabati described how a messenger had to be sent to Bhadreswar, 'a distance of about 3 miles to communicate the information' about picketing workers by phone. Even though the situation turned out to be peaceful, the complaint was underlined with the observation that it might have been very severe.[21] Since the train system was not as closely knit as on the eastern side of the river, the police needed to hire two buses from Serampore, in order to transport police forces in case of emergency.[22]

Workers' activities in areas where the BJWU was not present seem to have contributed to a sense of uncertainty and panic among sections of the Bengal police. Police reporters from Hooghly could not identify where the anticipated 'agitation' came from, and several rumours were afloat of meetings and movements, eventually affecting an area between Champdani and Howrah.[23] As police records would state later, a group of young terrorists had become active in Baidyabati, in support of the general strike. They do not seem to have been involved in labour struggles before 1929. Many of them owned small shops or studied in colleges in Calcutta.[24] The fact that this group was not known to local authorities was presumably an important reason why the police could not identify them.

The reaction to this tense yet hardly definable situation was immense police activity, in order to prevent a further spread of the strike. On 4 August, police reports mention the following incidents:

1.   Yesterday an information was received from the Deputy Commissioner, Special Branch, Calcutta, that a labour meeting would be held at Rishra

and that several members of Peasants and Workers Party and some members of Bombay Labour Union would address the meeting but no meeting was actually held at Rishra.

2.   From D.I.B., Howrah another information to the effect that strikers of this district [Champdani] would go in a body to attend the meeting at Howrah on the 3rd afternoon was received yesterday. But enquiries show no such body of men left the mill area.[25]

Similar reports abound – rumours are mentioned, as well as meetings, but only rarely is a concrete 'organizer' identified. Bankim Mukherjee and Kali Sen briefly tried to establish a presence in Champdani.[26] They were, however, prevented from further 'agitating' among workers by their arrest on 1 August in Serampore.[27]

In Howrah, on the other hand, where the anticipated unrest roused the anxieties of the police, local labour activists tried to facilitate the strike. They had announced a meeting on 3 August, for which 10,000 workers were expected to come from Champdani.[28] While the anticipated meeting in Howrah did not receive much attention from workers, it did from the police and wider public.[29] The *Times of India* wrote the next day, joining the expectations of a general strike:

> Although, at the moment of writing, only a small proportion of the mills are idle, strike fever as recently demonstrated, is an infectious disease difficult to isolate or circumscribe, once it appears in any part, however small, of a great industrial center.[30]

Thus, carried by the anticipations and expectations of various observers and participants, trying to prevent or to support the unrest, the situation in the jute belt of Bengal seemed increasingly chaotic. The hope for support of their specific struggle, for instance, brought the picketing strikers from Jagatdal into various other mill districts; the spread of the strike to Beliaghata increased the activities of both factions within the BJWU; revolutionary terrorists joined the ranks of labour activists in Hooghly; rumours and fears of a general strike triggered seemingly random police interventions and anticipations of a general strike induced local labour activists in Howrah to participate in the event as well.

On 3 August, Prabhabati Das Gupta called for a general strike in Jagatdal and Titagarh, to begin from 5 August.[31] One day later, the Metiaburuz Labour Union under Moni Singh followed and called for a general strike in the jute belt. This call was supported by Akhil Bandhu Banerjee from Beliaghata.[32] Given that only one further mill had actually joined the strike in Jagatdal so far and none in Titagarh, Prabhabati Das Gupta's decision might seem somewhat surprising. Her reasons can better be understood by keeping in mind the recent (and temporary) imprisonment of Kali Sen, who had turned into her main rival in the trade union. In this respect, the call for a general strike seems also to have been an attempt to settle the dispute over the political direction of the union, at a moment when her strongest opponents could not intervene.

Meanwhile, Moulavi Latafat Hossain from the moderate KLU also tried to intervene in the unfolding chain of events. At the Anglo-India Jute Mills, groups of weavers had temporarily left their workplaces, returning the same day. Moulavi Latafat Hossain arrived on the morning of 3 August at the mill gate with around 300 'loyal' weavers, who were supposed to work in the mills. This intervention led to violent attempts by workers to prevent these 'loyal' weavers from entering the mills.[33] The next day, when Moulavi Latafat Hossain again tried to prevent the anticipated strike from spreading, an angry 'mob' of mill workers attacked him. This was followed by massive police intervention in order to protect Hossain and to disperse the workers.[34] After these interventions by Hossain and by the police, the Anglo-India Jute Mills went on strike on 5 August. They were followed the same day by nearly all the mills in Jagatdal. On 6 August mills in Titagarh, Kankinarah, Champdani and Rishra, as well as the Clive Jute Mill in Garden Reach, joined the general strike.[35]

Altogether, then, the escalation of conflicts in the jute belt was shaped by two seemingly opposed moments: the centralization of the strikes' *political* representation under the BJWU – and, more specifically, under Prabhabati Das Gupta; and the escalation of conflicts beyond the realm of the BJWU's *organizational* representation. The former was marked by the tension within the BJWU over the question, of what kind of political representation the union wanted to provide for workers – a more moderate one, or a more radical and communist one. The increasing likelihood of a widespread general strike emerging in the jute belt contributed to a radicalization of the BJWU at this point, and, along with it, to a radicalization of the union president. Having objected to any strike action as late as 20 July, Prabhabati Das Gupta was calling for a general strike barely two weeks later. This was, of course, partly an attempt to contain the radicalization of the BJWU, but arguably it had the opposite effect.

Prabhabati Das Gupta's claim to the political representation of the emerging general strike was realized by the physical movements of workers, who carried the strike into different parts of the jute belt, and beyond the organizational reach of the BJWU. In conjunction with hectic responses by local labour activists, revolutionary terrorists and police forces, this development strengthened the formal political representation of the BJWU, while also undermining the trade union's control over the movement that was emerging. The question, often asked by historians, if strikes in Indian industries were triggered by workers' agency or trade unionists' activities, then, misses the point – at least when considering the situation in the jute industry. Rather than being shaped by a development that can be described in 'either-or' terms, the general strike in 1929 emerged *precisely within the tension* between the trade union activity and workers' agency.

4.3

The general strike

On 6 August, the BJWU under Prabhabati Das Gupta declared a general strike in the jute industry. By that day 120,000 jute workers had joined the strike.[1] Throughout the day, the union's president toured the northern part of 24-Parganas, announcing the strike and holding meetings.[2] A few days later she explained in an interview the demands of the workers as follows:

> Strike pay, proportionate increment, commission rate and 'khoraki' to mill workers in those mills where 'khoraki' were not given and the formation of the committee to meet the grievances of the strikers.[3]

In addition, the return to old bonus payments, which had been a demand by weavers in Jagadtal, was added as an official demand of the general strike. The general strike, then, was officially defined as a protest against the particular *modes* of implementation of the new hours of work by the IJMA. The association's decision to increase the hours of work was not in itself questioned nor were demands for higher wage rates part of the general strike. Workers' demand to restrict weekly hours of work to fifty-four hours had, as we have seen, never been supported by trade unions in the northern parts of the jute belt, such as the BJWA, nor was it supported by Prabhabati Das Gupta. Demands for an increase in wage payments, meanwhile, had been raised among workers in Beliaghata, who were organized by communist supporters of Kali Sen.

The declaration of a general strike by Prabhabati Das Gupta led to a near immediate escalation of conflicts within the jute belt. The *scale* of the conflict expanded within a matter of days, and by 8 August, just four days after the general strike was proclaimed, the number of workers reported to be 'idle' had almost doubled.[4] By 15 August, more than 240,000 jute workers had left their workplaces, and the strike had begun to spread into other industries as well.[5] While jute workers to the north and the south of Calcutta were involved in the general strike, then, the conflict soon risked turning into a general upheaval of workers in the industrial hinterland of Calcutta. With the involvement of several different sites in the increasingly militant struggle, the situation became muddled and chaotic. Prabhabati Das Gupta, once finally installed as the undisputed leader and representative of the general strike, was neither able to control the constantly emerging movement nor could she direct the trajectories in either faction of the BJWU any longer.

On 6 August, the same day as the general strike was proclaimed, a series of riots began in Naihati and Kankinarah, in the north of Jagatdal. For Naihati, the police had noticed so far 'no attention from the agitators', and in nearby Kankinarah trade unionists' attempts to establish themselves in workers' neighbourhoods had 'hitherto been repulsed by the workers'.[6] Reports about the movement of picketing workers from Jagatdal to Naihati were notably rare,

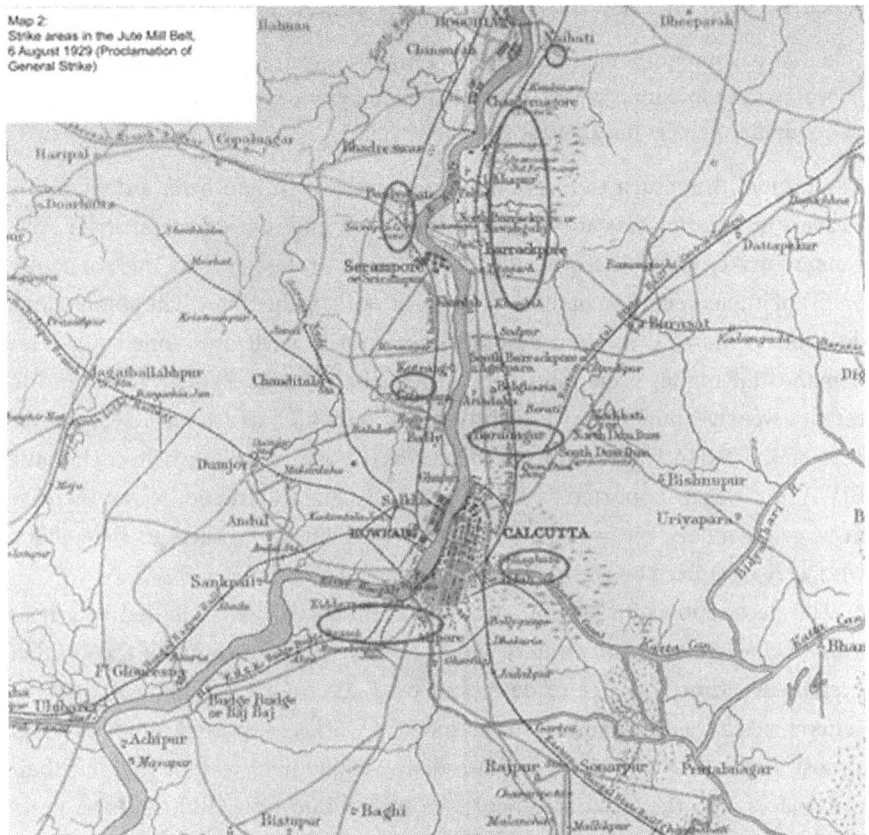

Figure 12 Strikes in the Jute Belt by 29 July 1929. / Map is based on: W.W. Hunter, *The Imperial Gazetteer of India Atlas*, Vol. 26. Oxford: Clarendon Press, 1931.

suggesting a rather vague boundary between the far north of the jute belt and the early centres of the strike. On 5 August, however, workers of the Nadia Jute Mills stopped work.[7] For the next day it was reported that picketing was expected in the nearby Gourepore Jute Mill and some police arrangements had been made, but a larger disturbance was not anticipated.[8]

When a group of strikers – according to *Liberty* about 500 in number – arrived at the mill, a 'band of Kabulis and Peshwaris' appeared suddenly, armed with knives and *lathis*, in order to prevent workers from going on strike. The correspondent of *Liberty*, while suggesting that 'some of them were drunk', also mentioned 'that about a hundred Kabulis live near the Gourepore Mills and carry on the business of money lending among the operatives of the Mills'.[9] This second piece of information provides an understanding of why the 'Kabulis' tried to interfere, given that workers usually had to borrow money at various points of their lives in mill towns, leaving them with debts to be paid. The 'Kabulis' accordingly had an interest in preventing workers from leaving their workplaces. The further events were reported as follows:

> The strikers who had assembled in front of the Mills at once demonstrated that they were only trying to persuade their fellow-workers to join the strike in a peaceful manner, and the Kabulis and Peshwaris had no business to interfere. At this, it is said, the Kabulis became enraged and suddenly whipped out big knives and attacked the strikers. As a result some of the strikers were seriously wounded.
>
> This news spread like wild-fire and the workers of the Gourepore Jute Mill came out and joined the strike. Then they attacked the Kabulis who, it is reported, were assaulting them with knives and lathis. [...]
>
> Being outnumbered, the Kabulis and Peshwaris fled to their quarters. But the workers followed them with lathis in hand. There was then a free fight between the Kabulis and Peshwaris on the one side and the strikers and workers of the Gourepore Jute Mill on the other side. As a result, four men lost their lives, several were seriously wounded and a large number of people received injuries. The houses of the Kabulis, it is reported, were set fire to, their cycles and other belongings were destroyed and documents regarding business torn to pieces.[10]

Police arrived at the scene soon afterwards and brought the situation under control by arresting twenty 'Kabulis'. Workers were only arrested two days later, when the police 'organised a raid on the coolie lines [...] to find out wounded participants in the Gourepore riot' and arrested about 100 workers.[11] The news of the riot on 6 August spread instantly to Kankinarah, where workers 'became infuriated and, it is said, began to attack the Kabulis residing there', causing three more deaths on the same day.[12]

On 7 August, the closing of all the jute mills in Naihati and two mills in Kankinarah was reported, as well as the posting of a strong police force in the region. Widespread panic among Kabulis and Peshwaris was further described:

> The Kabulis and Peshwaris are terror-stricken and many of them living at Bhatpara and the neighbourhood left for Calcutta, Hooghly and other places. The panic spread to Kanchrapara, a railway colony as well, and many Kabulis and Peshwaris who live there are also reported to have left the station out of fear.[13]

But also the opposite movement was noticed and the Deputy Commissioner of Police (South) reported on that some

> Kabuli money lenders [...] and others living in the jurisdiction of Matyaburz (B.P.) [Metiaburuz] left for Naihati yesterday. It is rumoured that they had gone there to render help to their own caste people who are in trouble.[14]

On the same day, on 7 August, another riot occurred in connection with the planned funeral of the three dead Kabuli moneylenders. A crowd of workers tried to prevent this funeral, approaching the houses of the moneylenders in the morning. The Kabulis, it was reported, fled in fear to the nearby police station, around which more and more workers gathered in the course of the day. The following events were reported:

> The situation became menacing late in the afternoon, when the crowd of mill-hands had swollen to three thousand, all firmly resolved not to allow the funeral. The *sardars* being informed that they would be held responsible for the conduct of the operatives, attempted to persuade the mob to disperse.
>
> Addressing the rows of squatting men they argued that the Peshwaris were Moslems and that the dead man should not be refused a Moslem burial. The crowd shouted in return 'These men are not our brothers. They killed our brothers.'
>
> The *sardars* replied that the Peshwaris at Kankinarah had nothing whatever to do with the fight at Naihati, but the crowd would not listen. Gradually, but without show of violence, they encircled the handful of police guarding the door of the house where the body lay.[15]

About half an hour later, workers started throwing brickbats at the police in an attempt to enter the *thana*. Fortunately for the police, who were hopelessly outnumbered, armed reinforcements arrived at the scene to disperse the workers just in time. The dead 'Kabulis' were buried that night under strong police escort.

The next morning, about 500 policemen entered workers' neighbourhoods near the Kankinarah Jute Mill. They arrested more than 230 jute workers and brought them to the police station in Jagatdal. On 8 August, however, 'thousands' of workers gathered and approached the police station in Jagatdal with the object of freeing the workers from Kankinarah. Police reinforcements arrived again just in time to disperse the strikers.[16] Kali Sen came along too, trying to prevent further violence. For the rest of the day, however, crowds 'stayed on the roadway', which connected different mill districts in the north of Calcutta.[17]

At the outset, the riots in Kankinarrah and Naihati reflected social tensions over the question of strike support, emanating with workers' neighbourhoods and the wider networks of social control that workers were part of. In the context of the ongoing general strike led by the BJWU, however, the riots also transcended the boundaries of the neighbourhoods, and took place in the jute belt at large. This was not merely on a symbolic level. 'Kabulis' joined the already spreading physical movements of workers and also of labour activists through the jute belt, each travelling along certain paths and yet each (foremost, obviously, the workers) breaking down the spaces allotted to them. In order to keep control over these movements of people, the police closed several ferries.[18] In the north of 24-Parganas, police buses, which came to be called the 'flying-police squad', started patrolling the industrial areas day and night, leaving the *thana* in tight intervals of thirty minutes.[19]

While the impressions of the general strike in Naihaty were marked by an apparent breakdown of social order, the situation in Jagatdal and Titagarh revealed considerable levels of organization. The police noted for Titagarh that workers helped to keep the roads clear from loitering men.[20] In the next days two-mile-long picketing lines were mentioned, connecting the early centres of the strike and of the BJWU's activities.[21] The fact that the BJWU had engaged with workers here since the beginning of the conflict probably had an impact on the modalities of how the strike was conducted in the area between Jagadtal and Titagarh on the one hand, and Naihaty on the other hand – where the BJWU had no previous presence. At meetings held by the group around Prabhabati Das Gupta, workers were asked not to resume work. She herself rarely appeared publicly in this period, partially because of orders prohibiting her from speaking.[22]

Prabhabati Das Gupta's role as the sole political representative of the movement was further developed and she was by now called 'mataji' regularly, and at times even 'Sakti personified'.[23] The political representation of the general strike, however, was at the same time increasingly directed away from an opposition to mill-agencies, to an opposition to the colonial state. The theme of solidarity and global support of workers for the strike in the jute industry vanished and the tone became more nationalistic and anti-British. 'Honour' and 'autonomy' still played an important role, but were now connected to political concepts such as 'injustice' and 'oppression' as well as 'freedom' and 'independence'. Consider for instance Jagannath Prasad, a member of the Barrackpore Congress Committee, who spoke as follows on 11 August at a meeting organized by Prabhabati Das Gupta:

> [The English] have [...] nationalism and that is why they are progressing and ruling us. They never buy any goods which are not [from] their own country. [...] In this country clothes used to be so beautifully made that even the English used to praise their workmanship in England and now Indians have to remain naked if Manchester does not supply them. The English cut the hands of the Indian weavers when they came here and saw their skill. Now Indians are working in English jute mills as spinners and weavers. [...] He told the audience that if they wanted to be treated like men and wanted to live, it was for them also to find out means and act up to them and not to depend on anybody else.[24]

In speeches like these, the fight seemed to become less one against the IJMA, and more one directed against the colonial state and colonial capital. With the increasing scale of the strike movement, members and supporters of the BJWU also discursively expanded the scale of the forces which the general strike sought to confront.

While the group around Prabhabati Das Gupta mainly worked from the northern parts of 24-Parganas, the group around Kali Sen worked on spreading the strike into the south of Calcutta. As early as 3 August, a group connected to Kali Sen arrived at the Fort Gloster Jute Mills in Bauria. However, they could not 'hold any meeting for want of audience'.[25] The next day, a new meeting was announced, with Kali Sen, Bankim Mukherjee and – as the rumour went – Philip Spratt's brother.[26] This announcement was more successful and about 3,000 workers gathered that day. Of the announced speakers, however, only Bankim Mukherjee spoke. When talking about the ongoing struggle in the north of the jute belt, he stated that workers there

> had included in their demands the case of Bauria for introduction [of the] double shift system [= multiple shift system] of work and he asked the workers to demand it from the manager when they would go to the mills the next day.[27]

This statement was not true – at least, not with regard to the demands that Prabhabati Das Gupta had officially defined as the demands of the general strike. On a broader level, the rising militancy among jute workers in the wake of the change in shift systems contributed to the escalation of conflicts in 1929. The immediate question of shift systems, however, was only reflected in workers' actions and demands at particular moments in the struggle. In 1929, only two mills introduced the single-shift system, and both of them were among the earliest mills to go on strike in Jagadtal.[28] The demand to reverse changes to the modalities of bonus payments, which was raised by weavers in this context, was presumably connected to demands made by workers from these mills. In Titaghur, in the meantime, the anticipation that the multiple-shift system would be introduced if workers failed to show their strength seems to have contributed to workers' support of strike action.

While the change in shift systems, then, was an underlying factor, it was hardly a dominant one in the dynamics in the events in the northern parts of the jute belt. With regard to the Fort Gloster Jute Mill in Bauria, the situation seemed different. In 1928, the mill had introduced a single-shift system, leading to one of the hitherto longest strikes in the jute industry against the change. Over a period of six months, workers stayed on strike, with the support of communist trade unionists, such as Phillip Spratt. Eventually, workers were forced to resume work unconditionally, and work under the new single-shift system resumed.[29] In 1929, the discontent over the change had not died down. The growing unrest among jute workers in the northern parts of the jute belt made it seem possible to take up this battle again – at least to Bankim Mukherjee, who tried to persuade workers to support the general strike on account of fighting for the multiple-shift system again.

In the next days, the strike spread rapidly, eventually affecting all the mills in the northern parts of 24-Parganas, as well as mills in Beliaghata, Garden Reach and in Hooghly. On 13 August, the Birla Jute Mill in Uluberia in the southern outskirts of the jute belt went on strike. The next day, the Shamgunj and the Fort Gloster Jute Mill at Budge-Budge and Bauria started a partial strike. The conflict increasingly affected the south of Calcutta as well.[30] Besides the regional spread, in this phase the strike began to involve other industries. After the riot in the Gourepore Jute Mill, workers at the nearby Paint Factory started sympathy strikes, eventually demanding higher wages.[31] On 14 August, the Britannia Engineering Works and a Rope Factory in Titagarh followed. Unrest was noted in Lillooah in cotton mills and in the railway workshop. At the Bengal-Nagpur railway workshop at Kharagpur, a parallel strike seemed possible, as well as in the railway colony of Kanchrapara in the north of Calcutta.[32] Unrest was noticed, too, among the oil workers in Budge-Budge, who formed their own union with

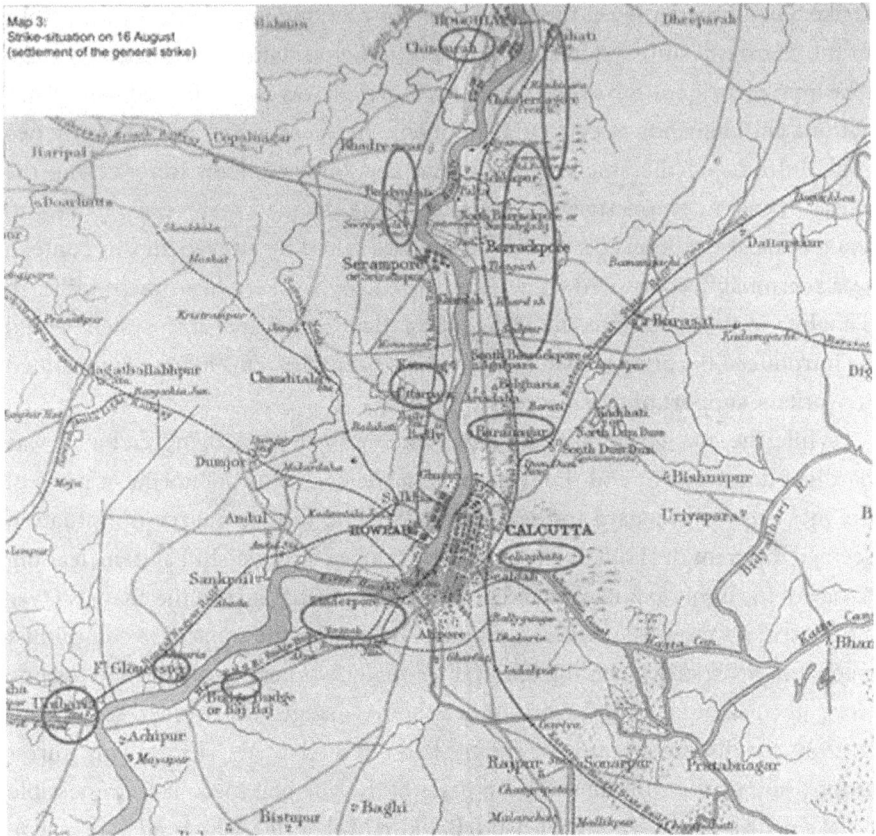

Figure 13 Strikes in the Jute Mill Belt on 16 August 1929. / Map is based on: W.W. Hunter, *The Imperial Gazetteer of India Atlas,* Vol. 26. Oxford: Clarendon Press, 1931.

the help of Subhas Chandra Bose. Further, rumours were afloat that the strike might spread to the sweepers of the municipality.[33]

The spread of the strike movement displayed networks of solidarity among workers which reached beyond the boundaries of the jute industry. In their everyday lives, workers had to rely on similar networks for finding work during periods of unemployment, or in order to find employment for friends and family members. What appeared as boundaries of workers' organization from the perspective of capital, state and trade unionists, presumably now appeared as part of a broader network that sustained workers in the jute belt. This was especially the case after a period of mass dismissals in the largest industry on the Hugli, during which dismissed workers were forced to seek and find jobs at other places.

Facing a potential general strike of workers, the colonial authorities tried to intervene in the conflict, in order to end the strike. The BJWU was not a registered trade union under the Trade Dispute Act. However, in a display of the urgency given to an immediate resolution to the situation, the government of Bengal invited Prabhabati Das Gupta to attend these negotiations as representative of the BJWU. In addition, the IJMA and the moderate KLU were part of the negotiations.[34] Not surprisingly, the mill-owners' association refused to negotiate with the BJWU, or even to accept that the general strike was a 'genuine' trade dispute. Managers argued that the conflict had been caused by 'outside-intervention' and that workers themselves had no genuine grievances.[35] On 13 August, the head of the IJMA claimed in an interview that 'there would be no prospect of a settlement so long as the outside influence did not cease to work'.[36]

Due to the pressure exerted by the government of Bengal on the IJMA, however, managing agencies had no option but to negotiate with the BJWU. On 14 August, in a last attempt to prevent the conclusion of negotiations, the IJMA assured workers that mill managers would concede the following demands, if workers resumed on their own:

(1) the wages paid shall be proportionate to the number of hours worked
(2) *khoraki* will be paid as at present
(3) there will be no victimization and
(4) maternity benefits will be extended.[37]

One day later, the IJMA was forced to give up its opposition to negotiations. Mediated by the government of Bengal, negotiations began between the government labour officer, R. N. Gilchrist, the IJMA, the KLU and Prabhabati Das Gupta for the BJWU, leading to a settlement the next day.[38]

Prabhabati Das Gupta was the only member of the BJWU invited, and several trade unionists afterwards expressed surprise that negotiations had taken place at all without their knowledge.[39] In the increasingly open-ended situation with regard to the scale of the strike movement and the degree of a breakdown of social order, it seems that a rapid settlement partly provided a possibility for Prabhabati Das Gupta to escape the political pressures created by the government and the management, the increasing political pressures within the union, as well as the difficulties created by the increasing loss of control over the general strike. The tensions between the scope of the trade union's political representation and its organizational scale, which had contributed considerably to the emergence of the general strike in the earlier phases of the event, had by now reached a breaking point, as Prabhabati Das Gupta could not control the movement she was leading anymore. This enabled the government of Bengal to intervene so quickly at a moment at which Prabhabati Das Gupta herself may have wanted to escape the struggles.

4.4

The end of the general strike and the return of localized strike movements

On 16 August, a settlement was arrived at, signed by Robert Laird for the IJMA, Moulavi Latafat Hossain for the KLU and Prabhabati Das Gupta for the BJWU. Work was scheduled to resume on Monday, 19 August. The settlement stated the following:

The Committee of the Indian Jute Mills Association have agreed to recommend

(i)   The correct proportionate increase in total earnings for the extra hours involved in the change from 54 to 60 hours a week;
(ii) Payment of *khoraki* on the same scale as before;
(iii) The same scale of bonuses as the workers used to get before July 1;
(iv) Provisions for maternity benefits; and
(v)   No victimization.[1]

This settlement is usually seen as a victory for jute workers and the BJWU.[2] At one level, this was certainly true. The IJMA was forced to agree to the main demands raised by the trade union on behalf of workers. For the first time in their history, the different managing agencies had, further, been forced to accept collective responsibility for the labour conditions in all their mills. The settlement was also a political victory for the BJWU. The government of Bengal, the IJMA and also the KLU had to accept the new union, which was not registered, as a political force. They had – as various newspapers pointed out – to accept that the trade unionists of the BJWU were 'asked to speak for' workers.[3] The settlement favourable to the demands of the workers also seemed to spell an end to the strike. A continuation of strike action, after all, would have disturbed the stability of the political compromise reached by the negotiations between the unions, the management and the government of Bengal.

The settlement, however, also displayed several crucial problems with the strike's resolution. First, with regard to the provisions of the settlement. With the exception of the provision relating to the return to the old scale of bonuses, the points mentioned in the agreement had already been offered by mill managers on 13 August. Workers and trade unionists alike had refused this offer, since it did not cover the demands raised by workers and trade unionists at several moments during the event. A tension between the formal demands raised by Prabhabati Das Gupta on behalf of jute workers, and the demands raised by trade unionists and workers themselves in the course of the event became apparent. In the course of the strike 'new' demands had come up, as workers in different parts of the jute belt joined the event. Workers in Beliaghata had demanded an increase in wage payments, while workers in Bauria anticipated the reintroduction of the multiple-shift system. In both cases, workers had been supported by in their demands by the BJWU – albeit by members of the faction around Kali Sen.[4] In Metiaburuz, at the same time, workers had posted their own demands on a sign board at the mill, including points such as an increase in wages, strike pay, 'no man to be dismissed within one year', the eight-hour day and the payment of *khoraki*, adding another voice to the conflict.[5]

This apparent instability was not principally the outcome of workers' rapidly changing demands. Rather, two elements contributed to this development. First, the conflicts that shaped the formation of the BJWU encouraged the apparent emergence of new demands, in the course of the union's efforts to convince workers to join the strike. Second, with the spread of the general strike, and with the emergence of a strike movement based on hitherto unprecedented levels of solidarity, demands that must have appeared as otherwise impossible to achieve – such as the introduction of the multiple-shift system – came to bear real potential. Thus, new demands were also the outcome of the general strike itself, as workers and trade unionists raised issues that they otherwise might not have raised.

Within the BJWU, discontent prevailed after the official end of the general strike and the sudden settlement. On 25 August, Prabhabati Das Gupta was expelled from the union and Kali Sen became its new president. Prabhabati Das Gupta founded (or re-founded) the Bengal Jute Workers' Association, whose president she became.[6] The union around Prabhabati Das Gupta, however, did not play an important role in future conflicts in the jute belt, in contrast to the BJWU.[7] The victory which Prabhabati Das Gupta had won by declaring the general strike and by becoming the accepted representative of the movement had turned out to be pyrrhic. The communists within the BJWU were now able to control and direct the trade union which had just organized and won the first general strike in the industry's history.

In the jute belt, the aftermath of the general strike of 1929 was marked by continuous outbreaks of industrial unrest. While the announcement of a settlement on 16 August led to an overall decrease in the number of labour conflicts, a considerable proportion of workers remained on strike, or left the site of production again, after having resumed work for brief periods. In addition, workers who had previously not joined the general strike left their mills. Until late September, strike movements remained omnipresent all along the Hugli. After a brief interlude towards the end of the year, during which the strikes seemed to have ended, workers went on strike again in a growing number of mills. Within two months, more than 30,000 jute workers were on strike, leading eventually to widespread anticipations of a new general strike to emerge. *Times of India* summarized public anxieties in an article with the rather dramatic title 'General Strike in Jute Mills. Fight to Finish'.[8]

Initially, contemporary observers tried to explain the continuance of strikes in the jute belt by pointing towards workers' apparent inability to understand the situation. Workers, who remained on strike after the settlement, accordingly, did not realize that the general strike had ended; or, alternatively, they could not make sense of the terms of the settlement and assumed that their employers had not applied the stipulations of the settlement.[9] The continuance of strikes in the jute belt, then, was essentially portrayed as a reflection of workers' irrational behaviour, as well as an expression of the fact that they did not understand the procedures of industrial dispute.

Since workers, however, did not resume work even weeks after the settlement, this interpretation of a 'misunderstanding' hardly offered a sufficient explanation for the situation. Local authorities, managers and trade unionists, after all, had in the meantime tried to persuade workers to resume work. Contemporary observers, then, declared the ongoing strikes to be entirely new protests, which bore no relation to the general strike. These new strikes were, further, not seen to reflect common grievances of jute workers, but, rather, appeared to be the outcome of local conflicts.[10] The strikes of jute workers were, accordingly, *localized* again.

It is of course true that the withdrawal of the BJWU – despite the tensions within it – marked some kind of conclusion to the general strike. Without the overall political representation embodied by union leadership, it was no longer possible to conceive of the continuation of industrial discontent within the parameters of a single, unified movement.[11] In more material terms, it meant that the support and sustenance which allowed for the generalization of the strike in the first place, such as the regular meetings or the distribution of food to some strike centres by trade unionists, also ended after the union and the IJMA concluded their negotiations.[12] In terms of state responses to industrial militancy, too, the extreme crisis marked by the general strike had clearly passed – police resources were no longer strained to breaking point in order to pre-emptively contain the spread of strike action.

Yet, neither the attributions of 'confusion' by contemporaries nor the notion that the ongoing strikes were marked by a break, seem sufficient to explain the continuities in workers' struggles in the aftermath of the general strike. Behind these confusions lies a fundamental duality in the character of the 1929 strike itself. On the one hand, the strike was, in its most obvious and immediate manifestation, an industrial dispute, framed by a specific set of formal demands, and concluded by negotiations between management and the union leadership, represented by Prabhabati Das Gupta. At the same time, however, the strike was part of an extended sequence of struggles, spanning from the mid-1920s to the onset of the Great Depression in the mills in June 1930. In this dimension, in contrast with its character as dispute, the strike is best grasped as part of an ongoing *movement*, which was far from concluded by the formal 'end' of the strike. At this level, in September 1929 the specific capital-labour tensions which grounded the general strike were still very much open.

The unexpectedly sudden announcement of the settlement by mid-August did indeed lead to 'misunderstandings' over the end of the strike – at least initially. These 'misunderstandings', however, were less a reflection of workers' confusion, than they were the result of the difficulties which workers, trade unionists and police forces faced, in spreading the news of the strike's conclusion throughout the jute belt. This was, for instance, apparent at the Birla Jute Mill, which was situated in the far south of the jute belt. On 18 August a police officer reported that workers here were 'unaware of the general settlement'. He therefore had 'the vernacular newspaper read out by a young schoolboy and distributed a few spare copies', in order to inform the workers.[13] He further proceeded to a nearby branch office of the BJWU, which had been opened up recently by labour activists from Dhaka. The rank-and-file members of the union, too, had not heard of the settlement. They agreed, however, to travel to Shamgunj, a bigger town in the area, in order to verify the information.[14] Meanwhile, in Jagatdal, trade unionists attempted to hold a meeting in order to inform workers of the end of the strike. This time, the local police did not seem to be aware of the settlement. Suspicious of the activities of the trade unionists, the police tried to

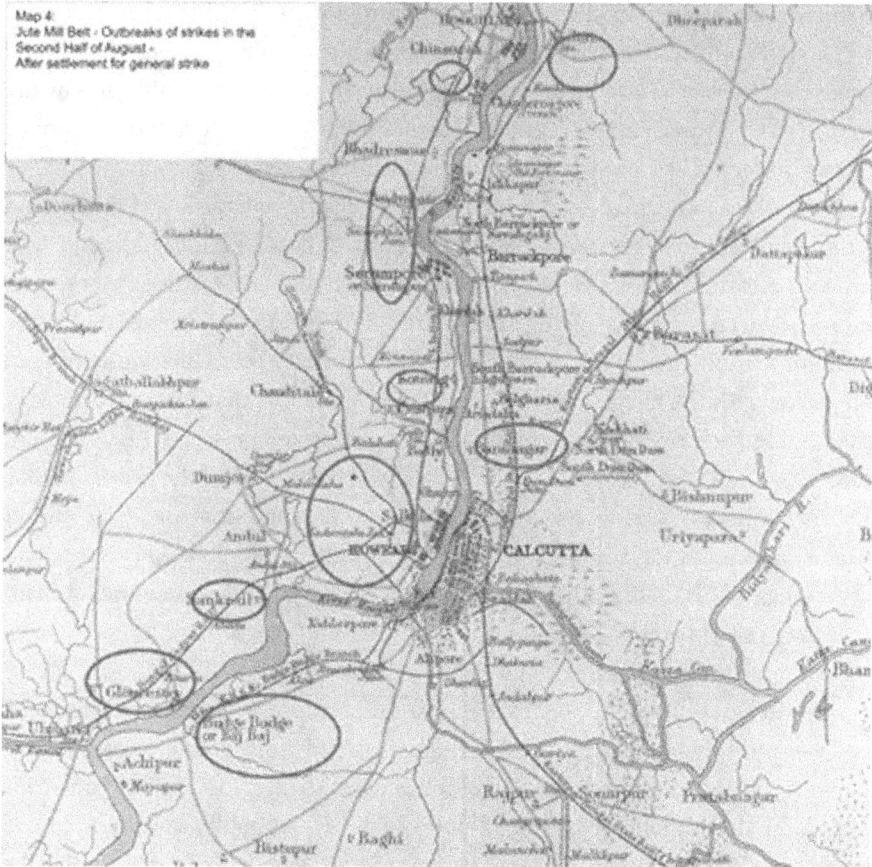

Figure 14 Strikes in the Jute Mill Belt in the Second Half of August 1929. / Map is based on: W.W. Hunter, *The Imperial Gazetteer of India Atlas*, Vol. 26. Oxford: Clarendon Press, 1931.

disperse the meeting. This intervention triggered a riot by '10,000 mill hands', which could only be quelled with the help of armed police forces.[15]

Another set of responses to the strike's formal conclusion concerned the terms of the settlement. Workers regularly raised the complaint that their demands had not been met. In Champdani, for instance, workers requested Prabhabati Das Gupta to demand an increase in wages when she informed them of the settlement. She denied support to this 'new' demand, arguing that this 'should be made after a year or so by which time the Union would be better organized and consolidated'.[16] In Titagarh, meanwhile, Ram Logan Sha 'could not explain in what way the workers have secured any benefit from the strike'. Only a 'heavy shower of rain' dispersed the workers, and 'gave him a chance to escape molestation'.[17] In the Clive and Union South Jute Mills in Metiaburuz, workers demanded that Moni Singh compensate them for one week of idleness, since 'the terms now offered were concluded and notified at the mill gates by the Manager' one week earlier already.[18] Moni Singh, too, was fortunate, as police reports noted, in escaping 'molestation' by angry workers.[19]

Difficulties in persuading workers of the successful conclusion of the general strike were not experienced solely in the early days after the settlement. In a number of cases workers went on strike again after having resumed work, and, more importantly, after having received their first wage payments under the terms of the settlement. For instance in the Kamarhatty Jute Mills, workers went on strike, with the allegation 'that they have gained less than those working in the double shift [= multiple-shift] mills according to the terms of settlement recently announced'.[20] In Jagatdal, one of the earliest centres of the general strike, workers resumed work without further protest. Discontent arose at the end of August, when the workers received their pay tickets. Prabhabati Das Gupta had difficulties in persuading the workers to resume work, and in convincing them that the problem was the belated implementation of the provisions, as the new adjustments took some time to implement.[21]

Another development was that industrial action also spread to areas that had been thinly affected until mid-August. In Howrah, where partial strikes had only occurred towards the end of the general strike, workers went on strike fully after the settlement had been published.[22] In Hooghly, the strike spread further in Champdani, Bhadreswar, Serampore and Rishra. In Budge-Budge, the strike did not only spread among jute workers, but oil-workers joined the strike too.[23] The majority of these 'new' strikes did not last for more than a week. In some instances, however, workers stayed out till the second half of September, outlasting the end of the general strike by about a month.[24]

Considering the chain of events which eventually led to these 'new' strikes, a clear-cut division between the general strike and workers' struggles in the second half of 1929 was hardly sustainable. In the district of Hooghly strike action had begun during the general strike. By mid-August it was already in the process of spreading in several subdivisions of the district, such as Rishra, Champdani, Bhadreswar and Telinipara. Similarly, in Howrah, partial strikes had occurred before the end of the general strike. Mills which had gone on strike turned into important centres for a further spread of industrial action after mid-August.[25] Budge-Budge, where workers demanded an increase in wages and a return to the multiple-shift system, became a centre of the union's activities. As early as 2 August, the group around Kali Sen tried to spread the general strike here, distributing leaflets and opening up a union-office.[26] When the workers joined the general strike about ten days later, they also joined hands with the oil workers of the municipality. While this area, then, had barely been part of the general strike in terms of active participation, the chain of events implies not only that the activities of trade unionists informed workers of the ongoing general strike, but that this information set in motion a distinct dynamic of conflict and solidarity in this locality, which involved networks among workers that reached beyond the limits of the jute industry.

In the second half of August, trade unionists tried to prevent the further spread of strikes in the jute belt. In particular the joint struggle of jute and oil workers in Budge-Budge turned into a focal point of union activities. The oil workers' union was run by Subhas Chandra Bose – whom neither of the factions of the BJWU were allied to. While it seems unlikely that Bose actually wanted to organize a new jute workers' union, he certainly made use of the situation, to present himself as an important labour leader, stating that

> many leading Jute Mill workers approached him in the office premises of the Union, asked for his advice and appealed to him to take their lead. He assured them of his full support in their struggle but he told them at the same time that they are the sole judges to decide whether they want to continue the fight or to join under the existing conditions. But this much he can say to-day that in face of the insulting behaviour meted out to them by the Manager of Budge-Budge Jute mills, he does not think that time has yet come for any honourable settlement; so they have no other alternative than to stay on and fight by organizing themselves into a powerful Union immediately. All workers signified their willingness to organize their Union under his leadership and unanimously resolved by show of hands to continue the fight until their grievances are redressed and a satisfactory settlement is arrived at.[27]

Members of the BJWU, the BJWA and even of the KLU, visited Budge-Budge in the following days. In meetings, the trade union activists addressed jute and oil workers with arguments that turned the rhetoric during the earlier phases of the event upside down. They highlighted the sufferings caused by the strike, and presented the workers' protest as irrational and without much hope of success. On 23 August, in a meeting jointly held with Bankim Mukherjee and Prabhabati Das Gupta, the trade unionists explained to the workers:

> He believed that [if] they can in a body hold out successfully, great results might come out of it but he seriously doubted if they were prepared to meet the consequences – the inevitable sufferings that must follow. Here the speaker was interrupted with all kinds of questions and remarks from the audience and

some said that they were not prepared to listen to all such fine speeches with which they already grew tired. Then Dr. Pravabhati Das Gupta rose to speak. She addressed doubt if the strikers really knew their own minds. [...] Pravabhati Das Gupta tried to bring home to the gathering that workers of the Jute Mills and Oil Companies stood on different grounds and their grievances were also different.[28]

Such attempts to stop the strike often ended with the audience shouting the speakers down or with workers leaving the meetings en masse.[29] Workers emphasized, on several occasions, the themes of their honour and the necessity of solidarity with the oil-workers. Jute workers, so the argument went, could not end the strike now that they had brought out the oil workers in a joint strike.[30] The patterns of solidarity among workers at those moments created a certain pressure to sustain the strike until it was successful. Despite the repeated attempts of the trade unionists to stop the strike and to separate the movements of oil and jute workers, the jute workers in Budge-Budge stayed out till the second half of September. By that time, conflicts within the workforce were increasing. In particular, 'up-country' workers were pushing for a resumption of work, since they could not sustain the absence of work any longer.[31]

By the end of September, the number of strikes in the Bengal jute belt was falling rapidly. In November it seemed that industrial conflicts had come to a halt, and the jute industry experienced a brief period without any strike actions. R. B. Laird, the head of the IJMA, elaborated with some hope the apparent stability of industrial peace in January 1930, stating that:

> Labour generally had settled down to peaceful and smooth working and it was safe to assume that such conditions would continue if the workers were not interfered with.[32]

His hopes, however, proved premature. In the same month, a strike broke out in the Angus Jute Mill in Hooghly, from where unrest soon spread to the nearby Champdany Jute Mill.[33] By February, protests were also noted in mills of the Titagarh area, which had been one of the main centres of the general strike. Workers, here, demanded an increase in wages – a demand which had already come up during the general strike.[34] The sudden spread of the unrest in the Angus Jute Mill, first within Hooghly, and then to the other side of the river, certainly raised anxieties among public observers that strike activities could intensify.

In early March, Prabhabati Das Gupta, who had gained some influence over workers in Titagarh in the course of the general strike, got involved in the mounting unrest in the area. She called for a day-long strike on 5 March, in order to demand wage increases in the mills of the IJMA. This brief strike was supposed to be led by mills in Titagarh and in Jagatdal, in order to give a warning to the IJMA.[35] With this step, she probably hoped to show that the BJWA could call for a general strike at any moment. In August 1929, she had promised workers that their wage demands would be taken up within a year as part of a fresh strike. The conflict between the different jute workers' unions, however, was certainly another element in her choice. The suggestion of a day-long strike, in this context, appears as an attempt to lead a 'controlled' strike movement, through which Prabhabati Das Gupta could display her influence over jute workers.

In Titagarh all the mills – with the exception of the Titagarh and the Khardah Mills – followed the call for a strike by Prabhabati Das Gupta, while none of the workers in Jagatdal went on strike. The limited response to the call for a strike was only one of the problems faced by Prabhabati Das Gupta. It soon transpired that she was not able to restrict the movement to a single day's strike action in Titagarh. Workers, instead, stayed on strike till the end of March. Making matters worse, the strike spread to the remaining mills in Titagarh, as well as to the Meghna Jute Mill in Jagatdal.[36] The attempt to stage a highly restricted moment of labour protest, then, immediately risked a loss of control over the strike movement.

One reason for the development seems to have been that workers in Titagarh assumed that the BJWA had, in fact, called for a proper strike. Discontent had prevailed in this area since the settlement of the general strike in August 1929, as workers had assumed that a 25 per cent increase in wages was part of the strike's demands – and, thus, part of the settlement.[37] A second element that contributed to the spread of strike was the dynamic of protest and militancy, which unfolded once workers had left their workplaces. The manager of the Titagarh Jute Mills described the impact of the first days of the strike in the area, and how it affected workers in his mill:

> Tuesday [4 March] was quiet but next day the workers were restless and did not show concentration at their work, although no actual stoppage took place. Several mills north of Titaghur were partially stopped on Wednesday and Thursday but both Titaghur and Khardah worked with a full complement. On the latter day however work at this mill was interrupted by crowds gathering round the gates and attempting to hold back the workers at the change of shifts. On Friday [...] just as the wages were being paid out, a crowd of about four hundred persons, mostly Spinners from other Mills rushed into the Spinning Department shouting and setting of the frames. Some difficulty was experienced

in clearing the department but this was successfully managed by the European Staff and when the crowd had been put out the Mill gates were closed and machinery restarted. [...] The mob was gradually driven to the crossing gate and here the rioters pounced on a trolley load of iron nearby and rushed the trolley against the gate which was smashed. During the melee the police arrived and the rioters were driven away.[38]

As in the early days of the general strike, then, the dynamics unfolding in the early days of this conflict demonstrated a high degree of solidarity, as well as militancy, among workers. The intervention by European supervisors, and, more importantly, by police forces, did not halt these dynamics, but, on the contrary, seemed to spur the spiral of solidarity and militancy among workers.

In Titaghar, the situation became more tense when a striker was arrested on 11 March. Within hours, '10,000' workers gathered in the local bazaar and attacked the police office in Jagatdal in order to free the arrested. The police, yet again unprepared for this outburst of workers' militancy and the direct assault on their power, were severely outnumbered. Reinforcements arrived eventually, putting an end to the riot. By that time, several constables and workers had been wounded, the mill building had been damaged, and its windows had been shattered to pieces by stones thrown from the angry crowd.[39] The next day the strike spread to the Meghna Jute Mill in Jagatdal, where the weavers of the mills left their machines first, followed by the rest of the mill.[40] With the spread of the movement into one of the earliest centres of the general strike, and with the apparent loss of control by the BJWA and local authorities alike, it seemed for a brief moment possible that a new general strike could emerge, or rather that the general strike of 1929 could be repeated.[41]

Public anxieties, however, proved to be unfounded. The strike in the Meghna Jute Mills was short-lived, and by the end of the month the workers in Titagarh also resumed work unconditionally. When the workers of the Champdany Jute Mills in Hooghly resumed work in early April, there seemed to be no surviving labour conflict in any jute mill. While in May and June strikes broke out in a number of mills in Howrah, these strikes did not seem to trigger similar anxieties about a sudden generalization of the dispute.[42] The absence of trade union involvement probably played a role in this difference of perception. Or, to put it differently: the absence of a recognized agent, who could have generalized these local struggles of workers, seems to have had a considerable impact on the ways contemporary observers responded to strikes of jute workers.[43]

In contrast to early 1929, a fragmented political representation of jute workers had been established by the end of the year. The different trade unions were not just openly competing with each other, but also had different bases of support in distinct parts of the jute belt. Prabhabati Das Gupta's BJWA was in this period almost solely active in the northern parts of 24-Parganas. The communist BJWU, on the other hand, was strongest in the south of Calcutta.[44] In Hooghly neither of the former factions of the BJWU seems to have gained a dominant presence. Rather, a group of terrorists and labour activists, which was connected to Bepin Ganguli, formed strike committees, and gained support among workers in the course of the general strike.[45]

The different local networks of support for trade unions, in the aftermath of the general strike, cannot be understood without considering older networks of trade unionism in the jute belt. In the north of 24-Parganas, Kalidas Bhattacharya and Santosh Kumari Gupta, as well as the KLU, had built up networks of trade unionism since the mid-1920s, while the communist unions had been active in building up local trade unions in the south of Calcutta in 1928.[46] In the case of Hooghly there seems to have been hardly any union activity before the general strike. The local group of revolutionary terrorists, however, could build on existing networks in the area and in Chandernagore. Connections ranged from an up-country priest active in workers' neighbourhoods, to an ex-soldier who was working on an irregular basis in jute mills, and who had participated in nationalist movements such as the Tarekswar-Satyagraha.[47] Already before the general strike, they tried to support workers in labour conflicts. They were for instance connected to the *Swadeshi Bazar*, where in April 1929 the article on 'The future revolution' had been published.[48]

Old and new networks among workers and local labour activists, which were mobilized in the course of the general strike, indicated another division in the jute belt between its northern and its southern parts. Whereas labour activists to the south of Calcutta tended to be connected to the Workers' and Peasants' Party, labour activists in the northern parts of 24-Parganas tended to be part of revolutionary terrorist networks. While not created by the general strike, the event seems to have solidified this division. In the run-up to the second general strike in the jute industry in 1936, then, police reporters noted that members of the Workers' and Peasants' Party started approaching workers in Metiaburuz and Budge-Budge. At the same time, police reports noticed that 'Comrade Bagchi' came from Kamarhaty to Titagarh, in order to talk to workers about the possibility of a general strike. 'Comrade Bagchi' was connected to the BJWU. He was connected to revolutionary terrorist networks in Titagarh, and owned a poultry business in Kamarhatty, in which he employed ex-detenus. He talked to, among others, a 'madrassi' worker named Narayana, who had first got involved in workers' politics during the general strike of 1929, led by Prabhabati Das Gupta. Narayana had, however, been disappointed by the outcome of that strike. When the Bengal Jute Workers' Union split after the general strike in August 1929, he had therefore joined the more radical wing, represented in his area by people like 'comrade Bagchi' and remained involved in it in 1936.[49]

5

'Fight to finish' – labour conflicts in the Bengal Jute Belt in the 1930s

The gradual abolition of the multiple-shift system throughout the 1920s culminated in 1931, when the single-shift system was introduced throughout the industry. The change in shift systems was implemented along with severe cuts in working hours and wages, due to the impact of the Great Depression. Workers in several mills protested the change. However, due to unprecedented levels of unemployment, labour's position had been weakened considerably, and protests against the change in shift systems ended soon.[1]

By the mid-1930s managers and managing agents introduced new measures of rationalization, designed to increase labour productivity and reduce costs of production. From the perspective of the industry, this new drive to rationalization was a response to a deepening crisis of overproduction, and to the escalating competition between managing agencies. Within the mills, however, these measures had another effect, as they ended up enforcing the formal regulations of deployment at the shop floor with new vigour. While cooperative practices between workers had formally been reduced under the single-shift system in the late 1920s, as we have seen in Chapter 3, managers could not completely control the movements of workers at the site of production. Instead, measures such as the speeding up of machinery, the redefinition of expected output or the further reduction of the number of workers deployed at machines in the spinning mill played a crucial role in expanding the introduction of the single-shift system. The combination of these steps implied an overall intensification of work throughout the mill, as well as an increased workload for workers deployed in the spinning mill.

Workers responded to this with strike action against the speeding up of machines, demands for increased output or in opposition to the installation of new machines. Both the intensity and frequency of workers' responses to the changes under the single-shift system surpassed that of conflicts in the past. While this development began in 1936, when the mills of the IJMA began to rationalize the process of production, it escalated in the second half of 1937 and in 1938, after the industry had witnessed its second general strike. The perceived novelty of the situation seemed to increase the distance between managing agents in the UK and managers in Bengal. When requested to keep agents in England informed on the events, Paul Benthal of the Bird company responded that:

> If however we telegraph to your side any reports of all the strikes, threats of strikes and terminations of strikes which go on here, we shall spend a lot of cables with very little advantage to anyone on your side.[2]

A representative of the Duff company, meanwhile, tried to explain the situation to his managing agents in Dundee, stating that:

> The changes have been so rapid and extensive that even many of us on the spot have not had time to adjust ourselves to view the changes from the standpoint which very evidently will have to do. [...] It seems almost absurd to say that such changes could take place in the matter of a few weeks, but such has been the case [...].[3]

What both men struggled to convey to their agents in Europe was, firstly, the level of militancy and organization among jute workers. In various mills, workers had formed workplace committees, through which strikes could be organized at short notice. Another representative of the Duff company, then, added that:

> It seems ridiculous that employers should be absolutely at the mercy of the workers, and that the hands can deliberately call a strike just when it pleases them [...]. If work is to be carried on in this manner for any length of time and Mills are to be continually going on strike and not knowing where they are with either labour, then industry is to become thoroughly disorganised [...].[4]

Industrialists' sense of crisis was compounded by the changing political situation in colonial Bengal, and in colonial India at large. Provincial elections, and the rising national and trade union movements, meant that conflicts over the organization of work, and conflicts over the ownership of industry, could hardly be distinguished anymore – at least not in the case of an industry that was dominated by colonial capital. Rumours, then, were circulating persistently in the jute belt, that if workers were on strike for more than three months, the new government of Bengal would be compelled to take over the mill, and would, in turn, help redress workers' grievances.[5] Compounded by the economic crisis of the industry, then, these developments indicated a reversal of the situation in 1931, as it was now capital that seemed in a weakened position.

The history of the jute industry in this decade has generally been analysed in terms of the development or transformation of workers' politics and labour conflicts, a tendency which also informed the analysis of labour conflicts in the late 1920s, as we have seen. This development, accordingly, started with a strike wave in the early 1920s, when nationalist labour activists entered the scene, and found its conclusion with a second general strike in 1937, when communist trade unionists had become dominant in jute workers' organizations.[6] The analyses, in other words, were guided by questions of the emergence of a wider trade union movement and its political conflicts. While labour conflicts in the second half of the 1930s occupied an important position in these histories, their histories were overshadowed by questions concerning the role of the Bengal Chatkal Mazdoor Union (BCMU, previously BJWU) in these strikes. The general strike of 1937, in which the trade union took a leading role, appeared as a culmination of conflicts starting in the early 1920s, and less as a point of departure for a wave of strikes that shook industrialists.

The subdued response to the abolition of the multiple-shift system, meanwhile, appeared in a number of studies as a moment marked by an absence of protest.[7] The change in shift systems occurred in tandem with severe cuts due to the impacts of the Great Depression systems, leading to the dismissal of 60,000 jute workers that year. Trade union leaders were not involved in the resulting strikes, and the protests were too short to make a meaningful impact on the wider working-class politics of the time. Pushing the argument about the absence of protest the furthest, Arjan de Haan suggested that workers did not protest against mass dismissals in 1931, because they were 'unsettled settlers'. Workers, then, could always leave for their 'up-country' homes, and dismissals did not even leave much of an impression on workers' memories. When an old worker that de Haan interviewed in Titaghar remembered the abolition of the multiple-shift system as significant event during the Great Depression, de Haan concluded that this response displayed a 'memory-gap' on the side of worker. This 'gap' of expected memories explained the proposed 'gap' of workers' protests.[8] The conclusion that workers could simply leave for their homes and, thus, 'forgot' about dismissals, confirmed the exclusion of workplace relations from workers' histories.

This chapter does not deny the growing importance of trade union politics in this period. As with the analysis of labour conflicts in the 1920s, however, it is clear that the omission of the changing organization of work from histories on the jute industry has led to serious gaps in our understanding of industrial relations and conflicts in the 1930s. While reasons for strikes were often read through the 'translations' of trade union representatives, workers' forms of organization at the shop floor were often overlooked. Capitalists' response to these protests – and, along with it, managerial attempts to regain control over their workforces, rarely seemed to enter analysis. This also affected the ways in which moments of crisis in capital labour relations were understood: it determined which kinds of protests were seen as significant, and which kinds elided or omitted in analyses.

Returning to the changing organization of work in the Bengal jute industry, we will trace the developments of the 1930s in this chapter. At the outset, the changing organization of work under the single-shift system can be described in terms of two distinct trends. First, it was marked by an *intensification* of regulation of workers at the site of production. This did not only include the formal rules of deployment, but workers' options for informal arrangements at the shop floor. Second, it was marked by an *expansion* of workers' regulation beyond the immediate realm of the workplace, and into workers' neighbourhoods. In order to regain control over workers, managers and managing agents introduced welfarist measures, such as the establishment of employment bureaus, as well as more immediate measures of control and influence, such as propaganda campaigns.

These two trends were interlinked. This was not in itself new. As we have seen with regard to the emergence of the multiple-shift system in the late nineteenth and early twentieth century, the increasing regulation of work gangs at the site of production had emerged in correspondence with wider changes in the industry, and the emergence of an industrial area in the hinterland of Calcutta. At this point, however, the interrelation between the two trajectories of regulation was largely a reflection of managerial concerns over the stability and the quality of the process of production. When the stability of production became less of a concern for managers, as an internal labour market had emerged in the jute belt, the tightening of the regulation of work gangs became increasingly possible. In the 1930s, in contrast, the interrelation between an intensification and expansion of regulation took another form. It was, in the first place, not an expression of managerial concerns, but, rather, an expression of workers' opposition to the changing organization of work, which managers were compelled to respond to. Correspondingly, the expansion of regulatory efforts outside the factory space took the form of managerial strategies designed to control workers outside their workplaces, rather than regulating the access of labour to the mill.

The Great Depression, the abolition of the multiple-shift system, the second end of the general strike

In 1930, the impact of the Great Depression began to be felt in the jute industry. Jute goods were nearly exclusively used as cheap packaging materials for trading goods. Not surprisingly, then, the industry was particularly prone to the crisis in global trade. The situation was worsened by the fact that the mills on the Hugli were already facing a crisis of overproduction, which had been the result of an increase in production in 1929. At that point, the IJMA had deliberately adopted a policy of 'controlled' overproduction in order to trigger a fall in prices for jute goods. This, the association hoped, would force competing mills out of the market. This step, however, came at a particularly bad moment. In 1930 the prices for jute goods did not simply drop as anticipated: they virtually collapsed. In particular, the export demand was at a critical low. Between 1928 and 1931, the prices for hessian bags were nearly halved. For sacking goods, the situation was not as dire; yet, here too the demand had dropped markedly.[1] In the next few years, the demand for jute products dropped further, sinking below even the levels reached before the First World War. At this point, the mills of the IJMA had installed 36,000 looms, whereas in 1930 the productive capacity of the industry had grown to 61,000 looms.[2] Only from the mid-1930s did demand rise again. Yet, even then it would prove to be lower than anticipated – a problem which indicated the magnitude of the crisis into which the jute industry had entered.[3]

Faced with a massive crisis of overproduction in 1930, the IJMA announced a series of cuts in an attempt to curtail production. In a first round of cuts, to be implemented by July 1930, the hours of work were to be reduced from sixty to fifty-four hours per week in all mills of the IJMA. In a second round of cuts in September, the hours of work were to be restricted further, to forty-two hours per week. This round of restrictions, however, did not imply an actual reduction

of working hours per week. Rather, the measure implied that the mills of the
IJMA shut their gates for one week per month. During the remaining three
weeks, they continued to work fifty-four hours.[4] Altogether, the reductions in
hours of work led to the dismissal of about 30,000 workers, as well as to a regular
lockout of those workers who had kept their jobs.[5]

While the prospect of large-scale dismissals throughout the jute industry
caused some concern among local authorities, the outlook of a monthly 'idle
week' created panic among the general public. Anticipations of an imminent
outbreak of industrial conflict, which might involve all jute workers at once,
dominated the responses. The fact that the IJMA announced the reduction of
hours of work in April, just after the latest attempt at a new general strike, gave
such fears a further boost.[6] Local authorities, whose limits had yet again been
tested in the previous strikes, however, had no power to intervene. The week-
long closure of jute mills was, after all, not in violation of the regulations of the
Indian Factories Act. They had, accordingly, no option but to await the pending
lockout, and prepare for the unrest anticipated among workers.

The IJMA, meanwhile, tried to divert the fears of industrial unrest. The
managers' association, firstly, decided to pay *khoraki* to their workers during the
week off.[7] They further agreed to pay compensation for the weeks when the mills
were closed. This was to be paid to workers who had worked continuously in the
week before the enforced 'idleness'.[8] This latter point, however, was not only a
response to public anxieties about labour conflicts but, maybe more importantly,
also reflected the fears of managers and managing agents that workers might
leave in the idle period, in order to work somewhere else. In other words, the
idle week could lead to new forms of labour shortage.[9]

In contrast to widespread anticipations and fears, the closure of jute mills
was not followed by waves of labour unrest. Workers did not seem to protest
against the measure, while managers even reported that workers in their mills
had been relieved to receive the first compensation payment, which they had not
expected.[10] The only problem mentioned was, indeed, a problem of temporary
labour shortages, which occurred when starting work again. The manager of the
Samnuggur North Mill, for instance, stated that after opening the mill, 'we have
been as many as 100 short in the Batching, Preparing and Spinning Departments'.
Hinting, further, at the fact that this problem was a recurrent one, he added
further that these 'departments gradually get filled up again, until the next off
week comes along when a similar occurrence takes place'.[11] The conclusion
which many contemporaries seemed to draw from workers' responses was that
the general strike of 1929 – as well as the continued unrest among jute workers

in its aftermath – had come to an end. The period of industrial peace, which R. B. Laird had already proclaimed in January, seemed to have finally arrived.

One crucial reason for the declining number of strikes in the aftermath of the cuts was certainly the increasingly insecure position of workers in the midst of unprecedented levels of unemployment. Mass retrenchments not only affected jute workers, but the entire industrial hinterland of Calcutta (as well, of course, other parts of colonial India). A considerable number of workers seem to have left the area for their original homes in Bihar and the United Provinces. Government officials like R. N. Gilchrist, then, reported at length about the fact that railway stations were crowded with dismissed workers for days and weeks after the cuts in the jute industry.[12] A significant number of workers, however, also remained in, or returned to, the jute belt. Unemployment turned into a visible and ever-present reality. Local authorities, consequently, noted a sudden increase in burglaries. In particular, reports about 'bands of wandering upcountrymen' in the subdivision of Barrackpore 'caused considerable alarm' among the general public.[13] Meanwhile, in Budge-Budge, police officers complained about a notice posted 'by some mischievous person to the effect that vegetables and sweetmeats would be sold at prices much below the market rate'. This claim, the further report stated, was 'readily believed, and when the shop-keepers refused to comply some looting of bazaar stalls took place'.[14]

Managers, however, showed some excitement about the new 'over-supply' of labour. The constant presence of unemployed workers, crowding outside the mill gates in the hope of finding a job for the day, certainly enabled management to increase the pressure on those workers who had retained their jobs. Due to new rounds of cuts and mass retrenchments in the years to come, the constant presence of unemployment in working class areas would continue to shape the situation. In 1934, the manager of the Titagarh Jute Mill remarked:

> No complaints can be made in this respect as there has been a plentiful supply of labour throughout the year. Those employed are giving more attention to their duties as they realise that their position can be easily filled from the number of unemployed workers in the district.[15]

Only from the mid-1930s did the situation improve, as levels of unemployment declined gradually.[16]

In March 1931, when levels of unemployment were still rising, a new round of cuts was implemented by the mills of the IJMA. This time, the mills on the Hugli reduced the hours of work to forty per week, and sealed 15 per cent of their looms. They further abolished the multiple-shift system completely, and introduced a single-shift system.[17] In contrast to earlier cuts, contemporary observers did not anticipate any resistance from workers. The absence of large-scale strikes during the weeks off, and, more importantly, the weakened position of workers, rendered this scenario unlikely. The anticipation of a 'peaceful' implementation of the new cuts lasted even when some mills went on strike in late February, just before the cuts had been introduced, and a police reporter noted that in the district of Hooghly district workers

> in one or two mills have ceased work, but despite the fact that thousands will be thrown out of employment by the introduction of the single shift system, the local police anticipate no serious trouble at present.[18]

This prediction proved to be wrong, and when the single-shift system was introduced, labour conflicts broke out in eleven jute mills.[19] In Howrah, workers went on strike instantly, while in mills in Titagarh, workers in the spinning mill refused their wages under the single-shift system.[20] Workers in Howrah resumed work after two weeks, while workers in Titagarh accepted their wages after three weeks.[21]

While the very fact of labour protests in the midst of the Great Depression was certainly remarkable, workers' responses to the introduction of the single-shift system did not find much resonance in contemporary reports. Rather, the situation in the jute belt seemed to revert to the state of the 1920s, when strikes were a regular occurrence among jute workers, while appearing principally at a local scale. These strikes did not trigger sudden police intervention, unlike in 1929. The responses of trade unionists, too, seemed to exhibit this return to the 1920s. Neither the BJWU nor the BJWA tried to organize or support workers' protest in 1931 beyond the level of individual strikes. While the communist BJWU supported the strikes in Howrah against the change in shift systems, Prabhabati Das Gupta, on the contrary, tried to prevent an open conflict on the matter. She travelled through Barrackpore, urging workers to demand 'a bonus for four months, a pension and a ticket to their homes'.[22] The general representation of jute workers at the level of trade union support, then, appeared to have come to an end as well for the time being.[23]

The demoralization of an increasingly vulnerable workforce opened up fresh possibilities for workplace restructuring, which were seized by mill managements in the course of the following months. Managers used the economic crisis as an opportunity to push through wide-ranging changes, which had hitherto appeared impossible to implement. In 1932, for instance, the mills of the IJMA began to prohibit the entry of young children into the mills. The Inspector of

Factories gave a vivid description of the implementation of these changes, and of its implications for the structure of the workplace:

> In past years, women employers were permitted to bring their infants and young children with them into the mills, the connection being that there was no one than their parents to look after them. During working hours it was an everyday sight in the mills to see young infants lying asleep beside the machines and on piles of sacks, while those able to run about roamed all over the mill. The dangers of accidents and the prejudicial effect on their health from the dust and fluff-laden atmosphere had long been realised, but until recently any attempt to interfere with the long and firmly established custom would undoubtedly have resulted in serious labour disturbances. As a result of the present trade depression, however, the supply of labour now greatly exceeds the demand and therefore the same need for countenancing the practice no longer exists. [...] Objections by the women employees were quickly overcome, the threat of dismissal in one case, and of suspension in another, having the desired effect.[24]

Other changes concerned, for instance, the question of safety. Workers employed on roving machines were compelled to wear shorts instead of *dhotis*, under 'penalty of dismissal if the order was not complied with.'[25] By 1933, the Inspector of Factories was able 'to report that all rovers, shifters and male coolies on roving machines in every jute mill in this district [Barrackpore] are now compelled by order of the management to wear' shorts 'whilst at work.'[26] The result of these changes was that the workplace in Bengal jute mills appeared to be an entirely different space from before. In several distinct ways, then, the crisis engendered by the Great Depression cleared the ground for a move towards the formalization of structures of industrial control.

Yet the defeat of labour was not a complete one. The reduction of working hours to forty per week was, yet again, implemented in an unusual way. The Inspector of Factories, reported on the matter as a side-line, saying that

> [i]n the jute industry, when the general change over to the single shift system was made, a regular four-day week of 10 hours per day was established in place of the previous four-day week of 13 1/2 hours per day with an idle week each month.[27]

The crucial information hidden in this remark was that the mills on the Hugli did not operate on a working week of five days. Instead, they retained a working week of four days, as they had done under the multiple-shift system. This was, arguably, not simply a choice of capital, but reflected a workers' demand. As we have seen in previous chapters, workers used their off-days to gain an extra income, gather firewood, or work in the fields. During the Great Depression, the distribution of hours of work marked a limit which industrialists could not cross. Managerial concerns over the degree to which wages could be reduced in jute mills presumably played an important role at this point, too. Nonetheless, another aspect was the anticipation of labour unrest. Or, as Paul Benthall asked in 1935, 'Why don't we work an 8-hour working day already? [...] On the whole, the answer must be that it would entail a strike'.[28] The weakened position of labour during and shortly after the Great Depression, which allowed for further wage cuts, then, also established a limit for capital, in the distribution of hours of work during the week.

'We are all more or less Socialists now' – the deepening crisis of the Bengal jute industry in the 1930s

Contrary to capitalists' anticipations, the end of the Great Depression did not lead to an end of the crisis of overproduction in the jute industry. Rather, the post-depression years seemed to reveal forcefully that the crisis of the industry was becoming terminal.[1] Despite the growth in global trade, the mills of the IJMA saw themselves forced to continue measures aimed at curtailing production in their mills, in order to prevent a further slump in prices. The productive capacity of Bengal jute mills far outstripped global demand. Members of the IJMA, then, continued to run with reduced hours of work, while keeping 15 per cent of their members' looms sealed, and the restrictive policy of the IJMA emerged, yet again, as a crucial point of conflict between capitalists.[2]

Unlike in earlier periods, however, the situation of the industry had changed significantly – and, along with it, so had the potential responses which the members of the IJMA could offer to counter the crisis. This was, on a more immediate level, apparent with the strategy to 'kill the competition' outside the IJMA by increasing hours of work. Debates around this strategy had dominated conflicts among capitalists in the 1920s. During the First World War, managing agencies on the Hugli had generated impressive savings, due to the immense growth in demand in that period. These savings could have sustained jute mills and also ensured stable returns to investors during a period of falling prices due to overproduction. When the Great Depression hit the industry, however, managing agencies used up these savings to meet investors' demands for high returns. In the mid-1930s, then, the members of the IJMA had no further recourse to the option of a strategic period of intensified overproduction. Instead, the potential failure to agree on new short-time agreements implied that a return to the 'survival of the fittest', which had accompanied moments of crisis of the industry in the late nineteenth century, was a real possibility at this point.

The abolition of the multiple-shift system further affected the range of options that managing agencies had recourse to. In case of a failure to agree on a restriction of hours of work, managing agencies could not access an excess supply of labour anymore. This problem points us less to the competition with 'outside' mills, and more to the competition among members of the IJMA. During each severe moment of crisis in the industry's past, those managing agencies that could sustain excess employment in their mills had retained an advantage over those agencies which worked with a single-shift system instead. Mills running on a multiple-shift system always had the option to run their machines longer hours than their counterparts, without breaking the restrictions of the Indian Factories Act. Under the single-shift system managers had no such option, and managing agencies began to increasingly focus on measures of rationalization, in order to prepare their mills for a period of intensified competition.

Trying to tackle the mounting risks of a failure to agree on short-term agreements, the IJMA also turned to the colonial state. Legal restrictions on the working hours in Indian jute mills were one major element of this push for a resolution. This, so the hope went, could replace the need for short-time agreements among members of the IJMA. Restrictions of the production of raw materials turned into a second possible legal resolution requested by the IJMA. The prioritized access to the raw material for Bengal jute mills would, it was anticipated, discourage jute industries emerging in other countries. The idea of turning to state authorities gained in importance in 1932, after the multiple-shift system had been abolished, and when the members of the IJMA were in the process of using up their savings.[3] The conflicts within the IJMA over how to sustain its global monopoly and its members' profits, then, could be solved by sidestepping resolutions from within the IJMA.

This new strategy marked a decisive shift from the IJMA's previous industrial policy. The chairman of the IJMA expressed the perceived radicalism of change vividly, explaining that:

> We are all more or less Socialists now, judged by Victorian standards; and if the ultimate good of any industry demands restriction of production, measures should be taken with vision and judgment[!] to interpret the handwriting on the wall. I hope I am not trying your patience over much, but I feel very sure of myself when I say that there will be no peace, no security in this industry, until the Government prevents any expansion of production by an emergency measure limiting the working hours of productive machinery to 54 hours weekly for 5 years, or until such time as all the looms now sealed are working 54 hours weekly.[4]

While the plan found support from the Bengal Chamber of Commerce, neither the Government of India nor the Government of Bengal was particularly impressed by the idea. Requests put to the Government of India for the restriction of hours of work and of the production of raw jute were refused outright.[5] A restriction of the legal limit of hours of work that was exclusive to the jute industry would, after all, have undermined core principles of the universal applicability of the Indian Factory Act, while wide-ranging interventions in the peasant economy of eastern Bengal on account of the Bengal jute mills did not appear feasible to the Government of India. The IJMA pinned its hope on the Government of Bengal instead, and focussed on the request to restrict the supply of raw materials, by restricting the areas in which jute could be grown in the province. This attempt initially failed as well, and the request was rejected.[6] While the IJMA did not give up on its attempts to push the Government of Bengal for a resolution of its internal conflicts, in the mid-1930s it seemed clear that this apparent solution to the industry's crisis was not going to be implemented any time soon.

At the same time as attempts to 'outsource' the resolution of the industry's conflicts to state authorities failed for the time being, tensions over the continuation of short-time agreements were rising. It became increasingly apparent that the anticipated growth in demand for jute goods, which would meet the productive capacity of the industry, was not imminent. Putting it bluntly, a report by the Government of Bengal stated that:

> It is difficult to foresee how long the present restrictive arrangements of the jute mills will last; we have already examined, it will be extremely hazardous to assume that the mills will revert to very much longer working hours in the immediate future. The odds are heavily against the restoration of the pre-restriction working hours, at any rate, during the currency of the Jute Mills Working Agreement.[7]

This realization was compounded by fears over the emergence of cheaper alternatives to jute products. Already in the 1920s, cheaper alternatives for jute products began to gain in importance. For instance, paper bags replaced jute bags as packing material for cement on the US American market.[8] By the mid-1930s, successful replacements of jute bags were still few in number, but experiments with alternative packaging materials were constantly being conducted.[9] The trend threatened to further reduce demand for jute goods, and it caused considerable concern among managing agencies. What was at stake here, after all, was the commodity value of jute products in the first place. Keeping prices for jute goods inflated by restricting production, then, turned into another risk for the industry – and into another reason for prioritizing intensified measures of rationalization instead.

The growing importance of Indian-owned jute mills, too, added to the growing difficulties in sustaining short-time agreements. The curtailment of production in the mills of the IJMA kept prices for jute goods stable, and, in turn, rendered investments in new Indian-owned jute mills profitable. Alexander Murray reported a meeting with G.D. Birla, during which the latter had told him that:

> He [Birla] was afraid that Europeans did not fully appreciate the mentality of this Marwari friends. There was any amount of money amongst them awaiting investment in industrial enterprise, and numbers of young men only too anxious to invest in the Jute industry. There was a great tradition behind that industry, and Indians believed that the risk of material losses on the manufacturing side was negligible. Experience showed that European Managing Agents would sooner or later enter into some Agreement that would prevent losses continuing.[10]

The exchange was reflective of growing tensions between colonial capital and Indian capital, which had been apparent in Bengal at least since the 1920s. When tensions over short-time agreements mounted in the mid-1930s, so too did anxieties that the restrictive policy of the IJMA prevented European-owned mills from competing with their Indian rivals.[11]

By the mid-1930s, then, short-time agreements no longer seemed feasible. While a majority of the members of the IJMA still supported restrictive agreements, a growing number of European managing agencies rejected them, rendering an agreement between the members of the IJMA difficult.[12] As a compromise, the mills agreed to implement a flexible restriction of working hours. Jute mills were accordingly allowed to work between forty and fifty-four hours per week.[13] Previously sealed looms, however, were to remain sealed, according to the agreement.

The result of this compromise was a spiral of loosening restrictions, and increasingly open competition between the members of the IJMA, which would shape the years to come. In March 1937, the mills decided to discontinue all restrictions on production, thus enabling its members to increase hours of work to fifty-four hours per week (or, to the legal limit under the Indian Factories Act), as well as to unseal the looms which had been standing idle since the Great Depression. In addition, the two Indian members of the IJMA seized the opportunity to introduce a (regular) double shift system, in order to increase working hours to twenty-two per day.[14]

One year later, the hours of work in Bengal jute mills changed again, when the Government of Bengal introduced the 'Jute Ordinance' in April 1938. This step was a concession to the earlier demand made by capitalists, and it restricted the area in which jute could be grown in Bengal.[15] In order to meet the now-restricted supply of raw jute, the mills of the IJMA reduced their hours of work to forty-five per week. This arrangement lasted until September 1939. With the outbreak of the Second World War, the demand for jute goods, particularly for sandbags and other war-related products, increased suddenly. This set in motion a fresh series of changes in hours of work, which increased with the advance of Japanese troops, and the resulting interruptions of transport routes.[16]

The escalating conflicts over hours of work among members of the IJMA by the mid-1930s were accompanied by a frenzy of rationalization in jute mills. This included measures to increase the output of production – such as the speeding up of machinery, new calculations for piece wages, measures to reduce labour costs by creating redundancies, as well as measures to improve the quality of production, by improving techniques of measuring output, and by increasing the number of workers that were dismissed due to insufficient work. At their outset, these measures were designed to increase productivity and lower the costs of production. They affected work processes across the mill, as machines were speeded up in all departments. One immediate consequence of this development was a significant increase in accidents. The Inspector of Factories noticed 'an increase of 580 in the total accidents' in 1935, and wrote that:

> It would appear that this increase is due largely to the restriction-of-production agreement, which has resulted in a general speeding up of the productive machinery with the object of obtaining maximum production within the working hours permitted by the agreement. This view is borne out particularly in regard to the looms. In most cases, these are now being worked at considerably higher speed than previously and the number of accidents due to flying shuttles, breaking straps and spindles, etc. show the greatest increase.[17]

While the Inspector of Factories focussed on the growing number of accidents among weavers in his reports, accidents were also rising sharply among other sections of the workforce, most markedly among spinners.[18]

Neither the Inspector of Factories nor mill managers discussed the reasons for increases in accidents in the spinning department. However, the gradual decline in overall accidents among spinners is indicative of the central role of the speeding up of mill machinery. From 1939, the jute industry experienced

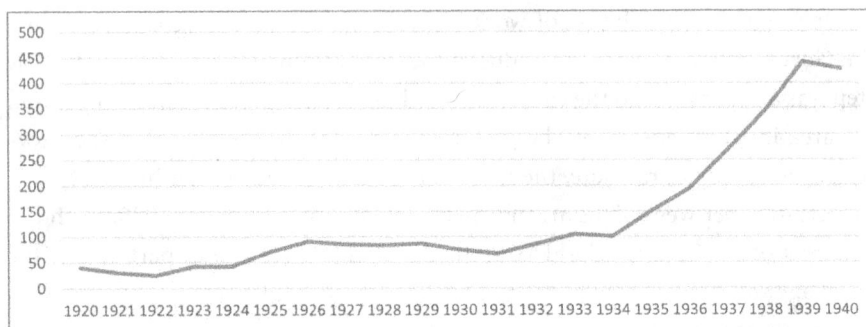

Figure 15 Total annual number of accidents in spinning departments of Bengal jute mills. / Data from: Annual Report on the Working of the Indian Factories Act in Bengal and Assam, 1920–40.

a tendency towards a shortage of skilled spinners.[19] This forced managers and managing agents to decrease the overall speed of spinning frames again, and, as a result, the overall number of accidents among spinners decreased as well.[20]

Beyond the general measures like speeding up of machinery, the spinning mill turned into a specific focus of managerial attempts to lower costs of production. New high-speed machinery was nearly exclusively installed in this side of the mill, leading to redundancies, while simultaneously increasing output. New roving machines, drawing machines and high-speed spinning frames were installed in a growing number of mills in the second half of the 1930s.[21] This had the potential to reduce labour costs significantly. In 1935, the manager of the Samnuggur North Mill calculated, after the installation of a set of new high-speed spinning frames, that ten workers were employed where previously twenty-three had been working, receiving altogether Rs. 25-12-0 per week, instead of Rs. 48-4-3.[22] The owners of the Union North Mill, meanwhile, reported in the same year that the installation of new machines in the departments of the spinning mill would lead to an increased output worth about Rs. 2,500 per week, while reducing labour costs by Rs. 500 at the same time.[23]

Measures of rationalization, however, were also aimed at improving the quality of production. This was a response to the changing global demand for jute goods, and in particular to a growing trend towards increased standardization of packaging material. Taking a look at the type of products listed for Bengal jute mills by the late 1930s in the coarser line of production alone, we get a glimpse of the variety of products that were commonly produced in the industry by that time:

Australian Cornsacks,
Egyptian Grain Sacks,
Cuban Sugar Bags,
Salt Nitrate Bags for Brazil,
Sugar Bags for Egypt and the Levant,
Java Sugar Twills,
Australian and the Cape Woolpacks.[24]

In addition to stipulations in terms of shape and size, jute bags had further specifications in terms of weight, or the type of yarn used.[25] With regard to the hessian side of production, the list of products and concrete specifications could be extended further, as the bulk of the more refined types of jute bags were produced in this side of the production process.[26]

A general trend towards further standardization and refinement of production shaped the history of the jute industry from its earliest days, as we have seen. The degree to which this trend shaped workplace relations, however, increased considerably in the 1930s, when the required levels of standardization reached new heights, and when the competition over declining markets for jute goods escalated. In the mid-1930s, in addition, questions of improving the quality of production had a more immediate political impetus: the IJMA still hoped to eventually gain support from the government of Bengal in their attempt to restrict the supply of raw jute. Producing a larger variety of jute goods in this context should also be seen as an attempt to prove that the mills of the IJMA had indeed tried various avenues – including modernizing their mills in order to counter the crisis of overproduction, instead of simply relying on government help to solve the problem.

Either way, attempts to gain more control over the quality of production became another source of managerial activities that acquired new urgency, in the midst of the ongoing crisis of the industry in these decades. It was, not surprisingly, the weaving factory where these concerns were most apparent. The threat of dismissal for insufficient or 'bad' work that had accompanied the introduction of the single-shift system was intensified, and the number of weavers who were dismissed for insufficient or 'bad' work rose. Techniques to measure the quality of production, too, improved. The manager of the Samnuggur North Mill reported:

> Chief amongst these improvements is the system of inspecting cloth received from the looms, and this unit of the calendering department now consists of 39 Inspectors and 13 darners. All the Hessian cloth is inspected and between

60 per cent and 70 per cent of the Sacking cloth. Weavers, making bad cloth and allowing it to pass into the calender find they have to interview the Overseer who uses his own discretion as to warning and fining and dismissal.[27]

In managerial reports, further improvements in measuring the quality of production turned into an important theme in the years to come. Given that this concern was also in the overall interest of the Bengal jute industry, representatives of managing agencies even toured different jute mills, in order to learn from improvements made in other mills, while also trying to use improvements in their own mills for competitive advantages.[28]

5.3

Revival of labour conflicts in the 1930s

The intensification of managerial attempts to change the organization of work in Bengal jute mills, together with changing hours of work, led to a fresh series of labour conflicts in the Bengal jute industry in the second half of the 1930s. After a period, in which strikes seemed to have ceased in the jute industry during the Great Depression, the number of militant labour conflicts in the industry rose again from 1936.[1] In February 1937, the Bengal jute industry experienced its second general strike. This was followed by a wave of strikes the following months, as well as in 1938. The number of strikes in the jute industry only seemed to reduce in 1939, but protests did not die out completely in this year either.[2] Workers' actions in these years, further demonstrated high levels of militancy, directed at mill buildings, machines and telephone wires, as well as against various figures of authority at the workplace, and against police officials.[3]

While managers had certainly been concerned by workers' responses to the change in the organization of work in the 1920s, the militancy and determination of working-class protest in the second half of the 1930s appeared new and alarming to many observers of the situation. Reporting to their directors in Dundee in 1937, mill managers of the Duff Company expressed their unsettlement:

It has been evident to all that the present labour unrest it entirely different in nature to anything that has ever been experienced before […].[4]/ *Shamnaggur North Mill*

At no time do we know of labour trouble which can compare with the conditions which prevailed at the time of this strike.[5]/ *Titagarh No 2 Mill*

Workers refused to accept the changes implemented at their workplaces, and undermined the authority of managers to decide how work should be conducted. Among the most common reasons that workers raised when going on strike were the dismissal of workers for reasons such as unproductivity, the speeding up of existing machinery or the installation of new machines.[6]

Probing this matter further, the manager of the Angus Jute Mill interviewed the weavers in the mill. The mill had gone on strike in August 1937, after the dismissal of six weavers for underproduction. The weavers accordingly argued that the mill management was

> justified in dismissing them for continuous bad work, but they do say that dismissals for short production and undue absence such as staying too long when going for a drink, must cease.[7]

They further explained their position, as the manager reported:

> They pointed out that they wished to be in a position and be allowed to leave their looms for prayers and stay away as long as they wished, adding that although the normal wage of a weaver may be say Rs. 8/- per week, it was none of our business if a weaver wished to take things easy and earn only Rs. 5/- per week.[8]

This conflict revealed limits of managerial control, which persisted despite the abolition of the multiple-shift system. While managers had dismissed workers employed in excess of the requirements of production, and while they had further closed the entries to the mill, they could not fully control the movements of regularly employed workers at the point of production. The changing regulations of deployment under the single-shift system, together with increased threats of dismissals for 'bad' work, served to curb these practices, but not to abolish them completely. In the midst of large workplaces, filled with machines, dust and workers bringing material from one place to another, workers still found ways to substitute one another in the course of the day within the confines of the single-shift system.

During the Great Depression, managers in Bengal jute mills did not seem particularly concerned with the options of sharing work which regularly employed workers created for one another within the confines of the single-shift system. It was, rather, the frenzy of rationalization that set in in the mid-1930s which, effectively, ended up enforcing the changes in the organization of work that managers and managing agents had begun in the 1920s with new rigour. By speeding up machines in the spinning-mill, and by increasing the number of pieces to be produced in the weaving factory, managers effectively demanded that workers continuously expend their labour power at their machine. In addition, weavers in particular were affected by new targets of production, as 'insufficient' production turned into an important cause for dismissal. The process of production under these conditions could not have been sustained if workers were prepared to periodically take over a colleague's machine as well.[9]

In 1936, managers were not willing to give in to the workers' demands. Not only was the industry going through a severe crisis, but, maybe more importantly, workers had, from the perspective of managers, no right to intervene in their choices in organizing the process of production. The manager of the Anglo-India Jute Mill expressed this starkly after his interview with the weavers of his mill, stating that:

> If labour has reached the stage of practically demanding control of industry, in my opinion there can be only one course open to employers, and that is to fight to the last ditch regardless of cost.[10]

A report by a representative of the Bird Company, meanwhile, informs us about a plan to use a planned renovation as a pretext to close the mill completely. After an extended closure with a corresponding loss in wages, so the hope went, workers would not be willing to go on strike, even if managers had changed the rates of production and the speed of machines in the meantime. The renovation, then, was seen as an 'excellent opportunity' of rationalizing production further without the risk of 'bad blood owing to strikes'.[11] Or, in other words: as an opportunity to discourage workers from opposing managerial authority by withholding work and wage-payments for a period of time.

Dismissals of workers turned into an important source of conflict beyond the pretext of insufficient work. In the second half of the 1930s, jute workers regularly protested dismissals due to redundancies – such as after re-arrangements in the process of production, or in the context of the installation of new machines. In addition to protesting lay-offs of sections of the workforce employed at the mill machinery, conflicts also included strikes over the dismissal of individual workers, as well as over the dismissal of workers who were not employed in the process of production, and who were not employed as regular workers either.[12] A brief (and far from exhaustive) list of examples may give an impression of this aspect of labour conflicts in this period. In January 1938, a strike broke out in the Naihati Jute Mill, when 200 women workers were dismissed. In February the same year, meanwhile, a conflict ensued in the Wellington Jute Mill, after the dismissal of one spinner. In the same month, a strike broke out in the Reliance Jute Mill, after an oil-engine worker was dismissed. One year later, the dismissal of a temporary sweeper led to the shutdown of the mill within half an hour of the incident.[13]

The crisis unfolding in the jute industry was compounded by the changing political situation in colonial India. With the Government of India Act of 1935, the coming of provincial (limited) autonomy was announced, and elections were held in January 1937 in all the provinces of British India. These elections catalysed new hopes. The parties in the fray made campaign promises about better welfare measures and rights for workers, and new expectations arose of the changes to come when the new government was elected.[14]

In Bengal, the election was won by the Krishak Praja Party-Muslim League coalition. H. S. Suhrawardy, who was to be chief minister of Bengal during the lead-up to Partition, was Labour Minister in the coalition headed by Fazlul Huq after the elections in January.[15] Trade union politics, meanwhile, had seen a revival of the Communist left in the mid-1930s. The alliances between Congress nationalism and the left in the 1935–39 period, which took different forms across the country, was accompanied by a new wave of strikes throughout colonial India, which seemed to surpass the previous wave in terms of militancy and determination among workers and trade unionists alike.[16]

From 1935, then, police reports noticed rising activities among labour activists working among jute workers, which were increasing in intensity in 1936. Local labour activists approached jute workers in different parts of the jute belt, or supported them during labour conflicts. In 1935, A.M.A. Zaman supported workers in strikes in the Hooghly district, calling himself the president of the Samnuggur Textile Workers' Union.[17] In January 1936, meanwhile, members of the Workers' and Peasants' Party of Bengal approached jute workers in Howrah, and to the south of Calcutta. They organized *bustee* meetings among workers, and distributed communist literature among them.[18] In April 1936, police reporters noted that 'Comrade Bagchi' came to Titagarh, in order to speak about the possibility of a general strike.[19] The second half of the year witnessed a growing number of meetings among labour activists who had become active in the jute belt. This served to re-establish networks among labour activists in different parts of the jute belt, and to coordinate them under the leadership of the BCMU. While communist trade unionists, who were aligned with the Workers' and Peasants' party, concentrated their efforts on organizing workers to the south of Calcutta, A.M.A. Zaman expanded his influence in Hooghly. Saumyendranath Tagore, meanwhile, took over the responsibility of coordinating networks among local labour activists to the north of Calcutta, where revolutionary terrorists had been dominant.[20]

One month after the election of the new provincial government in Bengal, a strike broke out in the Ganges Jute Mill in Howrah, after the mill manager had dismissed four weavers.[21] Five days later, the IJMA announced the suspension of all agreements regarding the restrictions of hours of work and the sealing of looms. This led to a further escalation of labour conflicts in the jute belt.[22] The strike, which had started in the Ganges Jute Mill, soon spread to other mills in Howrah, and workers demanded a 'restoration of the 1932 cuts'.[23] The BCMU supported these strikes, and formed a central strike committee, which comprised the different networks of communist and nationalist trade unionists in the various parts of the jute belt. In February and March, the strike movement spread in the south of Calcutta. In April, mills in Barrackpore went on strike as well, followed by mills in Titagarh and Hooghly.[24] On 24 April, about 240,000 jute workers were on strike all along the Hugli, and the industry was at a near standstill.[25]

The escalation of workers' militancy, immediately after the election, seemed to reveal that the new government was not capable of running the province. Trying to put a stop to the strike, Suhrawardy travelled through the jute belt in order to convince workers that their strike was meaningless, since the Government of Bengal would soon implement new welfare measures on their behalf.[26] He further encouraged the foundation of a white trade union for Muslim workers in jute mills, in order to break the emerging strike movement, as well as in order to counter the influence of communist and nationalist trade unionists in Bengal jute mills.[27]

The new government also exerted pressure on the IJMA to end the strike in their mills. Jute mills could, accordingly, only expect support from state authorities – such as the police – if managers were willing to engage with the situation constructively.[28] This meant, among others, that the IJMA was pushed to negotiate with the newly founded white union for Muslim workers. Behind this demand lay the argument that the strike was not only the fault of communist and nationalist trade unionists who had confused workers, but that capitalists, too, were to be blamed for the situation. The IJMA refused to negotiate with the new trade union, which its members did not recognize. The IJMA further refused the underlying assumption that capital was to blame for working-class discontent. Instead, the mill-owners' association questioned the capacity of the new government to deal with the situation, declaring that the strike was the

> direct result of the recent general election at which vast promises were made by members of the new Bengal Assembly, including some of the present strike leaders, of the imminence of a new heaven and a new earth in Bengal's green and pleasant land. Used thus democracy is a dangerous thing.[29]

The confrontation between capital and state at this point was a rather immediate reflection of the changing political situation in Bengal: members of the colonial elite were ill-prepared to deal with their weakening position, while members of the new government sought to assert their authority over colonial capitalists in their province. Both sides, however, agreed that trade unionists, supported by the Workers' and Peasants' Party and by the Indian National Congress, bore the bulk of the blame for the general strike.

At this point, however, communal tensions were already heading towards polarization in the jute belt.[30] On 8 March, the general strike was called off, as riots between Bengali and 'madrassi' spinners, who were predominantly Hindus and supported the BCMU, and 'up-country' weavers, who were organized in the new union founded by Suhrawardy, seemed to become an increasingly real possibility. In order to prevent a further escalation of violence, an agreement was drafted, according to which the IJMA agreed to consider workers' demands favourably, if they returned to work. The agreement was published as a preliminary settlement of the strike. Negotiations, however, did not continue after the strike's official end.[31]

The end of the general strike did not end the hopes and anticipations generated among workers nor did it improve the weakened position of British capitalists. In the colonial context, the latter had been used to a position that granted them exclusive access to the state, among other privileges. In localized labour conflicts in the aftermath of the general strike of 1937, members of the IJMA repeatedly tried to suppress strike action by requesting the deployment of riot police in the affected mill areas. In contrast to earlier years, however, the new government was less willing to respond to such requests favourably, instead demanding that managers first engage with their workers via moderate trade unions.[32] The members of the IJMA also faced increasing pressures from the Government of Bengal to prevent further strike movements – and, thus, to prevent an advance of left-wing trade unions.[33] The implementation of the Jute Ordinance in 1938, through which the Government of Bengal restricted the areas in which jute could be grown on behalf of the IJMA, increased the dependency of the industry on the local Government, and, along with it, the urgency felt by capitalists to suppress strike movements in their mills.

Among workers, strikes in the second half of the 1930s were sustained by remarkably strong forms of shop-floor organization. In particular, workers in the spinning department had organized themselves, and had built workers' committees in several mills along the river. A conflict over the dismissal of a worker, then, could lead to a strike on short notice. Giving an impression on the chain of events that unfolded in Bengal jute mills regularly in this period, let us consider a report from a strike in the Angus Jute Mill. In this mill, weavers, too, had been incorporated into the structure of workers' committees. After a strike in July 1937, the mill manager reported on the events:

Twenty workers were dismissed from the Spinning Department for not carrying out their duties properly and immediately thereafter several of the Committee members signalled to the workers to stop work as a protest and both [spinning] Mill and [weaving] Factory were stopped for about 1 1/2 hours. The members of the Working Committee assured the Manager that if he reinstated these 20 workers, work would be carried on normally and with this assurance, the Manager reinstated the dismissed spinners and work was resumed. In the afternoon 6 women workers in the Preparing Department were suspended in the usual way owing to there being an excess of material. They were told to come back the following morning, but this was taken exception to by a few Committee members, so the entire place again closed down but was started up 15 minutes later.[34]

The workers' committee in the Angus mill included workers from core sections of both the spinning mill and the weaving department. In mills where such committees were principally arranged around workers in the spinning mill, similar patterns of workers' control at the workplace were reported, and dismissals (including from the weaving factory) could lead to the instant closure of the mill. The predominant position of spinners in this context, however, could also lead to conflicts with sections of the weaving department, on occasions when weavers did not want to sustain another loss in wages.[35]

In colonial reports, workers' committees appear to emerge in the aftermath of the general strike of 1937. However, it seems unlikely that these forms of workplace organization had come up spontaneously, given how widespread they were, and given how efficiently these committees seemed to function at moments of conflict. Police reports mentioned that trade unionists had suggested the formation of workers' committees to jute workers in the mid-1930s. Labour activists, then, seem to be an important source of this development. This does not mean, however, that workplace committees relied on trade unionists to sustain themselves once they had been established. Labour activists, who had been important in addressing workers, could lose influence among workers, while workplace committees gained importance in the aftermath of the general strike. A.M.A. Zaman, who had exercised considerable influence among workers in the Hooghly district (among them, workers in the Angus Jute Mill mentioned above), lost his influence after promises he made during strikes could not be sustained.[36] On the other side of the river, meanwhile, revolutionary terrorist networks were considerably weakened after the Titaghur Conspiracy case, during which more than 200 people were arrested. 'Comrade Bagchi', who had established networks among workers after the general strike 1929, was among them.[37]

The dominant role of spinning departments, however, does point us to the initial importance of labour activists in the spread of the idea of workplace committees. In the southern parts of the jute belt, where spinning mills were dominated by Bengali workers, trade unionists had already in the late 1920s established stronger connections to these sections of the workforce than to up-country weavers. In the northern parts of the jute belt, meanwhile, spinning mills were dominated by 'madrassi' workers. In studies on the jute industry, this section of the workforce has often been overlooked, due to the assumption that they could not communicate with trade unionists because of linguistic barriers. However, children of 'madrassi' workers regularly learned some Bengali, in order to do odd jobs at local *bazaars* and elsewhere, as we have seen in pervious chapters. This was a condition for them to contribute to the family income before they were old enough to work in the mill. It is not surprising, then, that in the northern parts of the jute belt, too, sections of the spinning mill turned into an important point of contact for trade unionists.[38]

The changing organization of work after the abolition of the multiple-shift system provides an additional backdrop against which we can understand this development in particular in the spinning mill. The introduction of the single-shift system had altered established hierarchies among the workforce, as spinners had received relatively higher wage increases than the highest paid weavers. In addition, their work was increasingly becoming more skilled. The absence of informal options of training themselves at their machines, after all, led to an increasing shortage of trained spinners in the jute industry. Their bargaining power, in other words, increased in this period, while conflicts between spinners and weavers also indicated attempts by the former to assert themselves within the new workplace hierarchies of the Bengal jute mills.

Managerial responses to the situation, and in the context of the political changes of the late 1930s, ranged widely, from 'listening to workers' to mass dismissals. Whereas the former strategy was designed to display managerial goodwill, the latter was aimed at reducing the influence of communist and nationalist trade unionists, whom managers blamed for the unrest. In May 1937, for instance, spinners in the Titagarh Jute Mill went on strike demanding the employment of more spinners per spinning frame. After meeting a delegation of workers, and after learning that neighbouring mills deployed more workers per spinning frame, the general manager of the Duff company came to the conclusion that the workers' demand was justified. He accepted their demand somewhat dramatically, declaring that 'it was clear where our duty lay'.[39]

One year later, however, spinners in Titagarh went on strike again, this time over the dismissal of workers. The BCMU got involved briefly, in the anticipation that a new general strike could emerge. The strike, however, soon led to conflicts between spinners and weavers, which, in the midst of Hindu-Muslim tensions in the area, erupted into communal riots. The BCMU withdrew its support, and police forces suppressed riot-turned strikes in the following weeks. After the conflicts ended, managers dismissed all workers employed in the spinning department, and evicted them from their houses in the mill compound.[40] The brief involvement of communist trade unionists, as well as the violent riots between Hindus and Muslims, probably rendered such a mass dismissal possible, despite the pressures from the government of Bengal to 'listen' to workers.

In other cases, managers simply ignored what they considered minor infringements, in order to avoid triggering labour conflicts. When workers returned to the Angus Jute Mill after a strike, for instance, departmental overseers noticed that they were wearing *dhotis* instead of shorts. The wearing of *dhotis* at the workplace had been discontinued in 1931, under the purview of the Indian Factories Act. While posing an increased risk for accidents, the mills' manager simply accepted the violation of the rule, and noted that this was a problem for the Inspector of Factories, not for him.[41] In July, several managers admitted at a meeting of the IJMA that production in their mills had not been restored to normal levels since the resumption of work in May. They did not give many details on the exact conflicts, but it seems that workers objected in particular to the speeding up of machinery. The managers stated that they had dared to intervene, in order to prevent further strikes.[42] Managing agents, meanwhile, sent notices to their managers that dismissals were not to be made by European overseers, but only by managers themselves, and only after 'the case had been thoroughly investigated'.[43] In contrast to the ongoing labour struggles after the first general strike, then, the conflicts in the immediate aftermath of the general strike of 1937 seemed to reveal a situation in which workplace relations had been suddenly reversed – at least for the time being.

Regaining control at the site of production

From the perspective of managing agents, the conjuncture of economic crisis, labour conflicts and political change seemed to suggest that the changes in the industry needed to go beyond measures of managerial control at the point of production, or punitive dismissals in localized mills. Whereas the crisis of the industry had led to an increase in competition and an escalation of measures of rationalization, the widespread response by workers, as well as the industry's changing position vis-à-vis the state, seemed to push managing agencies in the opposite direction, of cooperation. The focus shifted from managerial control over workers to what we might call industrial control over the workforce. Whereas the former was in the hands of individual managing agents, the latter required cooperation between different groups.

Cooperation between managing agents in local mill areas played an important role here. As we have already seen, managers tended to refer to practices of work in surrounding mills when responding to demands such as an increase in the number of workers per loom or per spinning frame. Mill localities turned into crucial points of reference for legitimizing managerial choices. Further rationalization attempts and changes in hours of work, in turn, began to rely on the joint decisions of managing agencies that happened to run mills in the same area.

Managing agencies running mills in the same locality tried to gather information about workers by employing informants during strikes. While this had already been established as a practice during the 1929 general strike, the scale and importance of gathering information on workers increased markedly in this period.[1] Informants hired by jute mills moved into workers' neighbourhoods, in order to gain workers' trust. This was combined with propaganda measures, aimed at convincing workers that their strike was futile and could only result in the loss of income. This included flyers in Indian languages detailing the futility of labour unrest, which were distributed among workers and *sirdars*. Posters, too, were produced and hung up around workers' neighbourhoods. Managing agencies running mills in the same locality shared the costs for informants and for propaganda measures with one another.[2] During the general strike of 1937, the production of propaganda material was expanded and, more importantly, centralized. The IJMA took over the responsibility for producing propaganda materials. These were then given to the agencies organized in mill localities for distribution. The costs were covered by regular membership fees that the IJMA received.[3]

This information-gathering – not at the shop floor but in workers' neighbourhoods – also played an important role in debates about labour officers, which gained in importance in the aftermath of the general strike of 1937. Such labour officers were supposed to act as conciliators, and 'generally acting as a liaison Officer between the Management and workers'.[4] While mediating between workers and managers in order to avoid conflicts, they could also gather information and statistics for managers.[5] The IJMA experimented with this format too, employing a small number of labour officers of their own.[6] After the success of the initial trial, the IJMA scheme was expanded in 1939. Taking the tendency for localized cooperation between managing agents as a basis, the jute belt was divided into five divisions or areas, and one labour officer was deployed per division. Describing the change in more detail, the manager of the Titaghur No. 1 Mill reported that:

> A night office has been opened in a central area for this district and the Labour Officer is in attendance during certain hours each evening to listen to any grievance a worker may bring forward. When such evidence as he may receive justifies an investigation, a full report stating the case is submitted to the Manager for his careful consideration.[7]

As the mills on the Hugli were working on short-time agreements at that point, the labour officers were also tasked with the inspection of the mills in their division, to ensure that the restriction in working time was applied.[8]

Labour officers proved useful in gathering information about workers by visiting workers' neighbourhoods, and in coordinating between managers and local authorities during labour conflicts. Due to their additional task of investigating infringements of working time agreements, they further helped to reduce the levels of mutual distrust among managing agencies, which was an outcome of a long history of violations of such agreements. Workers, however, seem to have largely avoided consulting them.[9] Distrust about the objectives of these labour officers seems to have been an important reason here, and workers feared negative consequences for raising grievances in this context.

A second scheme, which the members of the IJMA implemented in 1939, was the establishment of employment bureaus. These served, firstly, to regularize the modalities of employment of workers, and reduce the control of *sirdars* at this point. They further enabled managers and managing agents to gather information on workers throughout the industry more systematically. In each mill, employment registers were created for all workers, containing photographs and fingerprints of each registered worker, information on their address (both in mill towns and, with regard to migrant workers, at their rural homes), duration of employment and information on skill and work performance. The scheme also included registers for *badli* workers. The manager of the Victoria Jute Mill explained the working of the latter in his report, stating that:

> Each Overseer will require to fill up a requisition from whenever vacancies occur in his Department and sent this form to the Bureau who will supply workers from their relieving workers' lists to till the vacancy. These workers will be given a duplicate requisition form to be given to the Overeer-in-Charge when they report for work. [...] The Overseer will however report on the work of all relieving workers and, at the termination of employment, these workers will be sent back to the Bureau with a report on the quality of their work. In the event of an adverse report being received the worker's name will not be put back on to the relieving workers register but all workers with satisfactory reports will be added to the register.[10]

Workers in a number of mills refused to cooperate in the process of taking their photographs and fingerprints. Fears over repercussions for workers engaged in strikes played a central role here – not only could managers dismiss workers and share their photographs with other mills, in order to prevent them from finding employment there, but managers could also share photographs with police authorities and increase the risk of their arrest. Especially after the dismissal of the entire spinning department in the Titaghur Jute Mill in 1938, these fears seemed well founded. However, conflicts over employment registers were also triggered by rumours circulating the jute belt that women workers were expected to pose naked for their photographs. Workers were, either way, forced under threat of mass dismissals to accept the measure, and cooperate in the process of setting up employment registers.[11]

The system of registration of employment was expanded one year later with regard to *badli* workers. Based on the records of work performances of *badli* workers, which had been recorded since 1939, *badli* workers were categorized into three groups, which signalled their experience, reliability and skill. Workers employed in the first group had the best chance of being employed temporarily, and, more importantly, they had the best chance of being employed as permanent worker if another worker left. Workers in the third group were only employed in emergencies, and only for short durations.[12]

The regularization of employment of workers and surplus workers proved important in the process of re-establishing control over workers. In contrast to labour bureaus, where workers had and exercised the option of not co-operating, the registration of workers and *badlis* was compulsory. While the photographing of workers led to a growing number of strikes, the simultaneously established register of surplus labour meant the dismissal of large sections of the workforce was less of a problem. Managers, after all, had access to information on skilled and 'loyal' extra workers. When workers protested against the introduction of employment bureaus, then, the manager of the Victoria Jute Mill simply dismissed '173 undesirables', as 'a plentiful supply of labour was available'.[13] In the following year, however, the registration of workers came to a sudden end, due to the outbreak of the Second World War, and a growing instability in employment among workers.[14]

Attempts to expand the control of managing agents over the workforce were interrupted by the events of the 1940s. The Second World War, and in particular the participation of Japan on the side of the Axis powers, led to the dislocation of labour as workers fled the jute belt in 1942. Employment registers, thus, proved to be outdated just after they had been finalized. One of the largest military bases of the allied forces, meanwhile, was set up just outside of Calcutta, employing large numbers of workers on better terms and better wages than in jute mills. In addition, shortages of coal supplies and blockages of shipping routes led to temporary mill closures. During the same period, India's independence was taking shape, and neither managers nor managing agents had much hope of continuing working in Bengal after the war.[15]

In 1947, when India and Pakistan gained independence as separate countries, the jute industry faced what was probably its most severe moment of crisis. The partition of the former colony was, firstly, accompanied by severe communal riots that were particularly strong in Bengal and in Punjab. Flights of workers were one of the results. In particular, Muslim workers, who often dominated the more skilled sections of the workforce in the weaving department, fled the area due to exceedingly bitter violence.[16] The partition meant, secondly, that the areas in which raw jute was grown were now in the newly formed East Pakistan, while the jute mills that worked with these raw materials were in India. After a brief blockage of exports of raw jute to India, the Pakistani government allowed the plant to be exported with a number of restrictions.[17] The Bengal jute industry, then, was drawn into the political conflicts of the time in a more existential sense than even in the 1930s.

Adding to the impression of comprehensive change, the 1940s and 1950s also witnessed the emergence and elaboration of a new industrial regime that would come to shape industrial policy in post-colonial India. An economy characterized through much of its modern existence by *laissez-faire* was transformed into an economy defined by strict state controls, and one where the state itself would rapidly emerge as the biggest industrial employer by far, setting up, managing and regulating both production and capital-labour relations. Industrial conflict came to be increasingly regulated by legislation and by judicial intervention: rather than 'free' collective bargaining, what emerged was a state-regulated structure of industrial relations in which labour courts and tribunals played a major role, and where the 'compulsory arbitration' of labour disputes was introduced – initially to ensure the smooth functioning of industries in wartime, but subsequently acquiring a life of its own.[18]

This move towards a more 'controlled' system of industrial relations was also marked at the site of production itself. Wage-payment, working hours, worker welfare and recruitment came to be regulated more strictly: this was visible in particular in the new nationalized industries, but also marked in industries – such as jute and cotton – where private capital controlled production. Worker welfare on a more expansive basis became a feature of the larger industries, private and state-controlled alike: employer-provided creches, canteens, dispensaries and schools sprang up on factory sites and in factory neighbourhoods.[19]

With regard to the jute industry, an industrial tribunal was set up in 1947, to investigate the complaints of workers, and to enforce changes in the industry. The tribunal reached its conclusion in 1948, detailing decisions on a wide range of issues:

(1) Recognition of trade unions by employers.
(2) Standardization of occupational nomenclatures and categories of workers.
(3) Minimum basic wages for manual workers and clerks.
(4) Revision of piece rates.
(5) Grades of wages for manual workers and clerks.
(6) Revision of dearness allowance.
(7) Bonus (1) for past years and (2) for the future. Profit-sharing bonus.
(8) Payment for period of involuntary unemployment.
(9) Procedure for retrenchment and payment of compensation.

(10) Revision of working hours and of spread-over period.

(11) Abolition of contract labour and *sardar* system.

(12) Standing orders and rules of service [...]

(13) Rules of Leave [...]

(14) Provision for provident fund, gratuity and pension.

(15) Housing and house allowance.

(16) Revision of medical facilities.

(17) Improvement of working conditions and sanitary arrangements [...]

(18) Cheap canteen.

(19) Provision for rest and recreation.

(20) Provision for creches.

(21) Arrangements for educational facilities for adult workers and their children.

(22) Free supply of implements to mechanical workers and carpenters [...].[20]

While many issues raised in this list point us in the direction of changes that managing agencies had previously tried to avoid or at least limit, the development of the industry in the pre-war years still proved an important point of departure for the tribunals' decisions, as well as for the industry's implementation of these provisions. Categories of groups of workers that managing agencies had developed in cooperation with one another when setting up employment bureaus, for instance, turned into a basis for wage revisions or rules of service. Employment bureaus, meanwhile, were crucial in providing for the payment of a food allowance during periods of involuntary unemployment. During the Second Word War managing agencies had introduced equal bonus payments in the industry through the IJMA. The mill owners' association continued to regulate these payments after the publication of the tribunal.[21]

Welfare measures and the recognition of trade unions were issues that managers and managing agents had previously avoided engaging with on an industry-wide basis. With regard to the former, this basically meant that such measures were implemented at the level of individual mills, with the result, for instance, that the quality of medical facilities varied even between mills belonging to the same managing agency. In response to the tribunals' decisions, the IJMA took a leading role in coordinating some of these measures – such as deciding on concrete holiday and leave regulations. In their majority, however, the implementation of welfare measures continued to be organized by individual managing agencies.[22]

With regard to the recognition of trade unions, meanwhile, the industry had until that point opposed cooperation. The employment of labour officers in the late 1930s was, in fact, also aimed at establishing paths for workers to raise their demands that avoided the involvement of trade unions. After the decision of the tribunals, the IJMA's labour officers turned nonetheless into an important element in implementing the new relations. They were responsible for mediating between trade unions, managers and state institutions. During labour conflicts, managers could refer to the labour officers to represent them and the industry.[23]

A point that stood out in the list was the abolition of the contract labour system, as this is the only issue referring more immediately to the organization of work at the site of production. Under this heading, the tribunal discussed the practice of deploying workers outside the process of production under the system of gang work that had been dominant among workers in the spinning side of the mill before the 1920s. It affected workers engaged with the loading and unloading of jute, but also carpenters, oilers and *mistries* (engineers employed for repair work).[24]

The eventual abolition of previous practices of gang work among these sections of the workforce marked a conclusion to a problem that had emerged in the 1920s. Managers and managing agents had at that point focussed their measures on re-arranging the process of production. Workers who were not employed at the mill machinery were, accordingly, not affected. However, already at that point, managerial attempts to regulate the motion of workers at the site of production implied regulations of the workforce throughout the mill space and the mill compound. Managers, in other words, could not completely separate the line of production from the regulation of the factory space. The enforcement of a change in the organization of work of all workers employed in the mill space, in turn, appears a logical conclusion to this development. It marked the workspace as a site of formalized labour relations.

The early 1950s did not see an immediate end to strikes in the jute industry. The implementation of the tribunal, in fact, caused new problems, as the standardization of wage payments throughout the industry meant that the hierarchies of wage payments changed in individual mills: an outcome which workers protested against.[25] Most of these conflicts did not last long and were resolved soon. The one exception was a protest of *mistries* and other workers who had previously been employed in workgangs. They refused to work according to the new mode of deployment and continued to work in gangs instead.[26] Unlike in the 1920s, managers had no particular stake in enforcing discipline in this matter. Not only had this change been imposed on them as well, but, more importantly, Scottish managers and overseers were gradually departing from India. Their stakes in the Bengal industry, in other words, had changed.

Instead of enforcing the new rules, they simply referred the matter back to state authorities and the factory inspector. The conflict lasted until 1952, when the *mistries* eventually accepted the new rules determined for them.[27] The abolition of older types of gang work among workers not employed at the mills' machines in the 1950s can be seen as a completion of this process, as the factory space emerged as a site not only of managerial control, but also of state regulation.

6

Conclusion

In this study, two perspectives on the changing organization of work in the Bengal jute industry have emerged. The first points us towards a specific long-term process, whereby labour was subjected to more and more stringent control at the point of production. Adjustments to the process of production, the types of raw materials and the ways in which workers were arranged around the machines, all contributed to the *intensified managerial control* that was exercised at the workplace. Practices of cooperation at the shop floor were regulated at various moments, by reducing levels of excess employment, regulating – and eventually abolishing – work gangs, and by rationalizing production under the single-shift system.

This extension of managerial control was also reflected in the increasing levels of standardization of an expanding set of jute goods. In the 1860s, the industry was unable to develop an export trade due to the uneven quality of production. By the 1870s, the decade when work gangs began to be regulated in the spinning mills, it had turned into an important export industry, exporting standardized sacking cloth. After the 1890s, the Bengal industry established a global monopoly over the production of jute goods. In this period, finer hessian goods became part of the portfolio of Bengal jute mills, as weavers were subjected to new forms of regulation. By the late 1930s, as employers extended their suppression of practices of cooperation at the shop floor, the mills were producing to a still higher level of standardization.

The second perspective points us more specifically to the period between the 1920s and the 1930s, which witnessed an *accelerated dynamic of transformation* at the workplace. While this should not be seen as strictly separate from the long-term intensification of managerial control, the new dynamics of transformation still implied new degrees of managerial intervention and a shift in their focal points. The interventions in the organization of work that managers and managing agents undertook after the First World War concerned the basic modalities of labour deployment at the site of production: work gangs were abolished at the mill machinery. This intervention was a condition for increasing managerial control over workers in the 1920s, and also the basis on which managers pushed for further measures of rationalization and standardization in the 1930s.

This development not only interfered with the concrete practices of work at the shop floor; more importantly, it interfered with the social formation of labour relations that had been established in jute mills. Practices common in the mills, such as the training of non-employed friends or family members at the machines, were embedded in social relations that sustained workers in mill towns and beyond. While the formal abolition of gang work under the multiple-shift system was one crucial moment in this acceleration of change, it did not conclude the transformation. Managers could not simply 'abolish' the social practices that workers relied on to sustain themselves and the process of production. Instead, the period of accelerated change continued into the 1930s, when practices of cooperation were further restricted under the single-shift system, at a moment of an escalating crisis of the industry.

This second perspective also indicates a shift away from a focus of managerial interventions at specific points in the process of production – such as the spinning mill, or the weaving department under the multiple-shift system – to the regulation of workers throughout the workplace. The discontinuation of gang work was, at the outset, a step that affected workers deployed at the mill machinery of every department. The control of individual workers at their machines, however, also implied the regulation of the motions of the workforce in the workspace, in the mill and the mill compound. The abolition of gang work, then, was combined with attempts to regulate workers' entry into the mill; restrict the movements of non-employed people – such as children; and to regulate the appearance of workers at the site of production. The workplace itself emerged as a focal point of regulation and labour control. With the establishment of employment bureaus and registers, new measures of managerial control over the workers' entry into the mill were introduced and soon expanded on. The cooperation between managing agencies in the jute belt played an important role here, turning Calcutta's industrial hinterland into a site of intensive capitalist regulation.

While these overall trends shaped the history of the industry, the concrete regulations introduced at various moments corresponded to the situation of the industry in the hinterland of Calcutta. The transformation of work organization in the jute industry, then, linked the spatial conditions in which mills and workers had to operate to the requirements of the process of production and of labour control. In the 1870s, this meant the regularization of excess employment at an extended moment of insecurity in the supply of labour. The expansion of the multiple-shift system in the 1890s implied a reduction of excess employment in those departments of the mill where a consistent supply of labour had been secured, by widening the networks of supply for workers in the weaving department. In the 1920s, those mills that deployed mostly 'local' Bengali workers in their spinning departments avoided introducing the single-shift system until the last years of the decade. Under the new system, the working days per week increased from four to five, while the working day was regularized, and workers needed to arrive at the mill at the same time. In the second half of the 1930s, the IJMA began to coordinate activities such as the introduction of liaison officers, in order to gain more information (and, along with it, control) over workers in their neighbourhoods.

This book has been a study of the transformation of jute factories as workplaces in colonial Bengal. It has attended closely to certain aspects of this process, such as the deepening crisis of capital invested in the jute industry, the emergence of a distinctive labour movement in the jute belt and the alteration of the conditions in which workers worked. But this analytical emphasis on the workplace has also involved a certain limit. Certain key developments of the period – such as changing gender relations, or communalized conflicts between sections of the workforce – have occupied rather less space in this study. This limit was necessary, in order to establish the workplace as a changing terrain of struggle and contestation, rather than the unchanging backdrop to the labour movement and capitalist development that it has been relegated to in much of the extant scholarship. However, once the historical dynamism of the workplace has been established, it should be possible to speculate a little about the implications this has for broader questions.

It thus seems useful in this conclusion, to revisit some of these themes, in order to conclude this study on the changing organization of work, and to analyse the implications of re-establishing the workplace as a changing terrain for wider questions of Indian labour history. I will begin this excursus by thematizing certain key aspects of the workplace history I have tried to unravel. These are, in order: the phenomenon of gang work in colonial Indian industries, questions of resistance and subversion and the changing structure of supervision in jute mills. Following this, I shall try to outline certain implications of workplace transformations for two key dimensions of wider social dynamics: changing gender relations, and communal antagonism.

Gang work

This book has shown that the multiple-shift system in Bengal's jute mills was based on the employment of 'excess' labour, of workers surplus to the immediate requirements of production. This necessitated the elaboration of specific forms of work organization, and the basic unit of labour was not the individual but the *work-gang*, a phenomenon whose different forms I have traced in different branches of the jute mill. My contention here is that this specific dimension which was so central to Bengal's jute industry – the deployment of work-gangs at the point of production – may be of some consequence for broader questions which exist in Indian labour history.

Work gangs were, of course, by no means unique to Bengal's mills: they were widespread across Indian industries. Contemporary descriptions of the 'irregularity' of work – the images of workers leaving the factory in the middle of the working day – underscore this aspect. In factory commissions and labour inquiries, these images were linked to narratives about 'pre-modern' habits of work. The deployment of work gangs was also reflected in descriptions of labour conflict. To take a prominent example: the reports of the 1890s describe conflicts over the pass-system in the Bombay cotton industry. Under this system, groups of workers received a pass which allowed their members to take limited 'irregular' breaks in the course of the day. Individual members of each group had the option of leaving the site of production by producing their group pass at the gate, while the other members of the group stayed behind. Once the time allotted to a group had been used up, its members could not leave the site of production any more, and received a new pass the next day. By the 1890s, the majority of cotton mills in Bombay seem to have used a pass-system to regulate work gangs. Conflicts arose when mills tried to reduce the time that workers were allotted per pass – thus reducing their scope to substitute one another.[1] Managerial attempts to intervene in the internal arrangements within work-gangs at the shop floor, then, were not an insignificant point of contention in this period.

Another feature of the Bombay cotton mills, analysed at length by Raj Chandavarkar, also has a correlative in the history of the Bengal jute industry, and is again linked to the phenomenon of the work-gang. This is the 'decline of the jobber': Chandavarkar notes that the role of the *sirdar* seemed to decline almost cyclically in Bombay's mills, and cites sources from different periods in the cotton industry's history to demonstrate this recursive observation about the declining jobber. If we introduce a comparison with the jute mills of Bengal, the common element in both industries – the persistence of gang-work – throws the question into sharper focus. The role of the *sirdar* was declining in the 1890s in the weaving department of Bengal's jute mills: in this decade, managers introduced a regulation of work gangs that brought sets of workers more immediately under the control of departmental supervisors, and also re-arranged the deployment of sets at the weaving looms. In the hessian side, four members of a group were deployed at specific looms, and that was determined by the mill, not by *sirdars* any more.

The role of *sirdars* was again seen to be declining in the 1920s, when the deployment of work gangs was formally abolished in Bengal jute mills. This step affected workers across the different branches of production, and managers declared the end of the '*sardari*' system. Decline was glimpsed yet again in the 1930s, first, when the speeding up of machines reduced the scope of workers to share their work informally, and second, when the first employment bureaus were established. Whereas the first implied an intensified regulation of the production process, the second meant that the role of sirdars was reduced at the point of workers' entry into the mill.

At the end of the 1930s, though, *sirdars* retained important positions in workers' everyday rhythms in the mill, since they still acted as line overseers, as middle-men between Scottish overseers and workers, and since they performed key functions in workers' neighbourhoods. Nonetheless, the ongoing decline of the *sirdars'* position in late colonial India points us to developments in which the articulations of groups of workers (which consisted of workers and their *sirdar*) were increasingly subordinated to the mills' extension of control over workers at the site of production. The 'decline of the *sirdar*' should thus be read as a formulation of this overall process at different stages of its development. The same motif – the decline of the jobber – actually concealed a plurality of changing situations of industrial control. While this development was contingent on the concrete situation of the industry, the growing demands for *standardization* of production played a key role at moments when managers and managing agents sought to extend and intensify their control over their workforce. What contemporaries described in terms of abolition or of permanency of practices of work, then, can better be described as an expression of changing configurations in the social formation of labour relations in this period.

Resistance and subversion

When practices of work that had previously served a function from the perspective of the industry were restricted or abolished, they turned into acts of subversion.

This was most clearly visible with regard to practices related to sharing work. Workers' absences in the course of the day, the 'informal' employment of friends or family members and the entry of 'ghost workers' emerged as practices that undermined managerial authority at the site of production. Given that this problem was linked to the developments pointed out above, the emergence of practices of subversion, too, can be seen in an almost cyclical manner in this period.

At a more immediate level, the line between the continuation of everyday social practices and active, volitional resistance to the mills' demands appears blurred. Whether we can understand workers' insistence on maintaining their practices of shared work in terms of social continuity, or as an act of resistance, hinges, in the first place, on the concrete moments in which we can identify conflicts over these issues. In the immediate aftermath of the change in shift systems in the late 1920s, a workplace conflict over the consequent dismissal of a worker might well be understood as triggered by the unwillingness of workers to change their work practices. In such cases, some of which I have discussed in Chapter 3, workers typically resisted managerial attempts to control the movement of friends and family members not employed by the mill. These can, therefore, be read as a defence of an older system of work organization at the moment of its downfall. By the mid-1930s, on the other hand, workers' resistance to dismissals occasioned by the enforcement of the single-shift system had changed qualitatively. Workers tried to alter the process of production by changing the number of workers per machine, and also wore clothes other than those prescribed by the mill. These conflicts, in contrast to those of the late 1920s, fall more clearly in the realm of active subversion of established managerial claims.

In either case, workers' responses to managerial interventions in the organization of work should also be understood as a defence of a variety of social practices through which workers had appropriated the spaces of the mill. Practices established in connection to the deployment of workers in groups were, for instance, linked to training friends and family members at the mill machinery. This could serve as an entry to mill work, connecting workers' networks at the site of production to their survival networks in mill towns. It could also serve as an entry into other departments of the mill (for instance, spinners could train themselves at weaving looms). Thus, such practices could become an important means of negotiating and asserting hierarchies within the mill. Practices of sharing work also enabled workers to negotiate age differences, allowing older workers to work shorter hours.

Measures that restricted the expressions of work gangs at the shop floor intervened in this complex set of social and cultural practices inside and outside the mill. Comprehensive changes, like the abolition of gang work by introducing the single-shift system, should, in turn, be seen as part of a process of change that was reflected in new problems emerging at the site of production, as well as in new strike demands. At the time when workers 'still' defended their right to substitute one another under the single-shift system in the 1930s, managers noted a growing gap in skilled workers, as the number of new workers who could train themselves had fallen. By the 1940s, demands for pension schemes began to be raised during strikes, as old workers could not work in the mill anymore. The success or failure of managerial interventions into the organization of work, in other words, appeared through shifts in the ways in which workers appropriated work, and in their position within the mill's hierarchies.

Structures of supervision

The expansion of managerial control at the shop floor also implied that decisions to intervene in the process of production were increasingly concentrated in Bengal. In the late nineteenth century, managers' and overseers' tasks were focussed on overseeing the regular work of groups of workers and *sirdars*. With the expansion of managerial control under the single-shift system, tasks related to departmental supervision expanded, and the frontiers of managerial agency in decision-making expanded. A representative of the Duff company wrote in the 1930s:

> The Mill works much shorter hours now than in the past, but supervision is much more strict and a higher degree of this is looked for nowadays. In addition, the assistant must use much more tact and intelligence in the running of his department.[2]

Managing agents tried to enhance the ability of Scottish overseers to 'get in touch' with workers. In an attempt to improve the levels of communication between Scottish staff and Indian workers, departmental overseers received bonus payments, when they learned Hindi, or Bengali.[3]

The expansion of the tasks of Scottish supervisors sat uncomfortably with the organizational structure of the managing agency system. By effectively giving supervisors and managers more agency to intervene in the everyday rhythms of the mill, a growing number of decisions were tied to the judgement of people who were not in London or Dundee. A fracture, then, was visible within the system of managing agencies itself, as the decisions taken by managers in the colony gained new weight vis-à-vis those taken by managing agents in the metropole. Compounded by the political situation in the 1930s and the coming of independence, the coordination of managing agencies in the IJMA further served to shift the weight of industrial control to Bengal. By the 1950s, the IJMA had developed into an organization that was central in coordinating the industry's response to the changing situation in India.

Gender and family

The transformation of labour relations in the Bengal jute industry also allows us to broaden our perspective on the changing position of women workers. As historians have pointed out in different regional contexts, the employment of women in organized industry declined steeply in the final decades of colonial rule. Bengal was no exception. Women were increasingly marginalized at the shop floor, and this was most powerfully marked by an overall decline in the number of women workers employed, and by the reduction of their employment options to particularly low-skilled and low-paid positions.[4]

Managerial strategies, reflected in the changing organization of work in the early twentieth century, did not so much single out women workers as a group which needed to be re-arranged at the site of production. Rather, the position of women workers came into the purview of managerial concerns when the employment of family units declined in importance as a strategy.

In the first decades of the twentieth century, mills had recruited 'madrassi' workers, who tended to come to the jute belt with their families. The objective was to improve the stability of production, at a time when the older strategy of excess employment emerged as a problem. 'Madrassi' workers were mostly employed in the spinning mill, where the stability of production was a major source of managerial concern. They depended on a joint family income to sustain themselves. In addition, mills provided cheaper housing for 'madrassi' workers, in order to bind them more closely to the site of production. If workers chose to work elsewhere, then, they had to find new accommodation as well.

Another section of the mill, where women workers dominated employment, was in the hand-sewing department. This department belonged formally to the finishing department. However, workers in the hand sewing department were not deployed at machines, and their work was considered particularly unskilled. The deployment of women here was again linked to their position within families: women workers tended to bring children that were too young to work to the shop floor. At the machines of the spinning mill, this meant that women workers took recourse to practices of work substitution in order to look after their children in the course of the day. In the hand-sewing department, it meant in addition that young children could take over the work of their mothers in the course of excessively long working days. They thus turned into substitute workers, allowing their mothers to take a break (for instance in order to prepare food) by providing unpaid labour to the mill.[5]

The changing position of women in this period can be described in two steps. Firstly, the emerging internal labour market in the jute belt in the early twentieth century, which was marked by an expansion of sources of labour supply, as well as by the establishment of a dense industrial hinterland around Calcutta, meant that the *functionality* of employing families was already losing importance at that time. Secondly, the formal abolition of gang work meant that practices of work that necessitated 'informal' breaks to look after children, or to prepare meals, turned into an *obstacle* to managerial control. Children who were too young to work were banned from the workplace during the Great Depression, signalling the mills' claim over the continuous deployment of their mothers' labour power. However, given that women workers were still subjected to social demands to look after their children, this signal did not end the 'risk' of subversion implied in their employment. This, arguably, contributed to their declining importance in managerial strategies.

Despite an overall decrease in employment levels, jute mills continued to employ women workers under the single-shift system. Important sections of the workforce were relying on the joint family income earned in mill towns. In the 1930s, they mostly entered managerial reports in the context of strikes and labour conflicts. These reports present the militancy of male workers as directed against, among others, women workers, who were attacked during strikes. Descriptions of such incidents, however, give us a rather clear pattern that underlay such events: during conflicts started by 'madrassi' spinners, spinners left their workplace and moved to the preparing sections of the mill, where their wives and family members were employed, with the objective of bringing them out on strike as well. Spinners' actions, then, point us not so much to hierarchies created by the overall dominance of male workers in the jute belt. They point us, rather, to patriarchal family relations.[6] Managerial reports, then, delinked the activities of protesting workers from the social relations that went into the making of the workplace, in order to dismiss strike action as illegitimate.

Trying to make sense of such moments, it is necessary to reconnect them by re-establishing the workplace as a complex site.

Conflicts vs riots

Labour conflicts over the abolition of gang work in the jute industry often demonstrated remarkable levels of solidarity among wide sections of the workforce. The abolition of gang work, after all, affected workers' practices throughout the mill. In strikes in the 1920s and 1930s, we have seen that industrial action, which started over the dismissal of small groups of workers in specific departments, often drew the support of wider sections of the workforce. This tendency shaped workers' response to the introduction of the single-shift system in the 1920s and 1930s significantly, and indicated limits to managerial strategies over the re-organization of work in this period.

The changing organization of work, however, also led to conflicts between sections of the workforce – foremost between spinners and weavers. In the midst of rising communal tensions in Bengal in the 1930s, these conflicts attained an increasingly communalized quality. Conflicts that began life as a strike often turned into communal riots. We have seen this for instance with regard to a strike in the Titaghur Jute Mill in 1938, where spinners had started strike action in December 1938. The strike evolved into a communal riot between Hindu spinners and Muslim weavers within a matter of days, followed by the withdrawal of support by the BCMU. Compounded by the escalation of communal conflicts in the 1940s, the number of riots between Hindu spinners and Muslim weavers increased in the final years of colonial rule.

At the outset, workers' participation in communal riots in this period can be understood against the backdrop of rising of communal tensions in workers' neighbourhoods and in mill towns, as well as in the context of the provincial politics of the late 1930s. The latter meant that the new government of Bengal actively tried to create 'white' trade unions that addressed Muslim weavers, in order to counter the dominance of communist and revolutionary terrorist trade unionists among Hindu spinners.[7] These developments originated, strictly speaking, outside the workplace. Returning, then, to the organization of work and its transformations, we can identify some pointers that we have touched upon in the course of this study, that help us to approach the question of how the workplace itself contributed to these developments.

Firstly, the arrangement of the workplace implied a potential for tensions between workers in the spinning mill and the weaving factory. The production of a sufficient amount of yarn was a critical condition for sustaining work in the weaving department. Inadequate production of yarn was a recurring problem of the industry and had a variety of reasons, ranging from the uneven quality of the raw material to labour conflicts in the spinning mill. The result was a loss of income for workers in the weaving department, who were employed as piece-workers (unlike their counterparts in the spinning mill, who were paid per working day).[8]

The abolition of gang work added new tensions to this basic division. These acquired communal connotations in the 1930s. The regularization of the working day under the single-shift system implied that workers in the spinning mill and in the weaving factory now had the same hours of work. Muslim workers, further, had no formal recourse to practices of sharing work, in order to leave the site of production earlier during *Ramadan*. Given the priority placed on the position of regulating weavers in the mill, managers and managing agents changed hours of work during *Ramadan*, and started work half an hour earlier, in order to close their gates earlier as well. While workers seem to have accepted this procedure in the immediate aftermath of the change in shift systems, managers' reports indicate tensions over the annual change in hours of work emerging in the second half of the 1930s. The jute mills in Titagarh, for instance, had to interrupt the practice of changing hours of work during *Ramadan* in 1937, when Hindu spinners refused to come earlier to the mill on account of Muslim weavers.[9]

Changing hierarchies within the workforce, combined with new wage structures, may also have contributed to tensions between Hindu spinners and Muslim weavers. Under the multiple-shift system, 'madrassi' workers – who were mostly Hindus – had started to use their position in the spinning department in order to secure an increasing number of jobs in the sacking side of the weaving department. Workers in the better paid hessian-side, meanwhile, had nearly exclusively been Muslim. The sudden shift of wage levels between hessian and sacking weavers reversed the relation between both sides of the weaving department.[10] In the 1930s, 'madrassi' workers were not mentioned any more in weaving departments (on either side), but seem to have been pushed back to the spinning department. This development implied that the reversal in wage levels initialized a re-appropriation of both sides of the weaving department by Muslim weavers, and, in turn, contributed to the increase in conflicts between spinners and weavers, as well as between Hindus and Muslims. Workers' attempts to assert their position at the workplace came to be intertwined with religious identities.

Managerial strategies added another layer to this development. In order to persuade workers to remain in the mill compound, a number of mills installed new tea stalls and sweetmeat shops for Muslim and Hindu workers, further increasing the visibility of religious identities in the everyday rhythms of workers. In the midst of ongoing labour conflicts in the second half of the 1930s, managers and departmental overseers, meanwhile, sought to 'get in touch' with a workforce whose dynamics and tensions they barely understood. The mills of the Duff company employed a retired clerk from East Bengal as a liaison officer, in order to improve communications between managers and workers. The company also hoped to improve its relations with the new government of Bengal, as the new liaison officer claimed to be a good friend of Suhrawardy (which turned out to be a false claim). The liaison officer's first and only engagement with workers on behalf of the Duff company was in Titagarh in 1938, when tensions arose that would eventually lead to the strike-cum-riots in the same year. Managers noted later that he spoke only to Muslim workers on that occasion, and refused to speak with Hindu workers. This episode reflected difficulties faced by managers in comprehending and navigating the rapidly changing situation in the jute belt of the late 1930s.

Notes

Introduction

1 Marie Imandt was the daughter of Peter Imandt, an early communist and friend of Karl Marx. The Dundee Courier had sent her together with Bessie Maxwell on a tour around the world, in an attempt to increase their women readership. They, thus, reported from Italy and Egypt, China, Japan or the United States of America. On their tour they also came through India, reporting from various places – here with a special focus on the jute industry in Bengal. / Susan Keracher, ed., *Dundee's Two Intrepid Ladies. A Tour Round the World* (Dundee: Abertay Historical Society, 2012).

2 The Hastings Jute Mill ran, more precisely, twenty-two hours per day during five days of the week, and twelve hours on Saturday. / John Leng, *Letters from India and Ceylon, Including the Manchester of India, the Indian Dundee, and Calcutta Jute Mills. Reprinted from the Dundee Advertiser* (Dundee: John Leng & Co., 1895), p 64.

3 *Manchester Evening News*, 1 June 1894; *Dundee Courier*, 17 November 1894; *Dundee Courier*, 13 August 1895.

4 *Dundee Courier*, 19 July 1894.

5 Ibid.

6 See among others: Indian Factory Labour Commission, Volume II. Evidence 1908, p 23.

7 *Dundee Courier*, 19 July 1894.

8 Summarizing these claims, the 1890 Factory Commission reported: 'The Indian factory worker is, in general, incapable of prolonged and intense effort; he may work hard for a comparatively short period, but even in such cases the standard attained is much below what would be expected, in similar circumstances, in any European country.' / Report of the Commission on Indian Factories, 1891, p 20.

9 Letter from Hajer Noor Mahomed Jackeriah, Secretary, Indian Trades Association, National Archives of India to the Under-Secretary of the Government of Bengal, 31 December 1878, National Archives of India (= NAI): Home (Judicial), A, Nos. 9-94 and K.W., January 1880.

10 See, among others: Memorandum prepared by the Manufacturers of Bengal for submission to His Honour the Lieutenant-Governor, 7 February 1879, NAI: Home (Judicial), A, Nos. 9-94 and K.W., January 1880. / This and similar interpretations were usually combined with the assumption that the 'Indian'

workplace would develop, and eventually catch up with its European counterpart. In principle, these themes have been widely discussed. See, among others: Rajnarayan Chandavarkar, 'Industrialization in India before 1947: Conventional Approaches and Alternative Perspectives', *Modern Asian Studies*, Vol. 19, No. 3 (1985): pp 623–68; Prabhu Mohapatra, *Situating the Renewal. Reflections on Labour Studies in India*, Labour History Series, 2 (Delhi: V.V. Giri National Labour Institute, 1998); Willem Van Schendel, 'Stretching Labour Historiography. Pointers from South Asia', *International Review of Social History*, Vol. 51, Supplement S14 (December 2006): pp 229–61; Chitra Joshi, 'Histories of Indian Labour: Predicaments and Possibilities', *History Compass*, Vol. 6, No. 2 (March 2008): pp 439–54.

11 In the 1870s, when the multiple-shift system was being introduced, the hours of work in Bengal jute mills were restricted by the daily hours of sun light. Jute mills, accordingly, worked between twelve to fourteen hours per day. In the mid-1890s, hours of work were increased to fifteen per day. One major exception was the Hastings Jute Mill which worked twenty-two hours per day. In the 1920s, in contrast, mills applying a multiple-shift system worked about 13½ hours per day. / Anon., *Jute Mills in Bengal. Described by the Special Correspondent of the 'Dundee Advertiser' in Calcutta* (Dundee: John Leng & Co., 1880), pp 10f; Leng, *Letters from India and Ceylon*, p 64.

12 In the course of the boom of the 1890s, the Bengal jute industry had expanded and was responsible for the consumption of 50 per cent of the global supply of raw jute (which was exclusively grown in Bengal as well). / Amiya Kumar Bagchi, *Private Investment in India, 1900–1939*, Cambridge South Asian Studies 10 (Cambridge: Cambridge University Press, 1972), p 79.

13 Gordon T. Stewart, *Jute and Empire. The Calcutta Jute Wallahs and the Landscapes of Empire* (Manchester: Manchester University Press, 1998), p 4.

14 Report of the Commission on Indian Factories, 1891, p 21.

15 Ibid.

16 As Ghosh put it: 'Propelled by colonial needs, industrialization in India, thus could be said to have resulted in a curious hybridization, the appearance of an atypical type.' / Parimal Ghosh, 'A History of a Colonial Working Class, India 1850–1946', in *Economic History of India from Eighteenth to Twentieth Century*, ed. Binai Bhushan Chaudhury (New Delhi: Coronet Books, 2005), pp 526f.

17 See, among others: Resolutions on the Factories Bill, 1878, NAI: Home (Judicial), A, Nos. 9-94 and K.W., January 1880; Report of the Commission on Indian Factories, 1891, Indian Factory Labour Commission, Volume II. Evidence 1908.

18 Letter from H.W.I. Wood, Secretary to the Bengal Chamber of Commerce to the Under-Secretary of the Government of Bengal, 22 February 1879, NAI: Home (Judicial), A, Nos. 9-94 and K.W., January 1880.

19 Report of the Commission on Indian Factories, 1891, p 14.

20 It may be pointed out here, that the result of this reading was also, that the opposition between the spheres of the 'pre-modern' and of the 'modern', which appeared as a contradiction when considering practices of work, was diverted into a type of opposition, in which 'only one genuine opposite exists'. We are, in other words, not dealing with a proper binary here anymore. Frederic Jameson aptly called this figure 'sun- and moon words', elaborating that in such cases 'one term turns out to be more defective than the other one, or in other words in which that second term radiates a kind of essentiality or plenitude which cannot be ascribed to its alleged opposite [...]; and the situation seems to be one in which the moon-term is the opposite of its other, while that other in its autonomy is the opposite of nothing.' / Frederic Jameson, *Valences of the Dialectic* (London: Verso, 2009), p 19.

21 See, among others: Report of the Commission on Indian Factories, 1891, p 14; Report of the Textile Factories Labour Committee, 1907, p 16; Indian Factory Labour Commission, Volume I. Report, 1908, pp 24f; R.K. Das, *Factory Labour in India* (Berlin: Walter de Gruyter, 1923), pp 30ff.

22 Report of the Commission on Indian Factories, 1891, p 20; Leng, *Letters from India and Ceylon*, pp 57f; Indian Factory Labour Commission, Volume II. Evidence 1908, p 253.

23 Report of the Commission on Indian Factories, 1891, p 18.

24 *Dundee Courier*, 19 July 1894.

25 Royal Commission on Labour (Whitley Commission), Volume 5, Part 1. Bengal (Excluding Coalfields and the Dooars), 1931. / This has also been noticed by other historians; see Chitra Joshi, *Labour History and the Question of Culture* (Delhi: V.V. Giri National Labour Institute, 2003).

26 *TOI*, 27 June 1934.

27 Rajnarayan Chandavarkar, 'The Decline and Fall of the Jobber System in the Bombay Cotton Textile Industry, 1870–1955', *Modern Asian Studies*, Vol. 42, No. 1 (2008): p 118.

28 For an overview over the historiography, see Jan Breman, 'At Work in the Informal Economy of India. A Perspective from the Bottom up', in *The Worlds of Indian Industrial Labour. Contributions to Indian Sociology*, ed. Jonathan Parry, Jan Breman, and Karin Kapadia, Occasional Studies 9 (New Delhi: Sage Publications, 1999), pp 1–44.

29 Morris David Morris, *The Emergence of an Industrial Labor Force in India. A Study of the Bombay Cotton Mills, 1854–1947* (Berkeley / Los Angeles: University of California Press, 1965), p 92.

30 Ibid., p 96.

31 Dipesh Chakrabarty, *Rethinking Working-Class History. Bengal, 1890–1940* (Princeton, NJ: Princeton University Press, 1989); Dipesh Chakrabarty, *Provincializing Europe: Postcolonial Thought and Historical Difference*, Princeton Studies in Culture/power/history (Princeton, NJ: Princeton University Press, 2000).

32   Chakrabarty, *Rethinking Working-Class History*, p 69.
33   For an overview over the critiques of Chakrabarty's work, see Sumit Sarkar, 'The Return of Labour to South-Asian History', *Historical Materialism*, Vol. 12, No. 3 (2004): pp 285–313.
34   Ravi Ahuja, 'Erkenntnisdruck Und Denkbarrieren. Eine Kritische Bestandsaufnahme Der Indischen Arbeitsgeschichte', *Soziale Welt*, Vol. 15, Sonderband (2004): pp 354f; Subho Basu, *Does Class Matter. Colonial Capital and Workers' Resistance in Bengal, 1890–1937* (New Delhi: Oxford University Press, 2004), pp 12f.
35   Chakrabarty, *Rethinking Working-Class History*, p 69.
36   Chakrabarty, *Provincializing Europe*, p 92.
37   Or, as Chakrabarty put it: 'In the eyes of the employers, then, certain aspects of working-class conditions gained priority over others and received more attention. And the knowledge produced as a result of this attention bore an unmistakable stamp of the employers' concern about the supply of labor.' / Chakrabarty, *Rethinking Working-Class History*, p 93.
38   Ibid., p 95.
39   See, among others: Rajnarayan Chandavarkar, *The Origins of Industrial Capitalism in India: Business Strategies and the Working Classes in Bombay, 1900–1940*, Cambridge South Asian Studies 51 (Cambridge / New York: Cambridge University Press, 1994); Rajnarayan Chandavarkar, *History, Culture and the Indian City* (Cambridge: Cambridge University Press, 2009); Jan Breman, *The Making and Unmaking of an Industrial Working Class. Sliding Down the Labour Hierarchy in Ahmedabad, India* (Oxford: Oxford University Press, 2004).
40   See, among others: Dilip Simeon, *The Politics of Labour under Late Capitalism. Workers, Unions and the State in Chota Nagpur 1928–1939* (New Delhi: Manohar, 1995); P. P. Mohapatra, '"Restoring the Family": Wife Murders and the Making of a Sexual Contract for Indian Immigrant Labour in the British Caribbean Colonies, 1860–1920', *Studies in History*, Vol. 11, No. 2 (1 August 1995): pp 227–60; J. Nair, 'Dangerous Labour: Crime, Work and Punishment in Kolar Gold Fields, 1890–1946', *Studies in History*, Vol. 13, No. 1 (1 February 1997): 19–61; Samita Sen, *Women and Labour in Late Colonial India: The Bengal Jute Industry*, Cambridge Studies in Indian History and Society 3 (Cambridge / New York: Cambridge University Press, 1999); Nandini Gooptu, *The Politics of the Urban Poor in Early Twentieth Century India* (Cambridge: Cambridge University Press, 2001); Chitra Joshi, 'On "De-Industrialization" and the Crisis of Male Identities', *International Review of Social History*, Vol. 47, No. 10 (November 2002): pp 159–75.
41   See, among others: Subho Basu, 'The Paradox of Peasant Worker: Re-Conceptualizing Workers' Politics in Bengal 1890–1939', *Modern Asian Studies*, Vol. 42, No. 1 (January 2008): pp 47–74; Arjan De Haan, *Unsettled Settlers. Migrant*

Workers and Industrial Capitalism in Calcutta (Rotterdam, 1994); Amal Das, *Urban Politics in an Industrial Area. Aspects of Municipal and Labour Politics in Howrah, West Bengal, 1850–1928* (Calcutta: Chandan Das, 1994).

42 Basu, *Does Class Matter*, pp 59ff.

43 Ibid. / see also: Basu, 'The Paradox of Peasant Worker', pp 47–74.

44 Chitra Joshi, *Lost Worlds. Indian Labour and Its Forgotten Histories* (London: Anthem Press, 2005), pp 143ff.

45 This impression is, to some degree, also apparent in economic histories. Industries like the jute industry were organized by managing agencies, which were part of a system of joint stock companies. Matters like sale of products, purchase of raw materials or the employment of staff – managers, salesmen, engineers and departmental overseers – were decided by managing agents and shareholders. The question of how the power relations between both were settled has been debated widely. For a brief overview of these debates, see: Chikayoshi Nomura, 'The Origin of the Controlling Power of Managing Agents over Modern Business Enterprises in Colonial India', *Indian Economic & Social History Review*, Vol. 51, No. 1 (January 2001): pp 95–132.

46 Wallace et al.

47 FN – changing labour supply.

Chapter 1.1

1 D.R. Wallace, *The Romance of Jute. A Short History of the Calcutta Jute Mill Industry 1855–1909* (Calcutta: W. Thacker & Co., 1909). / That the title of Wallace's book reflected the author's view on the history (and present) of the jute industry has been pointed out often. Janet Kelman, for instance, noted: 'The name at once suggests the point of view of the writer, and, it may be, brings a smile to the lips of those who are looking for something that might bear the name of romance in the lives of the workers whom the industry employs.' / Janet Harvey Kelman, *Labour in India. A Study of the Conditions of Indian Women in Modern Industry* (London: George Allan & Unwin Ltd., 1924), p 77. / See also: Stewart, *Jute and Empire*, p 147.

2 Indian Factory Labour Commission, Volume I, Report, 1908, pp 9f.

3 Indian Factory Labour Commission, Volume II. Evidence, 1908, p 252.

4 Ibid.

5 Contrast, for instance, the descriptions of the multiple-shift system in the notes of the Commission on Indian Factories in 1891, with those from the Indian Factory Labour Commission in 1908. / Report of the Commission on Indian Factories, 1891; Indian Factory Labour Commission, Volume II. Evidence 1908.

6   Indian Factory Labour Commission, Volume II. Evidence 1908.

7   Wallace, *The Romance of Jute*, [1909].

8   D.R. Wallace, *The Romance of Jute. A Short History of the Calcutta Jute Mill Industry. 1855–1927*, Second Edition (London: W. Thacker & Co., 1928).

9   Ibid.

10   Annual Report on the Working of the Indian Factories Act in Bengal and Assam, 1922–31.

11   Ibid.; Report of the Indian Jute Mills' Association, 1931.

12   Deepika Basu, *The Working Class in Bengal. Formative Years* (Calcutta / New Delhi: K. P. Bagchi and Company, 1993), pp 8f. / Sunil Kumar Sen, *Working Class Movements in India. 1885–1975* (Oxford: Oxford University Press, 1994), p 13; Ghosh, 'A History of a Colonial Working Class', p 662.

13   Ranajit Das Gupta, *Labour and Working Class in Eastern India. Studies in Colonial History* (Calcutta / New Delhi: K.P. Bagchi, 1994), p 340.

14   Ibid.; Sen, *Women and Labour in Late Colonial India*, pp 94f; Basu, *Does Class Matter*, pp 23f.

15   Urs Olbrecht, Bengalens Fluch Und Segen. Die Indische Juteindustrie in Spät- Und Nachkolonialer Zeit (Stuttgart: Steiner, 2000), pp 43ff.

16   Arjan De Haan, 'Migrant Labour in Calcutta Jute Mills. Class, Instability and Control', in *Dalit Movements and the Meanings of Labour*, ed. Peter Robb (Oxford: Oxford University Press, 1993); de Haan, *Unsettled Settlers*; Basu, *Does Class Matter*.

17   The term 'split shift' system was, in fact, one of the oldest names of the multiple-shift system. The term 'double shift' system, while in principle already used in the 1870s, emerged as a dominant term towards the end of the nineteenth century, and in the first years of the twentieth century. Terms such as multiple-shift system, or 'overlapping shift' system, in contrast, seem to have come up only in the first decades of the twentieth century. In the 1930s, when discussing the industry's past, terms such as 'double shift' system were not used anymore, leaving only the terms multiple-shift system, as well as 'overlapping shift' system. / For the usage of the term 'split shift' system, see among others: Anon., *Jute Mills in Bengal*; for 'double shift' system, see: Report of the Commission on Indian Factories, 1891; for multiple-shift system and 'overlapping shift' system, see: Annual Report on the Working of the Indian Factories Act, 1913; Managers' reports to the directors. Samnuggur North Mill, 1931, Dundee University Archives, MS 86/V/8/2/1; Managers' reports to the directors. Samnuggur South (No's. I and II Mills), 1931, Dundee University Archives, MS 86/V/8/2/2.

18   The problem of excess-employment, thereby, is often treated in an ambiguous way. While authors agree that jute mills tended to employ more workers than necessary, this problem is usually understood against the backdrop of the *badli*-system (or the

employment of daily workers), which mill managers accordingly regulated flexibly, according to *ad hoc* demands. / See, among others: Samita Sen, 'Gendering Class. Wives and Workers in the Jute Industrial Economy', in *A Case for Labour History. The Jute Industry in Eastern India*, ed. Arjan De Haan and Samita Sen (Calcutta: K.P. Bagchi, 1999), 196–245, pp 201ff; Arjan De Haan, 'The Badli System in Industrial Labour Recruitment. Managers' and Workers' Strategies in Calcutta's Jute Industry', *Contributions to Indian Sociology*, Vol. 33, Nos. 1–2 (1999): pp 271–301.

19 Chakrabarty, *Rethinking Working-Class History*, p 101. / Arjan de Haan treats the multiple-shift system in a principally similar way. The complexity of the system meant accordingly that effective labour control was difficult to establish. This created an instability in the everyday rhythms of work, which indicated the importance of migration patterns, as well as the 'fluidity of the "proletariat" and the existence of "alternative" forms of employment'. Yet, as we shall see in more detail later, the abolition of the multiple-shift system, too, seemed to indicate that workers were essentially 'unsettled settlers'. The changes in the form of work-organization at the site of production, then, accounted for the stability of other important features of the everyday rhythms of workers. / de Haan, 'Migrant Labour in Calcutta Jute Mills', p 211.

20 Tanima Ghosh, 'Income and Productivity in the Jute Industry across the 1947 Divide', in *A Case for Labour History. The Jute Industry in Eastern India*, ed. Arjan de Haan and Samita Sen (Calcutta: K.P. Bagchi, 1999), pp 56ff.

Chapter 1.2

1 Wallace, *The Romance of Jute*, [1928], pp 23ff.
2 Anon., *Jute Mills in Bengal*, pp 2f.
3 Ibid., p 3.
4 S. Waterhouse, Report on the Culture of Jute and the Importance of the Industry, Department of Agriculture Special Report, United States of America, Washington, 1883, p 12. / For new packaging materials made from jute goods, see: Chiranjiv Lall Mohindra, *Die Indische Juteindustrie Und Ihre Entwicklung*, Band 20, Volkswirtschaftliche Studien (Berlin: Emil Ebering, 1928), pp 15ff; R.J. Morris, *Relative Merits of Cotton and Jute Cement Sacks*, ed. Government of the United States of America, Technologic Papers of the Bureau of Standards, 1925.
5 Wallace, *The Romance of Jute*, [1928], p 53.
6 Report on the Transport & Marketing of Jute in India, Second Report, 1941, p 270. / The expression 'crude system of relieving-squads' is from an industrial report which was published in 1941. The introduction of the system in this time, however, was also mentioned in Wallaces's account, and in the descriptions which other

managers or managing agents gave. / Indian Factory Labour Commission, Volume
II. Evidence 1908, p 244; Wallace, *The Romance of Jute*, [1928], p 40.

7   Wallace, *The Romance of Jute*, [1928], p 40.

8   Indian Factory Labour Commission, Volume II. Evidence 1908, p 252.

9   In the late 1870s, managers and managing agents stated that 30 per cent of their
     workforce was employed in excess, whereas from the 1890s the number was said
     to be 25 per cent. Managers and managing agents gave no reason for the different
     statements on the degree of excess-employment. Given that the multiple-shift
     system came to be understood to be applied for the entire mill, it is possible that
     the incorporation of the 'rest' of the workforce into this calculation accounted for
     the change. Processes of rationalization appear only to a limited degree a possible
     source of this change. The speeding up of machines was mentioned already by
     Marie Imandt, while managers and managing agents improved the process of
     production in the spinning mill throughout the years. Such measures, however,
     did not change the fact that in the spinning mill degree in excess-employment
     was established in relation to the requirements of the process of production at
     any given moment (even if the requirements of production had been reduced due
     to measures of rationalization). / For the degree of excess-employment given by
     managers and managing agents in the late 1870s, see: Letter from D. Cochrance,
     Esq., India Jute Company, Limited, 18 February 1879, NAI: Home (Judicial), A,
     Nos. 9-94 and K.W., January 1880; for the degree in excess-employment after the
     1890s, see: Indian Factory Labour Commission, Volume II. Evidence 1908, p 250;
     for processes of rationalization, see: *Dundee Courier*, 23 July 1894; Wallace, *The
     Romance of Jute*, [1928], p 43; Director's Minute Books, Champdany Company,
     Glasgow University Archives, 1912–21.

10   This list could in principle be further extended, as the mills of the IJMA reduced
     their hours of work to an average of forty-two in 1931, due to the impacts of the
     Great Depression. This was, however, just one year before the final abolition of
     the multiple-shift system, and these measures, rather, made the limits of reducing
     hours of work with a fixed degree of excess employment visible, as we shall see in
     more details in later chapters. / Report on the Transport & Marketing of Jute in
     India, Second Report, 1941, p 270; Wallace, *The Romance of Jute*, [1928].

11   Dagmar Curjel, Enquiry into the conditions of Employment of women before
     and after child-birth, in Bengal Industries, 1923. / Royal Commission on Labour
     (Whitley Commission), Volume 5, Part 1. Bengal (Excluding Coalfields and the
     Dooars), 1931, pp 140ff. / The Hastings Jute Mill, where some historians saw the
     'origin' of the multiple-shift system, should be mentioned as another exception at
     this point, as the mill increased the number of sets deployed per day, in order to
     increase the hours of work to twenty-two per day. This procedure remained a short-
     lived experiment and was not applied by other mills. / Leng, *Letters from India and
     Ceylon*, p 67.

12 *Dundee Courier*, 26 July 1894.

13 As we shall see in more detail in later chapters, the structural features of the multiple-shift system implied crucial limitations for managerial control of workers. Leaving aside the complex arrangement of relays and sets, workers' presence at the site of production was controlled *sirdars*, rendering it difficult for managers to establish, who had actually been working and when. It should, thus, be added at this point that the five women gave the interview in the presence of the wife of the mills' manager. Their response concerning their hours of work, thus, can be safely assumed to refer to the formal rhythms of shifts, rather than (potential) informal arrangements among themselves. / Ibid.

14 *Dundee Courier*, 23 July 1894.

15 D. Cochrance, Esq., India Jute Company, Limited, 18 February 1879, NAI: Home (Judicial), A, Nos. 9-94 and K.W., January 1880.

16 See among others: Anon., *Jute Mills in Bengal*, pp 10f; Wallace, *The Romance of Jute*, [1928], p 40; Report on the Transport & Marketing of Jute in India, Second Report, 1941, p 270.

17 Indian Factory Labour Commission, Volume I, Report, 1908, p 11.

18 Ibid.

19 D. Cochrance, Esq., India Jute Company, Limited, 18 February 1879, NAI: Home (Judicial), A, Nos. 9-94 and K.W., January 1880, NAI: Home (Judicial), A, Nos. 9-94 and K.W., January 1880; Report of the Commission on Indian Factories, 1891; Indian Factory Labour Commission, Volume II. Evidence 1908.

20 Leng, *Letters from India and Ceylon*, p 64.

21 Shyam Rungta, 'Bowreah Cotton and Fort Gloster Jute Mills, 1872–1900', *Indian Economic & Social History Review*, Vol. 22, No. 2 (1985): pp 109–37; Das Gupta, *Labour and Working Class in Eastern India*, pp 56ff.

22 *TOI*, 13 February 1930.

23 Royal Commission on Labour (Whitley Commission), Volume 5, Part 1. Bengal (Excluding Coalfields and the Dooars), 1931, pp 118f.

24 W.A. Graham Clark, *Linen, Jute, and Hemp Industries in the United Kingdom. With Notes on the Growing and Manufacture of Jute in India*, ed. Department of Commerce [United States of America], vol. Special Agents Series No. 74 (Washington: Government Printing Office, 1913), pp 95ff.

25 Wallace, *The Romance of Jute*, [1928], pp 15f.

26 William Legatt, *The Theory and Practice of Jute Spinning. Being a Complete Description of the Machines Used in the Preparation and Spinning of Jute Yarns* (London: Simkin, 1921); Herbert R. Carter, *The Spinning and Twisting of Long Vegetable Fibres (Flax, Hemp, Jute, Tow & Ramie)* (London: Charles Griffin and Company Limited, 1904); Herbert R. Carter, *Jute and Its Manufacture* (London: Bale & Danielson, 1921); E. Nonnenmacher, *Die Jute. Pflanze und Fasergewinnung. Handel und Wirtschaft. Spinnerei* (Berlin / Heidelberg: Springer Verlag, 1930).

27 The lower quality of oil was still reflected in the limited range of products, which were produced by Bengal jute mills. The Borneo Mill, after several test trials, managed to produce cloths and bags, which were of a particularly coarse sacking-quality, with a fairly limited number of textures. They were, further, not standardized in wage or size. Improvements in the process of producing yarn were at the heart of the boom of the 1870s, as this enabled Bengal jute mills for the first time to produce standardized goods, and, thus, to export their goods beyond India and Burma. The boom of the 1890s was marked by another break-through in the production of jute goods, as Bengal jute mills managed to improve the production of hessian-products, leading, subsequently, to the expansion of this line of production. / On the development of the jute industry in Bengal, see: Wallace, *The Romance of Jute*, [1909], pp 17ff; on the usage of whale oil in Dundee, see: Clark, *Linen, Jute, and Hemp Industries in the United Kingdom*, p 108; Dennis Chapman, 'The Establishment of the Jute Industry. A Problem of Location Theory?', *The Review of Economic Studies*, Vol. 6, No. 1 (October 1938): p 34.

28 See among others: *TOI*, 17 August 1906; for the strike in the Hastings Jute Mill, see: *TOI*, 9 June 1911.

29 A. Crabbe, Esq., Manager, Champdany Jute Mills, 3 January 1879, NAI: Home (Judicial), A, Nos. 9-94 and K.W., January 1880.

30 Chakrabarty, *Rethinking Working-Class History*, pp 14ff.

31 For the Baranagore Jute Mill, see: Mary Carpenter, *Six Months in India*, Vol. I (London: Longmans, Green, and Co., 1868), p 248; for the Samnuggur Jute Mill, see: *TOI*, 29 July 1876.

32 W.W. Hunter, *The Imperial Gazetteer of India*, Vol. II. Bengal to Cutwa (London: Trübner & Co., 1881), p 32.

33 Leng, *Letters from India and Ceylon*, pp 76ff.

34 Anon., *Jute Mills in Bengal*, p 10.

35 Carpenter, *Six Months in India*, pp 248f.

36 Leng, *Letters from India and Ceylon*, 1895, pp 72ff.

37 The owners of the Hastings Jute Mill, after having increased their daily hours to twenty-two hours per day, in fact, claimed that the reason for this increase was the problem of labour supply. They, accordingly, received a 'rumour that another enterprising Glasgow firm contemplated putting up a large Mill close to Hastings, whereupon the proprietors of the later thought they might as well find employment for all the hands available in the neighbourhood'. / Ibid., p 78.

38 E.A. Bradbury, Esq., C.S., 15 April 1879, NAI: Home (Judicial), A, Nos. 9-94 and K.W., January 1880.

39 The Victoria Jute Mill was, more precisely, to be opened up on the river bank just opposite to the Samnuggur Jute Mill. The Victoria Jute Company, in either way, did not survive for long, and the Victoria Jute Mill was eventually taken over by the Duff Company, who also owned the Samnuggur Jute Mill. / Wallace, *The Romance of Jute*, [1928], p 46.

40 Both of these mills, by the way, went on a single-shift system in the late 1870s, just as the Seebpore Jute Mill, which was not far from the Howrah Mills. / Anon., *Jute Mills in Bengal*, p 11.

41 Ibid., pp 27f.

42 Another good example of a mill, which had been placed in a particularly difficult location, was the Champdany Jute Mill: 'They are about one mile from the railway station, and about 19 miles from Calcutta. As regards therefore their proximity and means of communication with Calcutta, the Champdany Mills are not inconveniently chosen. But the mistake has been made of locating the mill in a spot where labour was not readily obtainable, and much difficulty has been now and again experienced in getting hands; so much so that on one or two occasions, when sickness has been prevalent, much of the machinery has been standing in consequence.' However, also later observers, such as John Leng, or Dagmar Curjel, reported about similar problems. / Ibid., p 45.

43 Take, for instance, the location of the Samnuggur Jute Mill: 'The mill is very fairly supplied with labour, but the situation is unhealthy, and much fever prevails there during the rainy season. The wind blowing over an unhealthy tract of forest or jungle before it reaches the mill, it certainly is not the most desirable spot in a sanitary point of view upon which to have located a Jute mill.' / Ibid., p 43.

44 For the early years of the industry, Ranajit Das Gupta also pointed to the so called 'Burdwan' or 'Hugli' fever as a reason for diseases and tendencies to labour shortages. This fever spread in the second half of the nineteenth century in western and central Bengal. / Das Gupta, *Labour and Working Class in Eastern India*, p 64.

45 Annual Report on the Working of the Indian Factories Act for Bengal and Assam, 1930.

46 Annual Report on the Working of the Indian Factories Act for Bengal and Assam, 1932. / Indicating that this problem continued to constitute an important source of instability of labour supply in the years to come, the inspector of factories reported in 1934: 'As in previous years, malaria and intestinal diseases are still the chief cause of absenteeism, and it appears from the returns that in the factories which have suffered most are those situated in jungle areas or are surrounded by or adjacent to unoccupied land.' / Annual Report on the Working of the Indian Factories Act for Bengal and Assam, 1934.

47 Managers' Reports to the Directors, Victoria Jute Company Limited, Dundee University Archives, MS 86/V/8/14/6.

Chapter 1.3

1 Given that until the 1870s Dundee had mainly produced sacking-cloths, this was, in fact, the second time that the mills on the Hugli entered into a period of growth, by taking over markets, which had hitherto been served by Dundee. It is

no surprise, then, that this second boom raised serious concerns in Dundee, which were expressed in complaints about the long hours of work in the Hastings Jute Mill, and in Bengal jute mills in general – and which, in turn, were an important reason for the specific interest in the Bengal jute industry among journalists like Marie Imandt, whom we have encountered already. / Stewart, *Jute and Empire*, pp 38ff; Anthony Cox, *Empire, Industry and Class. The Imperial Nexus of Jute, 1840–1940* (London / New York: Routledge, 2013), pp 14ff.

2   Wallace, *The Romance of Jute*, [1909], p 58.

3   Indian Factory Labour Commission, Volume II. Evidence 1908, p 276.

4   Report on the Transport & Marketing of Jute in India, Second Report, 1941, p 270.

5   The problem of recruiting a sufficient number of skilled weavers, and to keep them in the mill, was already an important concern in the first jute mills in Bengal. / Rungta, 'Bowreah Cotton and Fort Gloster Jute Mills', pp 118f.

6   Beamers comprised the only section of the workforce deployed in a similar manner since the mid-1890s. In contrast to the weaving department, however, the beaming department belonged, technically speaking, to the spinning mill. It seems that the association of the beaming department with the spinning mill changed under the extended multiple-shift system. After the abolition of the multiple-shift system, beamers were 'returned' to the spinning mill. The movement of beamers between different modes of regulation in Bengal jute mill had a variety of other consequences, which concerned for instance the mode of wage payments. / For an overview over the departments which belonged to the spinning mill, see: Carter, *The Spinning and Twisting of Long Vegetable Fibres*; Legatt, *The Theory and Practice of Jute Spinning*: Nonnenmacher, Die Jute; for the association of the beaming department with the weaving factory under the extended multiple-shift system, see: Indian Factory Labour Commission, Volume II. Evidence 1908, p 23; for the formal transfer of the beaming department from the weaving factory to the spinning mill in the course of the abolition of the multiple-shift system, see: Managers' reports to the directors. Titaghur No. I Mill, 1931, Dundee University Archives, MS 86/V/8/2/3.

7   Ranajit Das Gupta, in fact, argued that the year 1895 was a crucial turning point in view to the composition of the workforce in Bengal jute mills. Until 1894, at least 50 per cent of the workforce was still Bengali workers, whereas this proportion changed rapidly from 1895. The expansion of railway lines in this period also contributed to this development, as has been pointed out. / Das Gupta, *Labour and Working Class in Eastern India*, p 9; de Haan, 'Migrant Labourers in Eastern India. A Structuration Approach', p 153.

8   de Haan, *Unsettled Settlers*, pp 55ff.

9   Das Gupta, *Labour and Working Class in Eastern India. Studies in Colonial History*, pp 31f.

10 On the strikes in this period, see: Dipesh Chakrabarty, 'Communal Riots and Labour. Bengal's Jute Mill-Hands in the 1890s', *Past & Present*, Vol. 91, No. 91 (May 1981): pp 140–69; Das Gupta, Das Gupta, *Labour and Working Class in Eastern India.*, pp 314ff; Subho Basu, 'Strikes and "Communal" Riots in Calcutta in the 1890s: Industrial Workers, Bhadralok Nationalist Leadership and the Colonial State', *Modern Asian Studies*, Vol. 32, No. 4 (1998): pp 949–83.

11 Report of the Commission on Indian Factories, 1891, Indian Factory Labour Commission, Volume II. Evidence 1908, pp 278f; Royal Commission on Labour (Whitley Commission), Volume 5, Part 1. Bengal (Excluding Coalfields and the Dooars), 1931, pp 144ff.

12 Rungta, 'Bowreah Cotton and Fort Gloster Jute Mills', p 116.

13 Royal Commission on Labour (Whitley Commission), Volume 5, Part 1. Bengal (Excluding Coalfields and the Dooars), 1931, p 119.

14 For the statement of the mill representative, see: Indian Factory Labour Commission, Volume II. Evidence 1908, p 254, for the weaving *sirdars'* statement, see: ibid., p 271.

15 In principle, this development can also be seen as signalling a shift in the way different sources of income could be combined in the jute belt. The fact that 'up-country' migrants often relied on small plots of land in order to sustain their social reproduction did not differentiate them from their Bengali colleagues. Yet, the cycles, in which both sections of the workforce returned to their rural homes, in order to sustain both sources of income, clearly differed. Whereas the former's cycles may be described as annual ones, Bengali workers returned to their homes on a daily basis. The development of a regularized working day in jute mills, however, implied that one part of this pattern – the work in mills – was more tightly bound to the space of the mill town. Another group, which came to play an increasingly important role in this period, were 'madrassi' workers. These workers often came with their families to the jute belt, where men, women and children worked. While following a rather different pattern of migration, then, the principal problem is still similar, as the joint income of the family could be combined better with the life in jute towns.

16 Leng, *Letters from India and Ceylon*, p 49.

17 Curjel, Enquiry into the conditions of Employment of women before and after childbirth, in Bengal Industries, Government of Bengal, 1923.

18 After the Titaghur Jute Mills in 1884, the Khardah Jute Mills opened up in 1895, the Standard Jute Mill in 1896, the Kinnison Jute Mills in 1897, the Kelvin Jute Mill in 1908 and the Empire Jute Mill in 1913. / see: Wallace, *The Romance of Jute*, [1928], pp 96f.

19 Review of the Industrial Position and Prospects in Bengal in 1908. With Special Reference to the Industrial Survey of 1890. Part II of Special Report, Calcutta, 1908, pp 2f.

20 Also Dr Curjel, who visited the jute belt in the early 1920s, reported that for instance in the Upper Hooghly Jute Mill, particularly many women were employed, whose husbands were working in the nearby Lilloah railway workshops. / Ibid.

21 Royal Commission on Labour (Whitley Commission), Volume 11 – Supplementary, 1931, p 359.

22 Ibid., pp 361f.

23 The calendar department was the first section of the finishing-departments in Bengal jute mills. / For the structure of weaving-factory, see: Clark, *Linen, Jute, and Hemp Industries in the United Kingdom*, p 107; E. Pfuhl, *Die Jute Und Ihre Verarbeitung Auf Grund Wissenschaftlicher Untersuchungen Und Praktischer Erfahrungen*, Zweiter Teil. Das Erzeugen der Gewebe, Herstellung der Säcke (Berlin / Heidelberg: Springer Verlag, 1891).

24 Royal Commission on Labour (Whitley Commission), Volume 11 – Supplementary, 1931, p 363.

25 Ibid., p 363.

26 Ibid., p 364.

27 Titaghur Jute Factory Co. Ltd., Reports of the directors, balance sheet, working account and profit and loss account, 1884–1976, Dundee University Archives, MS86/III/5/5.

28 In 1903, for instance, the directors reported: 'Labour has continued to be fairly satisfactory throughout the year, still proving the benefit of a mill being located in a good labour centre.' / Ibid.

29 He stated, in fact, that since 1914 'labour has never been scarce'. This insisted that the 'end of labour shortage' had come about due to wage increases, which jute mills implemented at the outset of the First World War. The members of the Whitley commission, in contrast, insisted that since 1912 there had not been any labour scarcities, as in this year the new amendments to the Indian Factories Act had been implemented. This resulted in a reduction of hours of work (at least in single-shift mills). The attempt of putting a precise date to the 'end of labour shortage', then, certainly reflected a conflict over the question, if capital or the state could claim the credit for this development. For workers, in either way, the combination of (potentially) reduced hours of work and wage increases was presumably both important. / Royal Commission on Labour (Whitley Commission), Volume 5, Part 1. Bengal (Excluding Coalfields and the Dooars), 1931, p 162.

30 Wallace, *The Romance of Jute*, [1928], p 130. / Indicative of the concentration of jute workers in different parts of the jute belt is also the number of mills per district. In 1906–7, thirty-three jute mills were counted in 24-Parganas, nine in Howrah and six in Hooghly. In terms of workers, this meant by the late 1929 that 205,093 jute workers were employed in mills in 24-Parganas, 77,353 in Howrah and 57,219 in Hooghly. / For the number of mills per district, see: Review of the Industrial

Position and Prospects in Bengal in 1908. With Special Reference to the Industrial Survey of 1890. Part II of Special Report, Calcutta, 1908, p 3; for number of workers per district, see: Annual Report on the Working of the Indian Factories Act in Bengal and Assam, 1929.

31 Interview, Dundee, 15 February 2012.

32 Annual Report of the Committee of the Indian Jute Mills' Association, 1929.

33 Budge-Budge riot case. Text of Judgements of original and appellate courts, 1914, India Office Library and Records (= IOR): L/PJ/6/1314, File 2124:21.

34 Footnote on general strike of 1929 – riots.

35 Rioting between Hindus and Moslems at Kankinara, Bengal, police report, report of the District Magistrate, 24-Parganas, 1924, IOR: L/PJ/6/1889, File 3669.

36 Ibid.

37 Reports from managers of managing agents, such as the Duff group of mills, the Bird Company as well as the Champdany Company deal with the topic of how to improve the production in the spinning mill regularly. In the latter case, for instance, the directors of the Champdany Company complained bitterly that one of their mills, the Wellington Jute Mill, had only managed to use 37 per cent of low-quality jute in their production, while the company's other mill, the Champdany Jute Mill, had managed to work with 61 per cent of cheaper raw-materials. / For the different amount of low-quality jute in the mills of the Champdany Company, see: Director's Minute Books, Champdany Company, Glasgow University Archives, 1912–21; for reports on the matter from other managing agencies, see: Managers' Reports to the Directors, Samnuggur Company Limited. South Mill, Nos. 1 & 2 Mills, 1936, Dundee University Archives, MS 86/V/8/6/3; Managers' Reports to the Directors, Titaghur Jute Company Limited. No. 1 Mill, 1932, Dundee University Archives, MS 86/V/8/3/3; Centre of South Asian Studies (University of Cambridge), Benthall Papers.

38 Nibaran Chandra Chaudhury, *Jute in Bengal*, Second Edition (Calcutta: W. Newmann & Co., 1921), p 183.

39 Managers' Reports to the Directors, Samnuggur Company Limited. South Mill, Nos. 1 & 2 Mills, 1936, Dundee University Archives, MS 86/V/8/6/3.

40 Managers' Reports to the Directors, Titaghur Jute Company Limited. No. 1 Mill, 1932, Dundee University Archives, MS 86/V/8/3/3.

41 Managers' Reports to the Directors, Samnuggur Company Limited. South Mill, Nos. 1 & 2 Mills, 1936, Dundee University Archives, MS 86/V/8/6/3.

42 Curjel, Enquiry into the conditions of Employment of women before and after child-birth, in Bengal Industries, 1923.

43 Royal Commission on Labour (Whitley Commission), Volume 5, Part 1. Bengal (Excluding Coalfields and the Dooars), 1931, p 143. / This problem was also noticed by other companies: 'The Multiple Shift System permits of drawing of

labour from long distances. This labour comes in as a relieving squad and does not start work, as a rule, before 8 A.M. and finishes at 6 P.M. with intervals or rest. This squad also comprises those who attend to House-hold duties – cooking, purchasing, bazaar, etc. In Single-shift Mills those workers who come from a distance would have to get up at 4 A.M. and would not return Home before 8 P.M. at the earliest.' / Annual Report of the Committee of the Indian Jute Mills' Association, 1927, p 100.

44 The proportion of single and multiple-shift mills was, more precisely, measured on the basis of the number of looms installed in each mill, which meant in early 1931 that 51 per cent of the looms were running in multiple-shift mills. / Report of the working of the Indian Factories Act in Bengal and Assam, 1931.

45 The Birla Jute Mill had, however, never abolished the multiple-shift system, as the mill had already applied a single-shift system when it opened its gates in 1922. / Annual Report of the Committee of the Indian Jute Mills' Association, 1926, p 237.

Chapter 1.4

1   Report on the Transport & Marketing of Jute in India, Second Report, 1941, p 270.
2   Ibid.
3   The testimonies of those managers, whose mills had not applied a multiple-shift system, for instance, generally describe the rhythm of work in their mills as being based on the deployment of a 'single-sets'. / Report of the Commission on Indian Factories, 1891, Indian Factory Labour Commission, Volume II. Evidence 1908.
4   Annual Report on the working of the Indian Factories Act in Bengal and Assam, 1912.
5   Anon., *Jute Mills in Bengal*, p 4.
6   Wallace, *The Romance of Jute*, [1909], p 28.
7   Bagchi, *Private Investment in India, 1900–1939*, p 8.
8   Anon., *Jute Mills in Bengal*, p 11.
9   Ibid., p 48.
10 Ibid.
11 Maria Misra, *Business, Race & Politics in British India* (Oxford: Oxford University Press, 1999), p 83.
12 Anon., *Jute Mills in Bengal*, p 18.
13 Letter from E. Benthall, 31 December 1928, Centre of South Asian Studies (University of Cambridge), Benthall Papers, Box 1, File 2.
14 Omkar Goswami highlighted the importance of a restrictive policy for the IJMA very well when stating that 'most industry associations tend to mention a few altruistic platitudes in their charters and leave the more real restrictive objectives

unsaid. IJMA was more forthright in this respect. From its inception and throughout the colonial era IJMA never fought shy of the fact that it was primarily a restrictive body'. / Omkar Goswami, 'Collaboration and Conflict: European and Indian Capitalists and The Jute Economy of Bengal, 1919–39', *Indian Economic & Social History Review*, Vol. 19, No. 2 (1982): pp 141–79, p 144.

15 Report on the Transport & Marketing of Jute in India, Second Report, 1941, p 270.

16 Indian Factory Labour Commission, Volume II. Evidence 1908, pp 252ff.

17 Report on the Transport & Marketing of Jute in India, Second Report, 1941, p 270.

18 Annual Report of the Committee of the Indian Jute Mills' Association, 1922.

19 Bishnupriya Gupta, 'Why Did Collusion Fail? The Indian Jute Industry in the Inter-War Years', *Business History*, Vol. 47, No. 4 (October 2005): p 538f.

20 The first Indian-owned jute mills which were opened in the 1920s – such as the Birla Jute Mill – became members, or associated members, of the IJMA. As associated members, they negotiated special terms, which allowed them to work longer hours than the older mills. / B.D. Bhatter and L. Nemenyi, *The Jute Crisis* (Calcutta: Thacker, Spink & Co., 1936), p 9f.

21 Gupta, 'Why Did Collusion Fail', p 538.

22 Omkar Goswami, *Industry, Trade, and Peasant Society: The Jute Economy of Eastern India, 1900-1947* (Delhi , New York: Oxford University Press, 1991), p 100ff; Stewart, *Jute and Empire*, pp 96ff.

23 Gupta, 'Why Did Collusion Fail', p 537.

24 Annual Report of the Committee of the Indian Jute Mills' Association, 1927.

25 Royal Commission on Labour (Whitley Commission), Volume 5, Part 1. Bengal (Excluding Coalfields and the Dooars), 1931, p 162.

26 Annual Report of the Committee of the Indian Jute Mills' Association, 1928.

27 Letter from E. Benthall to P. Thomas, 15 November 1928, Centre of South Asian Studies (University of Cambridge), Benthall Papers, Box 1, File 2.

28 Ibid.; *TOI*, 11 April 1930.

29 Annual Report of the Committee of the Indian Jute Mills' Association, 1931; Bhatter and Nemenyi, *The Jute Crisis*, pp 13f.

Chapter 1.5

1 Annual Report on the Working of the Indian Factories Act, 1914.

2 In 1922, once again, five mills, which abolished the multiple-shift system, but not the same ones which had done so before. In 1923, two more mills followed, and in 1924, four mills introduced the single-shift system. / Annual Report on the Working of the Indian Factories Act, 1922–4.

3 Annual Report on the Working of the Indian Factories Act, 1926–9.

4   While being framed in more general terms by the opposition between single-shift system and multiple-shift system, measures of rationalization were, in principle, not contradictory to the organization of work in sets or gangs. This was already reflected in the structural features of the multiple-shift system itself. The extension of the multiple-shift system to weaving departments in jute mills was, as we have seen, the result of concerns with controlling weavers at the site of production. Speeding up of machinery, too, was possible under the system. The organization of work in gangs, while not indicating the impossibility of rationalization measures, rather, seems to have posed a limit in this period, thus raising the single-shift system to the status of the condition of *further* rationalization measures.

5   Annual Report of the Committee of the Indian Jute Mills' Association, 1927. / The principal increase in measures of rationalization in this period has generally been acknowledged. See, among others: Das Gupta, *Labour and Working Class in Eastern India*, p 446; Das, *Urban Politics in an Industrial Area*, p 141.

6   The 'entire' workforce, however, should be specified here as workers engaged in the process of production. Other sections of the workforce which jute mills employed at various points – such as *mistries*, *durwans*, sweepers, boats-men, carpenters and carrying 'coolies' – were not part of the multiple-shift system; nor were they part of the single-shift system for that matter. For more details, see: Chapter 2.

7   Report of the Commission on Indian Factories, 1891, Indian Factory Labour Commission, Volume II. Evidence 1908, pp 278f; Royal Commission on Labour (Whitley Commission), Volume 5, Part 1. Bengal (Excluding Coalfields and the Dooars), 1931, pp 144ff.

8   For strikes in Bombay in the late nineteenth and early twentieth centuries, see among others: Morris, *The Emergence of an Industrial Labor Force in India*, p 179; Prashant Kidambi, 'Contestation and Conflict. Workers' Resistance and the "Labour Problem" in the Bombay Cotton Mills, C. 1898–1919', in Labour Matters, ed. Marcel van Der Linden and Prabhu Mohapatra (New Delhi: Tulika Books, 2009), pp 106–27; Sarkar, Aditya, *Trouble at the Mill. Factory Law and the Emergence of the Labour Question in Late Nineteenth-Century Bombay* (Oxford: Oxford University Press, 2018).

9   Report of the Textile Factories Labour Committee, 1906, p 17.

10 Indian Factory Labour Commission, Volume I, Report, 1908, p 6.

11 Ibid., pp 9f.

12 Bulletins of Indian Industries, No. 37: Indian Factory Legislation: A Historical Survey, 1926, IOR: V/25/600/98.

13 Annual Report on the working of the Indian Factories Act in Bengal, 1907, p 3.

14 Indian Factory Labour Commission, Volume I. Report 1908.; Indian Factory Labour Commission, Volume II. Evidence 1908.

15 Indian Factory Labour Commission, Volume I, Report, 1908, pp 33ff.

16 Ibid., pp 36f.

17 Bulletins of Indian Industries, No. 37: Indian Factory Legislation: A Historical Survey, 1926, Indian Factory Legislation: A Historical Survey, 1926, IOR: V/25/600/98.

18 Report of the Commission on Indian Factories, 1890. / Report of the Textile Factory Labour Committee, 1906.

19 Report of the Commission on Indian Factories, 1890, p 9.

20 Indian Factory Labour Commission, Volume I, Report, 1908, p 69.

21 Bulletins of Indian Industries, No. 37: Indian Factory Legislation: A Historical Survey, 1926, IOR: V/25/600/98; Annual Report on the Working of the Indian Factories Act for Bengal and Assam, 1912.

22 Letter from the Government of India, Department of Revenue, Agriculture and Commerce, 4 November 1878, NAI: Home (Judicial), A, Nos. 9-94 and K.W., January 1880.

23 Report of the Working of the Indian Factories Act in Bengal and Assam, 1928. / Or, as the Inspector of Factories put it two years earlier: 'The enforcement of the provisions of the [Indian Factories] Act regarding hours of labour entails the registration of all persons employed and, on account of the numbers involved, the multiple-shifts and the material on which the manager must rely for recording, this cannot be accomplished with that promptitude to enable the Inspector to ascertain compliance with the law or otherwise. Managers have given ample proof of their diligence to comply with the Act with respect to the labour they control, but they plead their helplessness to remedy matters under the multiple-shift system.' / Report of the Working of the Indian Factories Act in Bengal and Assam, 1926.

24 Annual Report of the Committee of the Indian Jute Mills' Association, 1930.

25 Royal Commission on Labour (Whitley Commission), Volume 5, Part 1. Bengal (Excluding Coalfields and the Dooars), 1931, p 193.

26 European overseers even filed a formal petition which was a unique procedure in the Bengal jute industry. / Proposed legislation to secure the closing of jute mills early on Saturdays, NAI: Home Department (Judicial), Proceedings, Nos. 6–11, June 1899.

27 Report of the Commission on Indian Factories, 1891, Indian Factory Labour Commission, Volume II. Evidence 1908, p 274.

28 Report of the Commission on Indian Factories, 1891, Indian Factory Labour Commission, Volume II. Evidence 1908, p 252.

29 Bulletins of Indian Industries, No. 31: Women's Labour in Bengal Industries, 1923, IOR: V/25/600/98.

30 This was most striking during the visit of the Whitley Commission. Considering, however, the internal reports by managers of the Duff company after the abolition of the multiple-shift system in their mills just two years later, it seems certain

that all managers of the company approved of the change enthusiastically. /
Royal Commission on Labour (Whitley Commission), Volume 5, Part 1. Bengal
(Excluding Coalfields and the Dooars), 1931, pp 140ff; Managers' reports to the
directors. Samnuggur North Mill, Dundee University Archives, MS 86/V/8/1/1;
Managers' reports to the directors. Samnuggur South (No's. I and II Mills), Dundee
University Archives, MS 86/V/8/1/2; Managers' reports to the directors. Titaghur
No. I Mill, Dundee University Archives, MS 86/V/8/1/3; Managers' reports to the
directors. Titaghur No. II Mill, Dundee University Archives, MS 86/V/8/1/4.

31 Nearly all of the statements against the multiple-shift system, which the members
of the Whitley Commission presented, were, ironically, the ones which Dagmar
Curjel had summarized after her visit to the jute belt in 1922, when managers had
been rather willing to talk about the problems of the system. / Bulletins of Indian
Industries, No. 31: Women's Labour in Bengal Industries, 1923, IOR: V/25/600/98.

32 Alexander Murray was, further, a very influential member of the Indian jute
industry. He worked for some of the largest managing agencies on the river, holding
also prominent positions in the IJMA and in the Bengal Chamber of Commerce.
In 1919, he had been the representative for capital in the delegation from colonial
India to the Washington Conference. / Annual Report of the Committee of the
Bengal Chamber of Commerce, 1919.

33 Government of India, Report of the Royal Commission on Labour in India
(Whitley Commission), Evidence, Vol. V, Part 1, 1931, pp 163f.

34 Alexander R. Murray, 'The Jute Industry', *Journal of the Royal Society of Arts*,
Vol. 82, No. 4263 (August 1934): 977–96, pp 977f. / This was in principle a concern
which Murray had already expressed in 1922, when Dagmar Curjel visited the jute
belt. Murray was at that point the manager of the Clive Jute Mill, and he informed
Curjel: 'He thought a number of maangers [!] did not realise that labour conditions
were altering in India, (whether they wished it or not). The best thing was to try
and see that there was increased efficiency along with the better conditions of
labour.' / Curjel, Enquiry into the conditions of Employment of women before and
after child-birth, in Bengal Industries, 1923.

Part 2

1 Royal Commission on Labour (Whitley Commission), Volume 5, Part 1. Bengal
(Excluding Coalfields and the Dooars), 1931, p 143; Curjel, Enquiry into the
conditions of Employment of women before and after child-birth, in Bengal
Industries, 1923.

2 Sime raised this complaint in 1926 at the annual meeting of the Indian Jute Mills'
Association. He had been one of the representatives of the industry who raised the

issue of the long working day in jute mills since 1908: 'It is one thing to work ten hours during an ordinary day, and quite another and altogether different thing for a man, and especially for a woman, to have to get up at 4 to 4.30 A.M. on a cold, foggy morning, and tramp (as many of them have to do) a considerable distance to the mill, or, when on the last shift, only to be able to reach their homes at 9.30 to 10 P.M., after which their cooking and preparation of the evening meal has to take place.' / Annual Report of the Committee of the Indian Jute Mills' Association, 1926, p 67.

Chapter 2.1

1   Oscar Ornati, 'Wages in India', *Economic Development and Cultural Change*, Vol. 3, No. 3 (April 1955): p 253. / Ranajit Das Gupta estimated the number of weavers in an average jute mill to being ever higher, stating that 'perhaps no less than one-fourth, of the labour force' was constituted by weavers. / Das Gupta, *Labour and Working Class in Eastern India*, p 340.

2   Ghosh, 'A History of A Colonial Working Class', pp 662ff.; Samita Sen, 'Gendering Class. Wives and Workers in the Jute Industrial Economy', pp 200ff.

3   Indian Factory Labour Commission, Volume II. Evidence 1908, p 271.

4   Managers and managing agents hardly discussed the structure of wages in jute mills in the mid-1890s. With regard to the shift to the bonus-system for weavers and *sirdars* in this period, however, one crucial indication in this respect came from Marie Imandt. In addition to the principal modalities of wage payments, the calculation of bonus payments for weavers changed from the amount of jute cloth produced (measured in yards) to the number of 'cuts' produced. A 'cut', in contrast, referred to the finished piece that was cut out of the cloth produced in the weaving department. Each 'cut' necessarily left behind a varying amount of wastage. Sections of cloth that were too damaged to be turned into a cut, too, turned into waste. The change, then, functioned to increase managerial control over the quality of production of weavers. / *Dundee Courier*, 23 July 1894; Olbrecht, *Bengalens Fluch Und Segen*, pp 69f.

5   Ghosh, 'A History of a Colonial Working Class', pp 662ff.

6   A principal problem was that excess-employment as a fixed category was only mentioned in regard to relay-sets. In the weaving factory, however, this number often remained vague. Contributing to the problem of establishing the number of 'extra' workers in this side of the mill were the conflicts over the abolition of the multiple-shift system, in the course of which supporters of the multiple-shift system tended to overestimate the number of workers that would be dismissed, if they were forced to introduce the single-shift system instead. While, then, managers and

managing agents claimed that the abolition of the multiple-shift system would lead to the dismissal of 25 per cent of the workforce, they also stated that those mills which had abolished the system had only dismissed about 10 per cent or less of their workforce. A considerable part of this difference was presumably due to the lower degree of 'extra' workers in the weaving factory in the late 1920s. Between the early 1900s and the early 1930s, the number of workers employed per loom was, meanwhile, falling due to measures of rationalization. / For contemporary statements on the number of 'extra' workers in jute mill, see: Indian Factory Labour Commission, Volume II. Evidence 1908, Indian Factory Labour Commission, Volume II. Evidence 1908; Royal Commission on Labour (Whitley Commission), Volume 5, Part 1. Bengal (Excluding Coalfields and the Dooars), 1931, p 142; Annual Report of the Committee of the Indian Jute Mills' Association, 1927; for the number of jute workers and looms in Bengal, see: Goswami, *Industry, Trade, and Peasant Society*, p 98.

7 Ibid.

8 Report on the Transport & Marketing of Jute in India, Second Report, 1941, p 20.

9 See Appendix 1 for an overview over the formal arrangements of work under multiple-shift system.

10 Report of the Commission on Indian Factories, 1891, Indian Factory Labour Commission, Volume II. Evidence 1908, p 269.

11 Working on two looms at a time was common in Dundee. Here, always one worker would be employed per two looms. This is probably also the reason why looms in jute mills were always constructed as a set of two. The machines were, after all, produced in Dundee, and not in Bengal. One main reason, why workers in Scotland managed to work on two looms for longer periods than workers in India, is, arguably, a difference in the kind of materials used in Bengal jute mills. In mills in Dundee, more precisely, whale oil was used in order to soften the jute. In Bengal, in contrast, mills used from the beginning mixtures of mineral oils, which did not soften the jute as effectively. The result of this difference was that the yarn, which weavers had to work with in Bengal, was of a coarser quality, and broke much easier, than in Dundee. / Clark, *Linen, Jute, and Hemp Industries in the United Kingdom*; Chapman, 'The Establishment of the Jute Industry. A Problem of Location Theory?' p 34.

12 Short supply of yarn was a problem, which was regularly raised in strikes by weavers, as we have seen in the previous chapter. Similarly, conflicts at the site of production indicate that the break-down of machinery could lead to serious tensions. For instance in 1913, a line *sirdar* had to be hospitalized after a conflict with a worker, which had come up 'because the machine at which he was working was out of order'. The constant expansion of the industry, which usually took the form of simply adding new looms to existing ones, constituted for another set of problems. On older looms, as the manager of the Titagarh Jute Mill specified in

1926, workers could hardly reach their weekly bonus payments in the first place, and these looms were, not surprisingly, often standing idle in the summer months, when some 'up-country' weavers returned to their homes temporarily. / Report of an assault against a European Assistant named Mr Henderson of the Telinipara Victoria Jute Mill, National Archives of India, Home Department/Police/1913/ Nos.196-Part B; Titaghur Jute Factory Co. Ltd., Reports of the directors, balance sheet, working account and profit and loss account, 1884–1976. Dundee University Archive, MS86/III/5/5.

13 After the abolition of the multiple-shift system – and after the discontinuance of the deployment of sets – *sirdars'* authority was, surely enough, abolished again, resulting in the impression of an ongoing decline of the *sirdar*, which bears similarities to the development which Chandavarkar noticed for Bombay / Chandavarkar, 'The Decline and Fall of the Jobber System in the Bombay Cotton Textile Industry', pp 117–210.

14 Another crucial pillar of *sirdars'* authority at the site of production points us to problems of fines, to which we will come in the following section.

15 Basu, *Does Class Matter*, pp 52f.

16 Whitley Committee Records, IOR: Mss Eur F303/120-130.

17 Indian Factory Labour Commission, Volume II. Evidence 1908, p 257; Royal Commission on Labour (Whitley Commission), Volume 5, Part 1. Bengal (Excluding Coalfields and the Dooars), 1931, p 166.

18 Royal Commission on Labour (Whitley Commission), Evidence Volume XI – Supplementary Part II, 1931, p 363.

19 Ibid., p 359.

20 Among jute workers in Dundee, hearing problem and deafness due to the noises of machines was a problem, which has been studied. Given that the machines were principally the same in Bengal, it can be assumed that this volume in Bengal jute mills was similar. / Thomas Oliver and Stephen Bonner, *Dangerous Trades. History of Health and Safety at Work*, Volume 2 (London: Continuum, 2004), p 660.

21 Interview, Dundee, 15 February 2012.

22 The importance of gestures may, indeed, not even have been established at the workplace at all, as gestures played an important role in Indian society, as David Arnold has shown in the context of the nineteenth century. / David Arnold, 'Salutation and Subversion. Gestual Politics in Nineteenth Century India', *Past & Present*, Vol. 203, No. 4 (2009): pp 191–212.

23 In larger mills, one overseer worked in the hessian and one in the sacking-side of the department. / Managers' reports to the directors. Samnuggur North Mill, 1931, Dundee University Archives, MS 86/V/8/2/1.

24 Attempts to improve the language skills of European overseers seem to have only increased in the period, in which the multiple-shift system was being abolished. While the IJMA, then, declared in 1931 that European overseers and mill assistants

'should acquire such a knowledge of the language as would enable them to make themselves clearly understood to the mixed crowd of uneducated workers with whom they come in contact curing the course of their duties', the first book for learning Hindustani for jute mills was published in 1932. / Annual Report of the Committee of the Indian Jute Mills' Association, 1931; Mohiuddin Ahmad, *Essentials of Colloquial Hindustani for Jute Mills & Workshops*, Third edition (Calcutta, 1947).

25 Indian Factory Labour Commission, Volume II. Evidence 1908, p 278.

Chapter 2.2

1   The reason, why the manager of the Titagarh Mills gave in this (rare and) more precise description of the problem of wage-payments, was, arguably, the conflict between capital and state at the time of the interview. The members of the Whitley-Commission pushed for the abolition of the multiple-shift system openly, arguing that the application of this system of shifts was essentially opposed to workers' interests. The manager of the Titagarh Mill, in an attempt to defend the multiple-shift system, appears to have tried to highlight how favourable the application of the multiple-shift system was for workers, thus pointing to the apparently 'generous' mode of wage-payment. / Royal Commission on Labour (Whitley Commission), Volume 5, Part 1. Bengal (Excluding Coalfields and the Dooars), 1931, p 76.

2   Gupta, *Labour and Working Class in Eastern India. Studies in Colonial History*, p 440.

3   Managers' Reports to the Directors, Titaghur Jute Company Limited. No. 2 Mill, 1930, Dundee University Archives, MS 86/V/8/1/3; Managers' Reports to the Directors, Victoria Jute Company Limited, 1931, Dundee University Archives, MS 86/V/8/2/4.

4   Managers' Reports to the Directors, Samnuggur Company Limited. North Mill, 1930, Dundee University Archives, MS 86/V/8/1/1.

5   Indian Factory Labour Commission, Volume II. Evidence 1908, pp 263ff; Managers' Reports to the Directors, Titaghur Jute Company Limited. No. 2 Mill, 1930, Dundee University Archives, MS 86/V/8/1/3; Managers' Reports to the Directors, Victoria Jute Company Limited, 1931, Dundee University Archives, MS 86/V/8/2/4; Managers' Reports to the Directors, Samnuggur Company Limited. North Mill, 1930, Dundee University Archives, MS 86/V/8/1/1.

6   Report of the Industrial Commission 1916–18, 1919, p 11. / Royal Commission on Labour (Whitley Commission), Volume 5, Part 1. Bengal (Excluding Coalfields and the Dooars), 1931, p 122.

7   Managers' Reports to the Directors, Titaghur Jute Company Limited. No. 2 Mill, 1930, Dundee University Archives, MS 86/V/8/1/3; Managers' Reports to the

Directors, Samnuggur Company Limited. North Mill, 1930, Dundee University Archives, MS 86/V/8/1/1.

8   Letter from P. Thomas to E. Benthall, 15 May 1937, Centre of South Asian Studies (University of Cambridge), Benthall Papers, Box 9; Managers' reports to the directors. Titaghur No. II Mill, 1934, Dundee University Archives, MS 86/V/8/14/5; Managers' reports to the directors. Samnuggur South (No's. I and II Mills), 1944, Dundee University Archives, MS 86/V/8/15/3; Managers' reports to the directors. Samnuggur North Mill, 1944 Dundee University Archives, MS 86/V/8/15/2.

9   Managers' reports to the directors. Titaghur No. I Mill, 1942, Dundee University Archives, MS 86/V/8/13/4.

10   Royal Commission on Labour (Whitley Commission), Volume 5, Part 1. Bengal (Excluding Coalfields and the Dooars), 1931, p 176.

Chapter 2.3

1   Letter from D. Cochrance, Esq., India Jute Company, Limited, 18 February 1879, NAI: Home (Judicial), A, Nos. 9-94 and K.W., January 1880; Report of the Commission on Indian Factories, 1891; Report of the Textile Factories Labour Committee, 1906; Indian Factory Labour Commission, Volume II. Evidence 1908; Royal Commission on Labour (Whitley Commission), Volume 5, Part 1. Bengal (Excluding Coalfields and the Dooars), 1931.

2   As we have seen in Chapter 1, the degree of excess-employment changed slightly between the late nineteenth century and the early twentieth century, dropping from 30 per cent to 20 per cent in the accounts of managers and managing agents. In the 1920s, a number of mills had, further, reduced the number of relay-sets to two, thus reducing the overall degree of excess-employment to 10 per cent of the requirements of the process of production. A discrepancy between the formally determined degree of excess-employment and the actual degree of excess-employment in the everyday rhythms of work would in principle have been the same in these cases, as the number of 'extra' workers did not affect the central problem of an apparent lack of managerial control at the point of ascertaining the attendance of workers.

3   Bulletins of Indian Industries, No. 37: Indian Factory Legislation: A Historical Survey, 1926, IOR: V/25/600/98.

4   Annual Report on the Working of the Indian Factories Act in Bengal, 1903.

5   Royal Commission on Labour (Whitley Commission), Volume 5, Part 1. Bengal (Excluding Coalfields and the Dooars), 1931, p 78.

6   The 'extra' person was according to the wage-structure employed on the feeder end of the machine. As a group, then, the three women attended to both sides of

the machine, while the wages were calculated in a way that two members of this set received lower wages than the third. The tension between the employment of individual workers and sets which was reflected in this structure, in turn, implied wage reductions for the set, as the mill arranged the positions of each member of the set accordingly. / Ibid.

7   Kelman, *Labour in India*, p 82f.

8   Ibid.; Curjel, Enquiry into the conditions of Employment of women before and after child-birth, in Bengal Industries, 1923; Annual Report on the Working of the Indian Factories Act, 1931.

9   Royal Commission on Labour (Whitley Commission), Volume 5, Part 1. Bengal (Excluding Coalfields and the Dooars), 1931, p 145.

10 Ibid.

11 Kelman, *Labour in India*, pp 252f.

12 Royal Commission on Labour (Whitley Commission), Volume 5, Part 1. Bengal (Excluding Coalfields and the Dooars), 1931, p 119.

13 Ibid.

14 Legatt, *The Theory and Practice of Jute Spinning*. / This problem was, in principle, also apparent in view to other machines in the spinning mill. Jute softeners in batching departments, for instance, consisted of '31 to 100 pairs of spirally fluted rollers', hinging on the type and age of the machine. / Carter, *Jute and Its Manufacture*, p 21.

15 Curjel, Enquiry into the conditions of Employment of women before and after child-birth, in Bengal Industries, 1923.

16 I am indebted to Dr Klaus-Peter Wittemann for pointing out the implications of the different structural features of spinning-frames and weaving-looms in regard to matters of labour control.

17 Indian Factory Labour Commission, Volume II. Evidence 1908, p 264.

18 Ibid.

19 In 1929, however, the Secretary to the Government of Bengal reported that Bengali workers in jute mills that 'in the case of jute mills situated in the south of Calcutta, where the four-day rule is in operation, the workers leave the mills on the last working day of the week, return to their own homes, do their home work and return to the mill again on Monday morning'. During the week, then, Bengali workers rented rooms in mill-towns. They did, thus, not return to their homes during lunch-break. The option to do this was common under the multiple-shift system, because the machinery ran four days per week. Under the single-shift system, mills worked five days per week, which, accordingly, rendered this practice uneconomical. In either way, the practice of renting rooms in mill-towns seems to have contributed another feature, which complicated the implications of the modalities of work under the system of relay-sets further. / Memorandum on Labour Conditions in Bengal for the use of the Royal Commission on Indian Labour, IOR: V/26/670/29.

20 Ghosh, 'A History of a Colonial Working Class', pp 662ff.

21 Royal Commission on Labour (Whitley Commission), Volume 5, Part 1. Bengal (Excluding Coalfields and the Dooars), 1931, p 145.

22 Ibid.

23 John F. Sime and Thomas Johnston, *Exploitation in India. By* Thomas Johnston, M.P., and John F. Sime (Secretary Dundee and District Union of Jute and Flax Workers). Issued by the Dundee Jute and Flax Workers' Union (Dundee: Jute and Flax Workers' Union, 1926), pp 9f; Royal Commission on Labour (Whitley Commission), Volume 1, Report, 1931, p 4.

24 Indian Factory Labour Commission, Volume II. Evidence 1908, p 264.

25 Royal Commission on Labour (Whitley Commission), Volume 5, Part 1. Bengal (Excluding Coalfields and the Dooars), 1931, p 78.

26 Recurring epidemics probably still led to temporary labour shortages. Other factors might have further complicated the relationship between workers and *sirdars* at this point. It has, for instance, been pointed out that relations among *sirdars* were rather competitive. Matters like the size of the work gang, which individual *sirdars* commanded, played an important role at this point. The resulting question, however, of how conflicts among *sirdars* and the relations within work gangs related to one another in different moments of the history of the jute industry, can only be flagged as a problem at this point. / Basu, *Does Class Matter*, pp 52f.

Chapter 2.4

1   The first Jute Tribunal Award in 1948 counted about 250 possible occupations in Bengal jute mills. / Award in the Matter of Industrial Disputes in the Jute Textile Industry in West Bengal between the Employers of 89 Specified Jute Mills and Their Workmen, 1948, pp 135ff.

2   Ibid.; Managers' reports to the directors. Titaghur No. I Mill, 1931, Dundee University Archives, MS 86/V/8/2/3.

3   Managers' reports to the directors. Angus Jute Works, 1950, Dundee University Archives, MS 86/V/8/21/1.

4   Royal Commission on Labour (Whitley Commission), Volume 11 – Supplementary, 1931, pp 356f.

5   Annual Report on the Working of the Indian Factories Act, 1928–1930.

6   Interview, Dundee, 6 March 2013; Interview, Dundee, 7 June 2013.

7   Royal Commission on Labour (Whitley Commission), Volume 5, Part 1. Bengal (Excluding Coalfields and the Dooars), 1931; Royal Commission on Labour (Whitley Commission), Volume 11 – Supplementary, 1931.

8   *TOI*, 20 February 1911.

9   Indian Factory Labour Commission, Volume II. Evidence 1908, p 271.

254 *Notes*

10 Ibid., p 264.

11 Disputes over sharing work at machines constituted a crucial field of conflicts in the aftermath of the abolition of the multiple-shift system, as we shall see in more detail below.

Part 3

1 Annual Report of the Committee of the Indian Jute Mills' Association, 1930.

2 Criminal prosecutions of certain Europeans for fatal assaults upon Indians: The Gouripur Jute Mill case, IOR: L/PJ/6/1919.

3 Ibid.

4 There were, in fact, two medical reports. Whereas the first report stated that the death of Jagnarain Singh had been the result of kicks which he received from J. Spence, the second report suggested that Jagnarain Singh could have already fractured his skull, and received the wound several days ago. Further, he might not have noticed this wound, only experiencing a headache. The encounter with Spence, in this reading, would only have caused Singh's death by intensifying the wound. The conclusion of this second report was, not surprisingly, that Spence was not to blame for the death of Jagnarain Singh. / Ibid.

5 Ibid.

6 *TOI*, 9 April 1926.

7 Calcutta Riots, 1924, IOR: L/PO/6/24.

8 *TOI*, 9 April 1926.

9 *TOI*, 10 June 1926.

10 Manju Chattopadhyay, 'Santosh Kumari Devi. A Pioneering Labour Leader', *Social Scientist*, Vol. 12, No. 1 (January 1984): pp 62–73; Das Gupta, *Labour and Working Class in Eastern India*, pp 406ff.

11 Criminal prosecutions of certain Europeans for fatal assaults upon Indians: The Gouripur Jute Mill case, IOR: L/PJ/6/1919.

12 See Appendix 2.

13 *TOI*, 20 April 1926; *TOI*, 25 May 1926.

14 *TOI*, 21 June 1926.

15 *TOI*, 12 November 1926.

16 See Appendix II.

17 Annual Report on the Working of the Indian Factories Act, 1926.

18 During the interview of the Whitley Commission with representatives of the IJMA, G.D. Birla made the prevalence of this interpretation very clear, while interrogating R.B. Laird, the head of the IJMA. Birla was an additional member of the Commission during the interviews in Bengal, and asked Laird if the IJMA

had taken 'the trouble of consulting the workers' about whether they preferred a multiple or a single-shift system. Laird, who supported the multiple-shift system, pointed to the recurring strikes against the single-shift system in order to answer this question. Birla, however, insisted further, asking: 'You will agree with me that the workers generally being under the thumb of the *sardars* cannot express their free opinion unless you take special care to consult only the workers, excluding the *sardars*?' Laird, stumbling over his own ideological assumptions at this point, saw himself forced to admit that strikes were merely an indicator of the opinions of *sirdars*, and not of workers' view on the matter. / Royal Commission on Labour (Whitley Commission), Volume 5, Part 1. Bengal (Excluding Coalfields and the Dooars), 1931, pp 156f.

19 Annual Report on the Working of the Indian Factories Act, 1926–8.

20 Ibid.

21 Riot at Fort Gloster Jute Mills, Bauriah, 1928, IOR: L/PJ/6/1963, File 2796.

22 Report of the working of the Indian Factories Act in Bengal and Assam, 1912.

23 Royal Commission on Labour (Whitley Commission), Volume 5, Part 1. Bengal (Excluding Coalfields and the Dooars), 1931, p 76. / Statements on the impacts of dismissals given by supporters or opponents of the multiple-shift system were certainly part of the escalating conflicts over the matter, which we have considered in Chapter 1. In Titaghur, for instance, as it would turn out in 1931 'only' 10,000 workers were dismissed, when the five mills in the municipality of Tithaghur changed shifts. / Managers' reports to the directors. Titaghur No. II Mill, 1931, Dundee University Archives, MS 86/V/8/2/4.

24 de Haan, *Unsettled Settlers;* Ghosh, 'A History of a Colonial Working Class'; Sen, *Women and Labour in Late Colonial India.* / Subho Basu can be seen to have followed a principally similar line of arguments. He stated that the IJMA had abolished the multiple-shift system in 1922, and reintroduced it in 1926. This, accordingly, led to the 'dislocation of labour', and, thus, contributed to the wave of strikes in this year. / Basu, *Does Class Matter*, pp 23ff.

25 Amal Das makes this assumption quite clear, explaining that, under the multiple-shift system, three shifts of workers had been employed in the course of the day. This was because mills worked continuously, and he added 'but under the present single-shift system, the machine was totally stopped during noon. So the third batch of workers who replaced the previous batch under the shift system during interval was dismissed from service'. This, then, also increased the workload, without managers having to introduce other measures of rationalization at all. / Amal Das, 'Jute Mill Strike of 1928. A Case Study', *Economic and Political Weekly*, Vol. 20, No. 4 (January 1985): pp 27–33, p 27. / See also: Das Gupta, *Labour and Working Class in Eastern India*, p 441.

26 Das, *Urban Politics in an Industrial Area*, p 158; Chakrabarty, *Rethinking Working-Class History. Bengal*, p 119.

27   Ranajit Das Gupta, *Material Conditions and Behavioural Aspects of Calcutta Working Class, 1875–1899*, Centre for Studies in Social Sciences, Occasional Paper, No. 20 (Calcutta, 1979): pp 30ff.
28   Dipesh Chakrabarty, 'On Deifying and Defying Authority. Managers and Workers in the Jute Mills of Bengal circa 1890–1940', *Past & Present*, No. 100 (August 1983): pp 127f.

Chapter 3.1

1   Annual Report of the Committee of the Indian Jute Mills' Association, 1927.
2   Managers' reports to the directors. Samnuggur North Mill, 1931, Dundee University Archives, MS 86/V/8/2/1; Managers' reports to the directors. Samnuggur South (No's. I and II Mills), 1931, Dundee University Archives, MS 86/V/8/2/2; Managers' reports to the directors. Titaghur No. I Mill, 1931, Dundee University Archives, MS 86/V/8/2/3; Managers' reports to the directors. Titaghur No. II Mill, 1931, Dundee University Archives, MS 86/V/8/2/4.
3   Managers' reports to the directors. Titaghur No. I Mill, 1937, Dundee University Archives, MS 86/V/8/8/4; Managers' reports to the directors. Titaghur No. II Mill, 1937, Dundee University Archives, MS 86/V/8/8/5.
4   Annual Report of the Committee of the Indian Jute Mills' Association, 1927, p 100.
5   Managers' reports to the directors. Titaghur No. I Mill, 1931, Dundee University Archives, MS 86/V/8/2/3.
6   Annual Report on the Working of the Indian Factories Act in Bengal and Assam, 1931.
7   Annual Report of the Committee of the Indian Jute Mills' Association, 1927; Managers' reports to the directors. Samnaggur North Mill, 1935, Dundee University Archives, MS 86/V/8/6/2.
8   The visiting director reported: 'They have no measuring machines. The Lapping machine does the measuring by counting the folds. The men who make up the cuts do this and again save the labour of measuring machines.' / Correspondence of directors while visiting mills in India with some related files (1932–68), J. Robertson, 1932–3, Dundee University Archives, MS 86/V/7/29.
9   In the late 1920s and in 1930, the inspector of factories collected wage data from Bengal jute mills and reported on the average wages in the industry in his annual reports. The tables on wage levels presented in this chapter are based on the data given in the report of 1930, when about 50 per cent of the industry applied either the multiple or the single-shift system. / Annual Report on the Working of the Indian Factories Act for Bengal and Assam, 1928–31.
10   Annual Report on the Working of the Indian Factories Act for Bengal and Assam, 1930.

11 For wage levels in the jute industry before the extension of the multiple-shift system, see: *Dundee Courier*, 23 July 1894; for wage levels after the extension of the multiple-shift system, see: John Leng, *Letters from India and Ceylon*, pp 53ff; Annual Report on the Working of the Indian Factories Act in Bengal and Assam, 1928–31; for wage levels after the abolition of the multiple-shift system, see: Award in the Matter of Industrial Disputes in the Jute Textile Industry in West Bengal between the Employers of 89 Specified Jute Mills and Their Workmen.

12 Under the 'single-shift' system, it seems to have been exactly reversed: someone remembered it precisely opposed: hessian-weavers missed their target more often than sacking-weavers and that, thus, sacking-weavers earned on an average more than hessian-weavers. / Interview, Dundee, 6 June 2013.

13 In the mills of the Duff Company, for instance, the basis for adjusting wages among weavers was the average output of the whole department under the multiple-shift system; which, in turn, implied a *quasi* accidental wage increase in relative terms for sacking-weavers, when both sides of the department were subjected to the same conditions of work. / Managers' reports to the directors. Titaghur No. I Mill, 1931, Dundee University Archives, MS 86/V/8/2/3.

14 Annual Report on the Working of the Indian Factories Act in Bengal and Assam, 1926; Annual Report on the Working of the Indian Factories Act in Bengal and Assam, 1931.

15 Managers' reports to the directors. Titaghur No. I Mill, 1933, Dundee University Archives, MS 86/V/8/4/4.

16 Annual Report of the Committee of the Indian Jute Mills' Association, 1927.

17 Royal Commission on Labour (Whitley Commission), Volume 5, Part 1. Bengal (Excluding Coalfields and the Dooars), 1931, 142.

18 Sen, 'Gendering Class', p 53 / Basu, 'The Paradox of Peasant Worker'.

19 Private Official Letters from Calcutta, 2 May 1939, Dundee University Archives, MS 86/V/7/8.

20 This procedure was, for instance, apparent during conflicts, after which members of managing agencies reported in more detail about the events at the shop-floor. / Managers' reports to the directors. Titaghur No. II Mill, 1931, Dundee University Archives, MS 86/V/8/2/4; Letter from MacDonald to Mason, 15 August 1939, Private Official Letter From Calcutta, 13 June 1939–28 December 1939, Dundee University Archives, MS 86/V/7/7.

Chapter 3.2

1 Report on Enquiry into the Conditions of Labour in the Jute Mill Industry in India, 1946.

2   Annual Report on the Working of the Indian Factories Act in Bengal and Assam, 1931.

3   Given that there some workers were usually absent, this also included the dismissal of 'ghost-workers' and, in turn, the amount of 'extra' income, which clerks, *sirdars* and workers could receive.

4   Letter from P. Thomas to E. Benthall, 31 December 1928, Centre of South Asian Studies (University of Cambridge), Benthall Papers, Box 1 File 2; Managers' reports to the directors. Samnuggur North Mill, 1931, Dundee University Archives, MS 86/V/8/2/1; Managers' reports to the directors. Samnuggur South (No's. I and II Mills), 1931, Dundee University Archives, MS 86/V/8/2/2; Managers' reports to the directors. Titaghur No. I Mill, 1931, Dundee University Archives, MS 86/V/8/2/3; Managers' reports to the directors. Titaghur No. II Mill, 1931, Dundee University Archives, MS 86/V/8/2/4.

5   Annual Report on the Working of the Indian Factories Act in Bengal and Assam, 1926; Annual Report on the Working of the Indian Factories Act in Bengal and Assam, 1931.

6   Managers' reports to the directors. Samnuggur South (No's. I and II Mills), 1931, Dundee University Archives, MS 86/V/8/2/2.

7   Letter from J. Williamson to E. Benthall, 31 July 1931, Centre of South Asian Studies (University of Cambridge), Benthall Papers, Box 8; Letter from MacDonald to Mason, 21 April 1938, Private official letters from Calcutta to Dundee, 1937–8, Dundee University Archives, MS 86/V/7/6.

8   Annual Report on the Working of the Indian Factories Act in Bengal and Assam, 1935.

9   Representatives of the Anglo-India Jute Mills (among others), when trying to indicate the advantages of a change in shift systems, thus, noted the dismissal of children as one major advantage of the single-shift system. / Annual Report of the Committee of the Indian Jute Mills' Association, 1927.

10   Sen, *Women and Labour in Late Colonial India*, pp 142ff; Emma Alexander-Mudaliar, 'The Special Classes of Labour. Women and Children. Doubly Marginalized', in *Labour Matters. Towards Global Histories. Studies in Honour of Sabyasachi Bhattacharya*, ed. Marcel Van Der Linden and Prabhu Mohapatra (New Delhi: Tulika Books, 2009), pp 131–51.

11   Managers' reports to the directors. Titaghur No. II Mill, 1931, Dundee University Archives, MS 86/V/8/2/4.

12   Kelman, *Labour in India*, p 82f.

13   Sen, *Women and Labour in Late Colonial India*, pp 241ff; Sen, 'Gendering Class'.

14   This, in turn, served to decrease the gap between the wage levels of 'coolies' and 'coolie-*sirdars*' – a development, then, which was the outcome of concerns over the re-adjustment in the process of production, which bypassed workers who were not directly employed on the mills' machines.

15   de Haan, *Unsettled Settlers*, pp 245f.

16   Royal Commission on Labour (Whitley Commission), Volume 5, Part 1. Bengal (Excluding Coalfields and the Dooars), 1931, p 79.

17   The Titaghur Jute Mills No. 1 & No. 2 were among the largest mills on the Hugli. While being in the same compound, each mill unit had a separate manager.

18   Managers' reports to the directors. Titaghur No. II Mill, 1931, Dundee University Archives, MS 86/V/8/2/4.

19   Managers' reports to the directors. Samnuggur North Mill, 1931, Dundee University Archives, MS 86/V/8/2/1.

20   Ibid.

21   Arjan de Haan expressed this tendency strongly when giving an overview of historiographical debates in Bengal labour history. He explained that 'one of the central characteristics of the Bengal labour historiography is that it deals only with non-Bengali labour'. This statement was, surely enough, meant to reflect a crucial theme in various debates on labour in Bengal, as well as a historical fact of industrial work in colonial Bengal – foremost its most prominent industry on the Hugli. / Arjan De Haan, 'Towards a "Total History" of Bengal Labour', in *Bengal. Rethinking History. Essays in Historiography* (New Delhi: Manohar, 2001), p 123.

Chapter 3.3

1   Royal Commission on Labour (Whitley Commission), Volume 5, Part 1. Bengal (Excluding Coalfields and the Dooars), 1931, for instance / but also managers' reports; Managers' reports to the directors. Samnuggur North Mill, 1931, Dundee University Archives, MS 86/V/8/2/1; Managers' reports to the directors. Samnuggur South (No's. I and II Mills), 1931, Dundee University Archives, MS 86/V/8/2/2; Annual Report of the Committee of the Indian Jute Mills' Association, 1927.

2   Union North Re-Construction Proposal, 2 August 1935, Centre of South Asian Studies (University of Cambridge), Benthall Papers, Box 8. / During the interviews of the Whitley Commission, too, one manager pointed out that in his mill, some 'extra' workers were still employed, despite the introduction of the single-shift system. / Royal Commission on Labour (Whitley Commission), Volume 5, Part 1. Bengal (Excluding Coalfields and the Dooars), 1931, p 145.

3   'Jhol-panni' is a Bengali expression for a small break. / Union North Re-Construction Proposal, 2 August 1935, Centre of South Asian Studies (University of Cambridge), Benthall Papers, Box 8.

4   Ibid.

5   Already in 1912, when a regular single-shift system was first introduced in the Bengal jute industry, workers protested against 'the locking of the mill gates during

the working hours as they cannot go out for meals any time they like as they were doing before'. The closing of mill gates continued to be step connected to the change in shift systems in the 1920s and in 1931. / *TOI*, 3 July 1912; Managers' reports to the directors. Samnuggur North Mill, 1931, Dundee University Archives, MS 86/V/8/2/1; Managers' reports to the directors. Samnuggur South (No's. I and II Mills), 1931, Dundee University Archives, MS 86/V/8/2/2; Managers' reports to the directors. Titaghur No. I Mill, 1931, Dundee University Archives, MS 86/V/8/2/3; Managers' reports to the directors. Titaghur No. II Mill, 1931, Dundee University Archives, MS 86/V/8/2/4.

6   Managers' reports to the directors. Titaghur No. I Mill, 1931, Dundee University Archives, MS 86/V/8/2/3. / In principle, workers in jute mills carried tokens since the amendment of Indian Factories Act in 1912. These tokens, however, hardly helped to regulate the employment of workers, as they merely served the purpose of complying with the formal regulations of the Indian Factories Act. The introduction of tokens with the objective of regulating employment under the single-shift system, then, should not be conflated with the previous introduction of tokens under the multiple-shift system. / For the introduction of tokens in 1912, see: Annual Report on the Working of the Indian Factories Act in Bengal and Assam, 1912; for problems with tokens under the multiple-shift system, see: Kelman, *Labour in India*, pp 252f; Royal Commission on Labour (Whitley Commission), Volume 5, Part 1. Bengal (Excluding Coalfields and the Dooars), 1931, pp 144f.

7   Indian Factory Labour Commission, Volume II. Evidence 1908, p 249.

8   Managers' reports to the directors. Titaghur No. I Mill, 1931, Dundee University Archives, MS 86/V/8/2/3.

9   Indian Factory Labour Commission, Volume I. Report 1908, pp 24f. / Another form of a pass-system seems to have existed in Cawnpore, where in 1888 a system was introduced, 'which allowed 20% of the workers in a room to be out at a time'. / Das, Factory Labour in India, p 29.

10 Managers' reports to the directors. Titaghur No. II Mill, 1931, Dundee University Archives, MS 86/V/8/2/4.

11 Managers' reports to the directors. Samnuggur North Mill, 1933, Dundee University Archives, MS 86/V/8/4/2.

12 One reason for this difference was certainly different income levels. Weavers were the highest paid group of workers at a time when sections of the workforce could not even afford to prepare tea at home. / Choudhury, Report on an Enquiry into the Standard of Living of Jute Mill Workers in Bengal, 1930.

13 Managers' reports to the directors. Angus Jute Works, 1937, Dundee University Archives, MS 86/V/8/8/1; Secret Communist 'cells' & secret labour committees in jute mills in Jagadtal area, 13 January 1938, Intelligence Bureau (West Bengal State Archives) (= IB): 59–38.

14 Interview, Dundee, 15 February 2012, 16 February 2012 and 7 June 2013.

15 Interview, Dundee, 16 February 2012 and 7 February 2013; see also: Stewart, *Jute and Empire*, pp 173f.

16 Managers' reports to the directors. Titaghur No. II Mill, 1931, Dundee University Archives, MS 86/V/8/2/4.

17 Chakrabarty, 'On Deifying and Defying Authority', p 131.

18 David Harvey, *The Limits to Capital* (Oxford: Basil Blackwell, 1982), pp 57ff.

19 Sen, 'Gendering Class', pp 200ff.

20 Managers' reports to the directors. Victoria Jute Company Ltd., 1939, Dundee University Archives, MS 86/V/8/10/6.

21 Managers' reports to the directors. Victoria Jute Company Ltd., 1940, Dundee University Archives, MS 86/V/8/11/6.

22 In an attempt to solve the problem, then, the manager of the Victoria Jute Mill reported that they 'encouraged' shifters 'to assist the spinners when opportunities occur and in time the Spinning Overseers may appoint the more proficient amongst them to be budli spinners'. / Ibid.

Chapter 3.4

1   *TOI*, 3 July 1912.

2   *TOI*, 21 May 1925.

3   Ibid., 29 May 1925.

4   Criminal prosecutions of certain Europeans for fatal assaults upon Indians: The Gouripur Jute Mill case, IOR: L/PJ/6/1919.

5   *TOI*, 10 June 1926.

6   Ibid., 9 April 1927.

7   Riot at Fort Gloster Jute Mills, Bauriah, 1928, IOR: L/PJ/6/1963, File 2796.

8   Superintendent of Police, Hooghly, 20 March 1929, IB: 303-I/26.

9   Stedman Jones refers to these two types of appropriation as 'appropriation of nature', and 'appropriation of the product'. Referring to Marx's Capital, he, further elaborates that: 'Like any other mode of production, the capitalist mode, as Marx defines it, is characterized by two distinct forms of appropriation. It is a specific mode of appropriation of the product and a specific mode of appropriation of nature. In other words, it embodies a double relation, a specific form of ownership of the means of production and a specific form of control over the labour process. These two types of appropriation are relatively autonomous. They cannot simply be reduced to one another, since – most obviously – their temporalities are different. ' / Gareth Stedman Jones, *Languages of Class: Studies in English Working Class History, 1832–1982* (Cambridge; New York: Cambridge University Press, 1983), p 45.

10 Ibid., p 53.

11 Ibid.

12 Ibid., pp 53f.

13 Das Gupta, *Labour and Working Class in Eastern India*, p 446; Sumit Sarkar, *Modern India. 1885–1947* (Macmillan, 1983), p 271.

14 Annual Report on the working of the Indian Trade Union Act, 1926 in Bengal, 1929.

15 Royal Commission on Labour (Whitley Commission), Volume 5, Part 1. Bengal (Excluding Coalfields and the Dooars), 1931, p 127.

16 K.C. Chowdhury, for instance, was asked by members of the Whitley Commission if his union supported the multiple or the single-shift system. He responded by more or less avoiding the question, stating that: 'Our union is really an advocate of shorter hours, and if a double shift permits of shorter hours we prefer a double shift; from our point of view our union advocates reduction of the present working hours.' / Ibid.

17 Chattopadhyay, 'Santosh Kumari Devi', pp 62–73.

18 Das Gupta, *Labour and Working Class*, p. 434.

19 Chattopadhyay, 'Santosh Kumari Devi', pp 62–73; Search of the Jute Workers' Union, Tittagarh, 24-Parganas, 1926, IB: 303 G/26; Search of the Bengal Jute Workers Association at 97 Barnwallis Street, Calcutta, 1926, IB: 303 H/26; Search of the Jute Workers Assoc., Mahesh Rishra, Hooghly, 1926, IB: 303I/26; Search of the Jute Workers' Association at Alambazar, 1926, Baranagar, 24-Parganas, IB: 303 D/26.

20 Narendra Nath Mukerji, P.W.-19, Meerut Communist Conspiracy Case (1929) Papers.

21 Chattopadhyay, 'Santosh Kumari Devi', pp 62–73; Das Gupta, *Labour and Working Class in Eastern India*, p 444.

22 Statement of Tulsi Das Ghosh 3/0 Akhaya Kumar Ghosh of Alambazar, Hedger Road, P.S. Baranagore, District Parganas, 20 March 1929, IB: 303 D/26.

23 He reported about the cooperation between his office and the BJWA in the two previous years in a similar manner. / Annual Report on the Working of the Workmen's Compensation Act During 1925–1927.

24 Annual Report on the Working of the Workmen's Compensation Act During 1928.

25 Statement of Tulsi Das Ghosh 3/0 Akhaya Kumar Ghosh of Alambazar, Hedger Road, P.S. Baranagore, District Parganas, 20 March 1929, IB: 303 D/26.

26 Superintendent of Police, Hooghly, 20 March 1929, IB: 303-I/26.

27 Report of D.I.B. Officer, 19 February 1929, IB: 448/28.

28 Das Gupta, *Labour and Working Class*, p 456 / Report of D.I.B. Officer, Hooghly, 19 February 1929, IB: 448/28.

29 Das Gupta, *Labour and Working Class*, pp 452ff.

30 This was to some degree a problem of language as well. Moni Singh gave an account of this principal, when describing how he got involved as a young man in a strike in the Keshoram Cotton mill in 1928: 'The workers began to explain

to us in chaste Urdu, why they had gone on strike. It was a language, which we did not know. Neither did we have any experience of textile mills. [...] Though we had no knowledge about these things, we came to a conclusion on the basis of our principle that the bourgeoisie could never do anything good for the workers. On this basis, we argued blindly. For we did not have the least idea about wages in a mill.' / Moni Singh, Life is Struggle, English Translation by Karuna Banerjee, People's Publishing House, New Delhi, 1988, p 21f / See also: Philip Spratt, *Blowing Up India. Reminiscences and Reflections of a Former Comintern Emissary* (Calcutta: Prachi Prakashan, 1955), p 46.

31 Statement of Tulsi Das Ghosh 3/0 Akhaya Kumar Ghosh of Alambazar, Hedger Road, P.S. Baranagore, District Parganas, 20 March 1929, IB: 303 D/26.

32 Ibid.

33 The problem, that single-shift mills had difficulties to make up time lost, because workers simply left was, in fact, a crucial reason for Benthal to contemplate the return to the multiple-shift system in the two mills of the Bird Company, which had made the change already in the 1920s. / Letter from P. Thomas to E. Benthal, 15 November 1928, Centre of South Asian Studies (University of Cambridge), Benthall Papers, Box 1, File 2.

34 Private Official Letters from Calcutta, 6 July 1939, Dundee University Archives, MS 86/V/7/7.

35 Royal Commission on Labour (Whitley Commission), Volume 11 – Supplementary, 1931, pp 358f.

36 In this context, one problem which a mill manager narrated to the Whitley Commission is rather telling. Workers apparently used the doors in their houses in the mills' coolie lines as firewood. While the manager, with this story, tried to highlight that workers did not understand urban life properly (or, in this case, that they did not understand the concept of 'door'), he also added that this was a very recent incident. It only happened in the late 1920s, when a growing number of mills worked on a single-shift system, operating on a five-day working week. It is thus likely that such incidents reflected the fact that workers had less time to gather enough firewood for the week under the single-shift system in the 1920s. / Royal Commission on Labour (Whitley Commission), Volume 5, Part 1. Bengal (Excluding Coalfields and the Dooars), 1931, p 283.

37 Managers' reports to the directors. Samnuggur North Mill, 1933, Dundee University Archives, MS 86/V/8/4/2; Managers' reports to the directors. Titaghur No. II Mill, 1933, Dundee University Archives, MS 86/V/8/4/5.

38 Choudhury, Report on an Enquiry into the Standard of Living of Jute Mill Workers in Bengal, 1930.

39 The reason that mills working with a multiple-shift system usually worked during a four-day week, however, was not so much that this was implied in the modalities of the multiple-shift system. Rather, this was a side-effect of the fact that the jute

industry worked with short-time agreements during most of the time, that the multiple-shift system was applied in their mills.

40 As we shall see in more detail in Chapter 5, mills of the IJMA did not introduce a five-day working week even when they reduced their weekly hours to forty per week during the Great Depression. Workers' opposition to this change was the primary reason for this. / see: Annual Report on the Working of the Indian Factories Act for Bengal and Assam, 1931.

41 Basu, *Does Class Matter,* Chakrabarty, 'On Deifying and Defying Authority'.

Part 4

1 The paper Swadeshi Bazar was published by a group of (ex-)terrorists – among them Bepinchandra Pal and Barindra Kumar Ghose, who had been key figures of the swadeshi movement in Bengal. But also Kali Sen, who came to play a central role in the general strike in the jute industry in 1929, was connected to the paper. / Publications: Swadeshi Bazar – a newspaper, Intelligence Bureau (West Bengal State Archives) (= IB): 387 – 28, 1928.

2 Anon., 'The Revolution of the Future', in: Swadeshi Bazar, 13 April 1929, [translation], Publications: Swadeshi Bazar – a newspaper, IB: 387 – 28, 1928.

3 Tanika Sarkar, *Bengal 1928–1934. The Politics of Protest* (Oxford: Oxford University Press, 1987), pp 49ff.

4 See among others: Nirban Basu, *The Working Class Movement. A Study of Jute Mills of Bengal 1937–1947* (Calcutta: K.P. Bagchi, 1994), pp 61ff; Basu, *Does Class Matter,* pp 208 ff; Das Gupta, *Labour and Working Class in Eastern India,* pp 1ff.

5 See Chapter 1.

6 Extract from I.B. Weekly Report dated 31st July, IB: 25/-29.

7 Poem recited by Puran Mall at a meeting of striking workers in Kankinarrah, 23 January 1938 / IB: 59–38.

8 Bengal Jute Workers Union, 1935, Special Branch of the Police, Calcutta: SW/521A/35.

9 Copy Extract from Weekly Report of the Director, Intelligence Bureau of the Home Department, Government of India, 8 May 1930, IOR: L-P&J-12/64; Extract from report from New Scotland Yard, 30 April 1930, IOR: L-P&J-12/64.

10 Indrajit Gupta, *Capital and Labour in the Jute Industry* (Bombay: AITUC, 1953); S.N. Sen and T. Piplai, *Industrial Relations in the Jute Industry in West Bengal. A Case Study* (Calcutta: Bookland Private Ltd, 1968), pp 11 ff.

11 The larger questions about the connection of memory and history have been explored in: Paul Ricoeur, *History, Memory, Forgetting.* Translated by Kathleen Blamey and David Pellauer (Chicago: University of Chicago Press, 2009).

12 See among others: Basu, *The Working Class Movement*, pp 61ff; Nirban Basu, 'Outside Leadership, Political Rivalries and Labour Mobilisation. The Jute Belt of Bengal, 1919–1939', in *A Case for Labour History*, n.d., pp 114ff; Amal Das, 'Outside Intervention in Jute Mill Strikes – Howrah, 1870–1930', in *A Case for Labour History*, ed. Arjan de Haan and Samita Sen (Calcutta, n.d.), pp 82ff; Das Gupta, *Labour and Working Class*, pp 406ff; Parimal Ghosh, *Colonialism, Class, and a History of the Calcutta Jute Millhands, 1880–1930* (Hyderabad: Orient Longman, 2000), pp 236ff.

Chapter 4.1

1   Stewart, *Jute and Empire*, pp 99ff.
2   Olbrecht, *Bengalens Fluch Und Segen*, pp 100f.
3   Letter from E. Benthall to P. Thomas, 15 November 1928, Centre of South Asian Studies (University of Cambridge), Benthall Papers, Box 1, File 2.
4   Bengal Jute Workers Union, 1935, Special Branch of the Police, Calcutta: SW/521-A/35.
5   Basu, *Does Class Matter*, p 209.
6   *Forward*, 13 January 1929.
7   Basu, *Does Class Matter*, p 209.
8   Ranajit Das Gupta, *The Jute General Strike of 1929* (Calcutta: Indian Institute of Management, WPS - 141 (90), 1990), p 14.
9   Ibid., p 10.
10 Ibid.
11 Suchetana Chattopadhyay, *An Early Communist: Muzaffar Ahmad in Calcutta, 1913–1929* (New Delhi: Tulika Books, 2011), p 153.
12 Ibid., p 201.
13 Bengal Intelligence Branch, *The Politico-Criminal 'Who's Who' of the Bengal Presidency*, revised up to the 1 July 1930 (Calcutta: Bengal Government Press, 1930), p 16.
14 R.W. Bell, Superintendent of Police, 24-Parganas, 1 August 1929, IB: 25/-29.
15 Local Government Reports, Bengal, July 1929, IOR: L/P & J /12/686.
16 R.W. Bell, Superintendent of Police, 24-Parganas, 1 August 1929, IB: 25/-29; see also: *Statesman*, 13 July 1929.
17 R.W. Bell, Superintendent of Police, 24-Parganas, 1 August 1929, IB: 25/-29.
18 *Statesman*, 7 July 1929.
19 R.W. Bell, Superintendent of Police, 24-Parganas, 1 August 1929, IB: 25/-29.
20 Ibid.
21 Report of A.D.I.B. Officer, 28 July 1929, IB: 25/-29.

22 Report of Watcher A.S.I., 25 July 1929, IB: 25/-29.

23 Report of D.I.B. Officer, 24-Parganas, 31 July 1929, IB: 25/-29, see also: Das Gupta, *Labour and Working Class*, p 465.

24 Report of Watcher A.S.I., 25 July 1929, IB: 25/-29.

25 Extract from I.B. Weekly Report, 24 July 1929, IB: 25/-29.

26 Extract from I.B. Weekly Report, 7 August 1929, IB: 25/-29.

27 Report of A.D.I.B. Officer, 26 July 1929, IB: 25/-29.

28 Ibid.

29 Ibid.

30 Ibid.

31 Ibid.

32 Bankim Mukharji joined meetings with Prabhabati Das Gupta at the initial stages of the strike. Only a few days after the meeting, he joined the group around Kali Sen, and did not join meetings with the unions' president until after the strike's end.

33 Ibid.

34 Report of D.I.B. Officer, 28 July 1929, IB: 25/-29.

35 Royal Commission on Labour (Whitley Commission), Volume 5, Part 1. Bengal (Excluding Coalfields and the Dooars), 1931, p 76.

36 Daily report on the Labour situation for 24-Parganas district, 11 August 1929, IB: 25/-29.

Chapter 4.2

1   *TOI*, 31 July 1929.

2   *Statesman*, 30 July 1929.

3   *TOI*, 30 July 1929.

4   Special Branch Office, 2 August 1929, IB: 25/-29.

5   Extract from I.B. Weekly Report, 7 August 1929, IB: 25/-29.The maps in this chapter are based on a map from: W. W. Hunter, *The Imperial Gazetteer of India Atlas*, Vol. 26 (Oxford: Clarendon Press, 1931).

6   Report of A.D.I.B. Officer, 31 July 1929, IB: 25/-29.

7   Extract from I.B. Weekly Report, 14 August 1929, IB: 25/-29.

8   Ashutosh Mahapatra, P.W.-27, Meerut Communist Conspiracy Case (1929) Papers.

9   W.H. Bemrose, Assistant Superintendent of Police, Barrackpore, 2 August 1929, IB: 25/-29.

10 Report of A.D.I.B. Officer, 31 July 1929, IB: 25/-29.

11 R.W. Bell, Superintendent of Police, 24-Parganas, 1 August 1929, IB: 25/-29.

12 Ibid.

13 Ibid.

14 *Statesman*, 18 August 1929.

15 R.W. Bell, Superintendent of Police, 24-Parganas, 1 August 1929, IB: 25/-29.

16 Ibid.

17 *TOI*, 1 August 1929; Copy No. 6418, 6 August 1929, IB: 25/-29.

18 See Chapter 5.

19 Private official letters from Calcutta. 29 October 1936 – 6 May 1937, March-April 1937, DUA, MS86/V/7/3/ Strike Report for 6 August 1929, IB: 25/-29; *TOI*, 4 May 1937.

20 R.W. Bell, Superintendent of Police, 24-Parganas, 1 August 1929, IB: 25/-29.

21 T. Meerza, Hooghly Police Office, 6 August 1929, IB: 25/-29 / Making matters worse, the Inspector General of Police for Bengal had just in the previous year complained that there was too little 'hospital space' in the area. / Annual Report on the Police Administration in the Bengal Presidency, 1928.

22 Ibid.

23 Ibid. / see also: Extract from I.B. Weekly Report, 14 August 1929, IB: 25/-29.

24 Baidyabati Conspiracy Case, 1936, IOR: L/PJ/7/1170.

25 T. Meerza, Hooghly Police Office, 4 August 1929, IB: 25/-29.

26 E.W. Duckfield, Superintendent of Police, Howrah, 5 August 1929, IB: 25/-29.

27 Ibid.

28 Ibid.

29 *Bengalee*, 4 August 1929.

30 *TOI*, 5 August 1929.

31 E.S. Jones, for Superintendent of Police, 24-Parganas, 4 August 1929, IB: 25/-29.

32 Extracts from I.B. weekly reports, 7 August 1929, IB: 25/-29.

33 W.H. Bemrose, Strike Report for 3 August 1929, IB: 25/-29.

34 Extracts from I.B. Weekly Reports, 7 August 1929, IB: 25/-29.

35 Ibid.

Chapter 4.3

1 Daily Report on the Labour Situation in the 24-Parganas District for 5 August 29, 6 August 1929, IB: 25/-29; *Statesman*, 6 August 1929.

2 *Liberty*, 6 August 1929; *Statesman*, 6 August 1929.

3 *Liberty*, 14 August 1929.

4 *TOI*, 8 August 1929; *Statesman*, 8 August 1929.

5 *TOI*, 15 August 1929.

6 Extract from I.B. Weekly Report, 7 August 1929, IB: 25/-29.

7 W.H. Bemrose, Assistant Superintendent of Police, Barrackpore, 6 August 1929, IB: 25/-29.

8 Ibid. / *Liberty*, 4 September 1929.

9 *Liberty*, 7 August 1929.

10 Ibid.

11 Ibid.

12 Ibid.

13 *Liberty*, 8 August 1929.

14 B.N. Bannerjee, Deputy Commissioner of Police, South, 8 August 1929, IB: 25/-29.

15 *Statesman*, 8 August 1929.

16 *Liberty*, 9 August 1929.

17 *Statesman*, 9 August 1929.

18 T. Meerza, Hooghly Police Office, 7 August 1929, IB: 25/-29.

19 *Statesman*, 8 August 1929.

20 Strike Report for 6 August 1929, IB: 25/-29.

21 *Statesman*, 7 August 1929.

22 T. Meerza, Hooghly Police Office, 13 August 1929, IB: 25/-29.

23 Report of D.I.B. officer, 11 August 1929, IB: 25/-29.

24 Ibid.

25 Report of Labour Situation in Howrah, No. 4, 5 August 1929, IB: 25/-29.

26 Ibid.

27 Ibid.

28 For mills changing shift systems in 1929 see: Annual Report on the Working of the Indian Factories Act in Bengal and Assam, 1931; for strikes in those mills, see: R.W. Bell, Superintendent of Police, 24-Parganas, 1 August 1929, IB: 25/-29.

29 Riot at Fort Gloster Jute Mills, Bauriah, 1928, IOR: L/PJ/6/1963, File 2796.

30 Reports on Labour Situation in 24-Parganas, 15 August 1929, IB: 25/-29; Labour Situation in the jute mills of Howrah, 15 August 1929, IB:25/-29.

31 Daily Report on the Labour Situation in the 24-Parganas, 15 August 1929, IB: 25/-29.

32 Extract from I.B. Weekly Report, 14 August 1929, IB: 25/-29.

33 Extract report on the Labour Situation of 24 Parganas District, 22 August 1929.

34 *Statesman*, 10 August 1929.

35 Ibid.

36 *TOI*, 13 August 1929.

37 *Statesman*, 14 August 1929.

38 *Liberty*, 17 August 1929; *Statesman*, 17 August 1929.

39 Das Gupta, *The Jute General Strike*, p 12.

Chapter 4.4

1 *Liberty*, 17 August 1929.

2 See among others: Basu, *The Working Class Movement*, pp 61ff; Basu, *Does Class Matter*, pp 208ff; Das Gupta, *Labour and Working Class*, pp 1ff.

3 *Liberty*, 17 August 1929.
4 Daily Report on the Labour Situation of 24-Parganas District, 14 August 1929, IB: 25/-29.
5 Extracts from the report of Deputy Superintendent of Police, 12 August 1929, IB: 25/-29.
6 Reports on Strike in and about Calcutta, 22 August 1929, IB: 25/-29; Kali Sen, 20 March 1930, IB: 25/-29; see also: Basu, *Does Class Matter*, pp 214f.
7 Das Gupta, *The Jute General Strike*, p 15.
8 *TOI*, 11 March 1930s.
9 Daily report about the various strikes in or about Calcutta, 20 August 1929, IB: 25/-29.
10 This tendency to localize strikes was already apparent on 17 August, only one day after the settlement, when the *Statesman* reported: 'This strike [in Budge-Budge], however, arose from a local cause but was connected with the change over to the 60 hours' week. It was not connected with the strikes further up the river'. / *Statesman*, 17 August 1929 / See, also: *Amrita Bazar Patrika*, 1 September 1929; *Liberty*, 4 September 1929; *TOI*, 7 September 1929.
11 This was in particular the case after the split of the BJWU, as both factions of the union presented the settlement as a victory for workers and trade union alike.
12 The Special Branch Officer reported that Bankim Mukherjee and other members of the BJWU had tried to organize more money, in order to support the pending protest at least in some cases. These attempts, however, seem to have failed. / Report of a Special Branch Officer, Calcutta, dated the 17 October, 1929, regarding the Labour Activities, IB: 25/-29.
13 Daily Report on the Labour Situation of 24-Parganas District, 18 August 1929, IB: 25/-29.
14 Ibid.
15 Ibid.
16 T. Meerza, Camp Champdani, 20 August 1929, IB: 25/-29.
17 Daily Report on the Labour Situation of 24-Parganas District, 19 August 1929.
18 Ibid.
19 Ibid.
20 Highlighting the fact that this conflict had come up in opposition to the multiple-shift system, *Liberty* summarized this development by stating that men working under the 'single shift system appear to be restive again'. / *Liberty*, 4 September 1929.
21 Daily Report on the Labour Situation of 24-Parganas District, 31 August 1929, IB: 25/-29.
22 Extract from I.B. Weekly Report, 14 August 1929, IB: 25/-29.
23 Summary Report of the proceedings of the Strikers meeting at Budge-Budge, 21 August 1929, IB: 25/-29.

24 Daily Report on the Labour Situation of 24-Parganas district for 28 August 1929, IB: 25/-29; Daily Report about Strike in and about Calcutta on 3 September 1929, IB: 25/-39; *Liberty*, 8 September 1929 and 12 September 1929.

25 T. Meerza, Camp Champdani, 21 August 1929, IB: 25/-29; Extract from I.B. Weekly Labour Report, 21 August 1929, IB: 25/-29.

26 Daily report on the Labour situation in 24-Parganas district, 2 August 1929, IB: 25/-29.

27 *Liberty*, 7 September 1929.

28 Summary Report of the Strikers' Meeting at Ram Chandra Aweshi – Rice Mills, Budge-Budge, 23 August 1929, IB: 25/-29.

29 Daily Report on the Labour Situation of 24-Parganas District, 26 August 1929.

30 Summary of Report on Proceedings at Budge-Budge, 25 August 1929.

31 *Amrita Bazar Patrika*, 1 September 1929.

32 *TOI*, 27 January 1930.

33 Ibid., 20 November 1929.

34 Managers' reports to the directors. Titaghur No. II Mill, 1930, Dundee University Archives, MS 86/V/8/1/4; *TOI*, 5 March 1930.

35 Managers' reports to the directors. Titaghur No. II Mill, 1930, Dundee University Archives, MS 86/V/8/1/4.

36 Fortnightly Report on the political situation in Bengal for the first and second half of March 1930.

37 *Liberty*, 5 September 1929; *TOI*, 5 March 1930.

38 Managers' reports to the directors. Titaghur No. II Mill, 1930, Dundee University Archives, MS 86/V/8/1/4.

39 *TOI*, 12 March 1930.

40 Ibid., 14 March 1930.

41 Ibid., 10 March 1930.

42 Fortnightly Report on the political situation in Bengal for the first and second half of May 1930; Fortnightly Report on the political situation in Bengal for the first and second half of June 1930.

43 One exception here would, arguably, be strikes in the immediate vicinity of Calcutta. In particular in the Clive Jute Mills in Metiaburuz, it is noteworthy that police and other state authorities tended to report more intensely on strikes – and, in turn, tried to intervene with the help of police forces – than when strikes occurred in the hinterland of Calcutta. / See, for instance: Disturbance at Clive Jute Mills, Calcutta on the 9 January 1929, NAI: Home Department, Police Branch, File No. 8/V/29-Police.

44 Extract from I.B. Weekly, 9 January 1930, IB: 497/27; Extract from I.B. Weekly, 2 February 1931, IB: 497/27; Extract from I.B. Weekly, 28 March 1931, IB: 497/27.

45 Baidyabati Conspiracy Case, 1936, IOR: L/PJ/7/1170.

46 Gupta, *Labour and Working Class in Eastern India*, pp 438ff.
47 Baidyabati Conspiracy Case, 1936, IOR: L/PJ/7/1170.
48 Kali Prosad Ghosh, 'The Friend', in: *Swadeshi Bazar*, 25 May 1929, [translation], Publications: Swadeshi Bazar – a newspaper, IB: 387-28, 1928.
49 H.O. 21 dated 7 April 1936, Special Branch, SW/521-A/35, 7 April 1936.

Part 5

1 Annual Report on the Working of the Indian Factories Act in Bengal and Assam, 1931.
2 Letter from E. Benthall, 29 June 1937, Centre of South Asian Studies (University of Cambridge), Benthall Papers, Box 9.
3 Private official letter from Calcutta to Dundee, 10 June 1937, Dundee University Archives, MS 86/V/7/6.
4 Correspondence of Directors while visiting Mills in India (1932–1968), J. Robertson, 1932–1933, Dundee University Archives (=DUA), MS 86/V/7/29.
5 Managers' Report for the Directors, The Angus Jute Works Company Limited, 1937, MS 86/V/7/1.
6 See among others: Ira Mitra, 'Growth of Trade Union Consciousness among Jute Mill Workers, 1920–40', *Economic and Political Weekly*, Vol. 16, No. 44/46 (November 1981): pp 1839–48; Basu, Does Class Matter, pp 225ff, Basu, The Working Class Movement, pp 61ff; Nirban Basu, 'Outside Leadership, Political Rivalries and Labour Mobilisation. The Jute Belt of Bengal, 1919-1939', in *A Case for Labour History*, n.d., pp 114ff; Das, 'Outside Intervention in Jute Mill Strikes – Howrah, 1870-1930', pp 82ff; Das Gupta, *Labour and Working Class*, pp 406ff; Ghosh, *Colonialism, Class, and a History of the Calcutta Jute Millhands, 1880-1930*, pp 236ff, Ghosh, 'A History of A Colonial Working Class', p 686.
7 Das Gupta, *Labour and Working Class in Eastern India*, pp 220ff; de Haan, *Unsettled Settlers*, p 27; S. Basu, 'Review on the Book: Unsettled Settlers: Migrant Workers and Industrial Capitalism in Calcutta by Arjan de Haan. Rotterdam: Verloren Publishers, 1994. pp 299', *South Asia Research*, Vol. 16, No. 2 (1 October 1996): pp 209–122, p 211.
8 de Haan, *Unsettled Settlers*, p 27. / Irrespective of the question of why this worker would remember the change in shift systems even as late as the 1980s, it also seems peculiar that the dismissals in 1931 should have stood out in his memory. A worker who had been part of the jute industry in any period between the 1930s and the 1980s, after all, would have been part of an industry which was experienced a long terminal decline – and continual dismissals, retrenchments and closures of mills – throughout his working life.

Chapter 5.1

1 Omkar Goswami, 'Then Came the Marwaris. Some Aspects of the Changes in the Pattern of Industrial Control in Eastern India', *Indian Economic & Social History Review*, Vol. 22, No. 3 (1985): pp 237ff.

2 Goswami, *Industry, Trade, and Peasant Society*, p 98.

3 Ibid., pp 237ff.

4 Annual Report of the Committee of the Indian Jute Mills' Association, 1930. / The reason, why the mills of the IJMA decided to implement a short-time agreement by shutting mills completely is uncertain. Yet, given that in the 1920s multiple-shift mills worked four days per week as they, accordingly, could not reduce the hours of work to less than 13½ per week due to the system of relay-sets, it can be assumed, that the application of the multiple-shift system in 50 per cent of the industry was a crucial reason, for adopting this mode of reduction of working hours.

5 Annual Report on the Working of the Indian Factories Act in Bengal and Assam, 1930.

6 Fortnightly Report on the political situation in Bengal for the first half of June 1930; Fortnightly Report on the political situation in Bengal for the second half of July; Fortnightly Report on the political situation in Bengal for the first half of August, 1930.

7 Fortnightly Report on the political situation in Bengal for the second half of July, 1930.

8 Managers' reports to the directors. Samnuggur North Mill, 1930, Dundee University Archives, MS 86/V/8/1/1; Managers' reports to the directors. Samnuggur South (No's. I and II Mills), 1930, Dundee University Archives, MS 86/V/8/1/2; Managers' reports to the directors. Titaghur No. I Mill, 1930, Dundee University Archives, MS 86/V/8/1/3; Managers' reports to the directors. Titaghur No. II Mill, 1930, Dundee University Archives, MS 86/V/8/1/4.

9 These fears were presumably also among the reasons why single-shift mills agreed to the procedure of closing their works for one week as well. For single-shift mills had technically the option to reduce their daily hours. Yet this would have implied a serious advantage, if, indeed, multiple-shift mills would have suffered labour shortages. More so, skilled workers could have simply found employment in single-shift mills, when multiple-shift mills were shut. These were options which probably would have prevented an agreement among the members of the IJMA.

10 Managers' reports to the directors. Samnuggur North Mill, 1930, Dundee University Archives, MS 86/V/8/1/1.

11 Ibid.

12 Labour Commissioner for the Government of Bengal (R.N. Gilchrist), Official Correspondence, July 1932, West Bengal State Archives (=WBSA): Commerce Department, 3C-1, Progs. B 322.

13 Fortnightly Report on the political situation in Bengal for the first half of August, 1930.

14 Fortnightly Report on the political situation in Bengal for the second half of November, 1930.

15 Managers' reports to the directors. Titaghur No. II Mill, 1934, Dundee University Archives, MS 86/V/8/5/5.

16 Directors' Reports to the Shareholders, Titaghur Jute Factory Ltd., 1937, Dundee University Archive, MS 86/III/5/5.

17 Directors' Minute Books, Samnuggur Jute Factory Company Ltd., 1931, Dundee University Archive, MS 86/I/1/22.

18 Extract from I.B. Weekly, 27 February 1931, IB: 497/27.

19 The Inspector of Factories reported that eleven jute mills went on strike after the change in shift systems. It seems, however, that he also included other mills. / Annual Report on the Working of the Indian Factories Act in Bengal and Assam, 1931.

20 Extract from I.B. Weekly, 4 April 1931, IB: 497/27; Managers' reports to the directors. Titaghur No. I Mill, 1931, Dundee University Archives, MS 86/V/8/2/3; Managers' reports to the directors. Titaghur No. II Mill, 1931, Dundee University Archives, MS 86/V/8/2/4.

21 Report on the Situation of Jute Mills in Howrah District, 15 April 1931, IB: 497/27; Managers' reports to the directors. Titaghur No. I Mill, 1931, Dundee University Archives, MS 86/V/8/2/3; Managers' reports to the directors. Titaghur No. II Mill, 1931, Dundee University Archives, MS 86/V/8/2/4.

22 Extract from I.B. Weekly, 2 February 1931, IB: 497/27.

23 The absence of trade union support in the northern parts of the jute belt may also have contributed to the peculiar form of protest in Titaghur. The strike in the previous year had been led by spinners of the mill, while other sections of the workforce – in particular weavers – opposed the strike. After the strikes defeat, the tensions within the workforce were rising. The rising unemployment and the absence of trade union support, then, prevented that these tensions could be overcome at this point. / Managers' reports to the directors. Titaghur No. I Mill, 1931, Dundee University Archives, MS 86/V/8/2/3; Managers' reports to the directors. Titaghur No. II Mill, 1931, Dundee University Archives, MS 86/V/8/2/4.

24 Annual Report on the Working of the Indian Factories Act for Bengal and Assam, 1932.

25 Ibid.

26 Annual Report on the Working of the Indian Factories Act for Bengal and Assam, 1933.

27 Annual Report on the Working of the Indian Factories Act for Bengal and Assam, 1931.

28   Union North Re-Construction Proposal, 2 August 1935, Centre of South Asian Studies (University of Cambridge), Benthall Papers, Box 8.

Chapter 5.2

1   Goswami, *Industry, Trade, and Peasant Society*, pp 239f / The crisis of the jute industry, was accompanied by a general decline of 'expatriate business houses in Eastern India', as B.R. Tomlinson put it in an article, which summarizes the debates on the matter well. / B.R. Tomlinson, 'Colonial Firms and the Decline of Colonialism in Eastern India 1914–47', *Modern Asian Studies*, Vol. 15, No. 3 (1981): 455–86, p 455.

2   Annual Report of the Committee of the Indian Jute Mills' Association, 1931; Report of the Bengal Jute Enquiry Committee, Vol. 1, 1934; *TOI*, 8 May 1934.

3   Nalini Ranjan Sarker, *The Jute Crisis. Proceedings of Conference, October 17, 1930* (Calcutta: J.N. Sen, 1930).

4   Annual Report of the Committee of the Indian Jute Mills' Association, 1932.

5   *TOI*, 6 November 1935.

6   *TOI*, 11 March 1936.

7   Report of the Bengal Jute Enquiry Committee, Vol. 1, 1934, p 20.

8   Morris, R.J., *Relative Merits of Cotton and Jute Cement Sacks*.

9   Report of the Bengal Jute Enquiry Committee, Vol. 1, 1934, pp 39f.

10 Correspondence of directors while visiting mills in India with some related files, Sir Alexander R. Murray, 1937–1938, Dundee University Archives, MS 86/V/7/33.

11 The objection of the Indian members of the IJMA to a restriction of hours of work, however, does not mean that Indian owners of jute mills refused working-time agreements in principle. The owners of mills outside the IJMA, such as the Sree Hanuman and Naskarpara Mills, for instance, proposed 'a Five Years Working Agreement', which would restrict their hours of work (though granting them longer hours, than the members of the IJMA). Other non-associated mills principally agreed to this proposal. / Working Agreement with Outside Mills, 20 August 1937, Centre of South Asian Studies (University of Cambridge), Benthall Papers, Box 10.

12 Directors' reports and accounts, Angus Co. Ltd, Jute and Engineering Works, 1934–1935, Dundee University Archives: MS 86/IV/5/1.

13 Giving an indication of the different choices, which managing agents took on the matter – and the resulting variety of hours of work in the jute belt, the general director of the Duff Company reported on 30 March 1936: 'Anderson Wright and Birds, like ourselves, are to work 45 hours a week, but while Khardah [Jute Mill] and our group are to work alternate weeks of 40 and 50 hours, Birds propose to work a week of 45 hours, viz. 5 days of 9 hours each. Douglas of Duncan Bros.

informs me that they are not quite settled as to what hours they are to work [...],
but he states that he has learned that Beggs have decided to work 45 hours [...]. I
have explained to Birds, Anderson Wright and Duncancs our view in connection
with working alternate weeks of 40 and 50 hours, how we can revert, if necessary, to
40 hours a week and avoid any complications with wages, how we can on Friday of
the 40-hour week do all our mechanical repairs, and probably close down entirely
the following week-end. [...] Gillanders, Birla and Hukumchand have signified
their intention to work 54 hours. Inchape and McLeods are apparently to adhere
to what they previously declared, viz: 50 hours a week [...]' / Private Official Letter
from Calcutta, 30 March 1936, Dundee, University Archive: MS 86/V/7/1.

14 In case of European-owned jute mills, this meant an increase in hours of work to
fifty-four per week; while the two Indian-owned jute mills seized the opportunity
and introduced a (regular) double shift system, in order to increase working hours
to twenty-two per day. / Private Official Letter from Calcutta, 30 August 1937,
Dundee, University Archive: MS 86/V/7/3.

15 Directors' reports and accounts, Angus Co. Ltd, Jute and Engineering Works, 1938,
Dundee University Archives: MS 86/IV/5/1.

16 For more details, see: Anna Sailer, 'When Mill Sirens Rang Out Danger. The
Calcutta Jute Mill Belt in the Second World War', in *Calcutta. Stormy Decades*, ed.
Sekhar Bandyopadhyay and Tanika Sarkar (New Delhi: Social Science Press, 2015),
121–50.

17 Annual Report on the Working of the Indian Factories Act for Bengal and Assam,
1935.

18 Ibid., 1935-1940.

19 The emerging shortage of skilled workers was, as we have seen, related to the
abolition of the multiple-shift system, which restricted workers' options to train
themselves at the machines.

20 S.R. Deshpande, *Report on an Enquiry into the Conditions of Labour in the Jute Mill
Industry* (Delhi: Government of India, Labour Investigation Committee, 1946).

21 Letter from J. Williamson to E. Benthall, 31 July 1931, Centre of South Asian Studies
(University of Cambridge), Benthall Papers, Box 8; Letter from MacDonald to
Mason, 21 April 1938, Private official letters from Calcutta to Dundee, 1937–1938,
Dundee University Archives, MS 86/V/7/6.

22 Managers' reports to the directors. Samnuggur North Mill, 1936, Dundee
University Archives, MS 86/V/8/6/2.

23 Enclosure 4 (Union North Re-Construction Proposal), 2 August 1935, Centre of
South Asian Studies (University of Cambridge), Benthall Papers, Box 8.

24 Report on the Transport & Marketing of Jute in India, Second Report, 1941, p 445.

25 Managers' Reports to the Directors. Samnuggur South Mill, 1935, DUA, MS
86/V/5/3.

26 Report on the Transport & Marketing of Jute in India, Second Report, 1941, p 445.

27 Managers' reports to the directors. Samnaggur North Mill, 1935, Dundee University Archives, MS 86/V/8/6/2.

28 Correspondence of directors while visiting mills in India with some related files (1932–1968), J. Robertson, 1932-1933, Dundee University Archives, MS 86/V/7/29.

Chapter 5.3

1 'The humble petition of the accused above named [Mahavir Sing]', 7 July 1936, IOR: L/P&J/12/138; *TOI*, 7 January 1936; *TOI*, 5 February 1936; *TOI*, 14 April 1936; *TOI*, 15 April 1936; *TOI*, 7 May 1936; *TOI*, 22 August 1936.

2 'Strikes in various Jute Mills in the district of 24-Parganas', 1937, WBSA: Home Department (Confidential) Political Branch, 128/37.

3 *TOI*, 16 April 1936; *TOI*, 19 April 1937; 'Strikes in various Jute Mills in the district of 24-Parganas', 1937, WBSA: Home Department (Confidential) Political Branch, 128/37.

4 Private Official Letters from Calcutta, DUA, MS 86/V/7/4, 3 June 1937.

5 Private Official Letters from Calcutta, DUA, MS 86/V/7/4, 10 June 1937.

6 Bengal Jute Workers Union, 1935, Special Branch of the Police, Calcutta: SW/521A/35.

7 Private Official Letters from Calcutta, DUA, MS 86/V/7/4, 10 June 1937.

8 Ibid.

9 Indicative of this was also that strikes over dismissals of weavers were at times also described as conflicts triggered over managerial attempts to 'implement the rules'. / *TOI*, 17 January 1936.

10 Ibid.

11 'Union North', 13 September 1935, Centre of South Asian Studies (University of Cambridge), Benthall Papers, Box 8.

12 See among others: Special Branch of the Police, Calcutta: SW/527/38 & SW/630/38.

13 For Naihati Jute Mill, see: Extract from the Bengal Police Administration, 15 January 1938, IB: 59/38 / for Wellington Jute Mill, see: Extract from the Bengal Police Administration, 14 February 1938, IB: 59/38 / for Reliance Jute Mill, see: Extract from the Bengal Police Administration, 19 February 1938, IB: 59/38 / for Victoria Jute Mill, see: Managers' Report for the Directors, The Victoria Jute Company Limited, 1939, Dundee University Archives, MS 86/V/8/10/6.

14 Sumit Sarkar, *Modern India. 1885–1947* (Macmillan, 1983), pp 349f.

15 Ibid., pp 354f.

16 Dilip Simeon aptly described the aftermath of the provincial elections in 1938 as the year, in which Indian 'workers began asserting themselves' – albeit, with regard to labour conflicts in and around Calcutta, we might rather speak of the 'years' in which workers asserted themselves. / Simeon, *The Politics of Labour*, p 236.

17 Report, Special Branch, SW/521-A/35, November 1935.

18 Report by Casual Agent, Howrah, SW/521-A/35, 10 January 1935.

19 H.O. 21 dated 7 April 1936, Special Branch, SW/521-A/35, 7 April 1936.

20 Bengal Jute Workers Union, 1935, Special Branch of the Police, Calcutta: SW/521A/35.

21 *TOI*, 5 February 1937.

22 Ibid., 10 February 1937.

23 Ibid., 12 February 1937.

24 'Strikes in various Jute Mills in the district of 24-Parganas', 1937, WBSA: Home Department (Confidential) Political Branch, 128/37.

25 *TOI*, 24 April 1937.

26 *TOI*, 19 April 1937.

27 Letter to Dundee, Correspondence of directors while visiting mills in India with some related files. 1932–1968, Alexander R. Murray, 28 December 1937, 1937–1938. MS 86/V/7/33.

28 Private Official Letters from Calcutta, Dundee University Archive, MS 86/V/7/4, 1. July 1937.

29 Ibid., 4 May 1937.

30 'Strikes in various Jute Mills in the district of 24-Parganas', 1937, WBSA: Home Department (Confidential) Political Branch, 128/37.

31 *TOI*, 8 May 1937.

32 Private Official Letters from Calcutta, DUA, MS 86/V/7/4, 1 July 1937.

33 Labour Conditions in the Jute Mills, 31 July 1937, Centre of South Asian Studies (University of Cambridge), Benthall Papers, Box 10; Private official letter from Calcutta to Dundee, 20 May 1937, Dundee University Archives, MS 86/V/7/6; Private official letter from Calcutta to Dundee, 8 July 1937, Dundee University Archives, MS 86/V/7/6; Private official letter from Calcutta to Dundee, 21 August 1937, Dundee University Archives, MS 86/V/7/6; Private official letter from Calcutta to Dundee, 5 December 1938, Dundee University Archives, MS 86/V/7/7; Private official letter from Calcutta to Dundee, 23 June 1939, Dundee University Archives, MS 86/V/7/8.

34 Managers' Report for the Directors, The Angus Jute Works Company Limited, 1937, MS 86/V/7/1.

35 Sailer, Anna, 'Spinners', *'Madrassis' and 'Hindus': Jute Workers' Strikes in Titagarh in the Late 1930s*, in: Südasien-Chronik/South Asia Chronicle, Vol 6/2016, 276f.

36 Managers' reports to the directors. Angus Jute Works, 1937, Dundee University Archives, MS 86/V/8/8/1.

37 H.O. 21 dated 7 April 1936, Special Branch, SW/521-A/35, 7 April 1936.

38 Sailer, Anna, 'Spinners', *'Madrassis' and 'Hindus': Jute Workers' Strikes in Titagarh in the Late 1930s*, in: Südasien-Chronik/South Asia Chronicle, Vol. 6/2016, 273.

39 Private Official Letters from Calcutta, DUA, MS 86/V/7/4, 27 May 1937.

40 Private Official Letters from Calcutta, DUA, MS 86/V/7/6, 19 December 1938.

41 Managers' reports to the directors. Angus Jute Works, 1937, Dundee University Archives, MS 86/V/8/8/1.

42 Private official letter from Calcutta to Dundee, 15 and 22 July 1937, Dundee University Archives, MS 86/V/7/6.

43 Managers' Report for the Directors, The Angus Jute Works Company Limited, 1938, MS 86/V/8/1; Annual Report of the Committee of the Indian Jute Mills' Association, 1937.

Chapter 5.4

1   Managers' Reports to the Directors, Titaghur No. 1 Mill, 1939, DUA, MS 86/V/8/10/4.

2   Private Official Letters from Calcutta, DUA, MS 86/V/7/4, 22. April 1937, 20 May 1937.

3   Private Official Letters from Calcutta, DUA, MS 86/V/7/4, 20 May 1937.

4   Managers' Report for the Directors, The Angus Jute Works Company Limited, 1938, MS 86/V/8/1.

5   Private Official Letters from Calcutta, DUA, MS 86/V/7/4, 21 April 1938.

6   Private Official Letters from Calcutta, DUA, MS 86/V/7/4, 21 April 1938, 19 April 1939.

7   Managers' Reports to the Directors, Titaghur No. 1 Mill, 1939, DUA, MS 86/V/8/10/4.

8   Ibid.

9   Ibid.

10 Managers' Report for the Directors, The Victoria Jute Company Limited, 1939, MS 86/V/8/10/6.

11 Ibid.

12 Managers' reports to the directors. Samnuggur North Mill, 1940, Dundee University Archives, MS 86/V/8/11/2.

13 Managers' Report for the Directors, The Victoria Jute Company Limited, 1939, MS 86/V/8/10/6.

14 Sailer, 'When Mill Sirens Rang Out Danger'.

15 Ibid.

16 Managers' Reports to the Directors, Angus Jute Works, 1950, DUA, MS 86/V/8/21/1.

17 Labour Conditions in the Indian Jute Industry, India Office Library and Records (= IOR): L/E/8/6457.

18 Ravi Ahuja, 'A Beveridge Plan for India? Social Insurance and the Making of the "Formal Sector"', *International Review of Social History*, Vol. 64, No. 2 (2019): pp 207–48.

19 Ibid.

20 The first Jute Tribunal Award in 1948 counted about 250 possible occupations in Bengal jute mills. / Award in the Matter of Industrial Disputes in the Jute Textile Industry in West Bengal between the Employers of 89 Specified Jute Mills and Their Workmen, 1948, p 8.

21 Managers' Reports to the Directors, Angus Jute Works, 1948, DUA, MS 86/V/8/19/1.

22 Managers' Reports to the Directors, Angus Jute Works, 1949, DUA, MS 86/V/8/20/1.

23 Managers' Reports to the Directors, Angus Jute Works, 1948, DUA, MS 86/V/8/19/1.

24 Managers' Reports to the Directors, Angus Jute Works, 1949, DUA, MS 86/V/8/20/1.

25 Managers' Reports to the Directors, Titaghur No. 2 Mill, 1948, DUA, MS 86/V/8/19/5.

26 Managers' Reports to the Directors, Angus Jute Works, 1949, DUA, MS 86/V/8/20/1.

27 Managers' Reports to the Directors, Samnuggur South Mill, 1952, DUA, MS 86/V/8/23/3.

Chapter 5.5

1 Report of the Commission on Indian Factories, 1891.

2 Private Official Letters from Calcutta, DUA, MS 86/V/7/4, 5 June 1939.

3 Confidential Report on the Merits of Managers, Assistant Managers and Mill Clerks in Samnuggur, Titaghur, Victoria and Angus, Private Official Letters from Calcutta, Dundee University Archives, MS 86/V/7/8.

4 Sen, *Working Class Movements in India. 1885–1975* (Oxford: Oxford University Press, 1994).

5 Dagmar Curjel, Enquiry into the conditions of Employment of women before and after child-birth, in Bengal Industries, 1923.

6 Sailer, Anna, 'Spinners', 'Madrassis' and 'Hindus': Jute Workers' Strikes in Titagarh in the Late 1930s, in: Südasien-Chronik/South Asia Chronicle, Vol 6/2016, pp 276.

7 This is also what Historians have pointed out:.... .

8 For instance in the Metiaburuz Jute Mills, a conflict escalated when hessian weavers demanded to leave work earlier due to a short supply of yarn. The workers pointed

out, that the early closing of the mill in such cases was a common practice. The departmental overseer, who had only recently started to work in Bengal, refused the demand. The weavers went on strike the same day, commencing work a few days later. A low supply of yarn from the spinning mill also resulted in wage losses for weavers, as workers in the weaving factory were principally remunerated according to the number of pieces they had produced – in contrast to workers in the spinning mill, who were categorized as time-workers. In the Hastings Jute Mill, for instance, weavers went on strike in 1911 due to the recurring problem of an insufficient amount of yarn, which arrived at their machines, as this resulted in a loss in wage payments for them. When the weavers left their workplace, mills' manager shut the weaving factory, but kept the spinning mill running. The production of yarn, after all, could be sustained without the weaving factory, but not vice versa. It was only when several weavers tried to enter the spinning mill violently that the mills' manager decided to stop work in the side of the mill as well. / For the strike in the Clive Jute Mill, see: TOI, 17 August 1906; for the strike in the Hastings Jute Mill, see: TOI, 9 June 1911.

9 Managers' reports to the directors. Titaghur No. I Mill, 1937, Dundee University Archives, MS 86/V/8/8/4; Managers' reports to the directors. Titaghur No. II Mill, 1937, Dundee University Archives, MS 86/V/8/8/5.

10 As we have seen, hessian weavers used to earn more than sacking weavers under the multiple-shift system. This was reversed, when the single-shift system was introduced, and hessian weavers suffered a relative decline in wage payments.

Bibliography

1 Private Papers

CAMBRIDGE, CENTRE FOR SOUTH ASIAN STUDIES
Papers of Sir Edward Benthall

2 Records

A. GOVERNMENT RECORDS

CALCUTTA, WEST BENGAL STATE ARCHIVES, GOVERNMENT OF BENGAL
FILES
Home Department (Confidential) Political Branch
CALCUTTA, WEST BENGAL STATE ARCHIVES, INTELLIGENCE BUREAU
ARCHIVE
Records
CALCUTTA, SPECIAL BRANCH OF POLICE ARCHIVE
Records
LONDON, GOVERNMENT OF INDIA FILES HELD AT THE INDIA OFFICE
LIBRARY AND RECORDS
Economic Department Records
General Department Miscellaneous Branch
Political and Secret Department
Public and Judicial Department
India Office Records Publication Series
NEW DELHI, NATIONAL ARCHIVES OF INDIA, GOVERNMENT OF INDIA FILES
Home Department Judicial Branch
Home Department Police Branch
Home Department Political Branch

B. RECORDS OF ORGANIZATIONS

DUNDEE, THOMAS DUFF & COMPANY LTD., DUNDEE UNIVERSITY
ARCHIVES
Correspondence of directors while visiting mills in India, 1933–37

Directors' Minute Books, 1900–40
Directors' Reports to the Shareholders, 1900–59
Managers' Reports to the Directors, 1930–59
Private Official Letters from Calcutta, 1933–40
Private Official Letters to Calcutta, 1936–39
GLASGOW, CHAMPDANY JUTE COMPANY, GLASGOW UNIVERSITY ARCHIVE
Directors Minute Books, 1911–21

3 Newspapers and Journals

Amrita Bazar Patrika
Bengalee
Dundee Courier
Forward/Liberty
Manchester Evening News
Statesman
Times of India

4 Interviews

Interviews with a former Engineer, Bird Company: Dundee, 14 February 2012
    and 6 June 2013
Interview with a former Assistant Manager, Budge-Budge Jute Mill: Dundee, 15
    February 2012
Interviews with the son of the manager of the Megna Jute Mill: Dundee, 16
    February 2012 and 7 June 2013

5 Printed Reports and Gazetteers

Annual Report of the Committee of the Bengal Chamber of Commerce. Calcutta, 1919.
Annual Report of the Committee of the Indian Jute Mills' Association. Calcutta, 1922–37.
Annual Report on the Police Administration in the Bengal Presidency. Calcutta, 1928.
Annual Report on the Police Administration of the Town of Calcutta and Its Suburbs.
    Calcutta, 1937.
Annual Report on the Working of the Indian Factories Act in Bengal and Assam. Calcutta,
    1919–38.
Annual Report on the Working of the Indian Trade Union Act, 1926 in Bengal. Calcutta, 1929.

Annual Report on the Working of the Workmen's Compensation Act in Bengal. Calcutta, 1928.

Award in the Matter of Industrial Disputes in the Jute Textile Industry in West Bengal between the Employers of 89 Specified Jute Mills and Their Workmen. Government of West Bengal. Calcutta, 1948.

Choudhury, A.C. Roy. *Report on an Enquiry into the Standard of Living of Jute Mill Workers in Bengal.* Government of Bengal. Calcutta, 1930.

Clark, W.A. Graham. *Linen, Jute, and Hemp Industries in the United Kingdom. With Notes on the Growing and Manufacture of Jute in India.* Government of the United States of America, Department of Commerce, Special Agents Series No. 74. Washington, 1913.

Curjel, Dagmar. *Enquiry into the Conditions of Employment of Women before and after Child-Birth in Bengal Industries.* Government of Bengal. Calcutta, 1923.

Deshpande, S.R. *Report on Enquiry into the Conditions of Labour in the Jute Mill Industry in India.* Government of India, Labour Investigation Committee. Delhi, 1946.

Fortnightly Report on the Political Situation in Bengal. Government of Bengal. Calcutta.

Finlow, R.S. *Report on the Extension of Jute Cultivation India.* Government of Eastern Bengal and Assam. Calcutta, 1906.

Gupta, Indrajit. *Capital and Labour in the Jute Industry,* Bombay: AITUC, 1953.

Hunter, W.W. *The Imperial Gazetteer of India.* Vol. 2. Bengal to Cutwa. London, Trübner & Co., 1881.

Hunter, W.W. *The Imperial Gazetteer of India Atlas.* Vol. 26. Oxford: Clarendon Press, 1931.

Indian Factory Labour Commission. Volume I, Report. Government of India. Calcutta, 1908.

Indian Factory Labour Commission. Volume II. Evidence. Government of India. Calcutta, 1908.

Meerut Conspiracy Case (1929) Papers. Prosecution Witnesses, PW 190–263 (4 October 1930–3 December 1930), VIII, 1929–33.

Morris, R.J. *Relative Merits of Cotton and Jute Cement Sacks.* Government of the United States of America. Technologic Papers of the Bureau of Standards, 1925.

Report of the Bengal Jute Enquiry Committee. Vol. 1. Government of Bengal. Calcutta, 1934.

Report of the Committee on Industrial Unrest in Bengal, 1921. Servants of India Society. Calcutta, 1921.

Report of the East India (Factories) Commission. India Office. London, 1891.

Report of the Industrial Commission 1916–1918. India Office. London, 1919.

Report of the Textile Factories Labour Committee. Appointed by the Government of India, December 1906. London, 1907.

Report on the Transport & Marketing of Jute in India. Central Indian Jute Committee. Second Report, Calcutta, 1941.

Review of the Industrial Position and Prospects in Bengal in 1908. With Special Reference to the Industrial Survey of 1890. Part II of Special Report. Calcutta, 1908.

Royal Commission on Labour (Whitley Commission). Vol. 5, Part 1. Bengal (Excluding
  Coalfields and the Dooars). Government of India. London, 1931.
Royal Commission on Labour (Whitley Commission). Vol. 11 – Supplementary.
  Government of India. London, 1931.
The Politico-Criminal 'Who's Who' of the Bengal Presidency. Revised up to the 1st July
  1930. Bengal Intelligence Branch. Calcutta, 1930.
Waterhouse, S., *Report on the Culture of Jute and the Importance of the Industry.*
  Department of Agriculture Special Report [United States of America], Washington,
  1883.

6 Books and Articles

AhmadMohiuddin. *Essentials of Colloquial Hindustani for Jute Mills & Workshops.* Third
  Edition. Calcutta, 1947.
AhujaRavi. 'Erkenntnisdruck Und Denkbarrieren. Eine Kritische Bestandsaufnahme
  Der Indischen Arbeitsgeschichte', *Soziale Welt*, Vol. 15, Sonderband (2004):
  349–66.
AhujaRavi. 'A Beveridge Plan for India? Social Insurance and the Making of the
  "Formal Sector"'. *International Review of Social History*, Vol. 64, No. 2 (2019):
  207–48.
Alexander-MudaliarEmma. 'The "Special Classes" of Labour. Women and Children.
  Doubly Marginalized.' In *Labour Matters. Towards Global Histories. Studies in
  Honour of Sabyasachi Bhattacharya*, edited by Marcel van der Linden and Prabhu
  Mohapatra. New Delhi: Tulika Books, 2009.
ArnoldDavid. 'Salutation and Subversion. Gestual Politics in Nineteenth Century India.'
  Past & Present, Vol. 203, No. 4 (2009): 191–212.
BagchiAmiya Kumar. *Private Investment in India, 1900–1939.* Cambridge South Asian
  Studies 10, Cambridge: Cambridge University Press, 1972.
BahrMax. *Die Jute-Not!* Landsberg-Warthe: Jutespinner-Verlag, 1914.
BasuDeepika. *The Working Class in Bengal. Formative Years.* Calcutta; New Delhi: K.P.
  Bagchi and Company, 1993.
BasuNirban. 'Outside Leadership, Political Rivalries and Labour Mobilisation. The Jute
  Belt of Bengal, 1919–1939.' In *A Case for Labour History*, 114–43. Calcutta: K.P.
  Bagchi and Company, n.d.
BasuNirban. *The Working Class Movement. A Study of Jute Mills of Bengal 1937–1947.*
  Calcutta: K.P. Bagchi, 1994.
BasuSubho. 'Review on the book : Unsettled Settlers: Migrant Workers and Industrial
  Capitalism in Calcutta by Arjan de Haan. Rotterdam: Verloren Publishers, 1994.
  pp 299', *South Asia Research*, Vol. 16, No. 2 (1 October 1996): 209–122.
BasuSubho. 'Strikes and "Communal" Riots in Calcutta in the 1890s: Industrial
  Workers, Bhadralok Nationalist Leadership and the Colonial State.' *Modern Asian
  Studies*, Vol. 32, No. 4 (1998): 949–83.

BasuSubho. *Does Class Matter. Colonial Capital and Workers' Resistance in Bengal, 1890–1937*. New Delhi: Oxford University Press, 2004.

BasuSubho. 'The Paradox of Peasant Worker: Re-Conceptualizing Workers' Politics in Bengal 1890–1939.' *Modern Asian Studies*, Vol. 42, No. 1 (January 2008): 47–74.

BhatterB.D., and L. Nemenyi. *The Jute Crisis*. Calcutta: Thacker, Spink & Co., 1936.

BremanJan. 'At Work in the Informal Economy of India. A Perspective from the Bottom Up.' In *The Worlds of Indian Industrial Labour. Contributions to Indian Sociology*, edited by Jonathan Parry, Jan Breman and Karin Kapadia, 1–44. Occasional Studies 9. New Delhi: Sage Publications, 1999.

BremanJan. *The Making and Unmaking of an Industrial Working Class. Sliding down the Labour Hierarchy in Ahmedabad, India*. Oxford: Oxford University Press, 2004.

CarpenterMary. *Six Months in India*. Vol. 1. London: Longmans, Green, and Co., 1868.

CarterHerbert R. *The Spinning and Twisting of Long Vegetable Fibres (Flax, Hemp, Jute, Tow & Ramie)*. London: Charles Griffin and Company Limited, 1904.

CarterHerbert R. *Jute and Its Manufacture*. London: Bale & Danielson, 1921.

ChakrabartyDipesh. 'Communal Riots and Labour. Bengal's Jute Mill-Hands in the 1890s.' *Past & Present*, Vol. 91, No. 91 (May 1981): 140–69.

ChakrabartyDipesh. 'On Deifying and Defying Authority. Managers and Workers in the Jute Mills of Bengal Circa 1890–1940.' *Past & Present*, Vol. 100, No. 100 (August 1983): 124–46.

ChakrabartyDipesh. 'Conditions for Knowledge of Working-Class Conditions. Employers, Government and the Jute Workers of Calcutta.' In *Selected Subaltern Studies*, edited by Ranajit Guha and Gayatri Chakravorty Spivak, 180–222. New York; Oxford: Oxford University Press, 1988.

ChakrabartyDipesh. *Rethinking Working-Class History. Bengal, 1890–1940*. Princeton, NJ: Princeton University Press, 1989.

ChakrabartyDipesh. *Provincializing Europe: Postcolonial Thought and Historical Difference*. Princeton Studies in Culture/Power/History. Princeton, NJ: Princeton University Press, 2000.

ChandavarkarRajnarayan. 'Industrialization in India before 1947: Conventional Approaches and Alternative Perspectives.' *Modern Asian Studies*, Vol. 19, No. 3 (1985): 623–68.

ChandavarkarRajnarayan. *The Origins of Industrial Capitalism in India: Business Strategies and the Working Classes in Bombay, 1900–1940*. Cambridge South Asian Studies 51. Cambridge [England]; New York, NY: Cambridge University Press, 1994.

ChandavarkarRajnarayan. 'The Decline and Fall of the Jobber System in the Bombay Cotton Textile Industry, 1870–1955.' *Modern Asian Studies*, Vol. 42, No. 1 (2008): 117–210.

ChandavarkarRajnarayan. *History, Culture and the Indian City*. Cambridge: Cambridge University Press, 2009.

ChapmanDennis. 'The Establishment of the Jute Industry. A Problem of Location Theory?' *The Review of Economic Studies*, Vol. 6, No. 1 (October 1938): 33–55.

ChattopadhyayManju. 'Santosh Kumari Devi. A Pioneering Labour Leader.' *Social Scientist*, Vol. 12, No. 1 (January 1984): 62–73.

ChattopadhyaySuchetana. *An Early Communist: Muzaffar Ahmad in Calcutta, 1913–1929*. New Delhi: Tulika Books, 2011.

ChaudhuryNibaran Chandra. *Jute in Bengal*. Second Edition. Calcutta: W. Newmann & Co., 1921.

Chiranjiv Lall Mohindra. *Die Indische Juteindustrie Und Ihre Entwicklung*, Band 20, Volkswirtschaftliche Studien (Berlin, 1928).

CoxAnthony. *Empire, Industry and Class. The Imperial Nexus of Jute, 1840–1940*. London; New York: Routledge, 2013.

DasAmal. 'Outside Intervention in Jute Mill Strikes – Howrah, 1870–1930.' In *A Case for Labour History*, edited by Arjan de Haan and Samita Sen, 82–113. Calcutta, n.d.

DasAmal. 'Jute Mill Strike of 1928. A Case Study.' *Economic and Political Weekly*, Vol. 20, No. 4 (January 1985): 27–33.

DasAmal. *Urban Politics in an Industrial Area. Aspects of Municipal and Labour Politics in Howrah, West Bengal, 1850–1928*. Calcutta: Chandan Das, 1994.

DasR.K. *Factory Labour in India*. Berlin: Walter de Gruyter, 1923.

Das Gupta, Ranajit. 'Material Conditions and Behavioural Aspects of Calcutta Working Class, 1875–1899.' *Centre for Studies in Social Sciences, Calcutta* Occasional Paper, No. 20 (1979).

Das Gupta, Ranjit. *The Jute General Strike of 1929*, Calcutta: Indian Institute of Management, Working Paper Series - 141 (90), 1990.

Das Gupta, Ranjit. *Labour and Working Class in Eastern India. Studies in Colonial History*. Calcutta; New Delhi: K.P. Bagchi, 1994.

de HaanArjan. 'Migrant Labour in Calcutta Jute Mills. Class, Instability and Control.' In *Dalit Movements and the Meanings of Labour*, edited by Peter Robb, 186–224. Oxford: Oxford University Press, 1993.

de HaanArjan. *Unsettled Settlers. Migrant Workers and Industrial Capitalism in Calcutta*. Hilversum: Verloren, 1994.

de HaanArjan 'The Badli System in Industrial Labour Recruitment. Managers' and Workers' Strategies in Calcutta's Jute Industry.' *Contributions to Indian Sociology*, Vol. 33, Nos. 1–2 (1999): 271–301.

de HaanArjan. 'Towards a "Total History" of Bengal Labour.' In *Bengal. Rethinking History. Essays in Historiography*, 119–134. New Delhi: Manohar, 2001.

FarrisDavid H. *Shopfloor Matters. Labor. Management Relations in 20th Century American Manufacturing*. London: Routledge, 1997.

GhoshParimal. *Colonialism, Class, and a History of the Calcutta Jute Millhands, 1880–1930*. Hyderabad: Orient Longman, 2000.

GhoshParimal. 'A History of A Colonial Working Class, India 1850–1946.' In *Economic History of India from Eighteenth to Twentieth Century*, edited by Binai Bhushan Chaudhury, 525–698. New Delhi: Coronet Books, 2005.

GhoshTanima. 'Income and Productivity in the Jute Industry across the 1947 Divide.' In *A Case for Labour History. The Jute Industry in Eastern India*, edited by Arjan de Haan and Samita Sen, 54–81. Calcutta: K.P. Bagchi, 1999.

GooptuNandini. *The Politics of the Urban Poor in Early Twentieth Century India*. Cambridge: Cambridge University Press, 2001.

GoswamiOmkar. 'Collaboration and Conflict: European and Indian Capitalists and The Jute Economy of Bengal, 1919–39.' *Indian Economic & Social History Review*, Vol. 19, No. 2 (1982): 141–79.

GoswamiOmkar. 'Then Came the Marwaris. Some Aspects of the Changes in the Pattern of Industrial Control in Eastern India.' *Indian Economic & Social History Review*, Vol. 22, No. 3 (1985): 225–49.

GoswamiOmkar. *Industry, Trade, and Peasant Society: The Jute Economy of Eastern India, 1900–1947*. Delhi; New York: Oxford University Press, 1991.

GuptaBishnupriya. 'Why Did Collusion Fail? The Indian Jute Industry in the Inter-War Years.' *Business History*, Vol. 47, No. 4 (October 2005): 532–52.

HarveyDavid. *The Limits to Capital*. Oxford: Basil Blackwell, 1982.

JamesonFrederic. *Valences of the Dialectic*. London: Verso, 2009.

JoshiChitra. *Labour History and the Question of Culture*. Delhi: V.V. Giri National Labour Institute, 2003.

JoshiChitra. *Lost Worlds. Indian Labour and Its Forgotten Histories*. London: Anthem Press, 2005.

JoshiChitra. 'Histories of Indian Labour: Predicaments and Possibilities.' *History Compass*, Vol. 6, No. 2 (March 2008): 439–54.

Jute Mills in Bengal. Described by the Special Correspondent of the 'Dundee Advertiser' in Calcutta. Dunde: John Leng & Co., 1880.

KelmanJanet Harvey. *Labour in India. A Study of the Conditions of Indian Women in Modern Industry*. London: George Allan & Unwin Ltd., 1924.

KeracherSusan, ed. *Dundee's Two Intreprid Ladies. A Tour Round the World*. Dundee: Abertay Historical Society, 2012.

KidambiPrashant. 'Contestation and Conflict. Workers' Resistance and the "Labour Problem" in the Bombay Cotton Mills, C. 1898–1919.' In *Labour Matters*, edited by Marcel van der Linden and Prabhu Mohapatra, 106–27. New Delhi: Tulika Books, 2009.

LegattWilliam. *The Theory and Practice of Jute Spinning. Being a Complete Description of the Machines Used in the Preparation and Spinning of Jute Yarns*. London: Simkin, 1921.

LengJohn. *Letters from India and Ceylon, Including the Manchester of India, the Indian Dundee, and Calcutta Jute Mills. Reprinted from the Dundee Advertiser*. Dundee: John Leng & Co., 1895.

MisraMaria. *Business, Race & Politics in British India*. Oxford: Oxford University Press, 1999.

MitraIra. 'Growth of Trade Union Consciousness among Jute Mill Workers, 1920–40.' *Economic and Political Weekly*, Vol. 16, No. 44/46 (November 1981): 1839–48.

MohapatraPrabu. '"Restoring the Family": Wife Murders and the Making of a Sexual Contract for Indian Immigrant Labour in the British Caribbean Colonies, 1860–1920.' *Studies in History*, Vol. 11, No. 2 (1 August, 1995): 227–60.

MohapatraPrabhu. *Situating the Renewal. Reflections on Labour Studies in India.* Labour History Series, 2. Delhi: V.V. Giri National Labour Institute, 1998.

MorrisDavid Morris. *The Emergence of an Industrial Labor Force in India. A Study of the Bombay Cotton Mills, 1854–1947.* Berkeley; Los Angeles: University of California Press, 1965.

MurrayAlexander R. 'The Jute Industry.' *Journal of the Royal Society of Arts,* Vol. 82, No. 4263 (August 1934): 977–96.

NairJ. 'Dangerous Labour: Crime, Work and Punishment in Kolar Gold Fields, 1890–1946.' *Studies in History,* Vol. 13, No. 1 (1 February 1997): 19–61.

NomuraChikayoshi. 'The Origin of the Controlling Power of Managing Agents over Modern Business Enterprises in Colonial India.' *Indian Economic & Social History Review,* Vol. 51, No. 1 (January 2001): 95–132.

NonnenmacherE. *Die Jute. Pflanze und Fasergewinnung. Handel und Wirtschaft. Spinnerei.* Berlin; Heidelberg: Springer Verlag, 1930.

OlbrechtUrs. *Bengalens Fluch Und Segen. Die Indische Juteindustrie in Spät- Und Nachkolonialer Zeit.* Stuttgart: Steiner, 2000.

OliverThomas, BonnerStephen. *Dangerous Trades. History of Health and Safety at Work.* Vol. 2. London: Continuum, 2004.

OrnatiOscar. 'Wages in India.' *Economic Development and Cultural Change,* Vol. 3, No. 3 (April 1955): 241–59.

PfuhlE. *Die Jute Und Ihre Verarbeitung Auf Grund Wissenschaftlicher Untersuchungen Und Praktischer Erfahrungen.* Zweiter Teil. Das Erzeugen der Gewebe, Herstellung der Säcke. Berlin/Heidelberg: Spinger Verlag, 1891.

RicoeurPaul. *History, Memory, Forgetting.* Translated by Kathleen Blamey and David Pellauer. Chicago: University of Chicago Press, 2009.

RungtaShyam. 'Bowreah Cotton and Fort Gloster Jute Mills, 1872–1900.' *Indian Economic & Social History Review,* Vol. 22, No. 2 (1985): 109–37.

SailerAnna. '"Various Paths Are Today Opened." The Bengal Jute Mill Strike of 1929 as a Historical Event.' In *Working Lives & Worker Militancy. The Politics of Labour in Colonial India,* edited by Ravi Ahuja, 207–56. New Delhi: Tulika Books, 2013.

SailerAnna. 'When Mill Sirens Rang Out Danger. The Calcutta Jute Mill Belt in the Second World War.' In *Calcutta. Stormy Decades,* edited by Sekhar Bandyopadhyay and Tanika Sarkar, 121–50. New Delhi: Social Science Press, 2015.

SailerAnna. '"Spinners," "Madrassis" and "Hindus." Jute Workers' Strikes in Titagarh in the Late 1930s.' *Südasien-Chronik/South Asia Chronicle,* Vol. 6 (2016): 265–88.

SarkarAditya. *Trouble at the Mill. Factory Law and the Emergence of the Labour Question in Late Nineteenth-Century Bombay.* Oxford: Oxford University Press, 2018.

SarkarSumit. *Modern India. 1885–1947.* New Delhi: Macmillan, 1983.

SarkarSumit. 'The Return of Labour to South-Asian History.' *Historical Materialism,* Vol. 12, No. 3 (2004): 285–313.

SarkarTanika. *Bengal 1928–1934. The Politics of Protest.* Oxford: Oxford University Press, 1987.

SarkerNalini Ranjan. *The Jute Crisis. Proceedings of Conference, October 17, 1930.* Calcutta: J.N. Sen, 1930.

SenSamita. 'Gendering Class. Wives and Workers in the Jute Industrial Economy.' In *A Case for Labour History. The Jute Industry in Eastern India*, edited by Arjan de Haan and Samita Sen, 196–245. Calcutta: K.P. Bagchi, 1999.

SenSamita. *Women and Labour in Late Colonial India: The Bengal Jute Industry.* Cambridge Studies in Indian History and Society 3. Cambridge; New York: Cambridge University Press, 1999.

SenSunil Kumar. *Working Class Movements in India. 1885–1975.* Oxford: Oxford University Press, 1994.

S.N. Sen and T. Piplai. *Industrial Relations in the Jute Industry in West Bengal. A Case Study.* Calcutta: Bookland Private Ltd, 1968.

SharmaBrij Kishore. 'Bengal Jute Mill Workers' General Strike of 1929.' *Indica*, Vol. 44 (2007): 51–66.

SimeJohn F., and Thomas Johnston. *Exploitation in India. By Thomas Johnston, M.P., and John F. Sime (Secretary Dundee and District Union of Jute and Flax Workers). Issued by the Dundee Jute and Flax Workers' Union.* Dundee: Issued by the Dundee Jute and Flax Workers' Union, 1926.

SimeonDilip. *The Politics of Labour under Late Capitalism. Workers, Unions and the State in Chota Nagpur 1928–1939.* New Delhi: Manohar, 1995.

SinghMoni. *Life Is Struggle, English Translation by Karuna Banerjee*, People's Publishing House, New Delhi, 1988.

SprattPhilip. *Blowing Up India. Reminiscences and Reflections of a Former Comintern Emissary.* Calcutta: Prachi Prakashan, 1955.

Stedman Jones, Gareth. *Languages of Class: Studies in English Working Class* History, *1832–1982.* Cambridge; New York: Cambridge University Press, 1983.

StewartGordon T. *Jute and Empire. The Calcutta Jute Wallahs and the Landscapes of Empire.* Manchester: Manchester University Press, 1998.

TomlinsonB.R. 'Colonial Firms and the Decline of Colonialism in Eastern India 1914–47.' *Modern Asian Studies*, Vol. 15, No. 3 (1981): 455–86.

van SchendelWillem. 'Stretching Labour Historiography. Pointers from South Asia.' *International Review of Social History*, Vol. 51, No. Supplement S14 (December 2006): 229–61.

WallaceD.R. *The Romance of Jute. A Short History of the Calcutta Jute Mill Industry. 1855–1927.* Second Edition. London: W. Thacker & Co., 1928.

WallaceD.R. *The Romance of Jute. A Short History of the Calcutta Jute Mill Industry 1855–1909.* Calcutta, 1909.

Index